AF663547

A COMPARATIVE STUDY OF THE JAINA THEORIES OF REALITY AND KNOWLEDGE

LALA SUNDARLAL JAIN RESEARCH SERIES

General Editor
PROF. SATYA RANJAN BANERJEE

VOLUME II

A COMPARATIVE STUDY OF THE JAINA THEORIES OF REALITY AND KNOWLEDGE

Y. J. PADMARAJIAH

Foreword by
E. FRAUWALLNER

MOTILAL BANARSIDASS PUBLISHERS
PRIVATE LIMITED • DELHI

First Edition: Delhi, 1963
Reprint: Delhi, 1986, 2004

ISBN: 81-208-0036-2

MOTILAL BANARSIDASS
41 U.A. Bungalow Road, Jawahar Nagar, Delhi 110 007
8 Mahalaxmi Chamber, 22 Bhulabhai Desai Road, Mumbai 400 026
236, 9th Main III Block, Jayanagar, Bangalore 560 011
120 Royapettah High Road, Mylapore, Chennai 600 004
Sanas Plaza, 1302 Baji Rao Road, Pune 411 002
8 Camac Street, Kolkata 700 017
Ashok Rajpath, Patna 800 004
Chowk, Varanasi 221 001

Printed in India
BY JAINENDRA PRAKASH JAIN AT SHRI JAINENDRA PRESS,
A-45 NARAINA, PHASE-I, NEW DELHI-110 028
AND PUBLISHED BY NARENDRA PRAKASH JAIN FOR
MOTILAL BANARSIDASS PUBLISHERS PRIVATE LIMITED,
BUNGALOW ROAD, DELHI-110 007

"Sheth Shri Amritlal Kalidas Doshi. Founder,
Jain Sahitya Vikas Mandal Bombay"

This book is published with the permission and consent of Shri Jain Sahitya Vikas Mandal, 112 Swami Vivekanand Road, Irla Bridge, Vile Parle, Bombay 400 056

FOREWORD

An important point in the external history of Indian Philosophy which still remains unexplained to a great extent is the relationship between the various systems and schools. This may be due in part to the tradition of the texts the insufficiency of which does not allow us to see more clearly. Nevertheless it is striking how often important ideas and even whole systems are not being noticed beyond the limits of the own school.

Looking at things in general we may say that we encounter constructive discussion with opponent theories especially when there were different opinions on a certain subject, as for example on the problem of generality (*sāmānyam*) as the object of verbal cognition, or on the details of the act of cognition in the case of perception. Yet these are cases where the interest is concerned less with the opponent's theory as such but rather with the elucidation and defence of the own theory by discussing it with the opponent.

The discussion moves farther in the opponent's field if the topic is one of the fundamental theories of the other system. Of such kind are in the discussion with the Buddhists, for instance, the argument about the existence or non-existence of a soul, or with the Nyāya the problem of the existence of a supreme god. Very seldom the heterogeneous system is considered in its totality and if it happens the rendering of this system is usually not more than a rough description and the polemics more often than not repeat the traditional arguments only. An appreciative investigation of another system of thought is almost not to be found and it is the most important and profound philosophical ideas particularly which remain unregarded in these polemics.

The same can be said with regard to doxographic works. A glance into the well-known *Sarvadarśanasaṁgrahaḥ* of Sāyana Mādhava sufficiently proves this. It is natural that Sāyana Mādhava deals scantily with the old Buddhist systems, which at his time had lost their importance long ago. But from his book one does not get an idea of the philosophical importance of an Utpaladeva or even Rāmānuja either. Generally we can state that many of the most important philosophers of ancient India would be completely unknown or only very inadequately known if we merely knew them through the records of other schools and systems.

This holds good in a high degree in the case of Jinism. During the whole period of Indian philosophy Jinism has not been attended to very much by the other systems. Whatever the causes for this neglection might have been—the history of Jinism during this time is still a potential object of thorough research—the facts are, that schools like the Nyāya or the Mīmāṁsā hardly mention Jinism in their polemics. It is only since the time of Akalaṅka that the Buddhists pay more attention to Jinism. And it is actually striking when an author like Śāntarakṣita in his *Tattvasaṁgrahaḥ* is quoting and refuting the opinions of single Jaina teachers. This is even more astonishing since the literature of the Jainas on the other hand is extensively occupied with other schools and systems.

One is almost inclined to think of a continuation of this traditional fact finding Jinism likewise inadequately dealt with in modern descriptions of Indian philosophy. As an example I only refer to the extensive history of Indian philosophy by S. Dasgupta. And even in more detailed descriptions of Jinism like the well-known book by H. V. Glasenapp the philosophical import is of no account.

Under these circumstances it is to be feared that Jinism is not being adequately considered in the present-day endeavours of establishing a relationship between Indian and Western philosophy. From this point of view efforts like the present book are desirable and welcome. As the object of his investigation the author has aptly chosen those theories, which are of fundamental importance for the philosophical thought of Jinism. He arranges them according to clear aspects, comparing them with other Indian systems and similar phenomena of Western philosophy and thereby trying to clarify the connections. Thus his book offers plenty of suggestions and it is to be wished that it might help to introduce the valuable ideas contained in Jinism to the philosophical discussion of to-day.

Indologisches Institut
der
Universitat Wien
Wien 1, Reitschulgasse 2

E. Frauwallner

CONTENTS

INTRODUCTION

Constructive thinking thrives on vigorous criticism. The most formidable critical force ever directed against the schools of Brahminism and Jainism was Buddhism. After the disappearance of Buddhism from the scene of India, metaphysical thinking in the Brahminical and the Jaina schools became stagnant.

In the last few decades, however, a new life has stirred in the philosophical circles of India—thanks to the impact of Western ideas, philosophical and scientific, on the traditional patterns of thinking and study. One of the forms this life has taken is the desire to understand where the Indian and the Western trends of philosophical thought meet, and where they part. Concurrently the interrelations of ideas among the Indian schools themselves have been subjected to intensive investigation. In other words, the method of comparative study which springs from the extended bounds of our philosophical knowledge, is gradually gaining ground, often unwittingly, as an important organ of investigation. A closer investigation of problems on comparative lines may reveal deeper affinities as well as sharper divergences, in these fields of study, than hitherto suspected.

In pursuing the comparative method of investigation it is necessary to be on one's guard against superficial and misleading resemblances among ideas. One should bear in mind that the ideas nurtured in one mental soil do not easily lend themselves to comparison with the ideas springing from a different mental soil. But this thought should not deter the seeker from his efforts. He should remember that despite their alien circumstances Śaṅkara and Hegel (or more particularly F. H. Bradley) have, between them, more in common than Śaṅkara and Kumārila on the one hand and Hegel (or Bradley) and Bertrand Russell on the other.

The present comparative study has been undertaken with the awareness of these difficulties. The problems selected for study are of a fundamental character and have not been treated, at any rate in recent times, by the same methods as are adopted here, nor have they been discussed in such detail.

Except in the course of a brief lecture by an Indian scholar, the important problem of relation (*saṁbandha*) has not as yet been treated by any writer. A similar neglect is shown in the case of the central problem of identity-in-difference which occupies the major portion of the first part of this study. Topics such as causal efficiency (*arthakriyākāritvam*), the concept of uniqueness (*jātyantaratva*), the dialectical implications of the doctrine of manifoldness (*anekāntavāda*), and the interrelatedness of *anekāntavāda*, *nayavāda* and *syādvāda* have not received the attention they deserve from the exponents of Indian philosophy. All this can be traced to the fact that Jainism in general and the Jaina philosophy in particular have been a neglected branch of the Indian studies. The present work has been undertaken to fill, in some measure, the gap created by prolonged neglect.

The scope of the subject-matter of the present study has been given in the text itself. A few remarks may, however, be made here about its nature and limitations :—

This work presupposes a broad familiarity with the philosophical position of Jainism as given, for instance, in J. L. Jaini's *Outlines of Jainism*, or in A. Chakravarti's introduction to his edition of Kundakunda's *Pañcāstikāyasāra*, or in any of the historical works on Indian philosophy.

No references have been made, except incidentally, to the Jaina canonical works. This is mainly due to the fact that many of the well-developed metaphysical ideas are a product of the post-canonical period although some basic ideas such as that reality is of the nature of permanence and change are found in an embryonic form in the canonical texts. Moreover, some scholars have already brought out a few works on the canonical section of Jaina literature. Amongst these the most notable are : W. Schübring's *Die Lehre der Jainas*, A. Weber's *Sacred Literature of the Jainas* (E. T. by H. W. Smith in *Indian Antiquary*, 1888-1892), and N. Tatia's *Studies in Jaina Philosophy*, and, above all, Vijayarājendra's *Abhidhāna-rājendra*, a massive canonical lexicon (in Jaina Prakrit, 7 vols.), and Ratnacandra's *Ardha-Māgadhī Dictionary* (5 vols.).

The epistemological part of this study has confined itself mainly to the treatment of the methods of knowledge. Further epistemological problems, such as the 'ways of knowing' (*pramāṇas*) and the various issues connected with them, could not be discussed within the limits of this work.

Owing to the nature of the subject-matter no strict adherence to chronology has been possible. The sequence in which the names of the various thinkers and their ideas occur has been governed by logical considerations.

Discussions on Buddhistic ideas have been restricted, mainly, to the development of Buddhism in India.

The system of diacritical marks adopted in the course of this work is that of the Royal Asiatic Society.

A few footnotes have been rather lengthy because they deal with some basic notions (e. g., continuity, relativity and divisibility) which call for a somewhat elaborate treatment. The inclusion of this matter in the body of the main text would have introduced needless complication into the discussion of the main arguments in the text. Moreover any serious curtailment in their length would, it was felt, affect the requirements of clarity and proper documentation of the text.

In presenting the ideas of some *kārikās* and the *gāthās* a compromise has been adopted between a too literal translation and very free rendering into English.

In conclusion, the writer wishes to express his gratitude to Prof. T. Burrow, Prof. S. Radhakrishnan and Dr. F. W. Thomas, for the able guidance and constant encouragement he received from them while preparing this work. He is also grateful for the help accorded him by the authorities of the following libraries : The Old Bodleian, Oxford; The Library of the Indian Institute, Oxford; The Library of the School of Oriental and African Studies, London; The Library of the Commonwealth Relations Office, London; and The British Museum Library, London.

EDITOR'S NOTE

The ontological section (Pt. I) of this study begins with a search for a balanced view of reality in which the elements of identity (*abheda*) and difference (*bheda*) would find their due place. The search results in the formulation of a scheme involving five possible approaches to the problem of reality. Four of them, viz., reality is (i) mere identity, (ii) mere difference, (iii) identity-in-difference in which identity predominates, and (iv) identity-in-difference in which difference predominates, are examined with various illustrations and found wanting as adequate explanations of our total ontological experience. The last approach, (v) a co-ordinate view of identity-in-difference, put forward by the Jaina thinkers, is found to meet the requirements of a satisfactory explanation. This view is, then, further examined and the validity of its approach confirmed from the philosophical views of Kumārila Bhaṭṭa, Immanuel Kant, and A. N. Whitehead.

Next, certain flaws (*doṣas*), alleged to exist in the Jaina view, are enumerated, analysed and refuted individually. The critics' unfamiliarity with, or misapprehension of, the nature and significance of negation in the Jaina view of reality is shown to be at the back of their objections. Another misapprehension on the part of certain critics takes, it is pointed out, the form of confusing the Jaina view with a 'mixed' theory (*miśravāda*) in which identity and difference remain extraneous to each other. In the course of clearing up this confusion the integral and the unique (*jātyantara*) features of the co-ordinate synthesis of identity-in-difference are brought out.

There follows a discussion of two aspects of reality, viz., the relational structure and causal efficiency (*arthakriyā-kāritvam*). It is shown that these, like other aspects of reality, can exist and function only within the ontological framework of a co-ordinate identity-in-difference.

An attempt (i) to determine the meaning and content of the notion of *dravya* (substance) and (ii) to distinguish between the two concepts of *guṇa* (intrinsic attribute) and *paryāya* (extrinsic attribute) concludes Part One of this work. It should be added that several notions such as relativity or interrelatedness, continuity (and the allied notions of compactness and consecutiveness), divisibility and negation (*apoha*) have been touched upon, in appropriate places, in the course of this part.

The epistemological section (Pt. II) endeavours to present an analytical account and a critical estimation of the methods of knowledge, recognised by the Jaina thinkers, under the characteristic doctrines of standpoints and of conditional predications (*nayavāda* and *syādvāda*). The presentation of these methods is, however, preceded by an investigation into the nature and the logical evolution of the theory of manifoldness (*anekāntavāda*) because this theory is the basis of the methods just referred to. The analysis reveals that the principle of distinction inherent in the logic of any realistic school of philosophy, has been given full play in the development of this theory of manifoldness. Hence the claim that it represents the most consistent form of realism in Indian metaphysics. It is sought to justify this claim through the postulation of the various logical steps, the last one of which, it is maintained, represents the climax of the realistic procedure.

Finally the analytical method of standpoints (*nayavāda*) and the synthetical method of conditional or seven-fold predication (*syādvāda* or *saptabhaṅgī*) have been dealt with at some length. They are shown to constitute a comprehensive scheme of complementary methods designed to help the mind in grasping the indeterminate nature of reality in its unity as well as in its diversity. Each method has been individually treated under the scheme of these cognitive instruments and a critical evaluation of the two doctrines has been offered at the end of the chapters concerned. The essential implications of some of the more important notions such as *syāt* (a conditional particle) and *avaktavyam* (the inexpressible) have also been touched upon in their appropriate contexts.

The work has aimed throughout at a comparative treatment of the problems. Effort has been made to avoid strained and far-fetched comparisons and contrasts and to treat criticisms and controversies in a constructive spirit.

PART I

ONTOLOGY (The Nature of Reality)

CHAPTER I

A Preliminary Statement of an Important Vedāntic and Buddhistic Objection against the Jaina View of Reality, leading to the Formulation of Five Types of Approach to the Problem of Reality

CHAPTER I

An Objection Stated, and a Scheme of Five Types of Approach to the Problem of the Nature of Reality Formulated.

The present study aims at a critical and comparative exposition of certain ontological and epistemological problems centering round the most fundamental metaphysical presupposition of identity-in-difference in Jaina philosophy. It will be divided into two parts : Ontology (Part I) and Epistemology (Part II). The first part will comprise eight chapters in the course of which a critical examination will be undertaken, of the various non-Jaina schools—not excluding a few striking trends of Western schools—of philosophy, as well as of the Jaina school, from the point of view of the problem of the nature of reality as identity-in-difference. The latter part will include three chapters which contain, essentially, a treatment of some topics which have a bearing on the modes or methods of valid knowledge in Jaina philosophy. These topics are the doctrines of manifoldness (*anekāntavāda*), standpoints (*nayavāda*), and the dialectic of conditional predications (*syādvāda*).

A firm grasp of the Jaina view of reality as identity-in-difference can follow only when it is distinguished from the other views. We see among these other views several types : one of these types recognises mere *identity* as the ultimate nature of reality; another accords this status to *difference*; the third type treats *identity-in-difference* as the ultimate reality but considers identity as more primary than difference, while the fourth one adopts the converse viewpoint; and, lastly, the fifth type, represented by the Jaina view, considers identity and difference as being necessarily co-ordinate, or equal, elements in reality. Together, these types, each of which represents a basically distinctive viewpoint, give rise to a scheme of five-fold classification which will be referred to towards the end of this chapter.

Starting with an important objection made against the Jaina view of identity-in-difference by the Vedāntic and Buddhist thinkers, we shall, in the course of the present chapter, be led to a preliminary review of the basic metaphysical viewpoints of the two schools, and, eventually, to a formulation of the five-fold classification just referred to. A somewhat elaborate examination of these two schools as well as of several others—all of which come within the range of the five-fold classification—will then be attempted in the course of the following five chapters. In the course of this procedure a number of issues, connected with the development of the main problem of reality, will inevitably arise. They will also be touched upon according to their degree of relevance and importance in the present study.

Granting, for the moment, the validity of the Jaina conception of identity-in-difference, and equating this conception to that of being-cum-non-being—these and similar other equivalent concepts and epithets will be fully explained in their appropriate places—, we may begin with the statement of the Vedāntic objection.

The objection[1] runs as follows :—

"On account of the impossibility (of contradictory attributes) in one thing, (the Jaina doctrine is) not (to be accepted)" (*naikasminnasaṁbhavāt*).

Commenting on this aphorism of Bādarāyaṇa, Śaṅkara maintains that "...... it is impossible that contradictory attributes such as being and non-being should at the same time belong to one and the same thing; just as observation teaches us that a thing cannot be hot and cold at the same moment."[2] This charge of contradiction is made from the point of view of the philosopher of being or identity which has reached its logical perfection—or rather its extreme—in the metaphysics of Śaṅkara. The monistic foreshadowings[3] of the Upaniṣadic real have been forged with

---

1. *SBE*, Vol. XXXIV, p. 428. See also *BBSB*, p. 127, the *Vārtikam* and the *Pradīpaḥ* in *BSB*, p. 597 f., as well as the *Bhāṣyabhāvaprakāśikā* (by Citsukhamunim), printed at the end in the same work, p. 61, *Prakaṭārthavivaraṇam* (author unknown, ed. T. R. Chintamani, Madras University, 1935), Vol. I, p. 447 f., *Bhāmatī* (by Vācaspati Miśra, Kāshī Saṁ. Series, 1935), p. 291 f., and *Ratnaprabhā* (by Govindānanda in the *Aphorisms of the Vedānta*, ed. R. N. Vidyāratna, *Bib. Ind.*, 1863), Vol. I, pp. 583-84.
2. SBE, Vol. XXXIV, p. 429.
3. Cf: *eko devaḥ sarvabhūteṣu gūḍhaḥ sarvavyāpī sarvabhūtāntarātmā* / *Śvetāśvatara*, VI. 11. (*The Twelve Principal Upaniṣads*, TPH, Madras, 1931, Vol. I, p. 308.)

   tatra ko mohaḥ kaḥ śoka ekatvam anupaśyataḥ / *Īśa*, 7, *ibid.*, p. 8.

   īśā vāsyam idaṁ sarvam / *Ibid.*, 1, p. 5.

   Although such utterances signify the primary reality of a unitary principle they are not to be understood as signifying the unreality or illusoriness of the world as was done by Śaṅkara and his followers. See also the following f.n.

a radical transformation[1] into an identity-ridden (*sattādvaita*) ontological and logical scheme at the hands of Śaṅkara and his followers, who have reinforced the dialectical strength of their master. It is difficult to maintain that the Upaniṣads[2]

---

1. The transformation relates, among other things, to two important issues, viz., (a) imposing on the earlier Vedānta a two-plane reality (*nirguṇabrahman*, indeterminate absolute, and *saguṇabrahman*, determinate absolute, or Īśvara), and a corresponding two-plane truth (*parāvidyā* or 'higher knowledge' and *aparāvidyā* or 'lower knowledge'). Thibaut says, in this connection: "If we have not to discriminate between a lower and a higher knowledge of Brahman, it follows that the distinction of a lower and higher Brahman is likewise not valid". *SBE,* Vol. XXXIV, p. XCI); and (b) substituting *vivartavāda* (the theory of illusory world), in which the effect is unreal and the cause alone is real, for the earlier *pariṇāmavāda* in which both the cause and the effect are real. (Cf: "Is there anything in the early Upaniṣads to show that the authors believed in the objective world being an illusion? Nothing at all." E. W. Hopkins, *JAOS,* Vol. XXII, second half, p. 385 ff.)
2. " The Upaniṣads do not call upon us to look upon the whole world as a baseless illusion to be destroyed by knowledge, the great error which they admonish us to relinquish is rather that things have a separate individual existence, and are not tied together by the bond of being all of them effects of Brahman, or Brahman itself. They do not say that true knowledge sublates this false world, as Śaṅkara says, but that it enables the sage to extricate himself from the world—the inferior *mūrta rūpa* of Brahman, to use an expression of the Bṛhadāraṇyaka—and to become one with Brahman in its highest form. We are trying to see everything in Brahman, and Brahman in everything; the natural meaning of this is 'we look upon the whole world as a true manifestation of Brahman, as springing from it and animated by it'." He adds further that Māyāvāda also uses this saying but by "perverting its manifest sense". Thibaut, *SBE,* Vol. XXXIV, Intro. p. CXIX f. See also the following f.n. R. G. Bhandarkar confirms this fact when he observes: " The opinion expressed by some eminent scholars that the burden of *upaniṣad* teaching is the

or even the Brahmasūtras[1] consistently advocated the Śaṅkara view of *nirguṇabrahman* (pure, attributeless, or relationless identity) coupled with the unreality (*māyā*) of the world of difference and plurality if only for the reason that they are claimed, at least with equal, if not greater, validity, as the main source of the Brahminical schools such as the earlier Bhedābheda or the later Viśiṣṭādvaita metaphysics. The weight of evidence seems, on the contrary, to tilt the balance in favour of an integral view in which both identity and difference, being and becoming, the one and the many, are real or rather stand in a relationship of real cause to real effect. Several scholars suggest, and others definitely maintain, that Śaṅkara revolutionised[2], or even—in so far as he evolved the phenomenalist

---

illusive character of the world and the reality of the one soul only, is manifestly wrong and I may even say, is indicative of an uncritical judgement." *Vaiṣṇavism, Śaivism and Minor Religious Systems* (Strassburg, 1913), p. 2, f.n. 2.

1. Cf. "That the Māyā doctrine was not present to the mind of the Sūtrakāra further appears from the latter part of the fourth *pāda* of the first *adhyāya,* where it is shown that Brahman is not only the operative but also the material cause of the world. If anywhere, there would have been the place to indicate, had such been the author's view, that Brahman is the material cause of the world through Māyā only, and that the world is unreal, but the Sūtras do not contain a single word to that effect. Sūtra 26 on the other hand exhibits the significant term '*pariṇāmāt*'. Brahman produces the world by means of a modification of itself." Thibaut, *op. cit.,* p. XCIV f.

2. The revolution consists in the superaddition of phenomenalism (*māyāvāda*) derived perhaps from the Mādhyamika Buddhism (See Jacobi in *JAOS,* Vol. XXXIII, p. 54 and Sukthankar in the *Vienna Oriental Journal,* Vol. XXII, pp. 137-8), through Gauḍapāda, to the principle of identity derived from certain Upaniṣadic utterances. Cf. *HIP,* Vol. I, pp. 493-4.

view (*māyāvāda*) of the world—made a break with the prevailing realistic or evolutionary viewpoint according to which the unitary Brahman transforms itself into the manifold of the physical and vital universe without losing[1] its primordial nature of perfection or fullness[2]. The view maintained by Śaṅkara is appropriately characterised as *brahmavivartavāda* in contrast to its predecessor *brahmapariṇāmavāda.*

Brahman, according to Śaṅkara, is the sole reality which does not admit of any difference whatsoever. Ontologically, his view is, therefore, one of pure and undifferentiated being.

Advaitism then, affords the best example, in Indian metaphysics, of the philosophy of identity or permanence which is the exact antithesis to Buddhism which adheres, with equal tenacity, to the doctrine of total impermanence and the consequent idea of flux[3]. Except

---

With respect to the reality of one being, Bhartṛhari also seems to have influenced Śaṅkara. See S. N. Dasgupta's *Indian Idealism* (Cambridge, 1933), p. 196.

1. Cf. The schools of Bhartṛprapañca, Bhāskara, Yādava and Rāmānuja in the sequel.

2. Cf. *Om pūrṇam adaḥ pūrṇam idaṁ pūrṇāt pūrṇam udacyate /*
pūrṇasya purṇam ādāya pūrṇam evāvaśiṣyate //
—*The Twelve Principal Upaniṣads* (*TPH*), *Īśa,* p. 5.

3. Referring to the "two contrary philosophical systems" in regard to the problem of flux Stcherbatsky writes: "We are faced in India by two quite different theories of a Universal Flux. The motion representing the world-process is either a continuous motion or it is a discontinuous, although compact (*sāndratara*), one. The latter consists of an infinity of discrete moments following one another almost without intervals. In the first case the phenomena are nothing but waves or fluctua-

for the early sect of the Vātsīputrīyas[1] the ultimacy of

---

tions (*vṛtti*) standing out upon a background of an eternal, all-pervading, undifferentiated matter (*pradhāna*) with which they are identical. The Universe represents a Legato movement (*pariṇāmavāda*). In the second case there is no matter at all, flashes of energy (*saṁskāravāda*=*saṅghātavāda*) follow one another and produce the illusion of stabilized phenomena. The Universe is then a Staccato movement. The first view is maintained in the Sāṅkhya system of philosophy, the second prevails in Buddhism". (*Bud. Log.,* Vol. I, p. 83. The Sanskrit equivalents within brackets have been given in footnotes in the book.) For a contrast between the Buddhist view and the views of the Vaiśeṣika and the Naiyāyika on the nature of motion or change, see *ibid.,* pp. 99-107. For a further comparison with Bergson's view in the matter, see *ibid.,* p. 107, f.n. 9, and pp. 115-118. In spite of the overwhelming similarity between the Bergsonian and the Buddhistic view of change, in general, we should not fail to see an important difference between the two on the point of duration and moments : duration for the Buddhist is a mental construction and moments alone are real, whereas, for Bergson, the moments are "artificial cuts" in duration which alone is real. (Cf. *ibid.,* p. 115 and p. 118.) The "running reality" of Heraclitus of ancient Greece is another ontology which has a close resemblance to the Buddhistic view of momentary change. Here again a fundamental point of divergence, which is not often patent to a superficial observation, centers round the law of opposites or of contradiction. Buddhism roundly repudiates this law. (Cf. its famous universal dictum : *yo viruddhadharmādhyāsavān nāsau ekaḥ,* i. e., that (entity) of which two or more opposed characteristics are predicated cannot be one. Another expression of the same truth is: *viruddhadharmasaṁsargāt anyadvastu,* i. e., 'a thing is "other" if united to incompatible properties'. See *infra,* p. 23 and f.n. 3 thereon, and *NBTD,* p. 5.) Heraclitus, on the contrary, bases his theory on the "harmony of opposites". (Cf. *Bud. Log.,* Vol. I, pp. 425-7.)

The most admirable exposition of this school is found in Stcherbatsky's " The Soul Theory of the Buddhists" which forms "a special index" to the last chapter of Vasubandhu's *Abhidharmakośa.* The other works which give a statement and criticism of this school are the same author's *Bud. Log.*, Vol. I, p. 343 ff., Vol. II, p. 25, f.n. 2, p. 115, etc. and *The Central Conception of Buddhism*, pp. 70-71. See also *TSS*, *kārikās* 336-49, and S. Mookerji's *Buddhist Philosophy of Universal Flux* (Calcutta, 1935), pp. 185-192. Even this school which is referred to as " the only important departure from the original scheme" of Buddhism, "dared not readmit" the substance soul, nor was it "reluctant" to deny unity or "personality" (*pudgala*) among the separate elements of the aggregates (*saṅghāta*). Hence it is said to have resorted to a "dialectical" device and argued that the "personality was neither identical with the elements nor different from them". (Cf. *Bud. Log.*, Vol. I, p. 110.) Stcherbatsky's characterization of this hesitant or "feeble" attitude of the Vātsīputrīyas as a case of contradiction is right. But his comparison of this school with that of the Jainas is not well-founded : "This course of admitting dialectical reality", he writes, "and neglecting the law of contradiction reminds us of the dialectical method very popular among the Jainas and consisting in assuming everywhere a double and contradictory essence." (*Ibid.*). The Jaina theory of reality does not predicate contradictory attributes of the same subject at the same time and from the same point of view, although it admits the manifold (*anekānta*) nature of everything. Nor does it anywhere assume "a double and contradictory essence" in the nature of things. Mookerjee states the Jaina position as follows: "The Vedāntist starts with the premise that reality is one universal existence; the Buddhist fluxist believes in atomic particulars, each absolutely different from the rest and having nothing underlying them to bind them together....The Jaina differs from them and maintains that the universal and the particular are only distinguishable traits in a real." (*JPN*, p. 13.) Referring to the law of contradiction in relation to Jainism he further observes, " The Jaina also believes in the truth of the law of contradiction, but he insists that the law should be sought not in *a priori* thought but in concrete experience of the behaviour of a thing." (*Ibid.*, p. 14). Moreover, it emphatically affirms substantiality or identity as a co-ordinate (not contradictory) factor with that of difference in the real so that such a positive attitude becomes, in comparison with that of the hesitant Vātsīputrīyas, not a matter of difference in degree but one of kind.

change[1] or becoming[2] has been the unchanging bedrock of the great and complex development of Buddhistic thought from its beginnings : Like Bādarāyaṇa and Śaṅkara, Śāntarakṣita and his commentator Kamalaśīla direct, from the Buddhist point of view, the charge of self-contradictoriness (*viruddhadharmādhyāsa*) against the Jaina synthetic view of the co-ordinate existence of the substance[3] (*dravya*) and its modes or states (*paryāyas*): "If the oneness between the substance and the states is real" (not figurative or *agauṇa*), observes Kamalaśīla, "then the substance also becomes diversified (*vyāvṛttimat*) like the states. If (on the contrary) the states become pervasive (*anugatātmakāḥ*) in their character, then they become identical (*aikātmatā*) with the substance"[4]

---

1. "All things change....Change is the stuff of reality. There is neither permanence nor identity with regard to the world." *IP*, Vol. I, p. 368. Change, in Buddhism, does not mean a transformation occurring in an enduring medium. It is, so to say, a "revolution" rather than an "evolution", and, constitutes the sole reality. The thing must either remain or go, it cannot do both at once, changing and remaining. If it has changed, it is not the same (*na hi sa eva anyathā bhavati* or *naikasya anyathātvam asti*). The example of melted brass proves nothing. Melted brass and solid brass are "other" objects. (*Bud. Log.*, Vol. I, p. 98.) Therefore change is both total and perpetual.
2. "The becoming of all that is, is the central fact of Buddhism : Identity of objects is an unreality." *IP*, Vol. I, pp. 368-369 ff. "In his (Buddhist's) view there is no Being at all, and the only reality is Becoming". *OIP*, p. 211.
3. A real, according to Jainism, consists of substance and its modes (*dravyaparyāyātmakaṁ vastu*).
4. *TSS*, *kārikās* 317-18, E. T. mine. See also the next three *kārikās* and the *PK*. on all the five. In *kā*. 321 (given below) Śāntarakṣita clinches the argument against the Jaina thesis

Jitāri, another great Buddhist logician, adds his powerful voice to the attack in his *Anekāntavāda-Nirāsaḥ*.[1] The gist of his rather lengthy, but closely argued, polemic[2] against the *anekāntavādin's* theory of identity-in-difference may be stated as follows : When the *anekāntavādin* maintains that *dravya* and *paryāya* are identical, owing to the identity of their nature, it means that he affirms nothing short of their total identity (*ekarūpataiva*). Difference, based on (the

---

by the following criticism : Therefore, it must be admitted that either there is destruction of all, or that all is permanent: exclusiveness (*vyāvṛtti*) and inclusiveness (*anugama*) cannot subsist in any single entity. (*tato niranvayo dhvaṁsaḥ sthiraṁ vā sarvamiṣyatām/ ekātmani tu naiva sto vyāvṛtyanugamāvimau//*). The spirit of this criticism is that either the substance (identity, *dravya,* or *anugama*) perishes with the ever-perishing states (*paryāyas,* difference or *vyāvṛtti*), or the ever-persisting states become imperishable like the substance which supports them. This criticism is, of course, made against the Jaina theory of the real as a combination of the unity of a substance with the diversity of the states. It implies that the only two possibilities logically warranted by the Jaina position are either that substance should be pluralised like the inherent states, or the states should be integrated into a unity, the co-existence of unity and plurality being, according to the Buddhist, logically absurd. The adoption of either course knocks the bottom out of the Jaina metaphysics, driving it into the arms of either the eternalist Vedāntin or the fluxist Bauddha.

1. Printed as the last section in the *Tarkabhāṣā* and *Vādasthāna* of Mokṣākaragupta and Jitāripāda, edited by H. R. Rangaswami Iyengar, Mysore, 1944.

2. Its length forbids its full citation here. The gist of the argument stated above, however, gives the main issue raised. The whole account in the text is but an amplification of the issue and refers to the several finer shades of the argument. The issue is dealt with, in considerable detail, in the sequel from the Jaina point of view. See *infra*, Ch. V.

secondary consideration) number etc. (*saṅkhyādi*), will then be fictitious (*kalpanāmātrakalpitah syāt*). For, real difference (*pāramārthiko bhedaḥ*) between the two cannot proceed from the identity of their nature.[1] Or conversely, when the *anekāntavādin* pleads that *dravya* and *paryāya* are different, it means that he affirms their unqualified difference. Identity will then be fictitious. For real identity (*svabhāvabhedaḥ*) cannot proceed from the difference which is their basic and total nature. The truth about the whole position, according to Jitāri, is that one cannot have identity as well as difference by the same nature.[2] The entire argument, from the Buddhist side, may be said to have been grounded on the basic truth of the fundamental Buddhistic dictum : "It cannot be right to affirm and deny a thing at once, affirmation and denial being mutually contradictory".[3]

Thus we have seen that the same objection is raised by the two diametrically opposed systems of ontology, viz., the

---

1. *na hi yayoḥ svabhāvabhedaḥ tayoḥ anyathā pāramārthiko bhedaḥ sambhavati* / *Ibid.*, p. 112.

2. *na ca tenaiva svabhāvena bhedaś cābhedaśca* / *Ibid.*

3. *nahyekasya ekadā vidhipratiṣedhau parasparaviruddhau yuktau* / Again : *anyānanyayoḥ anyonyaparihārasthitalakṣaṇatvāt* / Kamalaśīla in *PK.* on *kārikās* 316 and 1795, respectively, in *TSS.* The implications of this argument are again set forth, in considerable detail, with particular reference to the *syādvādin's* view of the universal (*sāmānya*) and the particular (*viśeṣa*) in the section on "The Examination of *Syādvāda*" (*kārikās* 1709-1785 and the *PK.* thereon). The *kārikās* 1726-1735, together with the comm., specifically elucidate and refute the "mutually contradictory" position of the Jainas touching, incidentally, upon the idea of diversity as conceived by the *anekāntavādin.*

Vedānta and Buddhism, against the *anekānta* theory of reality.

The full significance, the necessity and the value of the Jaina defence, accompanied by a critical consideration of its opponents' fundamental assumptions governing their philosophical structure, can be fully appreciated only when the Jaina approach is viewed against the full background of Indian philosophy. Already a partial statement of the two principal opponent schools, viz., the Vedānta (Advaitism) and Buddhism, has been made mainly from the point of view of their criticism of the Jaina theory of reality. The identity-view of Advaita is, in this context, a comparatively straightforward and unequivocal position, despite an immense range of internal developments within the framework of its adherence to this fundamental viewpoint. Hence, except for a further brief review, no elaborate treatment of this school is called for. A somewhat fuller glimpse into the basic ideas of Buddhism is necessary in view of the great impact, ranging over several centuries,[1] of this system, on the development of *anekāntavāda*. In between these two extremes of Vedānta and Buddhism, either of which leads to a lop-sided view, there are several schools which endeavour, with varying degrees of success, a compromise or a synthesis between the identity or substance view and the difference or modal view.[2] These

---

1. Cf. "The principal actors on the Scene of 'The Indian Mediaeval School of Indian Logic' (460 A. D.–1200 A. D.) were, as is well-known, the Jainas and the Buddhists." *Vide, HIL,* pp. 157-158.

2. These are characterised, in the Jaina terminology, as *dravyārthikanaya* and *paryāyārthikanaya*, respectively.

schools also will have to be treated severally for two important reasons, viz., (a) that in common with the Vedāntin and the Buddhist, they (e.g., Viśiṣṭādvaita of Rāmānuja or Dvaita of Madhva) impute the charge of self-contradiction against Jainism; and (b) that they also afford rich material for a fruitful comparative study of the problem.[1]

In surveying the field of Indian philosophy from the point of view of the problem of the nature of reality we may adopt, as our guiding principle, the following five-fold classification which includes, within its scope, the different schools of philosophical thought in terms of their adherence to "identity" alone, or to "difference" alone, or to both in unequal or equal proportions. The five types of philosophy embodied in this classification are intended to include almost any school, whether or not specifically to be mentioned in the course of our comparative study, in so far as such a school comes within the purview of our inquiry into the nature of reality.

1. The Philosophy of Being or Identity.
2. The Philosophy of Becoming (Change) or Difference.

---

1. The Sāṅkhya, for instance, postulates the ultimate principles of *prakṛti* and *puruṣa* and yet swings, in the ultimate analysis, to the side of the Vedāntin by virtue of his predominant emphasis on identity as a *satkāryavādin*. Conversely, the logical end of the Vaiśeṣika's exclusive emphasis on the postulate of *viśeṣa* or particularity leads him to import *ab extra* the element of *samavāya* (the necessary relation, see Ch. VII), the untenability of which (the *samavāya*) is proved by the tremendous polemical storm that has been raised, in Indian Logic, over it. *Vide* the sections on the Sāṅkhya and the Vaiśesika in the sequel.

3. The Philosophy subordinating Difference to Identity.
4. The Philosophy subordinating Identity to Difference.
5. The Philosophy co-ordinating both Identity and Difference.

The Vedānta (Advaitism) as the school of Identity *par excellence* and Buddhism as the school of Difference *par excellence* are respectively brought under the first and the second categories in the above classification. The Sāṅkhya, the Bhedābhedavāda (of Bhartṛprapañca, Bhāskara, Yādava and Niṁbārka) and the Viśiṣṭādvaitavāda (of Rāmānuja) figure under the third category. The Vaiśeṣika and the Dvaita (of Madhva) systems come under the fourth type and Jainism under the last. Hegelianism, though a school of Western philosophy, will also be brought into this scheme owing to its being frequently cited as a close Western analogue or parallel of Jainism. On examination it will be found to align itself with the third category despite its agreement with Jainism in certain vital points. Incidentally the Śuddhādvaita of Vallabha (distinguished from the Kevalādvaita of Śaṅkara) will be referred to in a small footnote under Advaitism because of its exclusive emphasis on identity (Brahman) as in Advaitism. Where it differs from the latter is in being a *brahmapariṇāmavāda* and, therefore, in recognising the reality of the *jīva* (the finite self) and the *jaḍa* (physical world) as identical with Brahman (*brahmātmaka*). After the necessarily brief treatment, separate or incidental, of the various schools coming under the five categories of the classification, the Jaina theory of reality as a case of the meeting of extremes, and its answer to the common charge of self-contradiction and other errors believed to issue therefrom, will be outlined in its appropriate context. The other topics which more or less form corollaries of the theory will then be dealt with reserving, as already indicated, an inquiry into some epistemological problems for the second part of this study.

We may now proceed to consider the school or schools which have been first assigned to each of the five classes of approach indicated in the classification just formulated. Among these schools the Vedāntic absolutism and Buddhism which come under the first and the second categories respectively have already been dealt with. But the treatment has been very sketchy, at any rate of the latter system (Buddhism). Owing to the great importance of the issues involved a few additional remarks on the former system and a somewhat elaborate treatment of the latter one, will greatly help us in evolving a proper perspective in which the Jaina contribution to the effort of solving the ontological and the epistemological questions can be viewed.

CHAPTER II

A Study in Contrasts:

A. The Philosophy of Identity (or Being);

B. The Philosophy of Difference (Becoming or Change).

CHAPTER II

A. The Philosophy of Being or Identity

The Upaniṣads taught that Brahman is the ultimate reality[1] although they are not[2] definitely committed to the *vivartavāda* of Śaṅkara according to which the world is empirical or phenomenal (*māyā* or *vivarta*). Both the Vedic and the Upaniṣadic seers did not see any incompatibility[3] between conceiving Brahman with and without form (*rūpa* and *arūpa*), the whole and its parts and both unity and diversity. The difference[4] (*bheda*), between Brahman and the world was considered to be internal (*svagata*) or homogeneous (*sajātīya*) rather than external or heterogeneous (*vijātīya*). As a matter

---

1. The following Upaniṣadic utterances declare unity but do so without perhaps repudiating difference as *māyā* which is not unreasonably believed to have been foisted on them by Śaṅkara : *mṛtyoḥ sa mṛtyuṁ gacchati ya iha nāneva paśyati* (*Kaṭha* IV. 11, *Twelve Principal Upaniṣads*, TPH. Edn., Vol. I, p. 80). *vācāraṁbhaṇaṁ vikāro nāmadheyaṁ mṛttiketyeva satyam* (*Chāndogya*, VI. 1.4, *ibid.*, Vol. III, p. 189). *ekamevādvitīyam* (*Ibid.*, VI. 2.1, pp. 190-1).
2. See *supra*, pp. 15-18 and the footnotes thereon, for the views of Thibaut and Bhandarkar as well as for the references to the views of Jacobi and Sukthankar.
3. See Thibaut's remarks, *supra*, p. 16, f.n. 1 and 2.
4. The notion of difference has been conceived in three forms, viz., *sajātīya*, or the difference which exists between something and something else of the same class; *vijātīya*, or the difference which exists between something belonging to one class and another thing belonging to another class; and,

of fact it was conceived to be the nature of Brahman alternately to become the manifest world, i. e., to transform itself into the world, and to re-absorb the world into itself. We can, therefore, safely say that pre-Śaṅkara Vedānta was not a *vivartavāda* with its inevitable two-plane[1] reality—the one real and the other phenomenal—but a kind of evolutionary monism (*ekatvavāda*) or *brahmapariṇāmavāda* admitting, not altogether unconsciously, the dual reality of the transforming ultimate and its transformed manifestation of the world.

While Vedic-Upaniṣadic monism admitted of duality or difference and, therefore, characterised it (difference) in relatively positive terms, Śāṅkara Advaitism, employing a negativistic[2] method, perhaps under the influence of the Mādhyamika dialectic, attempted firmly to reject it. Consequently the former conceived *brahman* as the basic reality

---

svagata, or the difference which exists between the parts within a single body. The following stanza from *Pañcadaśī* (20) illustrates these forms :—

vṛkṣasya svagato bhedaḥ patrapuṣpaphalādibhiḥ /
vṛkṣāntarāt sajātīyo vijātīyaḥ sitāditaḥ //

1. Cf. *dve satye samupasṛtya buddhānāṁ dharmadeśanā /*
lokasaṁvṛtisatyaṁ ca satyaṁ ca paramārthataḥ //
ye 'nayorna vijānanti vibhāgam satyayordvayoḥ /
te tattvaṁ na vijānanti gambhīraṁ buddhaśāsane //

Mādhyamika Sūtra, XXIV. 8 f. See also Sukthankar's remarks in this connection, in the journal already referred to: *supra* p. 17, f.n. 2.

2. In framing his celebrated four-fold (*catuṣkoṭi*) dialectic the Mādhyamika is guided by the principle that every view (*diṭṭi*) is self-contradictory and is, therefore, self-convicted. The four 'moments' of the dialectic are *sat* ('is'), *asat* ('is not'), *sadasat* (both 'is' and 'is not') and *na sat naivāsat* (neither 'is' nor 'is not'). Assertion of any of these possibilities necessarily, implies, according to him, its opposite counterpart and, thereby

whereas the latter came to conceive it as the sole reality although both hold it to be permanent, homogeneous and universal. This divergence of views is traceable, mainly, to the distinction between the earlier concept of *vikāra*, or *pariṇāma*, or modification, and the later one of *vivarta* or illusoriness. Sadānanda clearly describes this distinction. He observes that "(When a thing) actually appears as another, it is called *vikāra*, when (it) falsely appears as another, it is called *vivarta*."[1] Or, to express the same idea somewhat technically : when an effect is a '*real* transformation' of its material cause (which is its essence), it is called *vikāra* or *pariṇāma*, but when it is a false or '*apparent* transformation', it is called *vivarta*.[2] This doctrine of *vivarta* is a bold innovation of Śaṅkara.

---

exhibits the fissure or contradiction at the heart of any view. He is protected against any criticism since he does not claim to take any definite attitude with regard to any question (*catuṣkoṭi vinirmuktam*).

Śaṇkara must have been influenced by this dialectical technique. He does not, however, extend this to *brahman*. His application of this destructive method is confined to the phenomenal world alone. The mode and the extent of his application of the above method are, of course, determined by various other circumstances like his adherence to the Upaniṣads, etc. Śrīharṣa, the greatest post-Śaṅkara dialectician, wields in his *Khaṇḍanakhaṇḍakhādya* this weapon with a devastating force against the opponents of Advaitism and serves his master in the same way as Zeno did Barmenides (See for instance the reference to Śrīharṣa's "Negative criticism against the notion of difference" in *HIP*, Vol. I, pp. 401-40).

1. *satattvato'nyathāprathā vikāra ityudīritaḥ /*
atattvato'nyathāprathā vivarta ityudīritaḥ //

Vedāntasāra, by Sadānanda, ed. with Intro. and E. T. by M. Hiriyanna, Poona, 1929, p. 8 (text), p. 54 (translation).

2. Cf. *upādānasamasattākaḥ pariṇāmaḥ /*
upādānaviṣamasattāko vivartaḥ //
Quoted, *ibid.*, Notes, p. 36.

It is on this bold innovation of the *vivarta* doctrine that Śaṅkara builds up his conception of the universe. The universe, which is either empirical (*vyāvahārika*) or phenomenal (*prātibhāsīka*), is intrinsically unreal (*mithyā* or *avastu*) from the point of view of the absolute which is the only true reality (*pāramārthika-sat*). It is the acknowledgement of the absolute as the only true reality (*ekamevādvitīyam*), which is identity (*abheda*) *par excellence*, that makes Advaitism the exemplar of the identity-view[1] in Indian philosophy.

---

1. Vallabha's *śuddhādvaitavāda* and Bhartṛhari's *śabdabrahmavāda* (or *śabdādvaitavāda*) come closest to Śaṅkara's Advaitism. *Śuddhādvaitavāda* has, or at any rate claims to have, a flavour of *brahmapariṇāmavāda* although its rigour as an identity-view is not thereby affected. *Śabdādvaitavāda* develops its identity-view from the angle of the philosophy of language. Reserving for a later occasion a brief reference to this linguistic trend of Advaitism a few relevant remarks regarding how Vallabha's doctrine tends to become an identity-view, may be made here :

   Vallabha's doctrine is referred to, as just noticed, as *śuddhādvaitavāda* or pure non-dualism in distinction from Śaṅkara's doctrine described as *kevalādvaitavāda,* or absolute non-dualism, or, more familiarly, Advaitism. Unlike the latter the former maintains the reality of the individual world (*jīva*) or souls, and the insentient world (*jaḍa)* and at the same time, it regards them, viz., the souls and the insentient world, as a real manifestation of *brahman* with which they are, therefore, said to be identical in essence (*brahmātmaka*). To express the same idea somewhat more specifically, their appearance and disappearance are attributed to the manifestation *(āvirbhāva)* and withdrawal (*tirobhāva*) of the will of *brahman.*

   The living and the non-living worlds are thus ultimately regarded, by Vallabha, as at one with *brahman.* Here we see the rift in the structure of the doctrine. The firm affirmation, in this doctrine, of the identity of essence between *brahman,* on the one hand, and the living and the non-living worlds, on

Giving wide berth to the modal principle (*bhedatattva*) is, of course, a necessary deduction from the logic of *vivarta-vāda*. But even Śaṅkara finds it hard summarily to dismiss this massive and obstinate principle. He constructs, after the manner of the Mādhyamika dialectic, an explanation by which he hopes to achieve the denial of this principle. But the explanation is more in the nature of a dialectical mystification than a genuine solution to the problem : it maintains that the universe, or the modal existence which is inherent in the universe, neither 'is'[1] (*sat* or *bhāvarūpa*), nor 'is not'[2] (*asat*, *abhāva*, or *tuccha*), but is something other than both 'is' and 'is not' (*sadasadvilakṣaṇa*)[3]. This unique something is also said to be inexpressible or

---

the other, is incompatible with the initial acceptance of the reality, which should mean the independent existence of the living and the non-living worlds. Hence *śuddhādvaitavāda* may be taken to affirm the ultimacy or reality of identity in the same measure as it eventually repudiates the intrinsic reality of the living and the non-living worlds. But since the repudiation of the intrinsic reality of the living and non-living worlds is, in the ultimate analysis, complete, the doctrine may be taken to be almost as strong an identity-view as Śaṅkara's Advaitism. This is so in spite of the professed inclination of Vallabha's doctrine towards *brahmapariṇāmavāda*, and the consequent denial of *māyā* as the source of the limitations such as indifference (*bheda*) and finitude.

1. See below f.n. 3.
2. See the following f.n.
3. Cf. "If it (i. e., the world arising from *avidyā*, or *ajñāna* or *māyā*), were real (*sat*), it would never be sublated; if unreal (*asat*), it would never appear (*saccenna bādhyeta / asaccenna pratīyeta /*). So it must be other than both (*vilakṣaṇa*)." See *Vedāntasāra* (Hiriyanna's edn.), Notes, p. 24. The words within the first brackets as well as the text quoted within the last brackets are of my inclusion.

anirvacanīya[1]. Being neither *sat* nor *asat* it is further suggested to be midway[2] between the two, a 'twilight', a 'real-unreal', or a 'true lie'.[3] It evidently indicates a 'third position' which aims at doing away with the contradiction with which *sat* and *asat* are supposed to be riddled.

But one doubts if this explanation offered in the form of a 'third position' is a real solution at all to the problem. It looks like an evasive device which, when shorn of its dialectical embellishments, harbours the very contradiction which it aims at banishing from its scheme. It is not, therefore, surprising if this position invokes against itself the charge which Kumārila makes in a similar context: he affirms that "that which does not exist, does not exist; and that which really exists is real, while all else is unreal; and, therefore, there can be no assumption of two kinds of reality".[4]

---

1. That is, *anirvacanīya* is that which cannot be said to be either 'is' or 'is not': *sadasadbhyām anirvacanīyam / Ibid.*, p. 2 (text) and Notes, p. 24. Also:

   pratyekaṁ sadasattvābhyāṁ vicāra-padavīṁ na yad /
   gāhate tad anirvacanīyam āhur vedānta-vedinaḥ //

   See *HIP*, Vol. II, p. 155, f.n. 2 (quoted from Citsukhi). This aspect of *anirvacanīya* will, again, be dealt with in its relation to the Jaina notion of *avaktavya,* in the ch. on *Syādvāda.*
2. Referring to the 'middle category' of *sadasadvilakṣaṇa*, A. Bhattacharya writes in his *Studies in Post-Śaṅkara Dialectics* (Univ. of Calcutta, 1936), p. 240: "It is a new category which shares in the characteristics of both position and negation and therefore a middle category between the two, positive-negative in its character."
3. The words quoted in this and the next sentences are from *Aspects of Advaita* (by P. N. Srinivasachari, Madras, 1949), p. 41.
4. *tasmādyannāsti nāstyeva yattvasti paramārthataḥ /*
   tatsatyam anyanmithyeti na satyadvayakalpanā //
   MSV, Nirālambavāda, kā. 10, E. T., S. V. Jha, p. 120.

The 'third position' is thus logically invalid although it is posited to exist somehow. Instead of bifurcating the entire course of reality into two compartments, viz., *brahman*, and the illusory universe which is *sadasadvilakṣaṇa*, and then investing *brahman* with the character of 'identity' (*abheda*, *advaita*) and relegating 'difference' (*bheda*) to an intrinsically illusory universe, it would perhaps be a more straightforward course to treat 'identity' and 'difference' as two complementary aspects of the entire concrete nature of reality. This procedure saves also the needlessly involved and paradoxical dialectic which initially treats the notions of *sat* and *asat* as contradictory and eventually combines them in a 'third position' which cannot but be contradictory but yet is believed to be somehow existent. As if these surprises are not enough Śaṅkara springs upon us yet another surprise by asserting that the difference-ridden illusory universe is mysteriously grounded in the identity-ridden real absolute.

These incongruities, however, do not deter Śaṅkara from converting the entire drama of reality into a grand monologue of the lonely absolute.

B. The Philosophy of Becoming (Change) or Difference

So far an attempt has been made to survey Advaitism as the most thorough-going instance of the philosophy of being or identity, the first among the five ontological approaches indicated in the previous chapter. A further attempt may now be made to review Buddhism as the unparalleled instance of the philosophy of becoming (change) or 'difference', the second typical ontological approach forming an antithesis to the first one. Buddhism is, as already noticed, a philosophy of total change[1] or difference[2] which divorces from the true or ultimate[3] reality all notions[4] like permanence (*nityatva*), identity (*tādātmya*), generality (*jāti* or *sāmānya*) and the subject-object relation, assigning them to the subjective

---

1. See *supra*, pp. 19 ff.
2. The sole and ultimately real (*paramārtha-sat*) in Buddhism, is the 'point-instant' or 'the moment' (*kṣaṇa*). Each moment is different from or 'other' than the rest in the series (*santāna*): "Whatsoever exists separately (*sarvaṁ pṛthak*) from 'other' existing things. To exist means to exist separately.....The notion of 'apartness' belongs to the essential feature of the notion of existence (*bhāvalakṣaṇapṛthaktvāt*)". *Bud. Log.*, Vol. I, p. 103. The words quoted within the brackets are from the footnotes in the same work. Again: "Thus every reality is another reality. What is identical or similar is not ultimately real". *Ibid.*, p. 105. See also *STBS*, p. 939. Stcherbatsky adds, in this connection, that "a difference in space-time is a difference in substance". *Bud. Log.*, Vol. II, p. 282f.
3. The moment which is the unique thing-in-itself (*svalakṣaṇa*) is the true or ultimate reality (*paramārtha-sat*). (See *NBD*, p. 103.) It is directly inaccessible to our understanding (*jñānena prāpayitum aśakyam*). What we apprehend as 'real' is only the constructed (*parikalpita*) or imagined reality which, though empirically real (*saṁvṛti-sat*) is an 'illusion' from the ultimate view-point (*paramārthataḥ*). Cp. *Bud. Log.*, Vol. I, p. 70 f.
4. Cf. "Everything past is unreal, everything future is unreal, everything imagined, absent, mental, notional, general: every Universal, whether a concrete Universal or abstract one, is unreal. All arrangements and all relations, if considered apart from the terms related, are unreal. Ultimately real is only the present moment of physical efficiency." *Ibid.*, p. 70 f., and p. 542.
5. Cf. *CCBS*, p. 58.

realm of 'mental construction'[1] (*vikalpa*, or *kalpanā*).

This emphasis on change is evidenced by the complex and varied history of the evolution of Buddhistic thought which took its rise from the three-fold truth of the Pāli Canons that everything (*savvam*) is impermanent (*anicca*),

---

1. *Vikalpa* or *Kalpanā* is an ideation, or an ideal construction, conceived by the mind. It does not originate from (*arthāt notpadyate*), or have any reference to the objective reality. Being thus independent of the objective reality (*artha-nirapekṣam*) and, therefore, purely mental or conceptual, both with respect to its form and its genesis, it is considered to "be unauthenticated and unreliable as evidence of objective reality". Cf. *anapekṣaṁ ca pratibhāsaniyamahetorabhāvāt aniyata-pratibhāsam / NBTD*, p. 11. The two phrases quoted above, in this passage, are also from the same work, p. 10 and p. 11 respectively. Cf. *The Buddhist Philosophy of Universal Flux* (S. Mookerjee, Univ. of Calcutta, 1935), pp. 283 and 345.

   Stcherbatsky suggests that *vikalpa* or *kalpanā* "covers, directly or indirectly, the whole range of thought, the active element in cognition". *The Conception of Buddhist Nirvāṇa* (Leningrad, 1927), p. 147, f.n. 2. When considered in relation to what has been pointed out in the above paragraph, this comes to mean that the lack of objective reference and, consequently, of reliable 'evidence' with regard to the objective world, affect almost 'the entire range of thought'. For an exhaustive account of *vikalpa or kalpanā*, see *TSS*, *kārikās* 1214-1311. A brief but lucid discussion is found in *NBTD*, pp. 9-11; *Nyāyapraveśavṛtti* p. 35f., and the *Pañjikā* (p. 75) thereon, both being commentaries on *Nyāyapraveśa* (attributed to Diṅnāga), Pt. I, ed. A. B. Dhruva, Baroda, 1930. In his Notes (pp. 89-94) to this work the editor draws our attention to (a) the critical references to the notion of *kalpanā*, made by some non-Buddhist thinkers such as Uddyotakara and Vācaspatimiśra; and (b) the different shades of meaning attached to the notion of *kalpanā* by the different schools of Buddhism. The distinction pointed out by Stcherbatsky, between *vitarka* or *vikalpa* and *vicāra*, though not of material importance, also deserves our attention, in this context. See *CCBS*, pp. 104-105.

soulless or substanceless (*anatta*) and the cause of pain (*dukkha*) as against the Upaniṣadic view of an *ātman* (soul) which is eternal (*nitya*) and pure bliss (*ānanda*). Philosophically the *anicca* and the *anatta* elements of the early Buddhistic thought resulted in the great and daring metaphysics of *nairātmyavāda*[1] (the doctrine of 'soullessness'[2] or

1. The central point of *nairātmyavāda* consists in the repudiation of an 'ego', or an enduring entity behind the so-called phenomenal changes in the world. The most effective disproof of an 'ego' is contained in the dialogue—not reproduced here for fear of length—between King Milinda and the monk Nāgasena as to the nature of Nāgasena and of the chariot.

   At the conclusion Nāgasena, in the sense of an 'ego', is discovered to be "a mere empty sound" and the chariot to be "but a way of counting, term, appellation, convenient designation, and name for pole, axle, wheels, chariot-body, and banner-staff". There is said to be nothing beyond the five aggregates (*skandhas*) constituting the phenomena in the world. Nāgasena quotes the following lines from Vajira in proof of this thesis: "Even as the word 'chariot' means that members join to frame a whole; so when the Groups appear to view, we use the phrase, 'A living being'." *Buddhism in Translations* (H. C. Warren, Cambridge, Mass., 1915), pp. 128-133. The other instances cited from the *Visuddhimagga* (Chap. XVIII) are of a "house", a "fist", a "lute", an "army", a "city", and a "tree". *Ibid.*, p. 133 ff. The following verse from *Visuddhimagga* (Chap. XVI) gives an effective expression of the *Nairātmya* truth:

   "Misery only doth exist, none miserable
   No doer is there; naught save the deed is found.
   Nirvāṇa is, but not the man who seeks it.
   The path exists, but not the traveller in it."

   Ibid., p. 146. Cf. also in this connection T. W. Rhys David's reflections on this subject in *Pottapāda Sutta,* the Dialogues of the Buddha (*Sacred Books of the Buddhists,* Vol. II, Pt. I, Intro., p. 242, especially para 3).

2. This and the next term are as translated by Stcherbatsky in *STBS*. La Vallee Poussin, however, prefers translating *nairātmya* into 'selflessness' to 'soullessness'. See *The Way to Nirvāṇa* (Cambridge, 1917), p. 34.

'no-substance' or substancelessness) which is in diametrical opposition to the *ātmavāda* (substance-view or identity-view) of the Upaniṣads and the other schools[1], and runs through all schools of Buddhism[2]—from the *Ābhidhārmika* (*Vaibhāṣika*) stage to that of *Yogācāra* (*Vijñānavāda*)—their internal differences notwithstanding. The quintessence of the *nairātmya*[3] attitude consists in the denial of the *satkāyadṛṣṭi*

---

1. See the following f.n.
2. Except the school of Vatsīputrīyas (or Sammatīyas) whose view has already been referred to, see *supra*, p. 19 f., f.n. 1.

   Yaśomitra cites a line which claims the unique right to Buddha for the teaching of *nairātmyavāda*: *anyaḥ śāstā jagati ca yato nāsti nairātmyavādāt.* Yaśomitra's *Abhidhammakosa-vyākhyā* (ed. Unrai Wogihara, Tokyo, 1932-1936), Pt. II, p. 697. Deriding Vardhamāna, Kapila and others who, like the Upaniṣadic thinkers, are held "in the clutches of the crocodile of the false doctrine of the 'soul' (or substance)" Śāntarakṣita says :

   idaṁ ca vardhamānādernairātmyajñānamīdṛśam /
   na samastyātmadṛṣṭau hi vinaṣṭāḥ sarvatīrthikāḥ //

   TSS, *kā*. 3325. We notice, in the second line, that the heretical philosophers (*tīrthikāḥ*) are said to be 'lost' (*vinaṣṭāḥ*) in the heresy of a soul (*ātmadṛṣṭau*). La Vallee Poussin points out, in this connection, an interesting distinction between 'a heresy' or *dṛṣṭi* and a sin in his *The Way to Nirvāṇa*, p. 46, f.n. 1. This is the central point in which Buddhism differs from many other schools which believe in the substance of a soul. This is why Udayana significantly entitles his refutation of Buddhism as *Ātmatattvaviveka* (an inquiry into the reality of the self).
3. Literally the word means 'the state of being devoid of Ātman' Vidushekhara Bhattacharya has drawn our attention to the meaning of '*atman*' as *svabhāva* or nature 'which never under goes any change'. He also refers to the two-fold distinction of *nairātmya*, viz., *pudgalnairātmya* and *dharmanairātmya*. *Vide*, *The Basic Conception of Buddhism*, Vidushekhara Bhattacharya, University of Calcutta, 1934, p. 73.
4. For the various derivations of *Satkāyadṛṣṭi* (Pali—*Sakkaya-ditthi*) see *ibid.*, p. 77 f., f.n. 30.

which signifies an enduring entity, the "something I know not what", as Locke puts it, behind the dynamic and discrete moments.

Perhaps the varied developments of Buddhism are a continual series of approximations to the spirit of the 'enlightenment' (*bodhi*) which dawned upon the Buddha who must have felt that this mischievous or dangerous idea of an enduring something behind the goings-on of our life and the world breeds a craving for possession and the consequent ills[1] of despair and suffering at loss. In the words of Stcherbatsky the history of Buddhism is "a series of attempts to penetrate more deeply into the original intuition of Buddha, what he himself believed to be his great discovery".[2] The same writer refers to "a sense of opposition or even animosity" as being "clearly felt" in the words of Buddha whenever he (Buddha) talked about *satkāyadṛṣṭi* or the doctrines of a permanent self or substance. Mrs. Caroline Rhys Davids also remarks[3] "how carefully and conscientiously this antisubstantialist position had been cherished and upheld" as the "central point of the whole bulk of Buddhist teaching".

Thus the original character of soullessness or substancelessness remains the fundamental attitude of Buddhism in spite of the fact that we find several different shades of idealism and realism within the range of its philosophical

1. *ātma-dṛṣṭau ca satyam ātma-snehādayaḥ kleśāḥ pravartante* / *STBD, Abhidharmakośavyākhyā,* p. 697.

2. *Ibid.,* p. 824.

3. Quoted: *ibid.,* pp. 824-5.

evolution[1]. Impermanence (*anicca*) and soullessness (*anatta*) are, according to this view, the 'pitiless' laws of all existence so that existence becomes a cinematograph[2] show, the discrete moments[3] of which flash themselves into being serially

---

1. Cf. *OIP*, pp. 197-8.
2. Stcherbatsky rightly compares this to Bergson's view: "Bergson compares our cognitive apparatus with a cinematograph which reconstitutes a movement of momentary stabilized snapshots. This is exactly the Buddhist view". *Bud. Log.*, Vol. I, p. 117. But comparing this Buddhistic viewpoint with that of Russell, who also illustrates it with the analogy of a 'cinematograph' would be even more appropriate in view of the fact that Bergson's real is an unbroken flow of duration, while that of Russell is one of atomistic, or discrete, ultimate particulars. Russell, illustrating his point, observes that ".... the cinema is a better metaphysician than common-sense physics or philosophy". "My meaning in regard to the impermanence of physical entities may perhaps be more clear by the use of Bergson's favourite illustration of the cinematograph. ......Where, in a picture palace, we see a man rolling down a hill....we know that there is not really one man moving, but a succession of films each with a different momentary man." Russell's statements, quoted in course of this f.n. are from his *Mysticism and Logic*, London, 1950, pp. 128-9. It is curious how such contrasting viewpoints as Bergson's and Russell's can use the same analogy of the cinematograph with equal effect. Bergson is a durationist and Russell is a logical atomist although both agree with Buddhism in conceiving the real as flux or a group of impermanent physical entities. For a further treatment of the relation between Buddhism, on the one hand, and some important notions of Russell's logical atomism and Bergson's durationism (especially of the former) on the other, see the rather lengthy f.n. 2 on p. 44 ff. below.
3. The doctrine of discrete moments, or of momentariness, is the logical outcome, or 'the furthest extreme', of the doctrine of impermanence which, according to Vidushekhara Bhattacharya, antidated Buddhism. *Vide, The Basic Conception of Buddhism*, p. 83. After suggesting the general distinction between impermanence and momentariness Bhattacharya rightly adds: "In dealing with the Buddhist position by impermanence we are

as it were and vanish without a trace (*niranvaya kṣaṇika*). Whatever story is imposed upon them is the colourful imposition of our fancy. The flow or the passage of these momentary flashings is all that there is in reality. This metaphysics of process or becoming of the discrete and unique particulars is considered to be midway between the two extreme views, viz., "everything is" (*nityavāda* or eternalism) and "everything is not" (*tucchavāda* or nihilism).

The main purpose of bringing in Buddhism here is to show that it concerns itself with what may be designated as the modal view of reality by its exclusive emphasis on the unique, momentary and absolute particulars which constitute reality which is becoming or flux. The particulars are absolutely unique, not sharing their essence with anything[1] else and, therefore, differ[2] totally one from another (*trailo-*

---

to understand this momentariness." *Ibid.* Hiriyanna, however, assumes a slightly hesitant position on this issue. See *OIP*, p. 144.

1. Each such particular is something which has "not the slightest bit of otherness" in it (*aṇīyasāpi na aṁśena aparātmakam*). See *Bud. Log.*, Vol. I, p. 557.
2. The moments are emphatically asserted to be unique and, therefore, different from one another in a series (*santāna*). But they are also said to have some affinity or 'correlation' with their immediately antecedent moments, and hence, to arise in a uniform succession as, for instance, a moment of flame being succeeded by a 'similar' moment of flame. This implication of 'similarity' or 'continuity' (or 'continuation') is based on the Buddhistic causal theory of *pratītyasamutpāda*, i.e. 'dependent origination' or 'functional dependence' in contrast with that of *adhītyasamutpāda*, i. e., the theory of production at random and is supposed to permit uniformity without the need of the much-abhorred enduring entity underlying the fleeting phenomena. (For a statement of the several implications of

pratītyasamutpāda, and of the relation between *pratītyasamutpāda* and *adhītyasamutpāda,* see Stcherbatsky's *The Conception of Nirvāṇa,* p. 39, f.n. 2, p. 123, f.n. 4, p. 124 and p. 240.) But admission of similarity or continuity seems to be an unsafe compromise if not a self-contradiction which is in direct proportion to the need of this element of continuity or co-ordination. Moreover, admitting something which transcends the solely real moment or point-instant (*kṣaṇa*) also leads, to that extent, to compromising the exclusive reality of the moment.

While considering the paradoxical admission of continuity in Buddhism the parallel instance of Bertrand Russell's acceptance of the same idea (continuity) in his "logical atomism" suggests itself inevitably. Besides offering a classic parallel to Buddhism, in the twentieth century, it reiterates the lesson that an essential principle surreptitiously comes back through the back door, if it is thrust away from the front. The following passage looks like the Buddhist argument in a modern garb: "The world may be conceived as consisting of a multitude of entities arranged in a certain pattern. The entities which are arranged I shall call 'particulars'; the arrangement of pattern results from relations among particulars. Classes or series of particulars, collected together on account of some property which makes it convenient to be able to speak of them as wholes, are what I call logical constructions or symbolic fictions. The particulars are to be conceived, not on the analogy of bricks in a building, but rather on the analogy of notes in a symphony. The ultimate constituents of a symphony (apart from relations) are the notes, each of which lasts only for a very short time. We may collect together all the notes played by one instrument; these may be regarded as the analogues of the successive particulars which common-sense would regard as successive states of one "thing". But the "thing" ought to be regarded as no more 'real' or 'substantial' than, for example, the role of the trombone. As soon as 'things' are conceived in this manner it will be found that the difficulties in the way of regarding immediate objects of sense as physical have largely disappeared." *Mysticism and Logic,* pp. 129-30. For a further demonstration of continuity, *vide* Russell's three famous physiological, psychological and logical arguments in *OKEW*, pp. 145-158. (The main thesis is summarily stated in the last paragraph on p. 158.)

Important as it is, the agreement between Russell and Buddhism, as regards continuity, is not complete. As a matter of fact his "logical atomism" and Buddhism differ more than they agree on the issue of continuity. Russell's scathing attack on the Bergsonian La Duree undoubtedly bears comparison with the age-long battle Buddhism has waged against eternalism (*śāśvatavāda*) although the latter has been more thorough and many-sided. As for the interpretation of continuity Russell's approach is mathematical and complex, whereas Buddhists' approach is dialetical and relatively simple : Buddhism understands by continuity a mere "consecutiveness" or a uniform "uninterrupted succession of similar events". For Russell even "the lowest degree of continuity", which is described as "compactness", is more complex than the Buddhist ideas. Russell writes : " Mathematicians have distinguished different degrees of continuity and have confined the word 'continuous' for technical purposes, to series having a certain high degree of continuity. But for philosophical purposes, all that is important in continuity is introduced by the lowest degree of continuity which is called 'compactness' ". *Ibid.*, p. 138.

This difference between the simple consecutiveness which is signified by the idea of succession and the more complex "compactness"—not to mention the kinds of "high degree of continuity" —becomes clear when we understand the definition of "compactness". "A series is called 'compact'," Russell writes, "when no two terms are consecutive, but between any two there are others." (*Ibid.*) The number of such terms coming between them may be (according to him) "infinite". He illustrates this point as follows: "Given any two fractions, however near together, there are other fractions greater than the one and smaller than the other, and therefore no two fractions are consecutive. There is no fraction, for example, which is next after 1/2; if we choose some fraction which is very little greater than 1/2, say 51/100, we can find others, such as 101/200, which are nearer to 1/2. Thus between any two fractions, however little they differ, there are infinite numbers of other fractions." (*Ibid.*) Critics (e. g. Stcherbatsky in *Bud. Log.*, Vol. I, pp. 142-4 etc., S. Mookerjee in the *Buddhist Philosophy of Universal Flux*, p. 17f., f.n. 1) are more ready in noticing the "striking" coincidence of Russell's position with that of Buddhism, in this connection,—it is, indeed "striking" as a matter of broad comparison—than in delving into the subtle but important

kyavyāvarta). They are sole[1] objects of perception and

---

differences between the two positions. But the existence of such differences does not affect the general tone of agreement between the two positions, on the solutions offered to the problem of continuity.

Finally, it should be said that in spite of the extraordinary ingenuity shown in his solution of continuity by his method of "logical construction" we cannot help feeling that Bertrand Russell has not succeeded in convincing us that "compactness" or even the highest degree of discrete "continuity" can offer a genuine substitute for identity or permanence. Buddhism fares no better in this respect. The strength of their polemics against identity or permanence indicates the strength of the persistence of identity or permanence as a complementary element in being as in knowing.

1. *Sa eva ca pratyakṣaviṣayo yataḥ tasmāt tadeva svalakṣaṇam* (*Nyāyabindu* with *Nyāyabinduṭīkā, Bibliotheca Buddhica*, VII, p. 13). Stcherbatsky translates this as: "Since it is just that thing which is the object (producing) direct perception, therefore the particular (i. e., the unique moment, the thing in itself) is the exclusive object of sense-perception." *Bud. Log.*, Vol. II, p. 36.

Although a unique particular is the object of perception its knowledge cannot be had at the perceptual level (see the following f.n.). It is only at the conceptual level that the mind can form a cognitive image or notion of the particular by imposing the conceptual forms, such as the universals, relations, etc., (Such forms are collectively designated, by the Buddhist, as *sāmānyalakṣaṇas* in contrast with the *svalakṣaṇas*) on it.

The curious thing about the notion of the object thus obtained is that it does not, according to the Buddhist, represent the object as such but represents, on the contrary, the negation, or "the rejection", of what is other than—or the opposite of—the object (*anyāpoha*). For instance, a cow is said to be the negation of non-cow (*agonivṛttiḥ.*) Similarly, "bitter" (*tikta*) is described as the negation of "non-bitter" and "sweet" (*madhura*) as the negation of "non-sweet". (See S.V. Jha, p. 317, f. n. 121-122.) While discussing "Inference" Randle states on the authority of Uddyotakara, "the real meaning" of *apoha*, a term to be presently referred to, as follows: "If you say A is B, your real meaning may be that A is not not B—or, if you prefer, that A is not not-B,—or again, that not-not A is B, or even that not-not A is not-not not-not B." (*Indian Logic in the Early Schools*, London etc., 1930, p. 182, f.n. 1; see also p. 261, f.n. 2 and 3.)

Apohavāda is the name given to this theory according to which an object is conceived to be the negation of its opposite. Diṅnāga is the earliest exponent of this theory. He expounded it in his *Pramāṇa-samuccaya* (ch. V; see *HIL*, p. 287) in the extreme negative form which has just been illustrated. This form is specifically designated as *anyāpohavāda* in distinction from other two forms which will presently be mentioned.

A powerful polemic has been directed against this negative theory by several Brahminical and the Jaina writers from the points of view of their respective schools. The most notable Brahminical writers are: Uddyotakara (*Nyāyavārtika, Bib. Ind.* II. 2.65; *TBV*, p. 200 f., and *TSS, kārikās* 982-1000), Vācaspatimiśra's *Nyāyavārtikatātparyaṭīkā, Apohavāda*, E. T. in *Bud. Log.*, Vol. II, Appendix V), Bhāmaha (*TSS, kārikās* 912-914; *kā.* 13 has been quoted below in a context similar to this. See *infra*, ch. XI.), Kumārila (*MSV*, the extensive ch. on *apoha*), Jayanta (*Nyāyamañjarī*, ed. Gangadhara Sastri Tailanga, Benares, 1895, Pt. I, p. 316) and Bhartṛhari (*Vākyapadīya*, ed. Gangadhara Sastri Manavalli, Benares, 1887, ch. II, *kārikās* 118-154). The following are the notable Jaina critics of this theory: Abhayadeva (an extensive treatment of the topic in his *TBV*, pp. 173-270), Prabhācandra (*PKM*, 43-451 and *NKC*, Vol. II, pp. 551-566), Haribhadra (*AJP*, Ch. IV) *Śāntyācārya* (*NVVS*, pp. 96-98) and Siddharṣi (in *Vivṛti* on *Nyāyāvatāra*, P. L. Vaidya's edn., p. 4 f.).

Most of the above critics point out that the total lack of any reference to a positive content in Diṅnāga's negative notion of *apoha* exposes the notion to a suicidal danger (e.g. *MSV*, *kārikās* 134, 142-145, 147, etc., *NKC*, Vol. II, p. 563, the end of para. 1; and *AJP*, Vol. II, p. 403, *kā.* 6). Among others Kumārila, Prabhācandra, and Śāntyācārya emphasise the fact that logically speaking, even the notion of *apoha* does, or at any rate should, refer to a positive content, or a real object. For according to them, negation does not refer to void, of which *apoha* is said to be a variant form (cf. *apohaśabdavācyātha śūnyatānyaprakārikā* /*MSV*., p. 576, *kā.* 36), but to some different positive entity (cf. *bhāvān-*

taram abhāvo hi / MSV, p. 566, *kā.* 2; *sarvathā asataḥ pratibhāsa ayogāt / AJP*, Vol. II, p. 351; *NVVS*, p. 97, lines 17-18; and *NKC*, Vol. II, p. 562, line 8). The significance of negation in the Jaina metaphysics will be treated at the appropriate place. (See *infra*, ch. V.)

As a result of the many-sided attack by the various critics, the most notable of whom have just been noticed, the Buddhist attitude towards *apohavāda* underwent what might be described after Hegel as a triadic course of development. The thesis of Diṅnāga that *apoha* signifies nothing but negation fails to commend itself to Śāntarakṣita and Kamalaśīla. These latter thinkers take a realistic view—which may be described as an antithesis to that of Diṅnāga—in which *apoha* signifies a positive content (*bāhyārthādhyavasāyī, arthapratibimbakam*—see e.g., *TSS*, *kā.* 1011 and the *PK* thereon). They treat negation (in the sense that 'the nature of this thing is not the nature of the other thing') as only an implication which does not form an integral part of the positive 'felt content' but arises later when reflection plays upon the 'felt content' (see *TSS*, *kārikās* 1013-1015 and the *PK* thereon.)

Ratnakīrti comes upon this scene, where we find an unbridged gulf between the negative and the positive views on *apoha*, and attempts a synthesis. As a necessary step in this attempt he rules out the realistic argument that *apoha* denotes a positive content only (*nāsmābhiḥ apohaśabdena vidhireva kevalo'bhipretaḥ / SBNT*, p. 3) and that the negative import is just a later logical implication following the elusive perceptual presentation of the positive ('felt') content. (*Ibid.*)

He is equally firm in repudiating the converse view of the 'Negationist' (*anyāpohavādin*) that *apoha* is purely negative (*nāpyanyavyāvṛttimātram / Ibid.*) and that its positive reference is a later logical deduction (*ibid.*). His own view is that *apoha* is both positive and negative in its meaning (or content), and that both these elements are presented at once (*anyāpohaviśiṣṭo vidhiḥ śabdānām arthaḥ / Ibid.* See also the Preface, p. 1, para 2, and Keith's *Buddhist Philosophy*, Oxford, 1923, p. 317).

Thus we find three decisive landmarks in development of *apohavāda*, viz., the purely negative view of the pioneer Diṅnāga, the positive view of Śāntarakṣita and his alter ego Kamalaśīla, and lastly, the reconciliatory view of Ratnakīrti.

In the triangular fight over the interpretation of the natue of *apoha*, Ratnakīrti emerges, as just noticed, as a victorious synthesist of the two opposing trends. This victory seems to point to the truth that the true nature of any aspect of reality, nay, of the entire reality, consists in a synthesis of the positive and the negative aspects. The realization of the need for such a comprehensive synthesis, within howsoever limited an aspect it may be, is the result of a bold departure from the purely negativistic beginnings of the theory. But even the bold genius of Ratnakīrti stopped short of breaking through the narrow framework of the nominalistic metaphysics of momentariness, and of extending the limited truth of his discovery over the whole range of reality. The reverence for the master Diṅnāga seems to be so overpowering that none of the dissenters from Diṅnāga, the champion of negativism, has had the courage to declare openly the fact that he is dissenting. Even Ratnakīrti is no exception in this matter. They have all tried to rationalize, or read their minds into the view of the master. (This aspect of whether *apoha* denotes a positive, or a negative, or both positive and negative, signification of objects, is one among the several aspects, such as the nature of the universal, the relation between the word and the object, and so on, with which *apohavāda* is concerned. As a matter of fact, even the present aspect of the theory seems to have been keenly debated, not merely between the Buddhist and the non-Buddhist thinkers—as indicated by the reference to the non-Buddhist critics and their works in this footnote—but also between many Buddhist thinkers themselves at various stages. For instance, Ratnakīrti hints two groups of philosophers who held the positive or the negative view of the theory. They are referred to as *vidhivādins* and *pratiṣedhavādins*, respectively, in his *Apohasiddhi, SBNT*, p. 3. Jñānaśrī belongs, as can be seen in *PVD*, 167 ff., to the latter one. The Tibetan literature on *apohavāda* is said to be "very vast" (see *Bud. Log.*, Vol. II, p. 404). Dharmottara also is said to have written a 'special work' on the subject. Von E. Frauwallner's articles on 'Beitrage zur Apohalehre' in the *Vienna Oriental Journal* (Vol. XXXIX, pp. 247-285; Vol. XL, pp. 51-94; Vol. XLII, pp. 93-102; and Vol. XLIV, pp. 233-287, including a Tibetan text) deal with this subject at some length.

perception is the only source of their direct[1] knowledge. There is nothing besides these ultimate constituents[2] (*paramārthasat*), which neither extend in space (*deśānanugata*) nor stretch in duration (*kālānanugata*) beyond the twinkling flashes of moments. Unlike the monads of Leibnitz which, though 'windowless' in relation to other monads[3] communicate with God, these unique reals of Buddhism are entirely self-contained and therefore form a procession of full-stops as it were, in the process of reality. They are entirely disparate or unconnected[4]. Connection or relation is, as has already been observed, imposed on them by our distorting imagination (*kalpanā*). Being exclusive or self-sufficient they do not change. Change is spontaneous[5] and they are, therefore, self-productive and self-destructive. Hence nothing can destroy a thing if the power of destruction is not inherent in its

---

1. But the so-called direct knowledge is 'speechless' or indescribable (*anabhilāpya*) because an attempt to describe the 'brute fact', or percept (i. e. perceived something) is necessarily accompanied by overlaying the percept with ideal or mental categories. Uddyotakara is, therefore, right in characterising that this percept is 'like a dumb man's dream' (*mūkasvapnavat*). Cf. Randle's *Fragments from Diṅnāga*, p. 84 and f.n. 1 thereon.
2. Dharmottara observes that 'ultimate reality is in its turn the ultimate particular' (see *NBT*, p. 17 and *Bud. Log.*, Vol. I, p. 192).
3. They differ also in respect of their being entities which reflect the entire universe which is pregnant with the past and the future—from their own points of view. The *svalakṣaṇas* (unique reals) are efficient rather than reflecting forces.
4. Although they are 'similar' to each other the 'similarity' or continuity does not, according to Buddhism, form part of their inmost nature (see *supra*, p. 44 ff., f.n. 2).
5. The following 'celebrated' verse, previously uttered by the Bodhisattva, is cited by Buddha on the eve of his (Buddha's) death. That change is two-fold ('growth' and 'decay') as well as spontaneous or inherent in all things ('their nature', there-

nature even as nothing can bring it into existence if such power is not already within it. A jar, for instance, appears to be destroyed by the blow of a staff but this is not really so. The destruction must be entirely attributed to the natural potency of the fleeting forces which previously emerged into existence to become the phenomenon that is the jar[1]. This potency for momentary self-emergence and self-destruction is called *arthakriyāsāmarthyam* and it is the very essence of reality (*arthakriyāsāmarthyalakṣaṇatvād vastunaḥ*[2]).

For the Buddhist, momentariness and efficiency are inseparable. Reality is momentary because it is efficient and it is efficient because it is momentary. Anything which is

---

fore, not something *ab extra*) is specifically uttered in the second and the third lines of the verse:

aniccā vata saṅkārā
uppādavvaya dhammino /
uppajjittvā nirujjhanti
tesaṁ vūpasamo sukho //

Mahā sudassana suttanta, The Dīgha Nikāya, Pali Text Society, Vol. II, p. 199. The following is the E. T. of the verse:

How transient are all compound things!
Growth is their nature and decay,
They are produced, they are dissolved again;
To bring them all into subjection—that is bliss.

Sacred Books of the Buddhists, Vol. III, p. 232. See also Intro., pp. 194-195.

1. Cp. *The Buddhist Philosophy of Universal Flux,* pp. 1-5.
2. For reference to the Buddhist works wherein this idea, Biz. *arthakriyāsāmarthyam,* is dealt with, see *infra,* ch. V.

What follows, is a Buddhist polemic against the possibility of causal efficiency (*arthakriyākāritvam*) in the substance-view (*dravyavāda*) of any description.

The Jaina has no objection to join the Buddhist in this polemical attack but he does so on two conditions: one, that the substance-view attacked by the Buddhist is of the extreme or

non-momentary and non-efficient is unreal[1]. This attitude puts the Buddhist in opposition to the Naiyāyika and others who subscribe to the notion of a permanent substance. If the substance is permanent, the Buddhist would argue, there are only two ways of its being efficient in the production of its effects : the one simultaneous, the other successive. Both lead to absurdity : in the first case, the substance ought to produce *all the effects* it is capable of in the very first moment of its existence. Nothing should stand in the way of the spontaneous production of its effects. But if it produces all its effects, as it should, at once, then its potency is exhausted and its continued existence in the subsequent moments will be empty and meaningless. If, however, it continues to exist even though it is not potent or productive, then another difficulty sets in, viz., the incompatibility between productivity (*sāmarthya*) in the first moment and non-productivity (*asāmarthya*) in succeeding moments. This militates against the fundamental law of all existence, viz., nothing which has opposed characteristics can be one entity[2] (*viruddhadharmādhyāsavān nāsāvekaḥ*).

---

exclusive type (*ekāntadravyavāda*) and, two, that it is also of the static type (*kūṭasthanityavāda*). These conditions will again be mentioned (see *infra*, ch. V) in the course of the section on *arthakriyākāritvavāda* (see *infra*, ch. V). A criticism against the Buddhist view of this *vāda*, in the light of the Jainas' own of the subject, will also be discussed in that section.

1. As a matter of fact, momentariness, efficiency, causality and reality are treated as synonyms and, conversely, what is non-momentary or non-efficient, non-causal, is unreal (*nissvabhāvatvāt*) or non-existent (*abhāvarūpa eva*) : *akāraṇam asad eva*/ *PK* on *TSS*, *kā*. 384; see also *Bud. Log.*, Vol. I, p. 124 ff.
2. See *supra*, p. 23 and f.n. 3 thereon.

Again, the Buddhist feels that his opponent fares no better in the other case also, viz., that the permanent substance can produce its effects successively. The Buddhists here ask why the permanent should not produce all its effects *at once*, instead of in succession. For if it is in the nature of the substance to produce a certain number of effects, then it is absurd, he would argue, to maintain that it cannot produce B while it has been producing A inasmuch as both are, as it were, in its womb. The Buddhist would drive this matter to an issue and plead that if the substance cannot produce B together with all the effects inherent in it, then it can never produce any effect at all and remains barren forever like a piece of stone. If, on the other hand, his opponent approves of the contention, then he is reduced to the plight of accepting the simultaneous productivity of the whole range of effects by the substance. Both these alternatives are therefore uncongenial to the substantialist thesis.

Furthermore, the Buddhist tries to silence the opponent who might plead that the substance does not produce all its effects *at once* owing to the absence of its auxiliaries[1] (*sahakāri*) and that it will bring out the effects gradually as the auxiliaries come to its aid. The Buddhist comes down upon his opponent here and asks the opponent whether or not the auxiliaries make a difference to the substance. If they make any difference then the efficiency of the permanent in produc-

---

1. In the estimation of the Buddhist the opponents' (the target is the Nyāya-Vaiśeṣika reality) notion of causality involves not merely the manifest absurdities, which are being so trenchantly criticised, but also the additional absurdity of being conceived on 'the anthropomorphic pattern' of *Bud. Log.*, Vol. I, p. 128 f.

ing the cause is compromised and becomes dependent upon other things in order to be efficient. If, on the contrary, they do not make any difference to its nature, then it is futile to plead for inoperative and ineffective (*akiñcitkara*) elements in a thing. Applying this logic to the instance of the seed and the plant, the Buddhist argues that the plant is not the result of the productivity of an identical seed helped by the auxiliaries of rain, etc., but is an entirely different thing. In other words, the seed in itself is different from the seed in combination with its auxiliaries and, therefore, difference is ultimate. Failure to comply with this conclusion would lead the Buddhist to say that the seed as modified by auxiliaries is opposed to its initial unmodified condition. Such opposition does violence to the law that no two opposed things are one entity. The Buddhist, therefore, would conclude that causal efficiency is the essence of the simple and unique moments each of which is totally different from the others[1] (*trailokya-vyāvarta*).

Thus we see that in Buddhism permanence (or continuity or being) is treated as a mere subjective imposition (*vikalpa*)

---

1. The exceptions, of course, are the Vātsīputrīyas (also called the Ābhidhārmikas or Vaibhāṣikas), whose partial divergence from the extreme antagonism to the substantialist view has already been touched upon (see *supra*, p. 19, f.n. 1) and the Mādhyamikas who treat any positive view—whether it be the substantialist view or, for that matter, the erroneous doctrine of momentariness, under their negative and destructive method of *prasaṅga* (a form of *reductio ad absurdum* by means of which the inherent weaknesses of the opponent's doctrine is claimed to be exposed; here one is reminded of a similar method used by Zeno and Śrīharṣa).

on the absolutely different discrete, simple, momentary and unique events which constitute the process of reality. The Buddhist has persistently rebelled against any trace of substantialist[1] influence.

This extreme attitude of denial regarding substantiality and the soul is a consistent development of the initial triple postulate of *anicca, anatta* and *duḥkha.* This denial is but the negative aspect of the positive creed of relentless 'becoming' resembling a vast show in which the atomic entities or snapshots ceaselessly race to tell a story which does not proceed from within themselves but is fabricated by the onlooker. Each real is a monad from which there is no way out and into which there is no entrance. Such a position cannot help becoming solipsistic[2].

---

1. In his comments on the following statement of Dharmakīrti Śāntarakṣita suggestively touches upon the essential points—both critical and constructive—bearing on the whole argument of *arthakriyākāritva* as stated here: *yadi na sarvaṁ kṛtakaṁ vā/ pratikṣaṇavināśi syāt akṣaṇikasya/ kramayaugapadyābhyām arthakriyā ayogāt/ arthakriyāsāmarthyalakṣaṇamato nivṛttam/ asadeva syāt/* etc. *VND,* pp. 7-8, and the *Vipañcitārtha* thereon. See also *HBT*, pp. 118 ff., *PVD*, II. 3-4](and the *MV* thereon), and *SBNT*, p. 74.
2. Dharmakīrti seems to have been aware of this 'danger' and therefore to have attempted to escape from it by trying to make out a case for his position in his special "Tract on the Repudiation of Solipsism" (or "Establishment of the Existence of Other Minds"). The case—judging from Stcherbatsky's 'short summary' of the tract which is available in Tibetan—does not seem to be strong enough to rid the Buddhist position from the solipsistic consequences because Dharmakīrti's argument seems to rest on the supposed weakness of his opponent's argument rather than on the inherent strength of his own. See *Bud. Log.* Vol. I, pp. 521-24.

The wealth of human adventure and evolution becomes one vast fiction built on—but does not actually rest on—the mere fleeting moments.

The ethical and spiritual motive underlying this repudiation of substance or soul is clear. It is to do away with a 'continuant' having a prior and posterior existence and offering an enduring basis for the mutations of life and matter. This is considered to be the basis of avarice and egoism which breed the ills of life. To relieve the world from suffering meant, on this theory, to rid the evil-stricken beings from their pre-occupation with that which endures and lures them away from the path of *prajñā*.[1] But in achieving this Buddhism has overshot the mark. Or rather, the logical result of this view is that in the attempt to be cured of ailments man tends to be cured of life itself. Furthermore, speaking ethically, man has no basis for selflessness once he has lost the self. This prescription is as radical and extreme as its Vedāntic opposite which over-reaches its aim by offering a universal but static self or the absolute, and denying the ultimate validity to the values of this 'mighty frame' of the mutating world which must form an integral part of reality. Reality flies on both wings—the right wing of the Vedānta with its allegiance to the Upaniṣadic being, and the left wing of the *nairātmya* metaphysics (becoming) descending from the deep intuition of Buddha.

---

1. Cf. "Having seen by wisdom all the passions and evils arising from the view of Ātman (*satkāyadṛṣṭi*), and having also known that the object of it is Ātman, a Yogin denies its existence." This is V. S. Bhattacharya's E. T. of a verse by Candrakīrti in *Mādhyamakāvatāra,* VI. 123. See *The Basic Conception of Buddhism*, p. 72 and f.n. 23 thereon.

An adequate metaphysics does not annul but conserves and transfigures the obstinate elements of permanence and change. No doubt both the great systems display a rigorous internal consistency, but they lack comprehensiveness. Unless the claims of the two brothers are evenly accommodated philosophy becomes a haunted house constantly assailed by the ghost of the maltreated brother. An inclusive view of reality is a sure corrective to the one-sidedness. It should, therefore, be based on a concrete conception in which the co-ordinate ideas of being and becoming, identity and difference, universal and particular are harmoniously comprehended.

The failure of each of the two great systems so far considered is at once grand and fruitful—grand because of the depth of insight each has revealed in bringing out a massive system of thought into which some of the sublime elements of human thinking are wrought and fruitful because each has exhausted all the weapons it could possibly bring into its fight against the other and thereby shown how the inadequate postulates with which it started inevitably lead to a partial reading of the secrets of complex reality. Great as it is, this failure points to the need for a sturdy synthesis of the elements 'permanence' and 'change', 'identity' and 'difference', and 'universal' and 'particular' at all levels —ontological, epistemological and logical. A brief account of each of the schools which have attempted such a synthesis is offered in the following chapters.

CHAPTER III

The Schools of Philosophy in Which Identity Subordinates Difference :

A. *The Sāṅkhya System*

B. *The Bhedābheda Systems of :*

  (i) *Bhartṛprapañca*

  (ii) *Bhāskara and Yādavaprakāśa*

  (iii) *Nimbārka*

  (iv) *Rāmānuja*

C. *Hegelianism*

CHAPTER III

A. The Sāṅkhya System

Having viewed, in the course of the two previous chapters, Advaitism and Buddhism, and found that the one upholds 'identity' and the other 'difference', we may endeavour, in the course of the present chapter, to examine a few systems of philosophy in which difference (*bheda*) is subordinated to identity (*abheda*). The systems which figure here, in the order of their treatment are: (A) The Sāṅkhya; (B) the Bhedābheda schools of (i) Bhartṛprapañca, (ii) Bhāskara and Yādavaprakāśa, (iii) Nimbārka, and (iv) Rāmānuja; (C) Hegelianism, an important school of Western philosophy, is added to the above notable systems of Indian philosophy for the reason of its striking resemblance to, as well as divergence from, the Jaina view, in respect of some important dialectical features.

Without going into highly controversial and not directly relevant questions like how early[1] (before

1. According to R. Garbe the Sāṅkhya and the Yoga are "the two oldest systems (of philosophy) which India has produced" (see his Intro. to the *Bhagavadgītā*, E. T., *Ind. Ant.*, 1918, p. 14). Incidentally, in his 'estimation', the Sāṅkhya is also "the most significant system of philosophy that India has produced". (See his Preface to Vijñānabhikṣu's *Sāṅkhyapravacanabhāṣya*, p. XIV.) H. Jacobi points out Kauṭilya's references in the *Artha-*

śāstra (about 300 B. C., according to him) to this system (see *The Early History of Indian Philosophy*, E. T., *Ind. Ant.*, 1918, p. 102 ff.).

In his *Early Sāṅkhya* E. H. Johnston has made an attempt 'to trace the evolution (or 'the historical development') of the (Sāṅkhya) doctrine up to its culmination in the *Sāṅkhyakārikās*' by the method of sorting out, and assessing, 'four classes' of evidence. An earlier part of the same attempt is embodied in his paper on 'The Numerical Riddle in the *Śvetāśvatara Upaniṣad*', *JRAS*, 1930, pp. 855-878. Previously, S. N. Das Gupta also has endeavoured to trace the early developments of the Sāṅkhya, particularly as they are found in the *Carakasaṁhitā* of Caraka (see *HIP*, Vol. I, p. 213 ff.). Johnston credits Das Gupta with being 'the first to bring to notice the historical importance' of Caraka's account. B. N. Seal's *Positive Sciences of the Ancient Hindus*, and P. C. Ray's *Hindu Chemistry*, offer highly suggestive remarks on the naturalistic side of the Sāṅkhya philosophy.

With regard to the relation between the Sāṅkhya and the Upaniṣads opinions vary : some hold that the Sāṅkhya sytem is 'almost as old as the Upaniṣads' and 'independent in origin'. (Bādarāyaṇa's rejection of the idea that the Sāṅkhya represents Upaniṣadic teaching is significant in this connection; see *OIP*, p. 267 f.). Others maintain that it is 'based on the Upaniṣads', that the leading conceptions of its philosophy are already found in the 'varied teachings' of the Upaniṣads, or, to express the same somewhat specifically, that 'the realistic tendencies of Upaniṣads receive emphasis in the Sāṅkhya 'conception of the universe', and that certain important divergences in the system from the Upaniṣads are the result of 'a natural process of criticism and development of one side of the Upaniṣadic teaching'. But the generality of writers (except those who suggest 'borrowings' by the Upaniṣads, of 'the doctrines already extant in the Sāṅkhya system'—a suggestion which is repudiated as 'methodologically unsound' in Keith's *The Sāṅkhya System*, p. 7) find an impact of the Upaniṣads, at any rate the earlier ones, on the Sāṅkhya, although some attribute to this impact certain positive doctrines in the Sāṅkhya, and others a keen 'opposition' or 'reaction' which led to the development of the doctrines in it. Keith, however, admits both results of the impact (*ibid.*). See, in this connection, *OIP*, p. 267; *TP*, Vol. I, p. 259 ff., Vol. II, p. 249 ff.; the article on 'The Sāṅkhya', *ERE*, especially p. 190; and Keith's work, already cited.

Īśvarakṛṣṇa[1], the great exponent of the classical form of this school) did the Sāṅkhya originate, and whether and to what extent, it is an original[2] system, we may safely affirm that this school represents one of the earliest attempts, among the orthodox systems, to effect a synthesis[3] between 'identity' or

---

With regard to the question of the relation between the Sāṅkhya system and Buddhism, Stcherbatsky, in his excellent and lengthy review of Vidushekhara Bhattacharya's *The Basic Conception of Buddhism*, observes that "the Sāṅkhya system preceded Buddhism in time and constitutes its (the latter's) philosophical basis". He cites names of scholars such as H. Jacobi, Pischel, H. Oldenberg and even R. Garbe, in support of his thesis. E. J. Thomas, like Senart, however, finds that "the most certain parallelisms (between the two schools) are crossed by evident discordances" (see his *History of Buddhist Thought*, pp. 80 and 91, as well as f.n. 2 thereon). Stcherbatsky's comparison between the '*dharmas*' of the Buddhists and the '*guṇas*' of the Sāṅkhyas, and between the '*pratītyasamutpāda*' of the former and the '*pariṇāmavada*' of the latter, are, like several other ideas touched upon in course of the review, of highly suggestive significance. The review, referred to in this paragraph, is entitled 'The Dharmas of the Buddhists and the Guṇas of the Sāṅkhyas' in the *Indian Historical Quarterly*, 1934, pp. 737-760 (see especially p. 753 f.).

For a few observations bearing on the relation between the Sāṅkhya and the Jaina systems, on matters such as *puruṣa* and *jīva*, and *prakṛti* and *ajīva*, respectively, see *PrSKU*, Intro., p. LXII ff.

1. It is generally acknowledged that Īśvarakṛṣṇa's *Sāṅkhyakārikā* is the earliest work available on the Sāṅkhya system. Max Müller, however, thinks that the Tattvasamāsa is the earliest. (See his *The Six Systems of Indian Philosophy*, London, 1928, p. 224 ff.)
2. In this connection it is observed : "Thus it remains a moot question to this day whether the Sāṅkhya represents an original doctrine or is only derived from some other". *OIP*, p. 13. See also *supra*, p. 61, f. n. 1.
3. For Hiriyanna's confusion of the Sāṅkhya notion of identity-in-difference with that of the Jaina, as wel s for a critical comment thereon, see *infra*, p. 68, f.n. 1.

permanence and 'difference' or change. Of the two primordia realms the Sāṅkhya recognises as together constituting the entire reality, the first is the realm of a plurality of statically permanent (*kūṭasthanitya*[1]) selves (puruṣas[2]) and the second of dynamically constant (*pariṇāmanitya*) nature (*prakṛti*). *Puruṣas* being pure (*svacchāḥ*) and static entities, or undifferenced identities, the problem of synthesising identity and difference is confined, exclusively, to the realm of *prakṛti*.

Prakṛti is conceived to be a permanent framework within which is set the cosmic play of change. Change consists in the evolution of different configurations or patterns resulting from the different combinations of the three *guṇas*, viz., *sattva*, *rajas*, and *tamas*, the ultimate or irreducible constituent elements of *prakṛti*. The configurations thus evolved, or the evolutes, eventually dissolve themselves in their matrix, *prakṛti*, this dissolution or involution being the other aspect of change. An eternal cycle of these alternating evolutions and involutions is conceived to be the inherent nature of *prakṛti*.

---

1. Cf. *na prakṛtir na vikṛtiḥ puruṣaḥ* / *Sāṅkhyakārikā*, *kā*. 3.
2. S. S. S. Sastry has noticed that the early Tamil work, *Maṇimekhalalai*, refers to one *puruṣa* only in the Sāṅkhya system. See his *Sāṅkhyakārikā*, Madras, 1948, Intro., p. 18, f.n. 4.

   Logically plurality of *puruṣas* (*puruṣabahutvam*) necessitates postulating plurality of *prakṛtis* since *prakṛti* is said to be meant for the enjoyment (*bhoga*) and salvation (*apavarga*) of a *puruṣa*. If the same *prakṛti* is imagined to play infinite roles to infinite *puruṣas* then it is hard to explain how the intrinsically non-intelligent (*aviveki*) can accommodate itself to the infinitely different needs of the individually peculiar *puruṣas*. The Sāṅkhya does not seem to have any satisfactory explanations for these difficulties.

Although change, in this system, is genuinely real[1], it is not[2] radical or total as it is conceived to be under the *ārambhavāda* (the doctrine of new creation) of the Nyāya-Vaiśeṣika philosophy. According to the *ārambhavāda* an effect, the result of change, is considered to be a totally novel creation completely different from the cause although it inheres in the cause as a quality does in a substance. The effect jar (*ghaṭa*), for instance, is described under *ārambhavāda* as the 'counterpart' of its antecedent non-existence (*prāgabhāva-pratiyogi*). That is, when the jar comes into being its prior non-existence ceases to be, the prior non-existence and the posterior existence being totally different from each other. This view, also called *asatkāryavāda,* is in sharp contrast to the Sāṅkhya view of *satkāryavāda*[3] (the theory of identity of the cause and its effect) according to which the cause abides[4] in the effect as, for instance, the yarns abide in the fabric, the difference between the two being that the latter manifests a particular arrangement (*saṁsthānabheda*) of the former[5].

---

1. Cf. *kāryaṁ prakṛtisvarūpaṁ virūpaṁ ca / Sāṅkhyakārikā, kā.* 8.
2. Cf. *infra,* Ch. VII.
3. For a discussion of the two contrasting doctrines of *satkārya-vāda* and *asatkāryavāda* (or *ārambhavāda*), see Vācaspati Miśra's *Tattva-Kaumudī,* comm. on *kā.* 9 (in G. Jha's edn., pp. 20-24)
4. Cf. *prasārya iha yathāṅgāni kūrmaḥ saṁharate punaḥ / The Mahābhārata,* XII, ch. 253. This illustration of the tortoise (*kūrma*) is beautifully elucidated by Mādhavācārya. See *SDSC,* pp. 225-226.
5. *evaṁ abhede siddhe, tantava eva tena tena saṁsthānabhedena pariṇataḥ paṭo, na tantubhyo'rthāntaraṁ paṭaḥ /.* See *Tattva-Kaumudī* (Jha's edn.), p. 22.

John Davies has noticed the following interesting statement in Sir William Hamilton's works: "What is the law of causality? Simply this....that all that we at present come to know as an

Thus lack of identity between the two terms (the cause and the effect) necessarily indicates the lack of any causal relation as, for instance, in the case of a horse and a cow. Accordingly, what is meant by the production and the destruction of an effect is simply the revelation (*āvirbhāva*) and the concealment (*tirobhāva*), respectively, of a particular form of *prakṛti* depending, as already noticed, on the preponderance or the diminution in the relative proportions of its three ultimate constituents.

One of the two important conclusions emerging from the treatment of *pariṇāmavāda,* as applied to *prakṛti,* in the Sāṅkhya metaphysics, is that change or difference is a genuinely real feature of reality. But this conclusion is overshadowed by the other, and more important, conclusion arising from the supreme importance attached to *satkārya-vāda* in the sphere of *prakṛti.* The truth of this doctrine, viz., identity of the cause and the effect, leads the Sāṅkhya to elevate the importance of identity to such level that change or difference, however genuine it may be considered to be, becomes dwarfed in importance.[1] Treating the effect as an

---

effect must have previously existed in its causes". *Hindu Philosophy,* 2nd edn., London, 1894, p. 33, f.n. 1.

1. Therefore, Hiriyanna's comparison of the Jaina notion of identity-in-difference with that of the Sāṅkhya, as indicated in the following statement of his, though true in a broad sense, is to be understood as subject to this important qualification. Contrasting the Sāṅkhya notion of causality with that of the Nyāya-Vaiśeṣika he observes : "The material cause and the effect are not taken here to be quite distinct, as in the Nyāya-Vaiśeṣika.., *they form, on the other hand, an identity in difference,* as in Jainism." *EIP*, p. 109. (Italics mine.)

entirely novel creation is of course an extreme view. But treating the cause as primary and the effect secondary amounts to disregarding the co-ordinate importance of change or difference. As a matter of fact a firm instance on the logic of *satkāryavāda* may even lead to a wholesale repudiation of difference. This is proved in the case of Advaitism[1]. As the philosophy of a realist the Sāṅkhya tries to reconcile the doctrine of *satkāryavāda* with that of *pariṇāmavāda*. Partiality for the former, however, so much dilutes the truth of the latter that 'difference' is subordinated to 'identity'. When the undivided supremacy of identity in the realm of *puruṣas* is considered in conjunction with the primacy of identity over difference in the realm of *prakṛti*, the Sāṅkhya's adherence to permanence as a more primordial principle of reality becomes an undoubted proposition.

B. (i) The Bhedābheda Philosophy of Bhartṛprapañca

Bhartṛprapañca[2] is an early thinker who lived long anterior to Śaṅkara and Sureśvara. He maintains a form of

---

1. As a result of treating difference as appearance, and not reality, Advaitism has been more appropriately described as *satkāraṇavāda*. This doctrine differs from *satkāryavāda* in the greater degree of emphasis it lays on the cause. The distinction between the two doctrines is, therefore, one of degree rather than of kind.
2. None of the works of the early thinker has come down to us. Reference to, and discussions of, the various aspects of his views are, however, found in some Vedāntic works which often quote expressions from his writings. A number of "Fragments of

bhedābhedavāda[1], or *dvaitādvaitavāda*[2], a doctrine of 'identity-in-difference'[3], or of 'unity-in-diversity'[4]. According to this doctrine *brahman,* the ultimate reality, evolves itself into the manifold world of objects and the selves (*jīvas*) and the relation between *brahman* on the one hand and the world and the selves on the other is one of identity and difference. Owing to the evolutionary character of *brahman* this doctrine may also be called a type of *brahmapariṇāmavāda*[5]. As *brahman,* in the metaphysics of Bhartṛprapañca, is "not robbed of its manifestations" or the evolutes, viz., the world and the selves, but possesses them, its nature is said to be *saprapañca*[6].

Some of the examples by which the dual nature of 'identity in difference', in *brahman* on the one hand and in the *jīvas* and the world on the other, is illustrated are 'the

---

Bhartṛprapañca" have been brought together, by Hiriyanna, in a paper bearing this title (see *Proceedings and Transactions of the Third Oriental Conference,* Madras, 1924, pp. 439-450). In the article 'Bhartṛprapañca: An Old Vedāntin' contributed to *The Indian Antiquary,* 1924, pp. 77-86, the same writer has attempted, "a tentative reconstruction of Bhartṛprapañca's doctrine in its broad outline". There have been practically no further attempts, before or since the publication of the two contributions, just mentioned. The two contributions named will be referred to as *FrBH* and *BOV*, respectively. The sources from which the 'fragments' are taken, and on which the 'reconstruction' is based, are mentioned in the course of the body and the footnotes of the two works.

1. See, for instance, *BOV*, p. 78 and *FrBH,* p. 439.
2. *BOV*, p. 82, and K. C. Bhattacharya's *Studies in Vedāntism*, Calcutta, 1909, p. 25.
3. *FrBH*, p. 439 and *BOV*, p. 78, etc.
4. *BOV*, p. 82.
5. *FrBH*, p. 439.
6. Cf. *BOV*, p. 7, f.n. 2.

snake and its coils, hood, etc.', the 'sun and its rays', and 'unagitated and the agitated ocean'[1]. Bhartṛprapañca does not see anything incompatible[2] in the idea of the homogeneous (*para*) *brahman* envolving itself into a heterogeneous (*apara*) universe of selves and objects. On the contrary he sees in the latter the fulfilment of the evolving urge in the former.

His view, that there is no incompatibility or 'discrepancy' between *bheda* or diversity and *abheda* or unity in the integrated principle of *bhedābheda,* which is described as "the ultimate Truth"[3], is further accentuated by his theory of knowledge designated as *pramāṇasamuccayavāda*[4]. According to this *vāda* perception explicitly gives diversity although unity also is implicit in perceptual truth. Similarly the scripture explicitly reveals unity, although diversity is also implicit in the scriptural 'truth'. Neither truth—perceptual (or empirical) or scriptural (or revealed)—is more true than the other; both are "equally valid"[5]. There is, therefore, no "conflict" between them[6]. This view is in sharp contrast with the Śaṅkara view that empirical knowledge is 'on a lower footing' than revealed knowledge, and, that, in the ultimate analysis, revealed knowledge (of unity) or *parāvidyā*

---

1. *BOV*, pp. 78-79, and *IP*, Vol. II, pp. 789-790.
2. Cf. *BOV*, p. 82.
3. *FrBH*, p. 440.
4. Cf. *BOV*, p. 82. Of this theoretical side *jñānakarmasamuccyavāda* is the practical counterpart, or 'corollary'. See *FrBH*, p. 440.
5. Cf. *svānubhavāddvaitasya advaitasya śrutivaśāt (prāmāṇyam)/* *BOV*, p. 82, f.n. 44. Elsewhere we meet with a statement that '*dvaitam*' (also) is '*paramārthasatyam*'; *evaṁ sarvam idaṁ dvaitaṁ paramārthasatyam.* See *IP*, Vol. II, pp. 789-790.
6. *BOV*, p. 82.

is alone the absolute or sole truth (not the empirical knowledge, or *aparāvidyā*, which is ultimately false). Thus while the former view affirms that the two kinds of knowledge are valid "in exactly the same sense", the latter one assigns them to two different spheres[1], between one being ultimately true and the other false.

This difference between the two views is indeed of a basic and far-reaching philosophical significance.[2] It is, therefore, no wonder that it evokes from Śaṅkara a sharp criticism against the *dvaitādvaita* thesis of Bhartṛprapañca. The criticism is that "although rules of action may admit of exceptions or alternatives, a truth does not; truth does not depend on any one's choice. Two contradictory attributes, *dvaita* and *advaita,* dual and single, cannot both be true of the same thing. Yet the sea and its waves are said to be identical-in-difference. In fact the union of contradictories is not denied of phenomenal objects, it is denied only of the noumenon, the 'simple' eternal object (*nitya-niravayavavastu-viṣayaṁ hi viruddhatvam avocāma dvaitādvaitasya na kārya-viṣaye sāvayave*)."[3]

The above criticism by Śaṅkara has, if anything, some abstract logical force derived from the unitary basis of his philosophy, but not any concrete ontological conformity. The relationless unitary ultimate has no appeal either to Bhartṛprapañca or, as will be evident from the following sections,

1. *Ibid.*
2. Cf. *BOV*, p. 78.
3. K. C. Bhattacharya, *op. cit.*, p. 25.

to any other *bhedābhedavādins*, within the metaphysical range of *brahmapariṇāmavāda*.

This is but a brief account of the principal features of the *bhedābheda* view of Bhartṛprapañca, based, mainly, on Hiriyanna's "tentative reconstruction of Bhartṛprapañca's doctrine in its broad outline". Even in course of this brief attempt one cannot help noticing the fact that Bhartṛprapañca displays, behind his valiant effort to accord equal validity to the principle of difference (*bheda*), an indisputable predilection for unity (*abheda*, identity), in the form of upholding *brahman* as the evolving basis of the world and the *jīvas*. This position necessarily involves the logical fact that *brahman*, like the *prakṛti* of the Sāṅkhya[1], is the matrix, and, therefore, the primary real from which everything else is derived. Merely designating the derived universe of matter and life as of equal reality to that of *brahman* is not warranted by the logic of *brahmapariṇāmavāda*. Therefore, in the battle for 'difference' Bhartṛprapañca obtains a partial victory.

B. (ii) The Bhedābheda Metaphysics of Bhāskara and Yādavaprakāśa

Bhāskara and Yādava are two of the most notable post-Śaṅkara thinkers according to whom reality is an evolution from *brahman* (*brahmapariṇāma*) exhibiting, simultaneously,

---

1. For a comparison between the doctrines of the Sāṅkhya and Bhartṛprapañca, see *BOV*, pp. 85-86.

the dual character of difference and non-difference or identity (*bhedābheda* or *bhinnābhinna*). The evolution is a real transformation of the unitary *brahman* into the manifold world and the finite selves. This position, like that of Bhartṛprapañca, is in sharp contrast with the *vivartavāda* according to which the world is a 'cosmic fiction' or a phenomenal appearance (*māyā*) occurring owing to ignorance (*avidyā*)[1] which is sublated when true knowledge (*jñāna*)[2] reveals itself. A further important divergence on the part of this position from that of the latter doctrine concerns causal relation: While the two thinkers under study treat the world as a finite, but real, manifestation, or effect, of the infinite ultimate (*brahman*)[3] the *vivartavādin* repudiates[4] the intrinsic reality of any causal relation between the world and the ultimate principle. This is so because, in the *bhedābheda* view of the former, the effects, say, the jar, the pot and the platter etc., are

---

1. For the distinction, in meaning, between *māyā* as 'the principle of cosmic illusion' (or 'cosmic fiction') and *avidyā* (ignorance) as the 'incidence', of *māyā*, on the individual, see *OIP*, p. 348, f.n. 1 and p. 365 f.

2. Evidently this doctrine strikes Bhāskara as propounding the view that the world (which is infected with *bheda*) is 'epistemic' in its being (*prātītikasattā*), or that it exists for the individual (*puruṣāpekṣayā*) in ignorance. Bhāskara sharply attacks this view and (cf. *narabhedān na hi jñeyā vastunaḥ sadasatyatā/ na hi rūpam anandhānāṁ satyam andheṣvasad bhavet/ Brahmasūtra* with the Comm. of Bhāskarācārya, ed. Vindhyesvari Prasada Dvivedin, Benares, 1903, p. 18) and affirms that our experience of *bheda* is not phenomenal but real (*tasmān na bhedadarśanam avidyā/ Ibid.*, p. 19).

3. See the somewhat lengthy but highly lucid comm. on II. 1.14. Bhāskarācārya, *op. cit.*, p. 9288.

4. See below f.n.

the genuine states[1] (*avasthās*) of clay, whereas, in the *abheda* view of the latter, the clay alone—by which is meant the ultimate principle—is real: *mṛttikety eva satyam*[2], the states, or the effects, of clay being phenomenal or intrinsically unreal. A further consequence arising from this difference between the two views is that the *bhedābhedavādins* consider the world as not merely real, as just pointed out, but also describable (*nirvacanīya*), since words, it is pointed out, are eminently expressive of the truth: *atha nāmadheyaṁ satyasya satyam*[3]. The *abhedavādin*, on the contrary, considers the world, which is *māyā*, as indescribable (*anirvacanīya*) or

---

1. Cf. *tasmāt bhedadarśanato'vidyā na mithyā paramātmano'vasthā, viśeṣaḥ prapañco'yam* etc. Bhāskarācārya, *op. cit.*, p. 96.
2. Śaṅkara stresses '*eva*' in this *sūtra* (of the *Chāndogya Upaniṣad*, VI. 1.4) in order to accentuate his view that the cause is 'really and truly nothing but clay', and that the effect is 'a name merely' (*nāmadheyam*), having its origin in 'mere speech' (*vācārambhaṇam*), and is, therefore, 'untrue' (*asatyam*). *See SBE*, Vol. XXXIV, Pt. I, p.320. Bhāskara puts this case as follows: *atra kecin māyāvādam avatārayanti mṛttikety eva satyam ity avadhāraṇāt kāraṇam eva satyaṁ kāryam anṛtam asatyam anādikālapravṛttāvidyāvaśāt ayaṁ bhedaḥ pratibhāsate na paramārthato'sti* etc. Bhāskarācārya, *op. cit.*, p. 93. This *vivarta* view, that cause alone is real (*kāraṇam eva satyam*), is incongruous because one cannot speak of a cause without its correlative effect, sharing the reality of the cause. The *vivartavādin* is indeed aware of the fact that the illusory world needs a basis (*āspada or adhiṣṭhāna*) for its appearance, and maintains, consequently, that *brahman* or *sat* provides the sole basis. He also concedes that *brahman* cannot be called 'the cause' in strictness. It is, according to him, called so by courtesy so to speak (*upalakṣaṇa*). This way of playing fast and loose with the principle of causality which is admittedly unreal, intrinsically, offends the logical conscience of Bhāskara as of many others. Cf. *ibid.*, p. 92 ff.
3. Bhāskarācārya, *op. cit.*, p. 93. See also P. N. Srinivasachari's *The Philosophy of Bhedābheda*, 2nd edn., Madras, 1950, p. 59 ff.

indefinable. This is the reason why the former group of thinkers feels that the tests like *neti neti* (not thus, not so), or *neha nānāsti kiñcana* (there is no plurality of existence), etc., deny plurality and finitude (*bheda*) *in the absolute* or *brahman*, but not, as the group interprets, plurality and finitude as such[1].

Both Bhāskara and Yādava sternly maintain that identity and difference co-exist in all that is[2]. Every object of experience is, they say, a blend of the generic basis and the specific transformations of the generic basis. *Brahman*, the ultimate basis of the manifold universe of objects and selves, is conceived as retaining its infinity, purity and perfection even while it finitizes itself into the universe of objects and selves[3]. It is, therefore, the infinite cause, or the unitary ground, of the finite diversities both of which form, in this view, not mutually incompatible[4], but correlative elements of the total reality.

Despite their agreement on the basic position of the *bhedābheda* or *bhinnābhinna* approach to the nature of reality Bhāskara and Yādava differ on a few points, two of which deserve mention here. In the first place, *brahman*, according to Bhāskara, is the unconditioned absolute which, by virtue of *upādhis*, or 'limiting adjuncts', conditions itself into the

---

1. Cf. *kāryarūpeṇa nānātvam abhedaḥ kāraṇātmanā / hemātmanā yathābhedaḥ kuṇḍalādyātmanā bhidā* // *Ibid.*, p. 18.
2. Cf. *tasmāt sarvam ekānekātmakaṁ na atyantam abhinnaṁ bhinnaṁ vā* / *Ibid.*, p. 101.
3. Cf. Srinivasachari, *op. cit.*, p. 144, and *IP.*, Vol. II, p. 670.
4. Cf. *IP.*, Vol. II, p. 671.

diverse world of objects and selves. *Upādhis* or limitations are conceived by him to be real[1] (*satyopādhis*), not fictitious (*mithyopādhis*). The conditioned state of the unconditioned is compared to an enclosed or limited space in a jar, and the enclosed space is, nevertheless, thought to be continuous with the universal space. This principle of *upādhis*, which is considered as the necessary condition of the evolution of the world from the unconditioned, or the unlimited, absolute, is brought in by Bhāskara to bridge the gulf between the infinite and unitary absolute and the finite and multitudinous world. Yādava, on the contrary, does not feel the need of postulating anything like *upādhis* to intervene between the evolving *brahman* and the evolved world. He is content with investing *brahman* with an inherent power, or *śakti*[2], by virtue of which *brahman* can finitize itself into the world of diversities just as an ocean can spontaneously break itself into waves, ripples, and foam.

Secondly, Bhāskara and his followers maintain that '*Brahman* has two parts, a spirit part (*cidaṁśa*) and a material part (*acidaṁśa*)', the latter being a medium through which *brahman* transforms itself into the finite world[3]. Yādava, on the contrary, gives his ontology a certain spiritualistic orientation by denying qualitative differences between God (*Īśvara* or *brahman*) and consciousness (*cit*) on the one hand, and between consciousness and matter (*acit*)

---

1. Cf. Srinivasachari, *op. cit.*, pp. 51, 69-72 and 144. For Rāmānuja's objections against the notion of *upādhis*, see pp. 214-215.
2. *Ibid.*, p. 144.
3. Cf. *ibid.*, p. 6.

on the other[1]. "*Acit*", observes Srinivasachari, describing Yādava's philosophy, "is the object which can develop into the subject and consciousness sleeps in the matter and wakes up in the sentient being[2]." Yet, strangely enough Bhāskara emphasises the *abheda* texts and, consequently, emphasises the ultimacy of identity (*ananyatva*), in spite of his professed dualism of *brahman* and *upādhis,* while Yādava emphasises the eternality of difference, as well as of unity, despite his belief in a kind of pan-spiritualism[3].

Whatever may be the differences existing between Bhāskara and Yādava with respect to certain specific issues, two of which have been just noticed, these two thinkers primarily aim at setting forth a metaphysical scheme in which reality is "neither a bare unity nor a mere plurality—but a vital synthesis of both".[4] But while they have succeeded in considerably weakening the vigour of the Advaitic claims for a pure being, or a 'bare unity', which is bereft of all determinations or diversities, they have not succeeded in escaping the consequences of incongruously endeavouring to rear an imposing structure of diversity (the world and the selves, *bheda*) on the foundation of unity (*brahman* or *abheda*). They credit unity with 'being' the source and the destiny

---

1. *Ibid.*
2. *Ibid.*, p. 145. Also cf. p. 6, f.n. 1, wherein a confirmatory observation, on this point, is cited from *Tātparya-dīpikā* of Sudarśanācārya.
3. On the entire question of this difference between the views of the two thinkers, see *ibid.*, p. 145, *IP*, Vol. II, pp. 671-672 and *Brahmavādin*, Vol. V, p. 470.
4. Cf. Hiriyanna's Foreword to Srinivasachari's *op. cit.*, p. VII.

of diversity. This necessarily leads to the ultimate elevation of unity to the status of the primal principle and to the corresponding degradation of diversity to the level of a secondary or derivative element, in reality[1]. The ingenuous devices like the concepts of *upādhi* and *avasthās* have not, therefore, prevented the *satkāryavāda* systems of Bhāskara and Yādava from assigning to *bheda*, the principle of 'difference', an intrinsically subordinate role[2] to which it (*bheda*) is assigned in all forms of *satkāryavāda*.

B. (iii) Nimbārka's System of Svābhāvika Bhedābheda

Among the *bhedābheda* schools, derived from *brahmapariṇāmavāda*[3], Nimbārka's *svābhāvika*[4] *bhedābhedavāda* goes farthest in recognising both identity and difference as

---

1. Cf. Bhāskarācārya, *op. cit.*, p. 141 where *abheda* is characterised as *svābhāvika* or 'natural' and *bheda* as *aupādhika* or 'adventitious'. Distinguishing the viewpoints of Śaṅkara, Bhāskara and Yādava L. Srinivasachar rightly observes : .... *śrīśaṅkarasiddhānte bhedābhedaviṣaye bhedaḥ avidyakaḥ abhedaḥ pāramārthika iti / śrībhāskarasiddhānte bheda aupādhikaḥ abhedaḥ svābhāvika iti / śrīyādavasiddhānte bhedaḥ vyaktilakṣaṇaḥ abhedaḥ śaktilakṣaṇa iti etan matatraye bheda aupādhikaḥ abhedo mukhya iti pratibhāti / Darśanodaya*, Mysore, 1933, p. 194.
2. Cf. *VPSN*, Pt. III, p. 194, the last two paragraphs.
3. Cf. *VPSN*, Pt. I, pp. 292-297.
4. See Nimbārka's *Vedānta-pārijāta-saurabha* (called a Comm. on *Brahmasūtras*), ed. V. P. Dvivedin, Benares, 1910, III. 2. 27 and 28; and Anantarama Deva's *Tattvasiddhānta-bindu*, Benares 1913, *ślokas* 12 and 24; and the same writer's *Vedāntaratnamālā*, Brindavan, 1916, *śloka* 45. These three works will be referred to hereafter as *Saurabha*, *Bindu* and *Ratnamālā* respectively.

'equally real' (*tulyabalatvāt*)[1] elements in reality. Referring to this point Ghate observes that "....if at all we insist on seeing in the *sūtras* one of the five systems[2] under discussion, it can be at the most the '*bhedābheda*' system of Nimbārka, according to which both *bheda* and *abheda* are equally real, without the idea of any subordination of one to the other"[3].

---

1. Cf. *Śrutyantasuradruma*, by Purushottama Prasada, Benares, 1908, pp. 67 and 69, and *Ratnamālā*, *ślokas* 47 and 48. Supporting the equal reality of *bheda* and *abheda*, *Bindu* (*śloka* 13) declares :

   abhedaḥ kevalo bhrāntiḥ tathā bhedo'pi kevalaḥ /
   śrutismṛtiviruddhatvāt vivekinām asammataḥ //

   For the erroneous consequences issuing from the two views of *atyantabhedavāda* and *atyanta(kevala)bhedavāda*, see *ślokas* 3, 4, 7 and 8. Nearly every work, under the present system, contains at least a short account of criticisms, in general, against the two views just mentioned, as well as criticisms, in particular, against the views of Śaṅkara's *māyāvāda*, Bhāskara's *aupādhika bhedābhedavāda*, Rāmānuja's *cidacidviśiṣṭaparameśvaravāda*. See, for instance, Devācārya's *Siddhānta-jāhnavī* (a gloss on the *Brahmasūtras*; together with Sundarabhatta's sub-comm. *Siddhāntasetukā*, Benares, 1906, pp. 30-56), Puruśottama's *Vedāntaratnamañjūṣā* (concerned mainly with '*māyāvādanirākaraṇa*'), *and Śrutyantasuradruma* (Benares, 1908), pp. 11 ff., and 61 ff. etc.; and Mādhava-Mukunda's *Para-pakṣa-giri-vajra* (a review of whose controversies with the non-Nimbārka, particularly *advaita*, views is given in *HIP*, Vol. III, pp. 416-439).

2. The five systems referred to here, are those of Śaṅkara, Rāmānuja, Nimbārka, Madhva and Vallabha.

3. V. S. Ghate's *The Vedānta*, Poona, 1926, p. 183 (Reference to the *sūtras* follows this passage). See also *Indian Antiquary*, Vol. II, 1939, p. 324; and P. N. Srinivasachari's *The Philosophy of Bhedābheda*, 2nd edn., Madras, 1950, p. 155 (for a reference to S. Majumdar's view). That the claim that there is no 'subordination of one to the other' is, eventually, incompatible with any form of *satkāryavāda* or *brahmapariṇāmavāda*, under which Nimbārka's school figures, has already been, and will again be, touched upon at the end of this section.

This system is designated as *svābhāvika* or natural particularly in distinction from *aupādhika*[1] *bhedābhedavāda* of Bhāskara in so far as difference (*bheda*), here, is conceived, not as an 'adventitious' (*aupādhika*) element, but as one which is as natural as identity. We may now consider the essential features of this system and then see how far the claim of the equal reality of both identity and difference is tenable.

Three reals are admitted by Nimbārka in his philosophy: *bhoktṛ* (the enjoyer, or the *jīva*), *bhogya* (the enjoyable, or the world) and *niyantṛ* (the controller, or *Īśvara*, or *brahman*[2]). The relation between *Īśvara* (God) and the *jīvas* on the one hand, and between *Īśvara* and the world on the other, is conceived to be one of non-difference-in-difference or unity-in-diversity (*dvaitādvaita*[3]). The relation is, as just noticed, not 'adventitious' (*aupādhika*) as in the Bhāskarīya system, nor is it unreal (*asatya*) as in the Śaṅkara system[4]. It is both natural (*svābhāvika*) and real (*satya*).

---

1. See *Vedāntaratnamañjūṣā*, pp. 6-7; *VPSN*, Pt. III, pp. 85-86 and 182 ff., especially, p. 197, para. 3 and *Siddhānta-jāhnavī* (and *Setukā* thereon), p. 30 ff.

2. *bhoktā bhogyaṁ niyanteti trairūpyaṁ ca yathārthakam // Ratnamālā*, p. 25. See also *Vedāntaratnamañjūṣā* (on *śloka* 7), p. 84.

3. Cf. *tasmāt svābhāviko bhedaḥ trayāṇām eva niścitaḥ / atha abhedo'pi vijñeyaḥ svābhāvikaḥ tathocyate // Ratnamālā, śloka* 37. See also the verses following this, *Siddhānta-jāhnavī*, p. 44, and *Setukā*, pp. 46-47.

4. See *Siddhānta-jāhnavī* (and *Setukā* thereon), pp. 30-33. Another important possible view is that of Rāmānuja's *viśiṣṭādvaita* or complex whole in which *brahman* represents the element of identity (*advaita*) or substance (*prakārin*), and the world (*acit*) and the individual selves (*cit*) represent the element of differ-

ence, or diversity (*viśeṣa*), or attributes (*prakāras*). This view, like the other two, comes in for sharp criticism in Nimbārka's *svābhāvika dvaitādvaita* philosophy. Deferring a somewhat lengthy treatment of *viśiṣṭādvaita* metaphysics until the next section, we may mention here two important points of difference between the two schools in order to get a clearer view of their respective viewpoints : In the first place Rāmānuja's conception of *viśiṣṭādvaita* is, as will be noticed elsewhere, one in which identity subordinates difference in a more emphatic way than it does in Nimbārka's conception of *svābhāvika dvaitādvaita*. It is more emphatic in the sense that, in the former case, less attempt is made to conceal the bias for identity than in the latter one. Being based on *satkāryavāda* both schools lead, inevitably, to a view in which identity has a superior role. Nevertheless the latter has to surrender itself to the final conclusion much against its intended aim (see the end of the next para here), while the former, when logically pressed, will, perhaps, accept its final position. This difference is implicit in the spirit as well as in the procedure of either system.

Before proceeding to the next point it is necessary to point out, here, a misconception, entertained by at least one modern critic, regarding whether identity or difference is more primary in the conception of *viśiṣṭādvaita*. This critic feels that identity is secondary for him (Rāmānuja) and not primary like difference (P. T. Raju in the *New Indian Antiquary*, Vol. II, 1939, p. 323). That this is his confirmed opinion is indicated by its reiteration on the next page of the same journal. This is definitely contrary to the spirit as well as the letter of Rāmānuja's *brahmapariṇāmavāda* in which *brahman*, *ex hypothesi*, holds undisputed supremacy over its 'attributes' of *cit* and *acit*. The whole trend of Rāmānuja's theory, with its emphasis on *Īśvara* as the only independent substance, and the source and sustenance of the modes, points to identity, not difference, as more primary (cf. *IP*, Vol. II, p. 755). Nimbārka, on the contrary, accords, in his metaphysics, an equal measure of reality, at any rate theoretically, to both identity and difference.

The second point of difference between the two schools arises from the difference in the treatment accorded to *cit* and *acit* in the two schools. In *viśiṣṭādvaita* school *cit* and *acit* are, as already noticed, attributes of *brahman*. Although, as attributes, they are, according to this school, at one with (*abhinna*) *brahman*, they do not, owing to their distinction from (*bhinnatvāt*)

Nimbārka impresses upon the truth of this non-different-in-the-different relation between *brahman* and the '*jīva-jagat*' by means of the stock Vedāntic examples like a serpent and its coils and the sun and its rays[1]. The serpent (*ahi*) in its coiling state (*kuṇḍalāvasthāyām*) is conceived to be different from the serpent as it is in its normal elongated posture (*svābhāvika lambāyamānāvasthāyām*); and yet the two serpents are also regarded as non-different (or identical) in so far as the coiled one is an effect of the (elongated or) normal one which is the cause. Being a *satkāryavādin* Nimbārka considers the effect as being pre-existent—or, more precisely, an undifferentiated[2] (*avyakta*) existent—in its

brahman, corrupt *brahman* with even a trace of their defects (*evaṁ cetanācetanayor brahmaviśeṣaṇatve'pi tadbhinnatvān na tadguṇasāṅkaryagandho'pīti / Siddhānta-jāhnavī*, p. 42). This view does not commend itself to the exponents of *svābhāvika bhedābhedavāda.* They maintain that the function of an attribute (*viśeṣaṇa*) is to differentiate (*vyāvartakatvam*) the particular object to which the attribute belongs from other object or objects to which it does not belong. *Cit* and *acit*, being attributes of *brahman,* should, they insist, differentiate *brahman* from other objects. But, they continue, there is no other object than *brahman* from which *brahman* could be distinguished. To say that the attributes, viz., *cit* and *acit*, distinguish *brahman* from themselves would therefore be, according to them, absurd owing to the fact that the attributes belong to *brahman* and, therefore, their task is not to distinguish the object, to which they belong, from themselves but from other objects which do not possess them. There being no such other objects the entire Viśiṣṭādvaitic thesis, concerning *cit* and *acit* as attributes, is, they conclude, erroneous. For a lucid exposition of this argument see *Siddhānta-jāhnavī*, p. 43 f., and *Bindu, ślokas* 17-22.

1. See *Saurabha,* III. 2. 27 and 28; *VPSN,* Pt. II (pp. 552–556); and *HIP*, Vol. III, p. 416, f.n. 1, and p. 434, f.n. 1 (for a lucid passage from *Para-pakṣa-giri-vajra*).
2. See *Ratnamālā, śloka* 103.

cause, and, therefore, identical (*ananya*), at any rate to that extent, with the cause[1]. The example of the sun and its rays also is understood in the same way : the sun and its rays are, it is believed, two distinctive manifestations, and yet are, at once, identical as light.[2] The truth conveyed by such analogies is that *brahman* or *Īśvara* is identical with the world and the selves as their causal basis and, at the same time, is different from the latter in that the latter are genuinely different or visible manifestations of the former, which is the invisible or transcendental support of all that is. This view is believed to obviate the incongruous dichotomy between *nirguṇabrahman* and *saguṇabrahman* since it is believed to affirm the dual nature of *brahman*, viz., the co-presence of transcendence and immanence.

Without going into a minute analysis of the various aspects of Nimbārka's philosophy we can, even from the brief sketch attempted here, deduce that Nimbārka's *svābhāvikabhedābheda* view fares no better than the other *bhedābheda* views of the *satkārya*, or the *brahmapariṇāma*, type, with respect to the principle of difference. The realm of difference, which consists of the world and the selves, has its source of being in *brahman*[3] and is, therefore, considered by Nimbārka as dependent (*paratantra*) in relation to the supremely independent (*svatantra*) *brahman*[4]. It is, therefore, not logical to invest

---

1. Cf. *tadananyatvaṁ kāraṇasadbhāve kāryopalabdheḥ* / *Saurabha*, II. 1.15; see also this comm. on the preceding and the next *sūtras*.
2. Cf. Srinivasachari, *op. cit.*, p. 157.
3. Cf. *upādānaṁ nimittaṁ ca brahmaiva jagataḥ param / kāryaṁ cāpi sadevedaṁ jāyate brahmaṇaḥ sataḥ* / *Ratnamālā*, *śl.* 102.
4. *Ibid.*, *ślokas* 48-65.

it with a status which is co-ordinate with that of identity (or *brahman*). In order to be mutually co-ordinate elements both identity and difference must be equally primary which, though claimed to be so, is not the case in Nimbārka's philosophy. That Nimbārka favours asserting that both the elements are "equally real" is due to the awareness of the equal importance of the element of 'difference' also in reality. There is, however, no logical warrant for the status or the degree of reality associated with difference in his system. This is inevitable in the case of any *bhedābheda* system which, like the present one, is a form of *satkāryavāda* or *brahmapariṇāmavāda.* As a matter of fact the persistent claim, made by this system, for the equal reality between the two unequally real spheres—unequally real because the one (viz. of *brahman*) is supremely independent, or primordial, and the other (viz. of the world and the selves) solely dependent, or derived—makes the system open to the objection of not mere incongruity but of contradiction. This is somewhat surprising in a system which accuses the Jaina view of self-contradiction.

B. (iv) Rāmānuja's Viśiṣṭādvaitism

Rāmānuja's philosophy of *Viśiṣṭādvaita*[1] (the doctrine

---

1. See *The Brahmavādin* (Madras, 1900), Vol. V, p. 425 for the E. T. of a brief but lucid passage, from Rāmānuja's *Vedāntadīpa*, giving a summary sketch of this doctrine. See also *Vedāntadīpa* (ed. Bhattanathaswamy, Benares, 1902), *Avatārikā*, pp. 1-8, and the comments on *sūtra* 2, p. 11 f., and *Vedāntasāra* (also by Rāmānuja, ed. Bhagavatacharya, Brindavan, 1905) on the same *sū.*, p. 2 ff.

of unity with difference[1]) is as opposed to *nirviśeṣasattvavāda*[2] (the doctrine of differenceless identity) of Śaṅkara, as it is to *bhinnābhinnavāda* (the doctrine of identity in difference) of Bhāskara, Yādava, Nimbārka, and other *bhedābhedavādins*[3]. It is based on the notion of *viśiṣṭaikyam* or the complex whole, in contrast with that of *svarūpaikyam* or absolute identity (of Śaṇkara). A complex whole includes both unity and difference (or diversity) as integral elements[4]

---

1. This doctrine is also variously described as qualified nondualism, pan-organismal monism, qualified monism and so on. Cf., for instance, Rangacharya's *Rāmānuja and Vaiṣṇavism*, Madras, 1909, p. 34; P. N. Srinivasachari's *The Philosophy of Viśiṣṭādvaita* (to be referred to as *Viśiṣṭādvaita*, hereafter), Madras, 1943, p. 614, *IP*, Vol. II, p. 661, and *EIP*, p. 178.

   The doctrine is called *viśiṣṭādvaitam* because of its insistence on "The non-duality of two different objects, *viśiṣṭayor advaitam*" (*IP*, Vol. II, p. 686, f.n.1). Describing the meaning (*artha*) of the term V. Krishnamacharya writes: "*tad evaṁ viśiṣṭādvaitam iti padasya eṣo'rthaḥ paryavasannaḥ viśiṣṭasya aśeṣa-cid-acid-viśiṣṭasya brahmaṇaḥ advaitam aikyaṁ viśiṣṭādvaitam iti / aśeṣa-cid-acid-viśiṣṭaṁ brahmaikam eva tattvam iti 'ekam eva advitīyam' ityādiśruter arthaḥ / Vedāntakāvali* (of Bucci Venkatacarya, ed. V. Krishnamacharya, Madras, 1950), *upodghātaḥ*, p. X. For the interpretation and elucidation of Rāmānuja's own statement of the meaning: *viśiṣṭāntarbhāva eva aikyam*, see *OIP*, p. 399, and f. n.1, and *EIP*, p. 178.
2. For a polemical exposition of Śaṅkara's *nirviśeṣavāda* and Rāmānuja's *saviśeṣavāda*, as well as for the refutation of the former and the demonstration of the latter—all based on Rāmānuja's *Śrībhāṣya*—see V. K. Ramanujachari's *The Three Tattvas*, Kumbhakonam, 1932, Sections III and IV; and the corresponding portions (under 'The Great *Pūrvapakṣa*') in the *Vedānta-Sūtras, with Comm. of Rāmānuja*, Tr. G. Thibaut, Oxford, 1904, pp. 20 ff.
3. See *The Three Tattvas*, Sections VIII and IX and *The Vedānta-Sūtras*, I. 1.1, pp. 189-197 and 459 f.
4. Contrasting Viśiṣṭādvaita with Buddhism (which recognises the concept of *viśeṣaṇa*, but not of *viśeṣya*) on the one hand, and

whereas an absolute or bare identity (*sanmātrabrahmavādam*) excludes difference as a delusive appearance[1]. In terms of modern philosophy while Rāmānuja upholds both the 'that' and the 'what', Śaṅkara adheres to the 'that' only.

The 'what' in Rāmānuja's philosophy is described as the attribute, or the mode[2] (*prakāra*) which is related to the 'that' or the substance (*prakārin*). *Acit*, or the principle of material objects, and *cit*, or the principle of individual spirits constitute the modes of the substance which is God (*Īśvara*) in this philosophy. The three together, viz., *acit, cit,* and *Īśvara,* form the ultimate triad[3] of Viśiṣṭādvaitism.

The individual or the finite selves and the world of matter etc., are also said to form the body (*śarīra*) of *Īśvara*, who is their indwelling (*antaryāmin*)[4], supporting (*ādhāra*) and

---

with Advaitic monism (which recognises the concept of *viśeṣya* but not of *viśeṣaṇa*) on the other, P. N. Srinivasachari writes : "The Buddhistic view of quality without substance is countered by the monistic view of substance without qualities and these extremes find their reconciliation in the Viśiṣṭādvaitic theory of the world as the *viśeṣaṇa* of *Brahman*". *Viśiṣṭādvaita*, p. 230 f.

1. Cf. *The Vedānta-Sūtras*, pp. 38-39 and the comments beginning with : *brahma ca sanmātrarūpam / astītyeva kevalaṁ vaktuṁ śakyate na tu īdṛśam tādṛśam iti* etc., in *Śrīmadbhagavadgīta* (with Rāmānuja's *bhāṣya* and Venkatanātha's Gloss thereon, ed. V. G. Apte, Poona, 1923), p. 20.
2. *Tattvatrayaṁ cidacidīśvaraś ca* / Lokācārya's *Tattvatrayam* with Varāvaramuni's *Bhāṣya*, ed. Swami Bhagavatacharya, Benares, 1899, p. 3. See also *SDSC*, p. 66.
3. See the opening verse of *Vedāntasāra*. Sakalācārya observes : *sarvāvasthacidacidvastunaḥ paramātmaśarīratvam*/ *Sakalācārya-matasaṅgraha,* ed. Ratna Gopala Bhatta, Benares, 1907, p. 6.
4. See Rāmānuja's *Vedārthasaṅgrahaḥ,* with Sudarśanasūri's *Tātparyadīpikā* (ed. Sridharanidhara Sastry, Brindavan, Sam. 1978) p. 11 f., and *Tattvatrayam and the Bhāṣya,* p. 89.

controlling (*niyantṛ*) cause (*kāraṇa*)[1]. The body is, therefore, defined by Rāmānuja as "Any substance which a sentient soul is capable of completely controlling and supporting for its own purposes, and which stands to the soul in an entirely subordinate relation"[2]. Thus Rāmānuja maintains that the absolute is a supreme organism consisting of a cosmic soul and its dependent (*śeṣa*)[3] bodily parts (the world and the selves) which serve its purpose. The bodily parts, or the modes, are conceived to be identical with (*ananya*)[4] God as they are at one with him in their substance. But they are also said to be different from (*svabhāva-bhinnāś ca*)[5] God, just as a body is different from its soul.

---

1. *Īśvara* in this philosophy is not merely the *upādāna* cause but also the *nimitta* and the *sahakāri* cause. This follows of course from the *Satkārya* basis of this philosophy. *Tattvatrayam and the Bhāṣya,* pp. 102 ff., especially p. 109. The views of the Vaiśeṣikas, the Sāṅkhyas and also of others are criticised here. See also Śrīnivāsa's *Yatīndramatadīpikā,* ed. Ratna Gopal Bhatta, Benares, 1907, p. 37.
2. *The Vedānta-Sūtras,* p. 424. As a matter of fact Rāmānuja believes that it is only *Īśvara* or the 'Supreme Soul' that can possess a body unconditionally : cf. "Everything in this world, whether individual souls or material things, form the body of the Supreme Soul, and therefore He alone can be said to possess a body unconditionally (*nirupādhikaḥ śārīra ātmā*)." V. A. Sukhtankar's 'Teachings of Vedānta according to Rāmānuja', *Vienna Oriental Journal,* Vol. XXII, pp. 128-129. See also f.n. 1 on p. 128 for an explanation of the word 'unconditionally'.
3. For "The evolution of the concept of *Śeṣa*", see *B. C. Law Volume* Pt. II, pp. 123-127.
4. *cetanācetanaṁ viśvam ananyaṁ brahmato bhavet* / Śrīnivāsācārya's *Śrī-bhāṣya-vārtika,* ed. Ratna Gopal Bhatta, Benares, 1907, p. 53, stanza 80; see also what follows.
5. Cf. Sakalācārya's description of *paramātmā* (God) as *atyanta-vilakṣaṇa* in relation to the modes on the authority of *Sṛṣṭi* in his *Sakalācārya-mata-saṅgraha,* p. 5. Cf. also Rāmānuja's own

Here a natural doubt arises as to why modes which are really different from God should not be claimed to be substances like God. Rāmānuja's reply to this doubt is that what makes a mode is its 'complete dependence' on a substance, and that *cit* and *acit*—irrespective of their being different from or identical with, or both different from and identical with, God—can, therefore, be only modes but not substances. This dependent relation of a mode to its substance is compared to the relation of an adjective (*viśeṣaṇa*) to a substantive (*viśeṣya*). Although an adjective has, it is believed, some distinctive existence of its own, it cannot be understood without reference to, or rather without dependence upon, the subject (the substantive) it qualifies.[1]

The relation between the substance (*Īśvara*) and the modes is said to be one of "inseparability" (*apṛthaksiddhi-sambandha*)[2]. This relation is said to hold between a sub-

---

observation: "In general, wherever we cognise the relation of distinguishing attribute and thing distinguished thereby, the two clearly present themselves to our mind as *absolutely different*". *Vedāntasūtras*, pp. 42-43 (the italics are mine). Here it is hard to resist the feeling that Rāmānuja himself has fallen into the error of contradiction with which he charges *bhedābhedavādins* and others. For one wonders if Rāmānuja can fully succeed in reconciling the notion of an *anyatvam* with that of *atyantavilakṣaṇatvam* within the limits of the same logic as he employs against others.

1. Cf. "Matter and self are the adjectives of the absolute only in the sense that the attribute cannot be known apart from its substance or subject." *Viśiṣṭādvaita*, p. 233. That the 'modal dependence' suggested by this statement, does not rule out the idea of the 'monadic uniqueness' on the part of an adjective or attribute, is further pointed out by the same critic from whom the statement is quoted here. *Ibid.*, p. 234.
2. Describing the nature of this *sambandha*, Hiriyanna observes:

stance and its attributes, or between one substance and another when one of them is spiritual. It is considered to be "the pivot on which his (Rāmānuja's) whole philosophy turns"[1]. By virtue of its internal character it often tends to be distinguished from the Nyāya-Vaiśeṣika idea of *samavāya* to which it is otherwise similar in regard to its recognition of the reality, the mutual necessity, and the distinctiveness of the relata in it.[2]

The complex unity which the above relation is designed to establish is pointed out to be clearly demonstrated in the great statement (*mahāvākya*) '*tat tvam asi*' (that thou art). In Rāmānuja's interpretation, *tat* (that), in the statement, signifies *brahman*, which is the source (*ādhāra*) as well as the indwelling (*antaryāmin*) force of the living and the non-living creation: *tvam* (thou) signifies the individual soul which is held to be "connected with non-intelligent matter". Together, the two, viz., the living and the non-living creation, form, as already noticed, the body of *Īśvara*. The central meaning of the text, in this philosophy, is the affirmation

---

"It connotes that one of the two entities related is dependent upon the other in the sense that it cannot exist without the other also existing and that it cannot be rightly known without the other also being known at the same time." *EIP*, p. 177.

1. *OIP*, p. 399.
2. The fact that *apṛthaksiddhi* or 'inseparability' is, except for its internal character, 'parallel to *samavāya*' does not come in the way of Rāmānuja's explicit rejection of *samavāya*. See *Vedānta-sūtras*, p. 498. For an account of *samavāya*, see *infra*, Ch. VII.

   Further, *apṛthaksiddhi* seems to be regarded by Viśiṣṭādvaitism more as the nature of, than as a relation between, the relata or the entities, although it is also sometimes spoken of as a relation. Cf. *OIP*, p. 398, f.n. 5.

of the complex, or the organic unity of the whole, viz., *Īśvara* and the souls in association with matter. In other words, the text signifies, according to Viśiṣṭādvaitism, the idea of a concrete unity—not the abstract Advaitic identity—which is constituted by *brahman* and the attributes of *cit* and *acit* qualifying *brahman*[1]. Rāmānuja invokes support for his interpretation of the above text from the notion of *sāmānādhikaraṇya* or the "grammatical principle of the co-ordination of words in a sentence"[2]. According to grammarians *sāmānādhikaraṇya*, or co-ordination, conveys the abiding of several attributes in a common substrate; or "the application to one thing of several words for the application of each of which there is a different motive"[3]. The aim of co-ordination is, therefore, "just to convey the idea of one thing being qualified by several attributes"[4]. Here 'one thing' evidently refers to the unchanging unitary principle of *Īśvara* and the 'several attributes' to the realms of *cit* and *acit* which are marked by difference, muta-

---

1. For a fuller discussion of the nature and implications of *tat tvam asi* in the present school, see *Śrībhāṣya* (text, Abhyankar's edn.), p. 110 ff., *Vedāntasūtras*, pp. 129-138, and *Śrībhāṣya*, Vol. I, E. T. by Mr. Rangacharya and M. B. Varadaraja Aiyangar, Madras, 1899, pp. 211-224, *Vedārthasaṅgraha*, p. 37, etc., and Sukhtankar, *op. cit.*, pp. 288-289. For the various interpretations of this *mahāvākya* by the different Vedāntic schools see *Viśiṣṭādvaita*, p. 594 ff.
2. *Viśiṣṭādvaita*, p. 38.
3. *Vedāntasūtras*, pp. 79-80. Cf. *bhinnapravṛttinimittānāṁ śabdānām ekasmin arthe vṛttiḥ sāmānādhikaraṇyam iti śābdikāḥ* / *Śrībhāṣya* (text, Abhyankar's edn.), p. 59. See also what precedes this statement and *Vedārthasaṅgraha*, p. 51.
4. *Vedāntasūtras*, p. 79.

tion and plurality.[1] The unchanging unity of *brahman* is thus understood, in this view, to be co-ordinate with the changing diversities of its attributes. *Brahman* (*Īśvara*), the substance, and *cit* and *acit*, the modes which are believed to be co-ordinately bound up with the substance, what is described as *prakāraprakāribhāva*, or the substance-attribute relation. It is questionable whether Rāmānuja does not overstrain the slender grammatical co-ordination in seeking from it a sanction for his theory of reality as a complex whole.[2]

Two important points to be noticed in Rāmānuja's view of reality are : (a) that he emphasises, as against Advaitism the reality, in the attributes, of difference, and concomitantly with difference, of change and plurality; and (b) that he affirms, as against the *bhedābheda* view of reality, the unchanging character of *brahman* which, nevertheless, is the source of all change in the modes, by virtue of its inherent powers. The distinction from Advaitism has already been pointed out by means of the contrasting notions of *viśiṣṭaikyam* and *svarūpaikyam*. The distinction from the *bhedābheda* view will be noted presently when the notable features of Rāmānuja's criticism against this view, as represented by Bhāskara and Yādava, are considered. Meanwhile it may

---

1. For a discussion of the principle of co-ordination in relation to Viśiṣṭādvaitism see *Śrībhāṣya* (text, Abhyankar's edn.), p. 59 ff. and *ibid.* (intro., and notes, pt. 2), p. 24; *Vedārthasaṅgraha* (as well as *Tātparyadīpikā*) p. 51 ff., *Śrībhāṣya* (M. Rangachari's edn.), p. 112 and f. n. 75 (wherein Kaiyyata's definition of this principle is cited and reference to Paṇini and Patañjali is made in this connection).
2. For two critical observations on this question, see *infra*, p. 96 f. and f. n. 3 and 1 thereon.

be observed that Rāmānuja's criticism against the *bhedābheda* philosophy is primarily directed against the common *bhedābheda* thesis of a self-contradictory reality of identity-in-difference. It is because they hold this thesis that *bhedābhedavādins* are described as '*jainagandhi*' (Jaina-like) Vedāntins, and, therefore, as indulging, like the Jainas, in expounding an 'untruthful' (self-contradictory) view of reality (*ayathābhāṣaṇacaturāḥ*)[1]. The curious irony of this situation is that Rāmānuja himself, like the *bhedābhedavādins* thus criticised, is a *brahmapariṇāmavādin*, and is even described, quite rightly, as attempting a "re-interpretation of *bhedābheda*"[2]. Consequently, Rāmānuja is nearer to, if not one among, *bhedābhedavādins* like Bhāskara and Yādava, than to any other type of Vedāntins, like Śaṅkara. Never-

1. Cf. *yadi bhāskarayādavaprakāśau nigamāntasthitinirṇayapravīṇau / aparaiḥ kimivāparāddham āryā ayathābhāṣaṇacāturīdhurīṇaiḥ // ata eva nirguṇabrahmavādinām pracchannabauddhaprasiddhavadanayor api jainagandhivedāntinau iti nāmadheyam anuśośrūyāmahe* / Vedāntadeśika's *Saṅkalpasūryodaya*, ed. V. Krishnamacharya, Adyar, 1948, p. 322 f., p. 86. Commenting on the phrase *ayathābhāṣaṇacaturaiḥ*, the commentator of *Prabhāvilāsa* (on the above work) observes : *syādasti syānnāsti ityayathābhāṣaṇacāturyadhurīṇaiḥ* / Writing under the phrase *jainagandhivedāntinau iti* the same commentator observes : *ekasya vastunaḥ aikarūpyakathanāt tathātvam* / In *Prabhāvali*, a further comm. on the above work, K we see the following comment on this phrase : *evaṁ jainaiḥ samānayogakṣematvāt jainagandhivedāntinau iti nāma jagati prasiddham* / See also what follows. *Ibid.* Some modern critics also confirm this view. See *Brahmavādin*, Vol. V, pp. 467-468, and Vol. VI, p. 233. A further amplification of the objection of *virodha* in Jainism is found in *Śrībhāṣyavārtika*, verses 125-129.
2. "Rāmānuja explicitly rejects the theory of *bhedābheda* in many places in his *Śrībhaṣyam*. But his *Viśiṣṭādvaita* is really a

theless Rāmānuja is as much against Bhāskara and Yādava as he is against Śaṅkara. The following are the notable points of Rāmānuja's criticism against Bhāskara and Yādava:

In the first place, the Bhāskarīya and Yādavīya thesis of reality as simultaneous distinction and non-distinction (*bhedābheda* or *bhinnābhinna*) is, as just noticed, self-contradictory. This is believed to be so on the ground that distinction and non-distinction cannot co-exist as they do in the *bhedābheda* philosophy, after the manner of Jainism. In brief, the *bhedābheda* thesis represents an effort to reconcile the irreconcilable.

Secondly, if in order to escape from the above difficulty, Bhāskara and Yādava seek to affirm that non-distinction, or identity, is genus and distinction, or difference, is species, and that both genus and species constitute the two aspects of everything, then it is held that they tend to divide the indivisible into two compartments. Further, this attitude on the part of *bhedābhedavadins* will, it is contended, not with any convincing reason on the side of Rāmānuja, lead to a situation in which difference will tend to be more primary. If true, as Rāmānuja believes it to be, this primacy of difference over identity will, of course, militate against the accepted thesis of a co-ordinate scheme of identity-in-difference.

Thirdly, if, on the contrary, *bhedābhedavādins* declare that the two elements of distinction (*bhinna*) and non-

---

reinterpretation of *bhedābheda*". *Identity-in-difference*, P. T. Raju, *The New Ind. Ant.*, Vol. XII, Nos. 1-6, 1939, pp. 321-322. See also p. 323 of the same article and his *Idealistic Thought in India* (London, 1953), p. 154.

distinction (*abhinna*) should, despite their difference, form a single entity, on the ground that their essence is *brahman*, then the critic will point out that they become liable to the opposite error of holding non-distinction, or identity, as the fundamental reality.

Thus none of the three possibilities, which correspondingly centre round the notions *bhinnābhinna* (simultaneous distinction and non-distinction), *bhinna* (distinction), and *abhinna* (non-distinction), is, according to Rāmānuja, tenable; and consequently *bhedābhedavāda*, it is concluded, falls to the ground.[1]

Bhedābhedavādins, however, defend themselves against this, as against Advaitic attacks, on the firm ground that the co-existence of *bheda* and *abheda* in reality is an indisputable, and, therefore, uncontradictable, verdict of *pramāṇa* or valid knowledge. If this co-existence is a valid truth, then the several objections of Rāmānuja will lose their force. The fact that *bhedābhedavādins* have not fully succeeded in defending this truth does not detract from the value of their recognition of the truth.[2] It is needless to go minutely into the polemical subleties of *bhedābhedavādins* in defence of their position. Some of the arguments from the *bhedābheda* viewpoint have been outlined in the course of our account of the several schools of *bhedābheda* philosophy.

---

1. Cf. *Vedāntasūtras*, pp. 134-135, 189-193 and 195 f.
2. Cf. the following observation which represents the general *bhedābheda* attitude to the problem : *pramāṇataś cet pratīyate ko virodho'yam ucyate / virodhe cāvirodhe ca pramāṇaṁ kāraṇaṁ matam //*

Rāmānuja's objections against the *bhedābheda* philosophy, however, serve, in a somewhat indirect manner, as an indication of his attitude towards the Jaina view of reality. A direct statement of this attitude, touching in particular the point of self-contradiction in Jainism, is made in the course of his comments on the well-known *sūtra* of Bādarāyaṇa: "Not so, on account of the impossibility in one"[1]. Commenting, Rāmānuja observes: "Difference (*bhinnatvam*)... consists in things being the abodes of contradictory attributes; non-difference, not any more than the generic character of a horse and that of a buffalo, can belong to one animal."[2] Concluding his comments, Rāmānuja reiterates, "Things which stand to each other in the relation of mutual non-existence cannot after all be identical."[3]

Deferring a treatment of the Jaina solution[4] to the above objection of self-contradictoriness urged not merely by Viśiṣṭādvaitism but also by the other Vedantic, as well as the Buddhistic, schools, a few critical observations may be made here on the implications of Rāmānuja's own theory of reality.

All the efforts of Rāmānuja to weave difference as an independent entity into the texture of a *brahman*-ridden reality have proved unsuccessful and resulted in what is, after all, a "temperate monism", as Max Müller calls it. No system which is dominated by an infinite absolute—an absolute which is the source and explanation of all that is finite, or

---

1. *Vedāntasūtras*, p. 516.
2. *Ibid.*, p. 518.
3. *Ibid.*, p. 518.
4. See *infra*, Ch. V.

diverse—can, as it has been repeatedly pointed out, result in a justly comprehensive scheme of reality in which the principle of difference, and all that it implies, can enjoy an intrinsically real and co-ordinate status. Despite its professions to the contrary, Rāmānuja's Viśiṣṭādvaitism must be counted among such systems, for it holds that *brahman* is the supreme reality and *cit* and *acit* are, despite their supposedly distinctive status[1] of existence, real only in so far as they derive their reality from *brahman*. Under this scheme the course of reality becomes a one-way traffic—that is, one in which reality flows only from the infinite absolute to the so-called real and finite world and the selves—but not a genuinely comprehensive synthesis resulting from an interaction of the independent, but complimentary, elements of identity and difference.

Thus there can be little doubt that in Rāmānuja's philosophy, identity, represented by *brahman*, is, as shown in the present account, the primary principle; and difference, represented by the modal elements of *cit* and *acit*, is the secondary principle having *brahman* for its source and

---

1. That *brahman* is, strictly speaking (*vastutastu*), the only real principle (*ekameva*), in *viśiṣṭādvaita* as in the other schools of Vedānta (*vedāntānām*) in the opinion of Śrīnivāsa : *vastutastu vedāntānāṁ cidacidviśiṣṭam advaitam ekameva brahmeti tātparyam / ata eva cidacidviśiṣṭaṁ brahmaikam iti upakramya tameva prakāraṁ nirūpitavān/ataḥ cidacidviśiṣṭo.... nārāyaṇa evaikaṁ tattvam iti viśiṣṭādvaitavādināṁ darśanam iti siddham* // Śrīnivāsa's *Yatīndramatadīpikā*, p. 47; see also p. 39, and cf. *evaṁ sarvāvasthāvasthitacidacidvastuśarīratayā tatprakāraḥ paramapuruṣa eva kāryāvasthakāraṇāvasthajagadrūpeṇa avasthita iti..../ Śrībhāṣya* (S. Abhyankar's edn., text, p. 119). See also *Vedāntasāra*, pp. 8-9.

explanation. This stands out clearly in spite of the fact that Rāmānuja has not evolved a clear and well-grounded conception of difference in all respects. The ambiguous treatment of difference is evident when we see, for instance, that it (difference) is considered, on the one hand, as a component and therefore a genuinely real and distinct element in the complex whole (*viśiṣṭaikyam*) of reality, and, on the other, as something which does not touch[1] —for contact would mean introducing the taint of imperfection—*brahman* which is believed to be unchanging in nature.

It has just been noticed that, however ambiguous may be its nature, difference is definitely believed to occupy a subordinate or secondary place in relation to identity, in Rāmānuja's metaphysics. Nevertheless, we find two critics—Rāju and Śrīnivāsācārya—who are inclined to take the view that for Rāmānuja difference is primary (*mukhya*) and identity secondary (*gauṇa*)[2]. That this view (somewhat casually hinted at, and not accompanied by any serious supporting arguments), is not tenable is clear from the main drift of Rāmānuja's viewpoint. Whatever plausibility there is for an equal or co-ordinate—certainly not any superior (primary)—status of difference, derives eventually from the grammatical principle of co-ordination, or *sāmānādhikaraṇya*.[3] There are

1. Cf. *supra*, p. 79, f.n. 4.
2. *The New Ind. Ant.*, Vol. II, Nos. 1-6, 1939, p. 321, f.n. 4. See also the same author's (Rāju's) *Idealistic Thought in India*, p. 154 f.n. 2. Śrīnivāsācārya's *Darśanodaya*, p. 194.
3. That *sāmānādhīkaraṇya* signifies not merely unity but also—and co-ordinately with unity—difference is clearly pointed out

at least two considerations which weaken this principle of co-ordination as a basis of the argument for a co-ordinate status of difference. First *sāmānādhikaraṇya* conflicts with the most fundamental basis of *satkāryavāda*[1] which governs the entire philosophy of Viśiṣṭādvaita. It is an established fact that in any form of *satkāryavāda* difference is subordinate, not equal, to identity. Secondly, deriving an ontological fact from the notion of *sāmānādhikaraṇya* amounts to, as it has been rightly pointed out, taking "the grammar of language for the grammar of reality"[2].

These various considerations point to the fact that the principle of difference is in essence subordinated to that of identity in Rāmānuja's metaphysics.

---

by Rāmānuja. Cf. "But if there be no difference of 'modes' there can be no *sāmānādhikaraṇya.*" Sukhtankar, *op. cit.*, p. 290.

1. For a full statement of *satkāryavāda,* or the doctrine that "the effect is non-different from the cause" *(kāraṇād ananyaṁ kāryam)* in Viśiṣṭādvaitism, and a comparison with the attitude of the Vedānta and other schools to the problem, see *ibid.*, pp. 142-149.

2. *EPI*, p. 179. In the twenty-fourth series (1953) of the Riddell Memorial Lectures, at the University of Durham, on Languages, Standpoints and Attitudes, (O. U. P.), H. A. Hodges observes how "insoluble problems were....created for metaphysics, merely because linguistic forms were misinterpreted into ontological theories", and how, "so much of metaphysics has consisted of errors like these, that many have come to think that metaphysics is nothing else but misuse and misinterpretation of language" (p. 20). Supporting these remarks Hodges again maintains: "Grammatical forms have been taken as evidence of ontological relations; because facts can be described in sentences, it has been thought, that the structure of a sentence reflects the structure of the existing world." etc., p. 19; see also what follows.

C. Hegelianism

Among modern philosophers in the West Hegel most nearly approximates to Jainism in that he evolves a systematic dialectical synthesis which comprehends both identity (substantivity) and difference (relativity) in the structure of reality. "Substantiality and Relativity are" says Caird, describing Hegel's philosophy, "thus seen to be not two ideas, but one, and the truth is to be found not in either separately but in their union; which means that nothing can be said to be substantial in the sense of having existence independent of relation, but only in the sense of including its relativity in its own being."[1] Neither 'Being' (Substantiality) alone, nor 'Non-Being' ('Relativity', 'Nothing' or 'Other') alone, but 'Determinate Being'[2] ('Becoming'), the union of the

---

1. Continuing, Caird writes, "In other words, nothing is substantial except in so far as it is a subject or self which maintains itself in change, because its change is determined by its own nature, and is indeed only the necessary manifestation of nature...... The real substance has to be sought for, not in the two things taken separately, but in the principle which divides and at the same time unites them........Thus that alone can truly be called a reality which maintains and realises itself in the process of differentiation and reintegration of differences." Edward Caird's *Hegel*, Edinburgh and London, 1883, pp. 174-175.
2. "Of course Being is sometimes imagined, for instance, as pure light, as the clearness of unclouded vision, and Nothing as pure night; and their distinction is thus connected with this well known sensuous difference. But in fact, if this pure seeing be imagined more exactly, it is easy to perceive that in absolute clearness as much or as little is seen as in absolute darkness, and that one kind of seeing, as much as the other, is pure seeing,

two[1], constitutes reality. As a matter of fact "Being" and "Nothing" are said to be contradictory[2] 'moments' (or

---

that is, a seeing of Nothing. Pure light and pure darkness are two voids which are the same. We can distinguish only in determinate light, that is, since light is determined by darkness in clouded light,—and, equally in determinate darkness, that is, since darkness; and this is just because clouded light and illumined darkness contain distinction in themselves and therefore are Determinate Being". Hegel's *Science of Logic* (tr. by W. H. Johnson and L. G. Struthers, 1929, London), Vol. I, p. 105.

1. "The simple idea of pure Being was first enunciated by the Eleatics, as the Absolute and as sole truth; especially by Parmenides, whose surviving fragments, with pure enthusiasm of thought first comprehending itself in its absolute abstraction, proclaim that "Being alone is, and Nothing is not at all".—It is well known that in oriental systems, and essentially in Buddhism, Nothing, or the Void, is the absolute principle.—Heraclitus was profound enough to emphasise in opposition to this simple and one-sided abstraction the higher total concept of Becoming, saying: "Being is no more than Nothing is", or "All things flow", which means, everything is Becoming.—Popular sayings, chiefly oriental, to the effect that everything which is has in its birth the germs of its decay, while death conversely is entrance to a new life, express at bottom the same union of Being and Nothing. *Ibid.*, pp. 95-96. Although Hegel is concerned, in the course of the present passage, with deriving confirmation, and, in some measure, authority or sanction, for his dialectic of synthesis (of being and non-being) from the illustrious ancient Greek, it is a well-known fact that the Greek thinker, viz., Heraclitus, is more correctly associated with propounding, in keen contrast with Parmenides, almost an uncomprising philosophy of change ('becoming used in a somewhat more one-sided sense than by Hegel') than with reconciling the two opposed trends referred to, by Hegel, here. This is indicated by the very fragment just cited by Hegel, viz., "All things flow" as well as by analogies of fire etc. This consideration does not, however, affect the truth of Hegel's argument for the reconciliation or synthesis of being and non-being.
2. Cf. "Being, first, is determined as opposed to Other in general." *Ibid.* 91.

Croce is inclined to treat the two 'moments' or elements as 'distincts' rather than as 'opposites' or contradictories in Hegel's philosophy. Distinguishing and defending this procedure Croce writes: "The logical category of distinction is one thing, and the category of opposition is another. As has been said (at many places in course of the chapter from which this passage is taken), two distinct concepts unite with one another, although they are distinct; but two opposite concepts seem to exclude one another. Where one enters the other totally disappears. A distinct concept is presupposed by and lives in its other which follows it in the sequence of ideas. An opposite concept is slain by its opposite." Elucidating this contrast further he adds that opposites "do not constitute peaceable and friendly couples" (e. g., true and false, good and evil, being and non-being, life and death etc.)...."Opposition gives rise to deep fissures in the bosom of the philosophical universal and of each of its particular forms, and to irreconcilable dualisms." B. Croce's *What is Living and What is Dead of the Philosophy of Hegel,* E. T. by Douglas Ainslie, London, 1915, pp. 10-11. (Words within the first pair of brackets are mine, and the examples cited within the second pair are selected from among Croce's own given in a passage on p. 11.) Croce draws the further implications of imposing the "deep fissures" of opposition on philosophical thinking. One of them, for instance, is the tendency to affirm one of the opposites and deny the other or *vice versa.* That which is affirmed tends to become the whole truth and that which is denied to become a "necessary illusion". Hence the two should, according to Croce, be regarded as 'one-sided truths' or 'fragments' awaiting 'integration'. (Cf. *ibid.*, p. 14 ff.)

Replacing Hegel's dialectic of contradictories by that of 'distincts' is indeed a significant contribution of Croce to Hegelianism and philosophy in general. But even Croce is finally ensnared by the magic of the Hegelian doctrine of the "Concrete Universal". (Cf. *ibid.*, pp. 20, 22, 32, etc. Reference to the 'integration' of the 'fragments', just noticed, also suggests the fact of this ensnarement.) Reserving our criticisms against this specific doctrine for a later occasion it may be observed here that Croce's modified form of the dialectic of 'distinct' is in greater harmony with the Jaina view of real as constituted by identity (*dhrauvya*) and difference (*paryāya*) which are mutually complementary elements. This complementary character of the element is particularly accentuated

abstractions) clamouring for reconciliation or synthesis. They represent the thesis and the antithesis leading to the synthetic whole, or concrete universal, which forms the basis of a new start in the working of the triadic law. Unlike the Vedāntin and the Buddhist, and very much like the Jaina, Hegel does not frame the picture of reality through the 'annulment' or obliteration of one of the opposing elements of identity and difference but by a sturdy constructive synthesis of identity-in-difference which alone, according to him, is the 'truth' of reality. The two elements are not believed to be connected by a *tour de force*; they hang together by 'inner necessity'.

Up to this point Hegel and the Jaina agree in most important respects. But when Hegel tries to derive synthesis from the Absolute, that 'far-off divine event' towards which everything proceeds, they part company. For Hegel the Absolute (the Idea, the Ideal, the Reason) is the supreme all-comprehending whole which operates as a presupposition[1] of each of its finite aspects. It is the bottom of the inverted pyramid of Hegel's philosophy supporting and sustaining the massive structure of finite and relative 'moments'. "All else", he tells us, "is error, confusion, opinion, strife, caprice and impermanence". It is the Absolute that is the supreme synthesis of all finite syntheses which are but 'transitions' or mile-stones in our 'ceaseless progression'

---

in the process of the repudiation of the fallacy of contradiction or *virodhābhāsa* by the Jaina thinker, in the sequel.

1. "This comprehensive development of the notion of the Absolute is the entire system of the philosophy of the Absolute." J. B. Baillie, *ERE*, 573. See also what follows.

toward it. Moreover whatever objectivity there is in Hegel is due to the 'self-externalization' of the Asolute.

By his predominant emphasis on the Absolute Hegel ends as the philosopher of 'identity' although he begins well by treating identity and difference as co-ordinate elements and is second to none in his attack upon the theory of pure Being as well as of its opposite abstraction. For the Jaina also identity and difference are co-ordinate, or equally vital, elements in reality. The real, for him, however, is not the rational ultimate (the Absolute), as it is for Hegel, although it is cognisable (*jñeya*) to the mind. In other words, rationality or thought, (which, in the final analysis is equated by Hegel to the Absolute), cognises, rather than constitutes, reality or the universe. Nor does reality or the universe derive its being or truth from the Absolute. It is, on the contrary, a self-moving concern. Further, the Jaina seems pre-eminently to base his findings on experience, whereas Hegel seems to do so on a logical analysis although both recognise the objectivity, at any rate the objective reference, of thought or judgment.

A further significant feature arising from the differing background of metaphysical assumptions concerns the nature of the dialectical analysis itself in the two schools. There is an inherent urge in the 'moments' or alternatives, under the Hegelian dialectic, for conjunction, synthesis or integration. The moments, which are least inclusive wholes, mutually integrate themselves into a wider synthetic whole. Thus they have the character of self-transcendence or self-dissolution stamped on them. We may, therefore, characterise this Hegelian synthesis as a conjunctive dialectic, or conjunctive synthesis.

Under the Jaina dialectic, on the contrary, each 'moment' or alternative, of experience, is conserved alongside other 'moments' in its distinctive individuality. In the total fabric of experience the 'moments' are, therefore, neither transcended nor annihilated but preserved, in all their distinctness, displaying a complex network of relation to other 'moments' of experience. We may, therefore, describe the Jaina dialectic as the disjunctive synthesis or the disjunctive dialectic. In virtue of these differences Hegelianism swings, despite its resemblance to Jainism in important respects as already noticed, to the side of the Sāṅkhya system and the other schools of philosophy in which difference of *bheda* is subordinated to identity or *abheda*.

CHAPTER IV

The Schools of Philosophy in which Difference Subordinates Identity :

A. *The Vaiśeṣika System*

B. *The Dvaita System (of Madhva)*

CHAPTER IX

CHAPTER IV

The Systems of Philosophy in which Identity is subordinated to Difference

Having observed, in the course of the previous chapter, how 'difference' is subordinated to 'identity' in the several systems including Hegelianism, we may now briefly turn to two noteworthy examples in Indian thought, in which the converse thesis is upheld, viz., subordination of identity to difference. The two examples to be now considered in so far as they have a bearing on the problem of 'identity-in-difference', are (a) the Vaiśeṣika system and (b) the Mādhva system of Dvaitism.

A. The Vaiśeṣika System

This system is an atomistic pluralism. It adopts a sixfold classification of categories or *padārthas*, viz., substance (*dravya*), quality (*guṇa*), activity (*karma*), generality (*sāmānya*), difference or particularity (*viśeṣa*) and intimate[1] relation

1. 'Intimate or necessary relation' is a better translation of *samavāya* than 'internal relation'. This is so because the term 'internal' indicates that the inner character of the relata will, as will be noticed below, in ch. VII, be affected and, consequently, the relata will tend to become an identity which abolishes otherness or distinction which is the very essence

(*samavāya*). Non-existence (*abhāva*) was later[1] on added as a seventh category.

This system attaches a predominant importance to the category of *viśeṣa*[2]. It maintains this category as a fundamental ontological and functional principle. Even the name Vaiśeṣika is derived from the term *viśeṣa*.[3] This term *viśeṣa* is used to denote every individual element of particularity or difference as well as the whole group of such elements the

---

of the Vaiśeṣika philosophy. For a further treatment of the contrast between necessary relation and 'internal' relation as describing the inseparable (*ayutasiddha*) nature of the relata in *samavāya* see the opening portion of the chapter just referred to.

1. See *ILA*, p. 204 f., *SP*, p. 7 (notes), H. Ui's *The Vaiśeṣika Philosophy*, ed. F. W. Thomas, 1917, London, pp. 123-124, footnotes 1 and 2 on p. 124, and p. 183, and *IP*, Vol. II, pp. 219-221. A. M. Bhattacharya and N. C. B. Bhattacharya clearly affirm that Śivāditya was the first to add *abhāva* as the seventh category to the traditional list of six categories (see their edn. of *Saptapadārthī*, 1934, Calcutta, Intro. p. X).
2. Owing to such predominant importance attached to *viśeṣa* the Vaiśeṣika becomes 'essentially a philosophy of distinctions' See *IP*, Vol. II, p. 176 and Garbe's observations quoted in the following footnote.
3. Garbe observes : "Difference (*viśeṣa*), the fifth category...... holds an important place in the Vaiśeṣika system, inasmuch as, by virtue of it the difference of the atoms renders possible the formation of the universe. The name, therefore, of the entire system, Vaiśeṣika, is derived from the word for difference (*viśeṣa*)". (See his article on 'Vaiśeṣika', *ERE*.) It should, however, be noted here that difference is attached not merely to atoms but also, as noticed below, to all the ultimate entities forming the basis of the distinctions among such entities. Also cf. *viśeṣapadārthas tu darśanāntarakāraiḥ na manyate, ata eva asya darśanasya viśeṣadarśana iti saṁjñā, etanmatānuyāyinām api vaiśeṣika iti saṁjñā......* / V on VD in *VD*, p. 458. See also *ILA*, p. 179, f. n. 1; *PDS*, p. 32; *OIP*, p. 225; and *SP*, p. 3 (notes).

number of which is said to be infinite (*te anantāh*[1]). Every simple or ultimate entity (*nityadravya*) is believed to have a *viśeṣa* rooted[2] in it. It is by virtue of the *viśeṣa* thus rooted in it that an entity can be differentiated[3] from all other entities. This is so not merely in the case of ultimate entities which are otherwise indistinguishable[4] from one another, e.g., one atom (*aṇu*) from another, one liberated soul (*muktātma*) from another or one *manas* from another[5], but also among all other[6] entities in the universe.

If *viśeṣas* are granted to be the differentiating elements

---

1. See Jinavardhanasūri's Comm. quoted in *SP*, p. 5 (notes).
2. *vināśārambharahiteṣu nityadravyeṣu anvākāśakāladigātmamanassu pratidravyam ekaikaśo vartamānaḥ......*/ *PB*, p. 691. See also *SP*, p. 5 (for the Comm. quoted) and *TRD*, p. 277.
3. Hence *viśeṣas* are characterised as *vyāvṛttibuddhihetevaḥ*. *PB*, p. 691.
4. *anyanimittasambhavāt* / *Ibid.*
5. *nityeṣu tulyakṛtiguṇakriyeṣu paramāṇuṣu muktātmamanassu* etc. *Ibid.*
6. The direct means of differentiation among the ultimate entities are of course *viśeṣas* themselves. The proximate means of differentiation among the non-ultimate or composite bodies are, however, the distinctions among the component parts constituting the bodies (*avayavabhedādavayavibhedaḥ*). But, in the ultimate analysis, even these distinctions among the component parts are based on the indivisible atoms from which the parts are formed. Hence all differentiations are based, directly or indirectly, on the *viśeṣas*. Cf. "Thus a jar is distinguished from a piece of cloth ; because the component parts of the first are distinct from those of the latter ; and so on we may argue, until at last we arrive at the ultimate constituents of matter viz., atoms, which are indivisible. The same reasoning cannot be applied to distinguish one atom from another, since an atom has no further component parts." *SP*, p. 5 (notes). See also *Saptapadārthī* (A. M. Bhattacharya and N. C. B. Bhattacharya's edn.) p. XXXVIII f., f.n. 63.

severally abiding in all entities, simple (ultimate) and composite, living and non-living, then the question arises how one *viśeṣa* is to be differentiated from another. It would, indeed, be a paradox if the distinguishing element itself remains indistinguishable (*aviśesasvarūpah*) from the other such elements. If, in order to avoid this anomaly, a further distinguishing (*vyāvartaka*) element for each *viśeṣa* is admitted there comes in the situation of *regressus ad infinitum*[1] (*anavasthā*). For, every additional *viśeṣa* (*viśeṣāntara*) postulated to account for the distinctness of a *viśeṣa,* gives rise to the need of a further *viśeṣa,* and the latter, again, to a still further *viśeṣa* and so on in an endless succession. Anticipating this insuperable difficulty Praśastapāda, and more particularly, his commentator Vyomaśiva, lay down that a *viśeṣa* is also self-differentiating (*svatovyāvartaka*). That is, a *viśeṣa* is not merely other-differentiating but also self-differentiating in its nature, just as a lamp (*pradīpa*) is both other-revealing and self-revealing.[2]

The unique place accorded to the principle of *viśeṣa,* or difference, in the Vaiśeṣika system has earned for the Vaiśeṣika the title of being semi-nihilistic (*ardha-vaināśika*), or, at any rate, semi-Buddhistic. This is so because the

---

1. See *PB,* p. 691 f., and the *Vyomavatī* thereon (p. 694 f.). Jinavardhanasūri refers to another fallacy, viz., *ātmāśraya,* arising from the theory of *viśeṣas,* see *SP,* p. 6 (Notes). For how the "modern school of Nyāya" treats the question of *viśeṣa,* see *ILA,* p. 196 and S. Bhaduri's ***Studies in Nyāya-Vaiśeṣika Metaphysics*** (Poona, 1947), p. 146 and f.n. 1 thereon, where reference is made to Raghunātha Śiromaṇi's work.
2. *Ibid.* See also *The Vaiśeṣika System* (B. Faddegon, 1918, Amsterdam), p. 125.

unique atomistic entities, viz., the *viśeṣas* conceived by the Vaiśeṣika philosopher, have, despite their divergent traits in other respects, a close resemblance to the unique and discrete particulars conceived under the Buddhistic doctrine of *svalakṣaṇavāda.* The Vaiśeṣika is, however, saved from propounding, like the Buddhist, a philosophy of total difference by introducing into the Vaiśeṣika theory of reality the principle of *samavāya*, or the necessary relation, which may be loosely described as the element of identity in the system.

Samavāya represents the relational bond between such two inseparable (*ayutasiddha*) relata as *dravya* (substance) and *guṇa* (property). It would, therefore, be better to describe it as a unifying or synthesising principle than as identity, although it is the nearest equivalent to identity in the Vaiśeṣika system. A somewhat closer treatment of it may be reserved for a later occasion.[1] It has, however, already been suggested[2] that *samavāya*, despite its being a so-called intimate or necessary relation, is after all external in nature and therefore does not make any difference to the inward being of the entities it connects. This external character, therefore, weakens its claim for being treated as genuine identity. In maintaining the external character of *samavāya*, the Vaiśeṣika is no doubt in keeping with the temper of his "philosophy of distinctions". It is difference rather than unity or identity which is the basic rule of the system. If *samavāya* were invested with a rich internal character it would cut at the root of his atomistic, pluralistic

---

1. See Chapter VII.
2. See Chapter VII.

and realistic philosophy of difference and incline it towards some kind of idealism. As it stands this system is, as already pointed out, one in which "diversity (or difference) and not unity (or identity) is at the root of the universe".[1] In other words this system subordinates identity to difference.

B. Madhva's Dvaitism

An even greater[2] stress than in the Vaiśeṣika system is laid on *viśeṣa,* the principle of difference, in Dvaitism which is built up on the two ultimate postulates[3], the Independent (*svatantra*) and the Dependent (*paratantra* or *asvatantra*), the former postulate representing the supreme God and the latter comprising the selves, the material world and non-existence.[4]

---

1. *OIP*, p. 225. (The words within brackets are mine.)
2. In the first place, although distinctions in the Vaiśeṣika system, even among the composite bodies, are ultimately derived from *viśeṣas, viśeṣas* are restricted to the simple or ultimate substances only (see above under the Vaiśeṣika system, p. 109, f.n. 6). In Dvaitism, however, *viśeṣas* are postulated not only in the case of (ultimate or eternal) substances but in that of all categories—even non-existence. Secondly, "...... while in the Nyāya-Vaiśeṣika (or the Vaiśeṣika) *viśeṣa* accounts for the difference which is assumed to exist between two things, here (in Dvaitism) it accounts for making difference where there is none". See *EIP*, p. 194 f. Considerations like how *viśeṣa* is of comprehensive and great importance and how it lends significance to identity will become clear in the course of the present section.
3. See *SDAC*, p. 87 and *RRS*, p. 168.
4. The selves, and the material world, called *cetana* principle and the *acetana* principle, respectively, are together treated as

Fundamental as it is in the Vaiśeṣika system, *viśeṣa* is even more so in Dvaitism, on account of the Dvaitic belief that the entire course of reality is directly within the 'relentless grip' of this 'power' or 'potency'.[1] Being at the heart of everything real, this 'power' is said, by no means figuratively, to be the very 'nature' (*svarūpa* or *svabhāva*) of everything. "*Bheda*", it is said, "is *dharmisvarūpa*."[2] "It exists, guides, and controls matters here and hereafter. Earth and Heaven, secular and spiritual, all concerns of daily routine life, and all concepts of the intellectual life, and conditions of scientific disciplines—all come under the relentless grip of difference. The fundamental form of objects is difference."[3] "Difference is thus the very stuff of the cosmos."[4] "By a mere stroke of the pen, by a mere fiat, a speculative gesture, or an adroit assertion, or a craze for unity-mongering it would be impossible to deny or annihilate the *difference* that is constitutive and foundational of all reality—of sentient and non-sentient creation."[5] Madhva, on whose writings the statements quoted above are based, himself declares: "Diverse and of diverse attributes are all things of the universe" (*bhinnāś ca bhinna-*

---

existence or *bhāva*, non-existence or *abhāva* being treated as a distinctive category. See *RRS*, p. 168 ff.

1. See *RRS*, p. 511, para 1.
2. *Ibid.*, p. 296. The following observations, also made by Madhva, are to the same effect : (i) *padārthasvarūpatvāt bhedasya / bhedastu svarūpadarśana eva siddhaḥ / asya bheda iti tu padārthasya svarūpam itivat / Ibid.*, p. 583. (ii) *bhedastu sarvavastūnāṁ svarūpaṁ naijam avyayam /* See *HIP*, Vol. IV, p. 155, f.n. 1.
3. *RRS*, p. 287.
4. *Ibid.*, p. 292.
5. *Ibid.*, p. 299.

dharmāś ca padārthā nikhilā amī[1]); or that "It (difference) lurks in everything" (*so'sti vastuṣvaśeṣataḥ*[2]). Such statements are stated to express the "general metaphysical position" of Dvaitism.[3] This is a position in which "The Cartesian Cogito should be considerably amended, if not completely altered. What does Descartes say? 'I think—therefore, I am.' Madhva would alter it to 'I differ—therefore, I am.' It is thus a position in which "Existence means difference, and difference means existence—though not literally."[4]

If the statement that "*Existence* means difference and difference means existence . . ." and perhaps similar other statements (e. g., that "Difference is. . . .the very *stuff* of the cosmos" etc.), which declare the identity of 'existence' and 'stuff', are not to be taken 'literally', it is difficult to see how Madhva and his followers treat *viśeṣa* as an ontological principle at all. As a matter of fact Dvaitins, like the Vaiśeṣikas, speak of an infinity[5] of *viśeṣas*, corresponding to the infinite diversity of the nature of an entity within itself, as well as to the infinite range of entities in the universe, from which a particular entity is differentiated. It is doubtful whether what is considered as the 'nature' or the 'power' of an entity can be treated as the entity itself. It sounds somewhat illogical that a 'power' is considered to

1. *EIP*, p. 187, and p. 210, note 9.
2. *RRS*, p. 298.
3. Cf. *EIP*, p. 187.
4. *RRS*, p. 298 f.
5. See *IP*, Vol. II, p. 746, and Jayatīrtha's *Vādāvali* (Adyar, 1943), Notes, p. 203.

be an entity. If it were not so considered it would not be possible to speak of an 'infinity' of *viśeṣas* which are further asserted to be downright perceivable facts.

By treating *viśeṣa* as a 'power' or 'potency' the Dvaitin seems to think that he has avoided the charge of infinite regress[1] to which Praśastapāda's view of *viśeṣa* as a distinctive entity is believed to be liable. It is affirmed that "*viśeṣa* (peculiar power and potency etc.) is *sui generis, self-sufficient* and *self-explanatory*".[2]

The main defensive argument advanced on behalf of the 'self-explanatory' character of *viśeṣa* is that it, like any 'ultimate category', cannot be explained, and that it, on the contrary, explains itself and 'others'.[3] This sounds more like a dogmatic assertion than a logical argument. Further the Dvaitin seems to make capital out of the position assumed by the Advaitin, his principal opponent, on the question of '*avidyā*'. The latter is stated to consider '*avidyā*' as being *somehow* there projecting the cosmic illusion.[4] If this could be regarded by the Advaitin to be sufficiently self-explanatory, then why not, the Dvaitin argues, treat *viśeṣa* as such, that is, as an 'ultimate category' which is 'self-explanatory'[5]. All this seems to be rather poor defence of a notion[6] which is invested with a fundamental significance in Dvaitism. Even Dasgupta, a favourable critic of Dvaitism,

---

1. Cf. *RRS*, p. 512.
2. *Ibid.*
3. *Ibid.*
4. *Ibid.*
5. *Ibid.*
6. *HIP*, Vol. IV, p. 179.

passes the verdict of a 'weak'[1] defence on a great Mādhva dialectician who does not seem materially to add to the argument for difference just noticed.

The exponents of Dvaitism credit the notion of difference, as seen above, with such fundamental and comprehensive significance that we are apt to understand the system as one of uncompromising difference. It is indeed not uncommon that this system is described as *śuddhabhedavāda.*[2] In his crusading zeal for *bheda* Madhva interprets the celebrated texts[3] in such a manner that they are made to yield a *bheda* view of reality. *Ātma tat tvam asi* (soul! 'that art thou'), for instance, is construed as *ātma atat tvam asi*[4] (soul! thou are not that) and thereby difference, not identity, is elicited

---

1. For (a) the five-fold distinction (*pañcabheda*) of *viśeṣa*, as well as for (b) how *viśeṣa* is *svābhāvika* or real, not *aupādhika* or conditional or fictitious, see (a) *SDSC*, p. 94; Helmuth von Glasenapp's *Madhva's Philosophie des Viṣṇu-Glaubens*, pp. 14-15, especially p. 15, f.n. 1 (where the relevant lines from *Anuvyākhyāna* and reference to other works are cited) and *RRS*, pp. 598, and 139, f.n. 4; and (b) *RRS*, pp. 135, 228 and 427.
2. See *The Brahmavādin* (Madras, 1900), Vol. VI, p. 233.
3. Adverting to Madhva's attitude in interpreting the *Brahmasūtras*, Ghate observes that "the very fantastic and forced manner in which he (Madhva) interprets many of the *sūtras* leaves no doubt about the fact that he would have set aside the *sūtras* altogether, but that their uncontested authoritativeness prevented him from doing so". V. S. Ghate's *The Vedānta*, Poona, 1926, p. 33.
4. See *SDSC*, p. 97, and *RRS*, p. 601 ff., especially p. 601, f.n. 22, and p. 604. See also pp. 212-215, 263 f., 278, 321 and 680. Gauḍa-pūrṇānanda-chakravartin, however, suggests a somewhat different interpretation of this text. He interprets it as "thou art not Its" (*tasya tvam asi*). See *The Tattva-Muktāvali*, *JRAS*, New Series, Vol. XV, p. 139 (text), verse 6, and p. 155, E. T. by E. B. Cowell and f.n. 4.

from it. Nevertheless Dvaitism does recognise identity also under a more comprehensive designation of its philosophy, viz., *saviśesābhedavāda*.

Saviśeṣābhedavāda[1] is described as a doctrine of "identity-in-difference"[2], or, more correctly, identity associated[3] with difference, or, identity 'amidst'[4] difference. The relation of a substance (*guṇi*) is believed to be identical with its attribute (*guṇa*) or attributes[5]. "... Attributes of the supreme *Nārāyaṇa* (God) are", for instance, "*identical* with Him"[6]. Yet this identity of the substance and its attributes is believed to depend upon "the operation of *viśeṣa*, which functions in all cases of identity".[7] It is on account of the 'operation' or 'function' of *viśeṣa* that we are said to understand that although the substance and its attributes are identical they are also different—or rather, they are identical

---

1. *RRS*, pp. 293, 510 and 628. See also *EIP*, p. 189 and the article 'The *Saviśeṣābheda* Theory' in *A Volume of Eastern and Indian Studies* (presented to Prof. F. W. Thomas), 1939, Bombay, pp. 230-235.
2. *RRS*, p. 293.
3. *EIP*, p. 189.
4. *RRS*, p. 293.
5. Cf. *EIP*, p. 191.
6. *RRS*, pp. 509, 510 etc. It sounds rather strange that not merely the attributes and 'similar determinations' are identical with God but also are 'identical with one another' : cf. "*Guṇa* (attribute), *Karma* (action and activity) and similar determinations of *Brahman* are of the essential, foundational and fundamental (sic) nature of *Brahman*. They are inseparable from the nature of *Brahman*. They are identical with *Brahman*. In virtue of this identity the attributes are identical with one another or devoid of all difference..." etc. *Ibid.*, p. 504 f. See also what follows.
7. *Ibid.*, p. 509.

because[1] they are different—as indicated by the very expression : substance and its attributes, which implies a distinction between the two.

There is an important trend in Dvaitism which deserves notice in our discussion of the role of identity 'amidst' difference. In spite of the claim that Dvaitism is a "radical pluralism" and that "everything is unique" etc., the only "independent entity" in this system is God and everything else is "absolutely dependent upon his will".[2] As a matter of fact, it is pointed out that "Madhva goes so far as to ascribe even the being of everything also to God".[3] It is not, therefore, surprising that Dvaitism maintains that all words are said ultimately to refer to God.[4] Even a moderate twist of his 'God-intoxicated' monotheism[5] will yield first-rate material for a monistic idealism which can install identity as the sole reality and, thereby, banish difference by which Dvaitism, rather incongruously, sets such a high store.[6]

---

1. Cf. "There is '*Viśeṣa*' which will step in and account for the fundamental identity between the essential nature of anything and the thing itself..." *RRS*, p. 506. Also, "The object and so many differences are identical with one another and yet separate from one another. There is no mystery in that sort of relationship. There is no miracle either. There is what Madhva calls *Viśeṣa* in every object". *Ibid.*, pp. 297-8. See also p. 511. This would mean that *viśeṣa* is not merely the basis of difference, as it ordinarily means, but also of identity although identity is secondary in relation to difference. The entire position, however, does not seem to hang together consistently.
2. *EIP*.
3. *Ibid.*, p. 519.
4. Cf. *ibid.*, p. 192, and *RRS*.
5. *RRS*, p. 500.
6. Cf. *EIP*, p. 190, para 2.

Dvaitism, as it stands, however, declares : "An individual or an object is what it is in virtue of its difference from other objects belonging to the same class or genus and difference *ipso facto* from members of another class or genus. Whether the linguistic medium is used or not, whether there is outward expression or not, difference is the essential constituent of an object or individual. An object is what it is only on account of its difference from other objects. Difference is emphasised. In accordance with the pragmatic purpose of the subject, and in accordance with the fundamental and essential constitution of the objects themselves, difference is stressed. *It is difference that lends significance to identity*".[1] This admission of faet that "It is difference that lends significance to identity" brings Dvaitism under the category of the Vaiśeṣika system in which identity is subordinated to difference. It is, therefore, not surprising that Madhva, like many of the other earlier commentators on *Vedāntasūtras*, finds in the Jaina view of reality, viz., a co-ordinate conception of identity-in-difference, 'an admission' which, it is stated, is not merely 'against all reason and proof' but even 'contradictory'.[2]

---

1. RRS, p. 239 (italics are mine). See also p. 509 where identity is referred to as a 'doctrinal fact'.
2. See *The Vedāntasūtras,* with Madhva's Comm., E. T. S. Subba Rau, Madras, 1904, p. 119. Cf. also : *Śrī Brahmasūtrārtha Saṅgraha* (The *Brahmasūtras* of Bādarāyaṇa, expounded in Kanarese, in accordance with the Commentary of Madhvācārya) P. Ramchandra Row, Madras, 1903, p. 97.

CHAPTER V

The Jaina Philosophy of Identity-in-Difference in which Identity is Co-ordinate with Difference

CHAPTER V

The Jaina Philosophy of Identity-in-Difference in which Identity is Co-ordinate with Difference

Our preceding inquiry has been based on the central thesis of our entire present contention, viz., that neither 'identity' or permanence alone, nor 'difference' or change alone, nor even the preponderance of either over the other, but a synthetic co-ordination of both the basic elements, will lead to a balanced and adequate metaphysical view of reality. In the process of the enquiry, we have been led to formulate an exhaustive classification of all the philosophical views into five major types the fifth one being represented by the Jaina as conforming to the requirements of a balanced and adequate metaphysical approach to the problem of reality. The critics have found fault with this co-ordinate approach of the Jaina thinkers and feel that it inherently involves the fatal error of contradiction which in turn gives rise to a series of other errors.

The Jaina has to vindicate his position against such charges. Such a vindicative effort necessarily presupposes a positive metaphysical position of his own. This position is broadly designated as *anekāntavāda* or the theory of manifoldness and indeterminateness. This comprehensive theory of manifoldness is an ontology or a theory of reality, as well as an epistemology or a theory of knowlege. The *anekānta* ontology postulates a reality which is immensely complex or manifold. Correspondingly, the *anekānta* epistemology postulates a theory of manifold methods of analysis (*naya-vāda*) and synthesis (*syādvāda*) by means of which the complex reality can be apprehended by the mind. Besides these methods the *anekānta* epistemology postulates what is generally described as a theory of the ways of knowing (*pramāṇas*). The ways of knowing are broadly classified by the Jaina thinkers into two categories, viz., *pratyakṣapramāṇa* and *parokṣapramāṇa.* The former is the direct or immediate way of knowing and the latter is the indirect or mediate way of knowing. Each category is subdivided into further stages or divisions.

It is impossible to deal with all the problems connected with the *anekānta* ontology and epistemology within the moderate compass of this work. In the case of the epistemological discussions, for instance, our attention is largely confined to a critical exposition of the two major methods of knowledge, viz., *nayavāda* and *syādvāda,* omitting, almost entirely, any elaborate references to the two ways of knowing, viz., *pratyakṣapramāṇa* and *parokṣapramāṇa,* as well as to the several problems therewith connected. Even in the case of the treatment of the *anekānta* ontology, our attention is mainly focused on the examination, the elucidation and the illustration of the most fundamental ontological presupposition, viz., the co-ordinate concept of identity-in-difference. The entire *anekānta* ontology is only an elaborate structure built up on this basic presupposition. The several topics dealt with in the various chapters like those on the Relations,

Jātyantaravāda, or *Arthakriyāvāda*, are intended to reveal the manifestations of this presupposition in the different departments of reality.

It is also necessary to point out here that no rigid separation between the ontological and epistemological discussions can be made in the course of our treatment of the various topics in this work. Nevertheless the three chapters beginning with *anekāntavāda*, especially those on *māyāvāda* and *syādvāda*, may be described as largely epistemological as against the others which are largely ontological. The only topic which could be treated in relative isolation from ontological considerations is the one which is concerned with the ways of knowing (*pramāṇas*). But it has been excluded from the scope of the present work for the reason already stated.

The main purpose of the present undertaking is to show, in the course of its progress, that the notion of identity-in-difference is the pivot on which the entire ontological and the epistemological development in the Jaina philosophy turn. *Anekāntavāda* is but an elaboration of the implications of this pivotal idea worked out in the various spheres of reality and knowledge. An exposition of this central idea of identity-in-difference, through a dialectical examination of its various implications as revealed in the various aspects of reality, is a necessary task. This is so especially for the reason that even competent scholars of Indian philosophy have often been inclined to consider the Jaina metaphysics as an "unsystematical system" in which "a mass of philosophical tenets" is not "upheld by one central idea". The phrases quoted here were uttered by Hermann Jacobi in the opening part of his address to the Third International Congress for the History of Religions in 1908. To quote him in full : "All those who approach Jaina philosophy will be under the impression that it is a mass of philosophical tenets not upheld by one central idea, and they will wonder what could have given currency to what appears to us an unsystematical system. I myself have held, and given expression to this opinion[1], but I have now learned to look at Jaina philosophy in a different light. It has, I think, a metaphysical basis of its own, which secured it a position apart from the rival systems both of the Brahmanas and of the Buddhists".[2] It is a pity that Jacobi did not give a fuller expression to his ideas after he "learned to look at Jaina philosophy in a different light". Nevertheless he has suggested, in the address just referred to as well as in a few other brief writings, the lines on which he thought about the subject. Nor do any other writers seem to have approached the subject at any considerable length, on the dialectical lines of investigating the pervasiveness of one central idea in the different ramifications of the Jaina metaphysics. After making these general observations concerning the present study we may now proceed to consider the ontological position of *anekāntavāda*.

The most celebrated text the implications of which form almost the entire theoretical foundation of the Jaina philosophy

---

1. In 1878, he wrote in his *Introduction to the Kalpasūtra of Bhadrabāhu* (Leipzig, 1879), p. 3, that the philosophy of Mahāvīra "scarcely forms a system, but is merely a sum of opinions (*pannattis*) on various subjects, no fundamental ideas being there to uphold the mass of philosophical matter."
2. *SJJ*, p. 48.

of being is: "The real is characterised by birth or origination, death or destruction, and sameness or continuity (*utpāda-vyaya-dhrauvya-yuktaṁ sat*)."[1] Everything real must have, according to the postulate embodied in this text of Umāsvāti, the triple character of productivity (*utpāda*), destructibility (*vyaya*), and, at the same time, permanence or persistence (*dhrauvya*) underlying it. Conversely whatever lacks the one or the other of this triple nature is a mental abstraction having no title to reality. Productivity and destructibility constitute the two aspects of change and may, therefore, be together characterised as the dynamic aspect of reality, the static aspect being represented by permanence or *dhruvatva*[2]. That is, *utpāda* and *vyaya*, being the two facets of the process of change, will be treated together, throughout this work, under the comprehensive single principle of change;

---

1. *TSUJ*, V. 30.
2. On being asked by Indrabhūti, his foremost apostle (*gaṇadhara*): "What is the nature of reality?" (*kim tattam*) Mahāvīra is reported to have first answered: "origination" (*uppaṇṇeï vā*) and then, after the same question was successively repeated, "destruction" (*vigameï vā*), and "persistence" (*dhuveï vā*). Cf. A. R. Kapadia's *The Canonical Literature of the Jainas*, 1941, Bombay, p. 3, and the extract from Haribhadra Sūri's Comm. on *Avassaya* and its *Nijjutti* in f.n. 4 thereon.

   Modification; becoming; difference; discreetness; plurality; manyness; manifoldness; the occurrent; and dynamism—are some of the epithets generally used in varying contexts, as synonyms for change (*bheda* or *paryāya*) which have, in Jaina metaphysics, the constituents of productivity (*utpāda* or *utpatti*) and destructibility (*vināśa* or *vyava*). Similarly, substantiality; substratum; being; identity; non-difference; continuity; continuance; unity; oneness; the continuant; statism, as well as endurance and persistence, are used for permanence (*dhruvatva, dhrauvya* or *anvaya*). Besides being a correlative to "becoming" the term "being" could also be taken in its wider acceptation as a "substance" or *dravya* which includes both "being" in its narrow sense and becomming. That is, it could signify either one, or the totality of the two aspects of a *dravya*, viz., permanence and change, but in which sense it is taken at a particular place will be evident from the context.

Often "non-being" (*asat* or *abhāva*) also is used as a correlative of "being" (*sat* or *bhāva*) when, of course, the latter is treated in its narrow sense. Here a doubt naturally arises whether "non-being" could be taken as equivalent to or at least as constitutive of "becoming" which is the obvious correlative of "being". The answer would be in the affirmative as will be evident, in the sequel. Meanwhile, it may be stated, in passing, that "non-being" as applied to a particular case, say, a jar, does not mean merely the affirmation of what the jar is in itself, but also the negation of the nature of a cloth, or a fruit, in the jar. In other words, the "non-being" of the jar consists in what the jar is not from the point of view (*kathañcit*) of the cloth or the fruit. This negation of the nature of the cloth or the fruit in the jar is, according to Jainism, an absolutely necessary part of the nature of the jar. For a full comprehension of the jar consists, on this view, not only in knowing what the jar is in itself, but also what it is not with reference to the cloth and the fruit etc. Thus in so far as "not-being" is a necessary complement to "being" in the make-up of an object, it touches the dynamic aspect of reality. In other words while being or affirmation in its narrow acceptation is constitutive of identity, non-being or negation is constitutive of difference.

The most widely used pairs of correlatives in course of this work are : identity and difference, the continuant and the occurrent, and permanence and change. In the case of the first pair the combined form, viz., identity-in-difference or identities of difference, is better adapted to express the coordinate subsistence of the two basic elements in reality, and the fact that identity precedes difference in the formula does not indicate any primacy of the former over the latter element as in the case of philosophies which subordinate difference to identity, since both elements have a co-ordinate status in reality. The second pair of "the continuant" and

and *dhrauvya*, being the enduring principle in the nature of things, will be represented as the principle of permanence underlying the ceaseless changes in things.[1] Thus the most fundamental truth laid down by Umāsvāti in the above *sūtra* is that permanence and change are entwined in everything real.

The fact that both the Vedāntin who adheres to a totally static view, and the Buddhist who adheres to a totally dynamic view, join issue with the Jaina who endeavours to blend both the static and the dynamic postulates into an integrated metaphysical view, is but inevitable. This is the case also with the other schools[2] of philosophy which follow suit with

---

"the occurrent" is taken from W. E. Johnson's *Logic* (Cambridge, 1924), Pt. III, Intro. pp. XVIII f., 80, 84-85, where it bears a more or less similar import to the correlation of *dhrauvya* and *paryāya*.

1. Akalaṅka explains *utpāda, vyaya* and *dhrauvya* as follows :
   svajātyaparityāgena bhāvāntarāvāptiḥ utpādaḥ /
   tathā pūrvabhāvavigamo vyayaḥ/
   dhruve sthairyakarmaṇordhruvatīti dhruvaḥ/
   (Under '*dhruvaḥ*' he adds : *dhruvasya bhāvaḥ karma vā dhrauvyam/*) *TRAG*, p. 238, *kārikās* 1, 2 and 3. See also *TSV*, p. 434.

   For the three derivative meanings of the term '*dravya*' in respect of its permanent aspect (*dhrauvyam*), as well as for a comparison of the Jaina notion of *dravya* with similar notions in other systems of Indian philosophy see *PMHS*, *Bhāṣāṭippaṇi*, pp. 54-55. See also *SHM* on *gā*. 28 in *VBJ* and Siddhasena Gaṇi's *Tīkā* on *Tattvārthādhigamasūtra* (H. R. Kapadia's edn.) V. 29. The meanings and the divisions of *paryāya* are extensively discussed in *STP*, III. 32-37, in Siddhasena Gaṇi's *Tīkā* (reference just given). The significance of these two ideas, viz., *dravya* and *paryāya* will, however, become increasingly clear in the process of our treatment of the various topics in the following chapters.

2. *Vide* the third and the fourth groups of systems in the fivefold classification (*supra*).

the Vedāntin and the Buddhist in claiming to detect, from their respective viewpoints, a radical self-contradiction in the Jaina synthesis of permanence and change.

The success of the Jaina synthesist in framing a durable ontological foundation for the entire edifice of the *anekānta* metaphysics is to be measured by the strength with which he would be able to vindicate his integrated viewpoint, not merely by pointing out that his viewpoint has an intrinsic validity, but also by bringing to bear upon it a dialectical power equal to the task. Matching an unerring vision with a robust rational defence is the work of a supreme philosophical genius. It is idle to dogmatise about whether the Jaina has stood the test successfully and triumphed over the obstacles in the way of his establishing his thesis. It is doubtful if any major philosophical problem can ever be solved by anybody or by any school once and for all. This much, however, may be said to his credit, viz., that he has at least perceived the problem and has gone some way at least towards achieving its solution.

Before proceeding to a dialectical examination of the most important implications of his metaphysical position, it would be worth while to see if his fundamental claim that permanence and change constitute the basic elements of reality is borne out by any major philosophical thinkers of the past and the present. That it is so, and, therefore, that the Jaina view in respect of its ultimate postulate of identity-in difference is not a lonely cry in a philosophical wilderness, may be confirmed by appealing to the impressive testimony of three great thinkers who, in spite of wide divergencies in respect of their tenets, countries and age, profoundly concur with the Jaina. These thinkers are A. N. Whitehead, Kumārila Bhaṭṭa and Immanuel Kant. Their confirmatory views may now be stated briefly in order of their mention here :

Whitehead

A. N. Whitehead finds the formulation of "the complete problem of metaphysics", viz., "the metaphysics of 'substance'", and "the metaphysics of 'flux'", in the two lines of the hymn :

> Abide with me ;
> Fast falls the eventide.

Elucidating how these lines embody "a full expression of the union of the two notions", viz., permanence and flux, he observes : "Here the first line expresses the permanences, 'abide', 'me' and the 'Being' addressed; and the second line sets these permanences amid the inescapable flux. Here at length we find formulated the complete problem of metaphysics. Those philosophers who start with the first line have given us the metaphysics of 'substance'; and those who start with the second line have developed the metaphysics of 'flux'. But, in truth, *the two lines cannot be torn apart in this way*; and we find that a wavering balance between the two is a characteristic of the greater number of philosophers".[1] This

1. *PrR,* p. 318. A little earlier also he speaks in the same strain : "The elucidation of the meaning involved in the phrase 'all things grow', is one chief task of metaphysics. But there is a rival notion, antithetical to the former. I cannot, at the moment, recall one immortal phrase which expresses it with the same completeness as that with which the alternative notion has been rendered by Heraclitus.

passage expresses, succinctly and beautifully, the need for an 'integral' viewpoint in which the ultimate postulates of 'permanence and flux' are harmoniously blended.

Kumārila

Kumārila maintains, almost in identical terms as the Jaina, the nature of reality to be of threefold character: Production (*utpāda*), Continuance (*sthiti*) and Destruction (*bhaṅga*). In the *Vanavāda* of his great *Vārtika*, Kumārila observes: "When the *Vardhamānaka* being broken up, a *Rucaka* is made (out of the same gold), then the person who desires to have the former, becomes sorry, while one desiring the latter ornament likes the process, while a third person who only desires gold remains indifferent, unaffected. Therefore, the object (gold) must be admitted to have a threefold character. Because, unless the object partook of *Production, Continuance* and *Destruction*, there could not be (with regard to it) the three notions (of like, dislike and indifference). There can be no sorrow (or dislike) without destruction of the object desired; and there can be no pleasure without production (or appearance of the object desired); and lastly, there can be no indifference without continuance or permanence (of the desired object)."[1]

This other notion dwells on the permanences of things—the solid earth, the mountains, the stones, the Egyptian Pyramids, the spirit of man, God". *Ibid.*, pp. 317-318.

1. *SVJha*, pp. 332-333. The *kās*. run as follows:
vardhamānakabhaṅge ca rucakaḥ kriyate yadā /
tadā pūrvārthinaḥ śokaḥ prītiś cāpyuttarārthinaḥ // 21 //
hemārthinas tu mādhyasthyaṁ tasmād vastu trayātmakam /
notpādasthitibhaṅgānām abhāve syān matitrayam // 22 //

Touching upon the absence of any contradiction in the co-existence of unity and diversity in the same object, Kumārila observes elsewhere : " As in the case of the variegated colour, we can optionally fix upon any one of the various colours (without any contradiction), simply because the object (colour) is of a variegated character—so, in the same manner we could fix upon the diversity or unity. . . "[1]

Finally, it is significant to note that Kumārila recommends a 'middle position' (*madhyasthatā*) between the two extremes

---

na nāśena vinā śoko notpādena vinā sukham /
sthityā vinā na mādhyasthyam.........//

Cf. the following *kā.* of Sāmantabhadra :
ghaṭamaulisuvarṇārthī nāśotpādasthitiṣvayam /
śokapramodamādhyasthyaṁ jano yāti sahetukam //
AMS, kā. 59. See also *VVas* and *AŚA* thereon.

In another *kā.*, following the above one, the same idea is illustrated by a different analogy. *Ibid.*, pp. 30-31.

Elucidating the word "*trayātmakam*" in *kā.* 22 cited above Parthasārathimiśra writes : *trayātmakam utpattisthitivināśa-dharmātmakam—ityarthaḥ / NR* on *kā.* 22, p. 619, and Bhaṭṭaputra Jayamiśra also adds, in the same context : *tasmād bhaṅgotpādasthityātmakarūpatrayayuktaṁ vastu pratīyate / SVTJ,* p. 84.

Malliṣeṇa draws our attention, in this connection, to Patañjali's theory of *nityānitya* (the abiding and the changing) nature of substance (*dharmi*), and its (*dharmiṇaḥ*) threefold modification (*trividhaḥ khalvayaṁ dharmiṇaḥ pariṇāmo dharmalakṣaṇāvasthārūpaḥ*), and, points out how the latter (*pariṇāma*) is accepted to be "at once distinct from and identical with the former" (*dharma*). *Vide SM* (text), p. 16, and *ibid.* (notes), p. 46, where Dhruva gives an extract from *Vyāsa-Bhāṣya* on *Patañjali-Sūtra,* III. 13.

1. *SVJha*, p. 292. The *kā.* is as follows :
citratvād vastuno'pyevaṁ bhedābhedāvadhāraṇam /
sāmānyāṁśe tu niṣkṛṣya bhedo yena prasādhyate //

Pārthasārathimiśra, commenting on this *kā.*, observes : *nānāvarṇe hi vastuni ya eva varṇo niṣkṛṣya darśayitum iṣyate sa eva śakyo darśayitum, evaṁ nānārūpe vastuni sarvasya bhedābhedādeḥ sambhava iti / MSV,* p. 561, *NR* on *kā.* 58.

of the *bheda* (*anya*) view and the *abheda* (*ananya*) view each of which (*aikāntikam*) is characterised as fallacious (*mṛṣā*).

Kant

"The actual objects of our experience," observes Watson, interpreting Kant's 'Analogies of Experiences', are necessarily conceived of as substances, i. e., as things which in all their changes, yet maintain their identity . . . If we suppose that substances could come into being or cease to be, we destroy the condition under which alone there is any unity in our experience . . . There is no experience, then, except of objects which are determined as permanent in the process of change."[2] Showing how 'both elements', viz., 'the succession' (change) and 'the permanent' ('the abiding') are 'indeed, inseparably involved' in all existence Norman Kemp Smith clearly states: "Substance, Kant insists, is not a bare static existence in which changes take place, but a dynamic[3] energy which by its very nature is in perpetual necessitated change. Change is not change in, but change of, substance.[4]"

1. *dūśitā sādhitā vāpi na ca tatra balābalam /*
   kadācin niścitaṁ kaiścit tasmān madhyasthatā varam //
   tato'nyanānyate tasya sto naṣṭaś ceti kīrtyate /
   tasmāccitravadevāsya mṛṣā syādekarūpatā // MSV, p. 633.
2. *PKEW*, p. 199.
   In the words of Kant himself : "I find that in all ages not only the philosopher, but even the common understanding, has preposited this permanence as a substratum of all change in phenomena; indeed, I am compelled to believe that they will always accept this as an indubitable fact. Only the philosopher expresses himself in a more precise and definite manner, when he says : "In all changes in the world the *substance* remains, and the *accidents* alone are changeable."
3. *CPRM*, p. 138, *CPRMax*, pp. 161-166.
4. *CKCPR*, p. 362.

Paton confirms this, emphasising at the same time the subtlety of the matter : "The concept of change," he observes, "has to be interpreted in the light of the doctrine that succession can be determined only in relation to the permanent. Coming into being and passing away are not to be taken as changes of what comes into being and passes away. A change is a way of existing which follows upon another way of the same thing's existing. That is to say there is an exchange, or substitution, of one state of a thing for another state of that thing, but the thing itself must remain the same thing. We cannot say that a thing has changed, unless it remains the same thing; and we can put this paradoxically by saying that it is only the permanent, or substance, which changes, while the transitory, or the accidents[1], do not change, but rather are exchanged, for one ceases to be and another takes its place."

---

1. Just as the *guṇas* and *paryāyas* are not inessential, but vital and positive traits in Jainism, so also the so-called 'accidents' in Kantian metaphysics are not really accidental or superficial and negative traits, but are "positive determinations of the essential character of the object". Emphasising this point Watson observes: "The determinations of substances are not 'accidents' in the sense of something without which the object would still be what it is : they are just the manner in which the substance exists, or they are positive determinations of the essential character of the object, not determinations related to the object negatively. It is true we sometimes speak as if the modes in which a thing exists were accidents that merely adhere in it and are not essential to its existence. But this mode of speech, though it is natural in certain cases, is not strictly accurate, and is apt to lead to the false notion that the substance can exist, and be what it is, independently of its accidents." *PKEW*, p. 197; *KMEP*, Vol. II, p. 217. Cf.: "A mere succession which is not a succession of states of something which remains identical in an unconnected series of endings and beginnings, and with respect to it, 'duration',

There are, indeed, vital differences between the Jaina and the Kantian metaphysics, e. g., the latter's transcendentalism with its concomitant notion of the thing-in-itself (*Ding-an-sich*), the treatment of space and time as the forms of sensibility, the phenomenality of the world, and several other doctrines with which the Jaina does not concur[1]. However, Kant's insistence on the need of the co-existence of permanence and change in the realm of the experienced world marks a significant confirmation of the cardinal Jaina doctrine of identity-in-difference with a Western system which is considered to be the watershed of modern Western metaphysics.

Having observed how the three great thinkers, Whitehead, Kumārila and Kant, agree with Jainism on the truth of the fundamental Jaina axiom of the co-existence of permanence and change, or identity-in-difference, a further critical analysis of the essential implications of Umāsvāti's *sūtra*, viz., *utpādavyayadhrauvyayuktaṁ sat,* may now be attempted.

The strength of the proof that identity and difference

---

which has meaning with regard to changes, i. e., succession proper, has no meaning at all." *KTKP,* p. 272.

Caird and others also make frequent references to this "two-fold aspect" of reality so that "all existence is summed up in permanent substances and their states". *CPKE* Vol. I, p. 488. See also, pp. 490 ff., *SCKCE,* pp. 152-153 and *Critic of Pure Reason,* p. 151, ff., Francis Raywood, pub. by William Pickering, 1948, London.

1. To the Jaina the thing-in-itself is inacceptable since he maintains the knowability of all reality. Nor does he consider space and time to be forms of sensibility since the two are intrinsically real and form a necessary part of the physical universe. As a realist he also repudiates the phenomenality of the world and considers it to be unreservedly real.

are in a co-ordinate synthesis marks also the measure of success and reasonableness of the Jaina metaphysical position. In order, therefore, to demonstrate that identity and difference are harmonious co-existents, and not irreconcilable or contradictory elements, a critical examination of the Jaina view may be attempted in answer to the following four questions :

(a) Does not identity infect difference with its own character, i. e., identity, and convert the latter, i. e., difference, into something of its own nature, in a substance?

(b) Or, alternatively, does not difference infect identity with its own character, i. e., difference, and convert the latter, i. e., identity, into something of its own nature, in a substance ?

In other words, (a) and (b) mean, respectively, that identity should eschew difference, or difference should eschew identity; and that either the one, or the other, but not the two together, can be the ultimate ontological postulate. Consequently, the truth of (a) indicates a triumph of the identity-view, and the truth of (b) of the difference-view.

If the truth of neither (a) nor (b) is conceded, and the ultimacy of the postulate of identity-and-difference is adhered to, then the following question would be raised :

(c) Does not the hypothesis of identity-and-difference in a substance invoke upon itself the combined evils of both (a) and (b)?

If the opponent still finds the Jaina, even under the threat of (c), not pleading guilty to the charge of the irreconcilability or self-contradictoriness with regard to his hypothesis of the ultimacy of the dual postulate, then an unequivocal answer would be demanded to the following question :

(d) Could the Jaina formulate a satisfactory theory which would avoid the objections under (a), (b) and (c) as well as suggest a constructive view of reality?

Of these four questions, the first and the second are evidently advanced from the points of view of the theorists of identity (*abhedavādin*) and of difference (*bhedavādin*) respectively. *Prima facie*, the third question is directed against the Jaina because the target of the criticism under question is some kind of identity and difference or *ubhayavāda*. The Jaina, however, does not identify himself with the kind of theory implied by (c) since it is, according to him, suggestive of a mechanical combination of the theories implied by (a) and (b). His own theory—which is undoubtedly a type of the philosophy of identity-in-difference, but sharply distinguished from the schools bearing the same description by its unmistakably unique approach to the nature of reality—is described as '*Jātyantaravāda*' which may be rendered as the theory of uniqueness or theory of unique synthesis. Besides avoiding the pitfalls under the above-mentioned first three questions, this theory is claimed to put forth a distinctive view of the nature of reality.

A consideration of the four questions may now be undertaken. In carrying out this procedure it will be both convenient and necessary to treat the first two questions, viz., (a) and (b), jointly, and the other two separately. A further treatment of the nature and content of identity in relation to an important problem in modern metaphysics and of an important distinction concerning the nature of difference, will also be found necessary to enable us to obtain a somewhat closer grasp of the Jaina solution to the problem of reality. This will also be found in the sequel[1].

Now the questions (a) and (b)—which lay down that either identity should obliterate difference or *vice versa*, owing to their inherent mutual opposition—may be jointly stated, together with all the further erroneous consequences[2] imputed to be entailed in their subsistence. The Jaina hypothesis that identity and difference can somehow (*kathañcit*)[3] exist together in the same medium is untenable (*na yuktam*) owing to *Virodha* (contradiction) and the other erroneous consequences (*doṣas*) implied (*upalakṣita*) by *Virodha*.[4] If, it is argued, the *paryāyas* are, in any sense, of the same nature[5] as the *dravya*, their continuant locus (*āśraya*), then

---

1. *Vide infra*, Chap. VIII. "Is *dravya* a concrete universal?" and "What is *Paryāya*?"—these two controversial problems will be discussed immediately after the Jaina attitude to the present questions is studied.
2. See *infra*, p. 141 ff.
3. The Jaina view is characterised as *kathañcit bhedābhedavāda* in contrast with the theories of absolute identity (*ekāntika abhedavāda*) and of absolute difference (*ekāntika bhedavāda*) which are rejected by the Jaina.
4. Hemacandra succinctly puts the argument as follows : *dravyaparyāyayor aikāntikabhedābhedaparihāreṇa kathañcid bhedābhedavādaḥ syādvādibhir upeyate, na cāsau yukto virodhādidoṣāt / PMHS*, p. 28.
5. Because the Jaina admits that the relation between *dravya* and its *paryāyas* is *bhedābheda*.

they also acquire (*prāpnuvanti*) identity[1] (*dravyatva*), since they are *ex hypothesi* at one with the *dravya* (*dravyād avyatiriktatvāt*). In other words, identity cannot accommodate (*dussādhya*) difference, owing to the law that "dual character can never subsist in any single thing[2]. Conversely, the same circumstance, viz., the sameness[3] (*abhedatva*), or the oneness (*ekatva*) of the *dravya* and the *paryāyas*, renders *dravya*—which is said to be of unchanging nature (*avikṛtam* or *abhinnasvabhāvatvam*)—into something indistinguishable from (*avyatiriktam*) the mutable *paryāyas*[4]. That is, difference (*paryāya*) does not allow identity to reside with itself in a real owing to its nature of "exclusiveness" (*vyāvṛttimad rūpam*). An attempt to weave identity into the texture of difference within the being of a real results, it is said, in the inevitable transformation of the former into the latter.

If the Jaina is not (in fact he is not) prepared to accept either of the alternatives of undifferenced identity or unqualified difference resulting from the two conflicting parts of the

---

1. *yad anugatātmarūpavyatiriktaṁ tad anugatātmakam eva, yathā dravyarūpam* . . . / *PK*, p. 120.
   Also,
   > *yadīva te'pi paryāyāḥ sarve'py anugatātmakāḥ /*
   > *dravyavat prapnuvanty eṣāṁ dravyeṇaikātmatā sthiteḥ //*

   TSS, *kā*. 318. See also *kā*. 320.
2. *samāveśo na caikatra tayor* (i. e., *sadasator*) *yukto virodhataḥ //* *TSS*, *kā*. 1675...... *dvirūpatvaṁ naivaikātrāsti vastuni* (ibid., *kā*. 1676). Again, *yatrābhedas tatra tadviparīto na bhedo'vakāśaṁ labhate*, etc., *PK*, p. 119.
3. *vyāvṛttimadrūpavyatiriktaṁ ca dravyam iti* / *PK*, p. 120.
4. > *agauṇe caivam ekatve dravyaparyāyayoḥ sthite /*
   > *vyāvṛttimad bhaved dravyaṁ paryāyāṇāṁ svarūpavat //*

   TSS, *kā*. 317.

joint question just stated, then he is confronted with the following *doṣas*[1] or fallacies, to which his *bhedābhedavādā* or *dravyaparyāyātmakavāda* is said to be liable :

1. *Virodha* (contradiction); 2. *Vaiyadhikaraṇya* or *Vyadhikaraṇatā* ('transfusion', or 'absence of a common abode'); 3. *Anavasthā (regressus ad infinitum)*; 4. *Saṅkara* (confusion); 5. *Vyatikara* ('Exchange of Natures'); 6. *Saṁśaya* (doubt); 7. *Apratipatti* (non-apprehension); 8. *Viṣayavyavasthāhāni* (indeterminability of the true nature).[2]

---

1. Excluding the one *kārikā* attributed to the Naiyāyikas (*yaugaiḥ*) by Vādideva, viz., *saṁśayavirodhavaiyadhikaraṇyasaṅkaram athobhayadoṣaḥ / anavasthā vyatikaram api jainamate sapta doṣāḥ ṣyuḥ // SRK*, p. 738. We do not come across anywhere among the works of the non-Jaina critics, where *doṣas* are fully mentioned. The non-Jaina critics mainly concern themselves with *Virodha*, although Śaṅkara (*BBSB*, II. 2.33) and Kumārila add *Saṁśaya* or *Sandigdha* (Kumārila has done so in the course of two *kās.*, in defence of "*anekatvavāda*" or "*anekāntavāda*". See *MSV, Vanavāda, kās.* 79 and 80. For a reference to this, see *infra.*) and Śāntarakṣita and his commentator Kamalaśīla *Sāṅkarya (Saṅkara)* to *Virodha. (TSS, kā.* 1722, and *PK* thereon.) Whether or not the *doṣas* other than *Virodha* are explicitly mentioned by the opponents of the Jainas, they are presumed to be implied (*upalakṣita*) by *Virodha* which is considered to be their main basis (*mūlādhāra*). Hence their individual enumeration and refutation is, however brief, necessary in any polemical examination of the Jaina view.
2. The number and the order of the *doṣas* in this classification are as adopted by Hemacandra and Malliṣeṇa (See *PMHS*, I. 1.30, p. 28, and *SM*, p. 150 (text)). Some writers like Prabhācandra cite *ubhaya* (or *ubhayadoṣa*) and omit No. 8 (*PKM*, p. 526) and others like Akalaṅka, the earliest Jaina logician to defend the Jaina position against such *doṣas*, and Vasunandi, cite *ubhaya* and *abhāva* omitting Nos. 7 and 8. (See *AGAV*, p. 103, and *VVAS*, on *AMS*, *kā.* 20). All these writers retain, in spite of the difference of one or two *doṣas*, a classification of eight *doṣas*. Abhayadeva and Vādideva, however,

1. *Virodha*[1]. Most of the schools of Indian thought, which are based on the *Brahmasūtras*, consider, as it has been observed under their treatment of the *sūtra* : *naikasmin na sambhavāt*, that *Virodha* is the most insurmountable difficulty vitiating the Jaina view of reality. *Virodha* is a state of

---

represent a trend of opinion which refers only to seven instead of eight *doṣas*. Between these two thinkers the former rejects Nos. 5, 7 and 8, just adding *ubhayadoṣa* to the remainder of the classification (See *TBV*, pp. 451-452, and *SRK*, p. 738).

Guṇaratna, however, enumerates as many as nine *doṣas* adding *Vyavahāralopa, Pratyakṣādiprāmaṇabādhā* and *Asambhava* in place of Nos. 7 and 8 (*TRD*, p. 232). For an explanatory note on these three additional *doṣas* as well as on *Ubhaya* and *Abhāva*, see *infra*, p. 146, f.n. 3.

1. Ordinarily *Virodha* signifies the particular *doṣa* of contrary or contradictory opposition. But it has also the collective significance of indicating all the other *doṣas*, enumerated here, by way of *upalakṣaṇā* (cf. *SM* (notes), p. 264).

Another noteworthy feature with regard to opposition is that Indian thinkers, particularly the realistic schools like Jainism, do not seem to make any sharp distinction between contrareity and contradiction as in Aristotelian logic. Contradiction, according to Aristotle, signifies bare and total negation whereas contrareity is a partial negation of a specific attribute, with an implicit affirmation of an opposite attribute. For instance, when I assert "this is not yellow" under contradiction the entire universe of discourse is divided into two spheres, "yellow" and "non-yellow", and the "non-yellow" sphere is sharply ranged over against the "yellow" sphere in the relation of a bare and total negation, the two spheres, between them, exhausting the entire universe of discourse. In contrareity, on the other hand, the same assertion, viz., "this is not yellow", signifies the negation of "yellow" with the implicit assertion of "this is red" or "this is blue" according to the suitability of the context. There are, no doubt, in Indian literature and philosophy the conceptions of *prasajyapratiṣedha* and *paryudāsa*, which are compared to be the Naiyāyika's *atyantābhāva* ('absolute or

mutual opposition[1], e. g., between 'blue' and 'non-blue' (*nīlānīlavat*), 'hot' and 'cold' (*śītoṣṇavat*) or 'light' and

total negation') and *anyonyābhāva* (mutual negation) respectively. Describing the distinction between the two, Cowell observes: Where the negation is prominent it is called *prasajyapratiṣedha*; but where it is not prominent, we have the *paryudāsa* negation (*SDSC*, p. 250, f.n. 1). But these seem to be more in the nature of literary conventions, than of ontological principles of contradiction and contrareity, which have a more adequate and precise philosophical significance. The editor of *AJP* quotes two verses from the *Sāhityadarpaṇa* describing the two conceptions. See Vol. II, (notes), p. 276.

The Jaina conception of opposition seems to be largely akin to the latter kind, at any rate insofar as it asserts that identity, or being, necessarily implies its corresponding correlative of difference or non-being. This approach is countenanced by the fact that the Jaina does not subscribe to the hyperlogical or more conceptualistic approach of a Śrīharṣa or Nāgārjuna, whose hyperlogicism lands them in an absolute of the bare *sat* (absolute affirmation), or an equally brave void (absolute negation). The extremes of a Śrīharṣa or a Nāgārjuna, the results of a logically subtle sophistication, seem to indicate the fact that truth lies between such extremes. The modest approach of the Jaina conforms to the rule that the laws of logic should closely follow the course of nature. In other words, experience should, according to him, determine logic but not the other way about. This partiality for the factual side of things makes the Jaina suspicious of all transcendental dialectics which drive a wedge between the *parāvidyā* and *aparāvidyā* or *saṁvṛtisatya* and *paramārthasatya*. In fact his dogged adherence to the facts of nature has earned for him, in his approach to the problem of reality, the reputation of being too empirical, like the Pragmatists in the West. Although the note of cynicism attaching to this reputation dubs the Jaina a slow-crawling earthworm rather than a high-soaring transcendent bird, the story of the scientific temper of all ages seems to confirm the fact that excessive preoccupation with the clouds seems to yield more poetry and grander mysticism, which are more often than not less true to the crude facts in the life of nature.

1. *parasparaparihārasthitilakṣano'yam virodha iti* / *AJP*, com., p. 11.

'darkness' (*chāyātapavat*) at the same place and the same time. A simultaneous affirmation of the two contradictory elements with reference to an identical situation is, therefore, a logical absurdity. Similarly identity (*abheda*) and difference (*bheda*) are, it is argued, mutually opposed, and therefore positing (*vidhi*) the one means denying (*niṣedha*) the other[1]. Since the two can never co-exist in the same substratum[2], any attempt to weld the two, viz., identity and difference, being and non-being, or affirmation and negation, into the structure of a real is too fanciful (*kalpita*) to be resorted to by any sane-minded person (*svasthacetasā*[3]).

2. *Vyadhikaraṇatā* is an error which arises when two entirely opposed natures or characters tend to subsist in a single abode (*adhikaraṇa*) while they ought to subsist in two different abodes. Identity and difference, being entirely opposed to each other, as has just been observed under fault

---

1. *sattvāsattvayoḥ parasparaparihāreṇa sthitatvāt śītoṣṇasparśavat* / *TRD*, p. 231. See also *SBT*, p. 81f.
2. Arcata observes: '*utpādavyayadhrauvyayuktaṁ sat*' *ity etad apy ayuktaṁ, dhrauvyeṇotpādavyayayor virodhād ekasmin dharmiṇya-yogāt* / *HBT*, p. 146.
3. *tadbhāvaś cātadbhāvaḥ parasparavirodhataḥ* /
ekavastuni naivāyaṁ kathañcid avakalpyate //
vidhānapratiṣedhau hi parasparavirodhinau /
śakyam ekatra no kartuṁ kenacit svasthacetasā //
TSS, *kās*. 1729 and 1830. See also *PK* thereon.
Haribhadra trenchantly puts the argument for the opponent: *katham ekam eva ghaṭādirūpaṁ vastu saccāsacca bhavati tathā hi sattvam asattvaparihāreṇa vyavasthitam, asattvam sattvaparihāreṇa; anyathā tayor aviśeṣaḥ syāt / tataś ca yadi sat katham asat? athāsat kathaṁ sad? iti ekatra sattvāsattvayor virodhāt; tathā coktam—*
yasmāt sattvam asattvaṁ ca viruddhaṁ hi mitho dvayam /
vastvekaṁ sadasadrūpaṁ tasmāt khalu na yujyate //
AJP, p. 11.

No. 1, cannot be found together without bringing about a "split in the integrity of the locus". An endeavour to locate the two in two different abodes will, it is said, violate the Jaina answer to the objection that the two characters refer to *two aspects of the same thing,* and not to two different things, and would in turn become the target of a new difficulty, viz.,

3. *Anavasthā* or *regressus ad infinitum*, for the following reason : *each* of the two 'aspects' of a thing—identity and difference—will have to be at once both identical with, and different from, the other, if at least for the reason of avoiding absolutism or extremism (*ekāntatva*), to which the Jaina objects. This bifurcation, once started, will go on *ad infinitum*.

4. *Saṅkara* or confusion is another difficulty which is assumed to overtake the Jaina in the pursuit of his theory. It arises when there is an incidence of two mutually opposed natures in either of the two elements, viz., 'identity' or 'difference'. That is, identity will be an abode both of itself and of its opposite[1]. Difference also will behave in a similar way. Such behaviour on the part of either is thought to introduce a state of confusion into the abode concerned.

5. *Vyatikara* or 'Mutual Exchange' of natures is yet another of the erroneous consequences attributed to the Jaina view. The incidence of the two opposed natures of identity and difference in a common abode leads, it is stated, to a 'mutual exchange[2]', of their natures. This would result in the

1. *yugapadubhayaprāptis saṅkaraḥ* / *PMHS*, f.n. 3. Vimaladāsa, however, describes it as: *sarveṣāṁ yugapat prāptis saṅkaraḥ* / *SBT*, p. 82.
2. Cf. *parasparaviṣayagamanaṁ vyatikaraḥ* / *SBT*, p. 82.

absurd state of identity behaving like difference and *vice versa*.

6. *Saṁśaya* or Doubt : The simultaneous prediction of both identity and difference of a real is said to bring about a lack of definiteness (*idam ittham eveti niścetum aśaktih*) or doubt, in our minds. For a mind which is confronted with two natures in a real would be unable to know definitely whether the one or the other of the two is the nature of the real. In other words, doubt hinders the grasp of the unique nature of a thing (*asādhāraṇākāra*[1]). Such a 'forked road situation' of mind is said to lead further to :

7. *Apratipatti,* or a failure to achieve a proper apprehension of anything. Then, finally, we are said to face

8. *Viṣayavyavasthāhāni*[2] or the impossibility of determining any coherence or order in the realm of objective reality[3]. These myriad discrepancies led by, or rather attri-

---

1. *vastuno'sādhāraṇākāreṇa niścetum aśakteḥ saṁśayaḥ* / *SM*, p. 151 (text).
2. Malliṣeṇa characterises it as *pramāṇaviṣayavyavasthāhāni.*
3. For a statement of these *doṣas, vide PMHS*, p. 28 ; *SBT*, pp. 81-82; *PKM*, p. 526 ; *AGAV*, p. 103 ; *TBV*, pp. 451-452 ; *TRD*, pp. 231-232 (Ref. in *BM*) ; *SVS* and *SKL* thereon, p. 266 f. ; *SRK*, pp. 737-738; and *SM* (text), pp. 150-151. In the last two works these *doṣas* are mentioned in the context of the relation between the universal (*sāmānya*) and the particular (*viśeṣa*) which is, after all, an aspect of the wider problem of the relation between identity and difference.

   A brief reference may be made here to the five other *doṣas* noticed by Guṇaratna and others (vide *supra*, p. 141, f.n. 2) : 9. *Pratiniyatavyavahāralopa*, or simply *vyavahāralopa*, 10. *Pratyakṣādipramāṇabādhā*, 11. *Asambhava*, 12. *Ubhaya* and 13. *Abhāva*. These are the five other *doṣas* not mentioned by Hemacandra and Malliṣeṇa.

   9. *Pratiniyatavyavahāralopa* is a *doṣa* which introduces chaos in the uniform, or orderly, nature of things. This is said to

arise from the Jaina belief in the manifold nature of all things (*sarvasyānekāntātmakatve'ṅgīkriyamāṇe*). If reality is of multiple nature, that is, if all natures or characters subsist in all things, then a person proceeding to get water (*jala*) may find himself getting fire (*anala*) and another person proceeding to get fire may find himself getting water.

10. *Pratyakṣādipramāṇabādhā* is what is contrary to all experience of reality by perception and other means of valid knowledge. That is, the *bhedābheda* nature of reality, as conceived by the Jaina, is not borne out perceptually or inferentially or in any other manner.

11. *Asambhava* may be described as impossibility, resulting from the supposedly absurd view of reality held by the Jaina. Cf. *TRD*., p. 232.

12. *Ubhayadoṣa* : In the *bhedābheda* structure of reality the *abhedatva* signifies unitariness or oneness (*ekāntenaikātmatva*) and the *bhedatva* signifies manyness or plurality such that there arises the twofold *doṣa* of unity (*ekasvabhāvatvam*) subsisting in plurality (*anekāntatve*) and *vice versa* (*anekasvabhāvatvam ekāntatve*). (*PKM*, p. 52, and *SRK*, p. 739.)

13. *Abhāva* : The nature of this *doṣa* is not clearly indicated. Abhayadeva, however, seems to understand it as a *doṣa* which is presumed to rest on the non-cognisability (*apratibhāsatve*) of the incongruous reality as supposed to be contemplated by the Jaina theory : An incongruous real is, as stated under *doṣa* No. 10 in this f.n., what is contrary to experience and consequently what is contrary to experience is as good as being non-existent (*abhāva*, cf. *TBV*, p. 452).

It is not possible to demarcate clearly and severally the specific features of these *doṣas* since they are highly overlapping among themselves in their character. For instance *ubhayadoṣa* which refers to *ekatva* or *anekatva* of the *bhedābhedātmakavastutva* may, with a slight turn in the expression be easily included in, or identified with, *vyadhikaraṇatādoṣa* which also refers to the need for more than one, instead of one abode or nature. Similarly there is very little or practically no significant difference between the *doṣas* Nos. 7 and 8 on the one hand and those of Nos. 10, 11 and 13 on the other. Eventually all other *doṣas* are derived from, and therefore traceable to, *virodha*, the supposedly root evil, against which the Jaina has to marshal out all his dialectical resources.

buted to the protean evil (*doṣa*) of *virodha* are said to befall the Jaina theory of reality which is variously described as identity-in-difference (*bhedābheda*), or being (*sat* or *bhāva*) and non-being (*asat* or *abhāva*), or affirmation (*vidhi*) and negation (*pratiṣedha*). Broadly speaking, *virodhadoṣa* is at the back of even the four questions under which we have been endeavouring to examine, critically and comprehensively, the ontological implications of the Jaina theory, although it (*virodhadoṣa*) has been enumerated as one of the several *doṣas* in this connection. Obviating this principal evil should, therefore, form the most important part of the Jaina defence against the dialectical charges of the opponent schools whether the charges be the four questions—the first two of which come under the present review—or the seven or more *doṣas* centering round, or deriving from, *virodha*.

There is, in this connection, an important idea which forms the nucleus of almost the entire defensive or refutational as well as of the constructive metaphysical endeavour of the Jainas. It concerns the operative method of combining identity and difference, or being and non-being, or affirmation and negation, into the discriminative synthesis of a real, in which they are necessary, complementary and equal elements. Realization of the vital significance of this idea will reveal it, not merely as a direct answer to the imputation of *virodha* to the Jaina view, but also as a key to a fuller understanding and appreciation of the comprehensive metaphysical edifice represented by the twofold superstructure of *nayavāda* (the theory of standpoints) and *syādvāda* (the dialectic of relativism) or *saptabhaṅgī* (the theory of sevenfold predication) which in turn are reared on the foundation of *anekāntavāda* (the doctrine of manifoldness). Deferring an allusion to *syādvāda* or *saptabhaṅgī, nayavāda* and *anekāntavāda* to a later stage, we may now address ourselves to an analysis of the central idea which offers the *modus operandi* of synthesising identity and difference, being and non-being, or affirmation and negation, as a necessary preliminary to the refutations of the charges made against the Jaina view :

Every entity comprises, within the fullness of its being, two constituent elements, both equally important, viz., what is *itself* (*svatattva*) and what is other-than-itself (*paratattva*). A jar (*ghaṭa*), for instance, is constituted not merely by all the traits entering into its making, but also by the numerous other traits which constitute entities like a cloth (*paṭa*), a fruit (*phala*) or a book (*pustaka*), which *are not*, or *are other than*, the jar. The former group of traits forms the positive element (*sat* or *vidhi*), that is, what the jar is *per se*, and the latter group the negative element (*asat* or *niṣedha*), or what-is-not (or what-is-other-than) the jar[1]. Both the positive and the negative elements constitute the two moments or the two poles of the entity, viz., the jar in the present instance.

If reality is considered on the one hand to be all positive, or merely existent (*ekāntabhāvātmake*), then everything would be everything else (*vaiśvarūpaṁ syāt* or *sarvātmakaṁ syāt*). On this hypothesis neither the distinctions among the entities, nor the diverseness of character within the same entity, could be explained : "If a thing had only *positive*

---

1. Cf. *sarvapadārthānāṁ svarūpeṇa sattvaṁ pararūpeṇa cāsattvam* / *TRD*, p. 234.

nature, the nature would not be *its own* ; it is because of its negative nature, its differentiation from other things, that a thing possesses its specific nature."[1]

Advaitism, owing to its consistent adherence to the principle : *ekam evādvitīyaṁ brahma,* therefore, explains away the principle of difference. If reality is considered, on the other hand, to be all negation or non-being (*ekāntābhāvātmakatve*) then everything would become devoid of any intrinsic nature (*nissvabhāvatā syāt*) and then the world would be, as has been conceded by the Voidist (Śūnyavādin) "a tissue of false things, falsely related[2] and would vanish like mist...when subjected to philosophic investigation"[3].

---

1. *SM* (notes), p. 165.
2. Cf. *anubhava eṣa mṛṣā.* Nāgārjuna's *Mādhyamika kā.* (St. Petersburg Edn.), p. 58. Quoted in *OIP*, p. 220, f.n. 1.
3. Regarding the controversy whether the Śūnyavādin is a nihilist, scholars like Hiriyanna, Dhruva and others maintain, against critics like Sogen and Stcherbatsky, that Śūnyavādin is a nihilist advocating 'void' or 'essencelessness'—also rendered as 'Emptiness' or 'Universal Void'—of all reality as the outcome of philosophic investigation. Hiriyanna observes: "Not the Hindus alone, but the Jainas also, hold the *Mādhyamika* to be a nihilist." *OIP*, p. 222. He also points out Candrakīrti's distinction between the genuine nihilism and the 'common or vulgar nihilism' as consisting in that the former is the result of 'a logical scrutiny', whereas the latter of merely 'a dogmatic or whimsical denial'. The 'result' or conclusion is, of course, the same, viz., all is negative (*sarvaśūnyataiva paraṁ tattvam*). *Ibid.*, especially f.ns. 1 and 3, in the latter of which two important Jaina authorities (from one of which the Sanskrit quotation just given within the brackets is taken) are cited. See also *SM*, Intro. p. CXVII. S. Mookerjee also writes to the same effect: "If non-existence were to be the sole and exclusive character of things, nothing would be existent and, consequently, neither affirmation nor negation of anything would be possible. Paradoxical as it may appear, this is,

The Nyāya-Vaiśeṣika no doubt accepts the reality of *bhāva* and *abhāva*, but as "things which are in themselves separate". This method of treating the two as being mutually exclusive[1] (*paraspara-vivikta*) does direct violence to the integral character of reality (hence the Jaina maxim: *sarvabhāvānām hi bhāvābhāvātmakaṁ svarūpām*[2]) "The Naiyāyika errs" a discerning critic observes in this connection, "by emphasising the one or the other as the exclusive characteristic. But the nature of reals, as has been sufficiently proved by the Jaina, is not exclusive or extremistic. It is existent-cum-non-existent."[3]

This conception of reality as bipolar is the cornerstone of the *anekānta* ontology. Its wide operative force will become evident in course of the account, in the sequel, of *syādvāda-saptabhaṅgī* and *nayavāda*, the two main methods originating from the fundamental conception of *anekāntavāda*, whose ontological aspect is suggested or hinted by the formula of Umāsvāti.[4]

---

however, the position seriously maintained by the Voidist (Śūnyavādin), if we are to believe the interpretation of Candrakīrti, the commentator of Nāgārjuna, and the criticism of the rival philosophers constitute a faithful representation of the position of Nāgārjuna". *JPN*, p. 82. Whether or not the Śūnyavādin believes in a transcendental realm of truth (*vivṛti-satya*) is immaterial in so far as he repudiates 'essencelessness' (*nissvabhāvatā*) in the so-called empirical world which, for the Jaina at any rate, is a genuine reality.

1. Guṇaratna, therefore, describes this school as: *Kāṇādayaugābhyupagataparaspara-vivikta-dravya-paryāyaikānta* / *TKD*, p. 231
2. *SM* (text), p. 91.
3. *JPN*, p. 68.
4. Regarding the identification of *anekāntavāda* or *anantadharmātmakavāda* with the truth of Umāsvāti's formula, viz., *utpāda-*

The positive and the negative elements of a real are not conceived to be related *ab extra*. They are, as already observed, mutually integral or organic and, therefore, the method for the obtainment of their integral connectedness is not by forging an external linking of them—for that there is no such external linking will be alluded to under the topic of relations—but by making a proper analysis of the internal structure of things, which exhibit, as the monads of Leibnitz do, a complex or manifold network of forces. The moment the fact that the positive and the negative elements form the two sides of the shield of reality is lost sight of, one goes the way of the Advaitin or Śūnyavādin. For the Advaitin created the positive aspect of the real, or identity, into the sole principle of reality, just as the Śūnyavādin allowed an unrestricted sway of the negative principle on his theorisings, which resulted in the negativistic absolute of the Void. Nor did the Naiyāyika fare better by treating each element as being in a severe isolation from the other. Whatever his other faults, the Jaina has maintained, steadily and firmly, the delicate balance of these two elements in the equilibrium of reality. There is due to his conviction that position and negation, or identity and difference, are not mutually opposed with any "aggressive repugnancy of two things that cannot co-exist without collision" but are compelling complements. Each shows 'ragged edges' without

---

vyayadhrauvyayuktaṁ sat, Guṇaratna observes: *anantadharmātmakasyaivotpādavyayadharmātmakatvaṁ yuktiyuktam* ... etc., *TRD* p. 229. He also gives here an inferential demonstration as well as an explanation of this idea.

the other. Or, more correctly, the one without the other is not so much half real as unreal.

Reserving a further reference to the several finer points of, and the supplementation to, this integral truth of the *bhāvābhāvasvarūpatva,* or *sadasatsvarūpatva,* of reality, we must take a somewhat closer view of the concept of negation. This is necessary for at least one important reason, viz., that it (negation) is frequently equated to the idea of difference (*bheda*) which seems to have, unlike pure negation, a positive implication : we have just observed that a concrete jar is the product of the dual principle of the position of jarness and the negation of what-is-other-than-jarness, which is inclusive of clothness (*paṭatva*), fruitness (*phalatva*) and so on. Negation, or 'what-is-other-than-jarness' in the present context, seems to have (in point of fact, it actually has), like its positive counterpart, a positive trait in so far as it signifies 'what-is-other-than-jarness'. This is so because although we negate 'clothness', 'fruitness' and 'bookness', etc., under 'what-is-other-than-jarness', in the jar the traits so negated are after all certain determinate traits having a peculiar existence of their own and being connected with[1]—

---

1. Cf. *MSV*, p. 476, *kā*. 12. The significance of this *kā*. is rendered as follows : "Every object has a double character : with regard to its own form, it exists (i.e., *as jar* a jar exists); while with regard to the form of another object, it does not exist (i.e., as *cloth* the jar does not exist). Both forms are equally entities; sometimes people cognise the one, sometimes the other". Continuing further to explain 'the sense' of Kumārila, it is clearly remarked "that the fact of the non-existence of the cloth in the jar simply means that the cloth *in its non-existent form* inheres in another object, the jar, and

without, of course, being confused with—their positive counterpart (*svatattva*) in an intimate union. If these negative traits were mere non-existents—'non-existents' (*tuccha*) in an unreal sense of the word—then they could not be described as 'clothness' or 'fruitness' etc. Total negation is one thing and negation of determinate, or even determinable, traits with reference to an existent is quite another. The latter type of negation is negative in a particular ontological setting, although in a different ontological setting these traits may assume a definitely positive character like the jarness in the present context. In other words, position and negation are relative terms and what is the one under one set of circumstances may become the other under a different set of circumstances.[1]

The factors determining whether an aspect of a particular factual situation is positive or negative depend upon the material (*dravya*), the place (*kṣetra*), the time (*kāla*) and the state (*bhāva*) attaching to the situation. The first and the last among these four factors specify the internal and the remaining two factors specify the external condition of the fact or the object in question. In other words, the material

---

as such, produces the cognition of its non-existent form in the jar". *SVJha*, p. 244. The italics and what is included within the brackets are as in the original.

Another *kā.*, also of Kumārila, bears out the same truth:

nāstītyapi ca saṃvittir na vastvanugamādṛte /
jñānaṁ na jāyate kiñcidupastambanavarjitam //

MSV, p. 478, ka. 16 and *SVJha*, p. 245.

1. Cf. *svadharmyapekṣayā yo dharmaḥ sattvādiḥ / sa eva svadharmāntarāpekṣayā dharmī / evam evānekāntātmakavyavasthopapatteḥ / TRD*, p. 235.

(*svadravya*), from which the object in question is made, the spatial and the temporal setting (*svakṣetra* and *svakāla*), in which it is located, and the state (*sva-bhāva*) it manifests in the specific context concerned, are the fourfold (*svadravyādi-catuṣṭaya*) factors, which differentiate the positive aspect of the object concerned from the corresponding negative fourfold factors (*paradravyādicatuṣṭaya : paradravya, parakṣetra, parakāla* and *parabhāva*), associated with the other or the concomitant negative aspect of the object.

A doubt is raised, at this stage, whether the positive aspect, comprising its fourfold determining characteristics, would not be after all the *same as* the negative aspect, comprising the corresponding fourfold negative characteristics.[1] This doubt is of course based on the assumption that the positive aspect, like its negative counterpart, belongs to an identical entity; therefore it (the positive aspect) ought to be the same as the other one. This amounts to the identification of position and negation, or being and non-being. The Jaina dialectician promptly objects to this treatment of the situation and reaffirms his position that the two are distinctive elements, although they refer to an identical entity and can, therefore, reside in the same entity since the entity is of a manifold nature.

Here he lays stress on the fact that identification of a part (*aṁśa*), viz., the positive aspect (*bhāva*), with the other part, viz., the negative aspect (*abhāva*), results in the dual fallacy of dissolving the *bhāva* in the *abhāva* (which means all that is

1. *svadravyādisattvam eva paradravyādyasattvam/* *AJP*, Vol. I, p. 38 ff.

positive in the entity), and, consequently, of treating *abhāva* as the entire content of the entity. When *abhāva* or negation becomes the sole content of the entity, the entity disappears without a trace. Like his opponents the *anekāntavādin* is well aware of the fact that predicating two opposing characters of *the same aspect* of an entity is of course a contradiction: *tenaiva svabhāvena sac cāsacceti viruddham etat.*[1] This contradiction is, as will be shown in the sequel, as objectionable to the Jaina as it is to his opponents. But what the opponents have persistently missed observing here is that the so-called 'opposing characters' refer to the two different aspects of an entity and, consequently, become necessary and complementary components of it.[2]

This negation, as observed in the concrete setting of the *anekānta* ontology, is an essential or organic element in the constitution of an entity, which is an intrinsic-extrinsic complex. It is not a vacuum subsisting alongside an unconnected positive existent in a compartmental entity. It is an almost axiomatic belief, on the part of the *anekānta vādin*, that nature, or reality, abhors vacuum. He maintains, therefore, that negation comprises manifold traits collectively

---

1. *AJP*, Vol. I, p. 44.
2. This repudiation of the attempt falsely to identify *bhāva* with *abhāva* contains within itself also the implicit condemnation of the converse attempt to identify *abhāva* with *bhāva*. There is, however, an interesting point which supplements the general trend of the repudiation: *abhāva*, if identified with *bhāva* becomes indistinguishable from the latter and, consequently the entity in question—or, for that matter the entire reality in general—becomes an indifferenced or negationless existence which is evidently fictitious.

designated as *otherness* (*paratva*) in every real. This otherness is nothing other than the principle of difference in the constitution of reality which is identity-in-difference.

Thus negation with the Jaina is a significant negation which embodies a rich content within itself and not a species of total vacuity.

The proportion of the 'content' comprised in the notion of negation or otherness depends, according to the Jaina thinkers, upon the range of reality engulfed within the context or situation concerned. A customer who wishes to buy a jar from a shop will be satisfied with bringing, under the aspect of otherness, the several kinds of wares which *are not* jars, whereas a *kevalin* (a realised soul) will have, in his vision which is *sub specie aeternitatis,* an illimitable plenitude of objects in their infinite network of complex relations present to him against a contemplated situation.

This relativistic trend of thought finds its consummate expression in the idea that the full knowledge of anything is inextricably bound up with the full knowledge of everything and *vice versa.*[1] This truth is lucidly expressed by a stanza which states that "he who knows one thing completely knows all things"[2], and that "he alone who knows all things knows anything completely"[2].

---

1. Cf. *evaṁ caikasminnarthe jñāte sarveṣām arthānām jñānam sarvapadārthaparicchedam antareṇa tanniṣedhātmanā ekasya vastuno viviktatayā paricchedāsambhavāt* / *SM* (text), p. 92.

2. *eko bhāvaḥ sarvathā yena dṛṣṭaḥ sarve bhāvāḥ sarvathā tena dṛṣṭāḥ / sarve bhāvāḥ sarvathā yena dṛṣṭā eko bhāvaḥ sarvathā tena dṛṣṭaḥ //* *SM* (text), p. 92 and *OIP*, p. 171.

A canonical *gāthā*, quoted by Malliṣeṇa, also runs to the same effect:

je egaṁ jaṇai se savvaṁ jaṇai /
je savvaṁ jaṇai se egaṁ jaṇai //

SM (text), p. 92.

The notion of relativity has had a long and varied history of development in Indian as well as in Western philosophy. Its influence, under several forms akin to the Jaina view of *anekānta* (manifold or indeterminate) reality, will be alluded to elsewhere. (See ch. IX.) Its application in Western philosophy ranges from Protagoras, the author of the well-known dictum: "Man is the Measure of all things", in ancient Greece, to Albert Einstein, the originator of the celebrated theory of Relativity, in physics today. The reverberations of the Einsteinian theory, of physics, on the numerous branches of human knowledge, including philosophy, have been heard in increasing measure, for about a quarter of a century.

The notion of relativity is associated with theories such as are not merely divergent but are, often, mutually opposed. For instance, Berkeleyan idealism and Humean scepticism are, despite their opposition in important respects, both described as relativistic on the common grounds that they maintain that the "inmost nature" of "things" is "unknowable, inscrutable, and inconceivable, not to us merely, but to every other creature" (see J. S. Mill's *An Examination of Sir William Hamilton's Philosophy*, 2nd ed., London, 1865, p. 10). This meaning of relativity is reminiscent also of Kant's "unknowableness of things in themselves" as well as of Herbert Spencer's "ever unknown" or "unknowable reality existing behind all appearances" (H. Spencer's *First Principles*, 6th ed., The Thinkers Library, London, 1937, p. 55). There are many thinkers, ancient and modern, who subscribe to this view (*vide* Spencer, *op. cit.*, p. 55, and Mill, *op. cit.*, p. 11). Sir William Hamilton's impressive "Testimonies", classical and other, substantiating the "relativity of knowledge", in the sense in which relativity is referred to in the present paragraph, are of considerable interest. H. Spencer's and J. S. Mill's chapters on "The Relativity of All Knowledge" and "The Relativity of Human Knowledge" in the *First Principles* (ch. IV) and *An Examination* (chapters II and III), just cited, are of no less interest.

W. Wundt, a great psychologist of the period prior to that of Einstein's theory of relativity, enunciates 'the law of relativity' which coincides, at any rate in one of the essential implications, with the Jaina conception of the manifold (*anekānta*) nature of conciseness (cf. ch. IX). His 'law', supported also by Thomas Hobbes and Alexander Bain, maintains "that every phase of experience is influenced by every other phase of experience of the moment, and also by the whole past history of consciousness" (see *Dictionary of Philosophy and Psychology*, Vol. II, ed. J. M. Baldwin, 1911, New York, p. 450; see also the editor's *Handbook of Psychology*, 2nd edn., London, 1890, pp. 58-63; James Ward's article on "Psychology" in *Encyclopaedia Britannica*, 11th ed., 1891, London, p. 558 ; H. Hoffding's *Outlines of Psychology*, E. T. by M. E. Lowndes, 1891, London ; and Mill's *op. cit.*, p. 6 and f. n. thereon). This 'law' has also been affiliated, by its authors, to the Berkeleyan and Humean tenet of the 'unknowableness' of the 'inmost' nature of reality. The implication of interrelatedness of each phase of experience to all phases of experience, according to this 'law' is therefore a superimposition upon the theory of 'unknowable' reality. The point of comparison between this 'law' and the Jaina conception of manifold reality does not, therefore, extend beyond the common point of interrelatedness between the two schools in question. Further, the 'law' is bound by two limitations with respect to the comparison: (1) that it is purely psychological and, on the side of Jainism, applies only to the sphere of consciousness and not to total reality of which consciousness is a part and (2) that it superadds to itself the philosophical theory of an 'unknowable' reality in sharp contrast to Jainism which subscribes to an attitude of direct access to, or cognition of, reality. A. N. Whitehead however, complements the truth of Wundt's psychological relativity, touching, by means of his principle of 'the signi ficance of events', the objective side of reality: "Returning to the significance of events", he observes in *The Principle of Relativity* (Cambridge, 1922, p. 26), "we see there is no such thing as an isolated event. Each event essentially signifies the whole structure. But, furthermore, there is no such thing as a bare event." (See also *The Concept of Nature*, Cambridge, 1920, p. 29, para 2, etc.) These two sides of the truth of relativity, viz., the subjective side as advanced by Wundt and the objective side as advanced by Whitehead, give, between them, of course in a rough and ready manner, the total scope of the meaning attached by the Jaina philosophers to the notion under consideration.

The Einstein theory of relativity has given rise to a new development of the notion of relativity in the framework of a four-dimensional reality (for the meaning of the 'fourth dimension' see the lucid passage in S. A. Eddington's *The Romanes Lecture on the Theory of Relativity and its Influence on Scientific Thought,* Oxford, 1922, pp. 15-16). Making allowance for the differences in the cosmological structure between the highly complex physical theory of Relativity of Einstein and philosophical theory of relativity in Jainism we observe that the two theories are governed by one or two important features which suggest a considerable mutual affinity between them. A brief indication of these features may be made here:

Stating the position of relativity in Einstein's theory Viscount Haldane observes (*The Reign of Relativity,* London, 1921, p. 85; see also p. 88, para 2): "Two systems at a distance from each other, moving in different directions and with different velocities, may, for observers in them of a common object, be productive of results signifying different truths, in the form of shapes and measurements of space and time as actually and correctly observed". In other words, an object is not just what it appears to be from one viewpoint and the other viewpoints are not deviations from, or distortions of, that one absolute or isolated presentation. An object is, in the words Sir A. Eddington, perhaps the greatest exponent of the Theory of Relativity so far in England, "a symposium of worlds presented to different viewpoints" (*The Nature of the Physical World* Everyman's Library, London, 1935, p. 275). "The more standpoints, the better" (*The Romanes Lecture*, p. 24). Bertrand Russell calls individual viewpoints 'aspects' or 'private worlds' and defines an object ('thing') as 'system of aspects', or a 'system of perspectives', or simply 'perspectives'. (Cf. 'The system consisting of all views of the universe, perceived and unperceived, I shall call the system of 'perspectives'. I shall confine the expression 'private worlds' to such views of the universe as we actually perceive....Thus an aspect if a 'thing' is a member of the system of aspects which is the thing." *OKEW*, pp. 95-6). Both Eddington and Russel admit the possibility of "correlation" among the "worlds" or "private worlds" which have their basis in the object or "the referent" (cf. *The Nature of the Physical World*, p. 275, and *OKEW*, p. 96). Otherwise such a lack of intercommunication among such "worlds" leads to a solipsistic world-view, an interpretation which H. Dingle makes of the theory of Relativity. The snag in any mentalistic hypothesis, such as that of Dingle and, in the ultimate analysis, of Eddington himself (as will presently be shown) is that it does eventually, lead to a solipsistic universe despite any professions to the contrary (see Part II, chap. IX for criticisms against idealism, in general, and for a controversy in this specific issue, between Dingle & others. Dingle is logical (but not necessarily truthful) in so far as he is aware of the solipsistic implications of his interpretation.

The elements of 'standpoints' and 'aspects', so far considered have an unmistakable resemblance to *anekāntavāda,* in general, and *nayavāda* and, to some extent, *syādvāda,* the two primary modes of *anekāntavāda,* in particular, although this resemblance does not admit of a close point-for-point correspondence. A *naya,* or a standpoint, offers, according to Jainism, a partial truth of a real (*vastvaṁśagrāhī naya*), whose full truth could be comprehended in a totality or 'symposium' of such partial truths or presentations, actual and possible. Similarly, the word '*syāt*' in '*syādvāda*' is indicative of the other inseparable but distinguishable 'aspects' or presentations in any complex entity. Further, the immense complexity of a real, under the theory of Relativity, answers, in general, to the manifold or indeterminate (*anekatva*) structure of reality under the Jaina theory of relativity.

Lastly, the question whether relativity is rooted in a subjective or an objective universe, according to the theory of Einstein, is closely bound up with the treatment of the notion of relativity in relation to Jainism. As Haldane points out (*The Reign of Relativity,* p. 53) there are two schools of thought which interpret Einstein's relativity. One of them tends towards "mentalism" and the other towards objectivism or realism. The great Eddington himself is a notable adherent to the former view, also called structuralism. In his exposition of the theory of Relativity he observes: "All through the physical world runs that unknown content, which must surely be the stuff of consciousness...... And, moreover, we have

Having gone, in considerable detail, into the way in which being and non-being, or identity and difference, have been integrated in concrete reality, we may now resume the treatment of the *doṣas* which have been already formulated, elsewhere. The leading *doṣa* is, as already observed, *virodha* or contradiction, and the other *doṣas* are only the expression of its various aspects. The refutation of *virodha* implies,

---

found that where science has progressed the farthest the mind has but regained from nature that which the mind has put into nature". Concluding this thesis he further remarks, "We have found a strange foot-print on the shores of the unknown. We have devised profound theories, one after another, to account for its origin. At last, we have succeeded in reconstructing the creature that made the foot-print. And Lo! it is our own." (*Space, Time and Gravitation*, Cambridge, 1920, pp. 200-201. See also the *Reign of Relativity*, p. 105, and Broad's elucidation and criticism of Eddington's thesis presented at the Symposium on "The Philosophical Aspect of the Theory of Relativity", *Mind, N. S.*, 1920, pp. 414-49). Giving us a "glimpse of Reality" "reached" by "the modern scientific theories" which evidently include the theory under consideration, the same thinker speaks: "To put the matter crudely, the stuff of the world is mind-stuff.... The mind stuff is the aggregation of relations and relates which form the building material for the physical world". (*The Nature of the Physical World*, pp. 266 ff.) A counterblast to this mentalism of some "experimental philosophers" like Eddington, and, at the moment, of H. Dingle, comes from an even larger number of equally competent "experimental philosophers" and others, the most notable among them being Max Born, A. N. Whitehead, Bertrand Russell, H. P. Ushenko and Henry Margenau. Reference is made elsewhere (see Part II, chap. IX), to the views, realistic or objectivistic, of the latter group of thinkers, excepting that of A. N. Whitehead since it has been referred to in this footnote. H. Dingle's view, as well as the criticisms thereon, may also be noticed thereunder. The relevance of some of the ideas considered in course of this footnote to the Jaina conception of reality will become even more evident at the later stages of this work.

therefore, a substantial part of the refutation—though a somewhat implicit one—of the others also. A brief reference to the criticism of each of the other *doṣas* is also made with a view to give completion to the dialectical examination of the ontological stand taken by the Jaina :

There are, according to the Jaina, three[1] possible forms (*rūpas*) in which *virodha* can occur : 1. *Vadhyaghātakabhāva* (the destructive opposition); 2. *Sahānavasthānabhāva* (the non-congruent opposition) and 3. *Pratibadhyapratibandhakabhāva*[2] (the obstructive opposition). The first one holds between two 'hostile' participants or factors one of which is stronger than and, therefore, destructive (*ghātaka*) of the other (*vadhya*) if the two are brought together (*saṁyoge*). The illustration cited under this form of opposition is that of the mongoose (*nakula*) and the serpent (*ahi*) between which the the mongoose is stronger and, therefore, the preying agent in relation to its prey, the serpent. The condition that the agent and the patient (the serpent) should be brought together in a single situation is important in view of the fact

1. On a closer examination the three forms, an account of which follows immediately, seem to make a cross division although each of the three has more or less a specific feature of its own. The opposition between a mongoose and a serpent has been instanced as coming under *vadhyaghātakavirodha*, although it would not be wrong to bring it under either of the two other forms of *virodha*. This overlapping division does not, however, affect the truth of the Jaina stand.
2. The English equivalents, though somewhat inadequately rendered, are adopted for brevity. When fully rendered they become : 1. The opposition of the destroyed and the destroyer, 2. The opposition of 'non-congruence', and 3. The opposition of the obstructed and the obstructor, respectively. The term 'non-congruence' is after S. Mookerjee's rendering.

that if they remain two independent or separate facts they would not be opposed. If opposition could come into play even when they are separate or unconnected factors, then no serpent could ever exist in a world which is inhabited by the species of mongoose. Similarly there would be no fire left in a world where there is water. The paradox of the situation is that the two factors cannot, however, be brought together into a state of lasting union owing to their inherent opposition to each other. Even if they are coerced into a union the stronger member would destroy the weaker one and become the sole occupant, or the content, of the situation. Such a union of being and non-being with an imminent danger of a destructive union hanging upon it is not admitted to exist even for a moment (*kṣaṇamātram api*) between *sat* and *asat* in the *anekānta* ontology. This is so because the participant factors are admitted to be of equal strength (*tulyabalatvāt*) and, therefore, of a co-ordinate nature which admits of no fissure, in a real which can be described as unified complex or a complex union.

2. *Sahānavasthānabhāva*, or the congruent opposition, is a form of contradiction which occurs in the case of two states which cannot exist together in one substratum. It is possible for the two states in question to exist at different periods of time (*kālabhedena*) but they cannot do so, it is stated, at the same period of time. In a raw state a mango, for instance, is green (*śyāma*). In a ripe state the same mango becomes yellow (*pīta*). But the raw and the ripe states cannot, it is admitted, exist together in the mango since the two states are, in the present case, consecutive (*pūrvottarabhāvinau*). The Jaina maintains that this form of *virodha* also cannot affect

his conception of reality as *astitvanāstitvarūpātmaka* in as much as both *astitva* and *nāstitva* are concurrently revealed to exist together in concrete fact. If the two states, viz., *astitva* and *nāstitva*, are consecutive, or exclusive, then when *astiva* prevails all would be indistinguishably existent, and similarly, when *nāstitva* prevails all would become totally non-existent. In such circumstance the occurrence of *astitva* when all is *nāstitva* and *vice versa* becomes an absurd proposition: *sarvathaiva sataḥ punar ātmalābhābhāvāt, sarvathā cāsataḥ punar abhāvaprāptyanupapatter naitayos sahānavasthānaṁ yujyate*[1].

Hence to avoid this anomaly it is appropriate to assume that *astitva* and *nāstitva* are concurrent in reality.

3. *Pratibadhyapratibandhakabhāva*, or the obstructive opposition, is said to occur between two events or facts when one obstructs the occurrence of the other. The removal of the obstructing fact is, under this form of contradiction, the necessary antecedent condition for the occurrence of the other. To quote a traditional example, under the protective influence of a 'moonstone' (*candrakāntamaṇi*, the fictitious gem with cooling property) the rays of the sun cannot, it is said, burn us. That is, the occurrence of the burning effect is conditional upon the removal of the heat-obstructing stone. Similarly heat, which is an obstructing factor to cold, needs to be removed before a body feels cold. The Jaina view of *astitvanāstitvasvarūpatva* of reality is not accepted to be liable to this form of *virodha* also. The obvious reason

---

1. *SBT*, p. 88.

advanced is that both elements are concurrently revealed to our observation.

At this juncture it is necessary to point out a grave misapprehension which has implicitly prejudiced the opponents of Jainism with regard to the Jaina attitude to the problem of contradiction: The Jaina has been generally assumed to indulge, almost wantonly, in contradiction, particularly in relation to the development of his theory of reality. He has, of course, continually repudiated this assumption. In fairness to the impartial canons of philosophical criticism it is obligatory on the part of critics to realise the distinction between an avowedly conscious attempt to build up an ontological scheme on the foundation of contradiction, and an attempt to frame an ontological scheme which might seem to some critics to lead to a contradiction. The former attempt does not, but the latter does, absolve the author of the scheme from the intention of entertaining contradiction as an important element in the scheme. The Jaina seems to have persistently met with such a misconception of his ontological endeavour at the hands of even such great thinkers as Śankara and Dharmakīrti—not to mention several others whose dialectical acumen is of a lesser order. The Jaina himself does not think even for a moment that his theory of reality is built upon, or even leads to, contradiction. He is as zealous in the avoidance of contradiction as any of his adverse critics. Nowhere has he been seen to compromise on this subject. The three forms of contradiction just referred to sufficiently indicate his adherence to a non-contradictory approach to the problem under consideration. In a proper dialectical evaluation of the essential concepts in a certain school of thought, understanding the concepts as their authors wish them to be understood before proceeding to find out their faults is not the least part of a critic's duty.

There is a deeper consideration underlying the repudiation of the forms of contradiction with regard to the Jaina conception of reality. It lies in the fundamental difference in the approach to the problem of reality between the Jaina and the non-Jaina—especially the idealistic Advaitic and the Buddhist—schools. The difference may be stated, in modern phraseology, to be one between aposteriorism and apriorism. Aposteriorism signifies a direct appeal to experience and apriorism to some kind of 'intuition' which is "pure and transcendental". The intuitional or the aprioristic view would not of course object to the idea of experience being the sphere of verification of a truth. But it objects to the treatment of experience as the sole determinant of the knowledge and of the validity of its truth. This point of view is clearly expressed in the following observatior : "The opposition between being and non-being is known *a priori* and does not stand in need of verification to validate it. Its validity is self-certified, and though experience may illustrate its truth it does not confer validity upon it. Its validity is intrinsic, being derived from the aprioristic constitution of our thought-principle. If experience is found to be in consonance with this law, as known *a priori,* it is true and valid, and if it is found to be at variance with it, it must be rejected as false".[1]

---

1. *JPN*, p. 18.

The aposterioristic view of the Jaina, on the contrary, takes the attitude that experience is the source of the knowledge as well as of the validity of its truth. There is, on this view, no transcendental or transempirical region of 'pure' thought, from which the so-called contingent and particular truths can derive their truthfulness or validity and universality. Experience which gives rise to a knowledge of truths also imprints on it the signature of their self-certitude and self-validity.

This assumption, viz., that experience is the source of knowledge and the validity of all truths, underlies the Jaina assertion that if experience does not vouch for contradiction[1], then contradiction itself is false[2] and not the experience. Hence the Jaina feels that his view of reality as existence-cum-non-existence (*bhāvābhāvātmaka* or *sadasadātmaka*) is irrefutably valid.

V

1. The refutation of *Virodha*, supposedly the most important of the *doṣas* attributed to the Jaina theory of reality, is

---

1. *pratīyamāne vastuny avirodhāt. PKM*, p. 93. See also *PHMS*, p. 28.
2. Pascal offers a corrective to those who are so obsessed with contradiction that they see it even where it is not. Although the Jaina does not subscribe to Pascal's view as indicated in the following passage, it is interesting to observe how Pascal gives a glimpse into the other side of the picture, as it were, than the one given by the idealistic enthusiasts:

   "Contradiction is", observes Pascal, "a poor sign of truth; much that is certain is open to contradiction, much that is false passes without contradiction. Neither is contradiction a mark of untruth, nor absence thereof a mark of truth". Pascal's *Pensees*, p. 95, H. F. Stewart, Routledge and Kegan Paul, London (1950).

believed to weaken considerably the strength of the other *doṣas*. These *doṣas* have already been formulated elsewhere and referred to as being eventually the various aspects of *virodha*. One or two points of criticism against each of them may, however, be briefly supplemented to the above account of the Jaina refutation of contradiction.

2. The *vyadhikaraṇatādoṣa* or the fault that the Jaina notion of reality as *bhāva* and *abhāva* requires two abodes, loses its point owing to the fact that both *bhāva* and *abhāva* are unconflictingly revealed (*pratibhāsanāt*) together in a single locus (*ekādhikāraṇatvena*)[1].

3. *Anavasthā* or the infinite regress, as applied to the Jaina theory, is claimed to need an endless progression of predicating *sattva* and *asattva* in their togetherness, of each aspect, viz., *sattva* and *asattva* of the continually-increasing series of the pairs of *sattvāsattva* characteristics in a substance. The Jaina adduces the following argument against this charge: *sattva* and *asattva* are, according to him, the attributes of substance (*vastu*) itself and cannot, therefore, be treated as further attributes of attributes which they would be if the opponent is right. This principle is clearly stated by Guṇaratna: *sattvāsattvādayo vastuna eva dharmāḥ, na tu dharmāṇām dharmāh, dharmāṇāṁ dharmā na bhavantīti vacanāt.*[2] Umāsvāti also authoritatively

1. *nāpi vaiyadhikaraṇyam; nirbādhabodhe bhedābhedayoḥ sattvāsattvayor vā ekādhāratayā pratīyamānatvāt* / *PKM*, p. 535, and *NEEP*, p. 371. See also *TRD*, p. 236, *PMHS*, p. 28, and *TBV*, p. 452.
2. *TRD*, p. 234. Cf. *NKC*, p. 371, and *PKM*, p. 536.

confirms this truth in the *sūtra*: *dravyāśrayā nirguṇāh guṇāḥ*[1]. *Sattva* and *asattva*, the attributes of a *vastu* only, cannot, therefore, give rise to further pairs of similar attributes. Hence the question of *anavasthā*, the Jaina concludes, does not arise in his case.[2]

4. *Saṅkara,* and 5. *Vyatikara* : Neither *saṅkara* (confusion) nor *vyatikara* (exchange of natures) between *bhāva* and *abhāva* would arise from the Jaina point of view owing to the admitted fact that the variegated character of reality is clearly evident as in the case of a multi-coloured gem (*mecakaratna*) or of a similar fabric (*citrapaṭa*). Moreover,

---

1. *TRAG*, p. 243.
2. Further, in course of his defence of the Jaina stand against this charge, Guṇaratna distinguishes two kinds of infinite regress (*anavasthā*) : one the 'vicious' infinite, and the other the non-vicious or the 'harmless' (*aśakta*) infinite. The names he gives them respectively, are *mūlakṣatikāri* (lit. that which cuts the root) and *amūlakṣatikāri* (lit. that which does not cut the root). They are so described because the first one tends to cut at the very root of the substance it analyses and the second one to 'save' the root. The second one is also described as being indicative or illuminative of the manifoldness of reality (*amūlakṣatikāritvena pratyutānekāntasyoddīpakatvāt*). See *TRD*, p. 234, and compare the stanza, quoted by Guṇaratna, with the one pointed out by Dasgupta as having been quoted by Jayanta (*HIP*, Vol. I, p. 160, f.n. 1). Although both of them describe the two distinctions of the 'vicious' and the 'harmless' infinites the latter half of the stanza quoted by Guṇaratna is adapted to express the '*ānantya*' or 'the *anekāntatva*' principle of Jaina ontology. It is, however, a pity that Guṇaratna does not fully work out the implications of his argument and show how the 'harmless' infinite—which he exalts as being a '*bhūṣaṇa*'—is directly applicable to the Jaina theory which is, *ex hypothesi*, accepted as being free from any kind of infinite regress.

among the diverse shades of colour in such objects no one shade is taken for another nor does any of them exchange its character for that of another. Because they all together form an intelligible and unitary pattern in which each shade has its own specific place and feature. Similarly the unitary *bhāva* would be empty without the diversified *abhāva*; and the diversified *abhāva* would be meaningless without the unitary *bhāva*. Once the mutual necessity of the two is realised the question of confusion and misplacement in regard to the two elements in reality would not arise.

6. *Saṁśaya*: that doubt or lack of definiteness (*adṛḍha-pratīti*) would haunt a mind confronted with the dual nature of reality is, according to the Jaina, also ill-founded owing to the vivid revelation of both being and non-being (*sattvāsattvayoḥ sphuṭarūpeṇaiva pratīyamānatvāt*) in a *vastu*[1]. An acute observation[2] of Kumārila also bears out this truth.

7. *Apratipatti*, and 8. *Viṣayavyavasthāhāni*: A complex structure as well as a coherent order being indubitably transparent in a real denial of either[3] would be, according to

---

1. *TRD*, p. 236, and *PMHS*, p. 28.
2. This occurs in the following passage where Kumārila also maintains the doubtlessness (*na sandigdhaṁ; suniścitam*) of the non-absolute character (*anekatva; anyanānyatva* or *sattvāsattvarūpatva*) of our knowledge of a *vastu*: "This fact of the non-absolute character of an object, does not render our cognition of it doubtful (or invalid). Because it is only where cognition itself is doubtful that we can have its invalidity. In the present case, however, our cognition is perfectly certain, viz., that the *object is of non-absolute... character* (and as such, the validity of this cognition cannot be doubted)". *SVJha*, p. 344.
3. *pratipanne ca vastuny apratipattir iti sāhasam* / *PMHS*, p. 28.

the *anekāntavādin*, untruthful.[1] Hence these two *dosas* also are inapplicable to the Jaina conception of reality.

Arthakriyākāritvavāda

Hitherto the various objects of the *abhedavādin* and the

---

1. With regard to the five *doṣas* noticed on p. 146, f. n. 3, there is nothing strikingly new beyond what has already been given under the statement of the *modus operandi* by which being and non-being are synthesised in reality, as well as of the eight *doṣas* hitherto dealt with.

The refutation of fault No. 9, viz., *pratiniyatavyavahāralopa*, by virtue of which there would be, it is contended, a 'chaos' in the order of things—a 'chaos' in which a person proceeding to get water might get fire and *vice versa*—is contained in the statement of the *modus operandi* by which *svatattva* and *paratattva* are combined (*supra*, p. 149 ff.). In other words, water or fire has its own specific nature which is distinguishable from everything else. Were it not so, chaos would certainly break out among things as well as in our cognitions of them (cf. *TRD*, p. 236).

Reference has already been made to the overlapping character of the refutations of the various *doṣas* on p. 146, f. n. 3, and p. 163, f. n. 1. This is particularly evident in the case of the remaining four faults; viz., *ubhaya* (no. 12), *pratyakṣādi-pramāṇabâdhā* (no. 10), *asambhava* (no. 11) and *abhāva* (no. 13), which have also been noted in course of the same footnote. The answer to the charge of *ubhayadoṣa* would be, as already indicated, a variation of the answer to the charge of *vyadhi-karaṇatādoṣa*. That is, just as *bhāva* and *abhāva* can reside in the same abode, so also oneness and manyness can.

Similarly, the faulty notions of 'being contrary to all experience', 'impossibility', and 'non-existence' (the last two of these being the consequences of the first one), which have been brought under no. 10, no. 11 and no. 13 respectively, have been repudiated, in spirit if not in letter also, under the one or the other of the eight *doṣas*, particularly under *virodha*, *apratipatti* and *viṣayavyavasthāhāni*. Cf. *TRD*, p. 236.

bhedavādin to the Jaina view of reality have been jointly stated and the answers from the Jaina point of view also have been outlined. There is, however, one important principle which the Buddhist claims to be closely connected with his *bhedavāda* and on which it is necessary to ascertain the Jaina stand. It is the principle of *arthakriyākāritva* or causal efficiency which is considered by the Buddhist to form the essence[1] of reality. The Buddhist's arguments against the applicability of this principle to any kind of *abhedavāda* or *dravyavāda* have already been considered[2] at some length. The Jaina shares[3] the Buddhist's opposition to *dravyavāda* almost entirely, although some Buddhist critics imagine[4], not rightly, as will be shown in the process of answering the present as well as the next question, that this opposition to *dravyavāda* affects the Jaina position as well, in so far as the Jaina theory is concerned with the *dravya* as an element of reality.

There are, however, two important points of difference between the Buddhist and the Jaina in the meaning they attach to *dravyavāda* in their common denunciation of the view which connects this notion of *arthakriyākāritva* with *dravyavāda*. First the Buddhist is against *dravyavāda* of any kind, while the Jaina is against *ekāntadravyavāda*. Secondly, the Buddhist's attack actually turns out, whatever his profession may be, to be on the hypothesis of the static (*kūṭasthanitya*) *dravya* whereas the Jaina's attack is also on

---

1. See *NBD*, p. 103, *NBTD*, p. 17, *PVD*, II. 3, and *HBT*, p. 145 ff.
2. See *supra*, pp. 52-56.
3. See, for instance, *TBV*, p. 327 ff., *PHMS*, pp. 25-26, AVP, St. 26 and the *SM*. thereon, etc.
4. See *infra*, p. 187, f.n. 4, p. 190, f.n. 1, and p. 193.

the same hypothesis but only as a contrast to his own theory of the dynamic (*pariṇāmi*) *dravya*. It is needless to recount the Jaina arguments against *ekāntadravyavāda* since they are largely on the same lines as those of the Buddhist[1], which have already been noticed earlier[2] except for the difference with respect to the connotation of *dravyavāda* just stated.

The Jaina dialecticians[3] like Prabhācandra, Hemacandra, Abhayadeva and Malliṣeṇa do not merely show, with the Buddhist, the inapplicability of the principle of causal efficiency to the hypothesis of *dravyaikāntavāda*. They also pursue the consequences of the application of this principle even into the sphere of the Buddhist hypothesis of *kṣaṇikavāda*, the *paryāyaikāntavada* or the *anityavāda*[4] as the Jainas would call it—which maintains that reality is a series

---

1. Cf. *TBV*, p. 729.
2. See *supra*, pp. 52-56.
3. Akalaṅka is perhaps the earliest Jaina writer to dispute the relevance of the idea of *arthakriyākāritva*, in its two modes (to be mentioned presently) to the *nityavāda* or the *dravyaikāntavāda* on the one hand and to the *kṣaṇikavāda* or the *paryāyaikāntavāda* on the other. He observes:

   arthakriyā na yujyeta nityakṣaṇikapakṣayoḥ /
   kramākramābhyāṁ bhāvānāṁ sā lakṣaṇatayā matā //

   AGAM (and *AGAV* thereon), p. 4. See also *PKM*, pp. 498-499, *PMHS*, pp. 25-27, *TBV*, pp. 324-331, 400-403 and 728-729, *SM*, pp. 18-20, *NVVS*, p. 91, *AVV*, p. 202 and *SRK*, p. 731.

   Vācaspatimiśra, Jayantabhaṭṭa and Bhadanta Yogasena are among the early non-Jaina critics of the Buddhist idea of *arthakriyākāritva*. They all, of course, criticise it from the points of view of their respective doctrines. See *NVTT*, pp. 554-556, *NM*, pp. 453 and 464, *TSS*, *kās*. 428-434, and *PK* thereon.
4. *ekāntanityavadanitye'pi kramākramābhyām arthakriyāsambhavāt* / *PKM*, p. 499. See also *NVVS*, pp. 91-92.

of discrete moments without the thread of an inner connectedness. They try to show how *arthakriyākāritva*—a principle so dearly cherished by the Buddhist, who went, at certain stages, even to the extent of deriving[1] his very conception of reality, viz., *kṣaṇikavāda*, from it, or, at any rate, of identifying it with *kṣaṇikavāda*—deserts him when the consequences of its application to his theory of reality are examined. Without going into much detail the main features of the Jaina argument may be outlined as follows :

The Jaina contends that causal efficiency is incongruous[2] with the doctrine of momentariness or *kṣaṇikavāda*—also

---

1. We can distinguish three meanings in the evolution of the principle of *arthakriyākāritva* from the early times. At first it conveyed the simple meaning of 'the fulfilment (*siddhi*) of any need', then it meant 'action' (*anusthiti*) and finally it came to mean the efficiency of causing any action or event or simply the causal efficiency, which became 'the universally accepted definition of existence'. See *HIP*, Vol. I, p. 163, f.n. 1.

   Or to express its development in a somewhat different way at first, it was treated as 'a criterion of knowledge', then as a 'criterion of existence', and lastly, as 'the other name of existence' (that is *arthakriyākāritva* came to be regarded not merely as a characteristic of reality but as reality itself : *arthakriyākāritvameva sattvaṁ tacca kṣaṇikānāmeveti. HBT*, p. 145). Das Gupta draws our attention to the fact that athough it was historically derived from the prior doctrine of momentariness, later on, momentariness itself was sought to be proved as 'the logical result of the doctrine of *arthakriyākāritva*'. *Ibid.*, p. 154, f.n. 1, and p. 209, f.n. 2. But whatever the variations in its meaning may have been, fundamentally *arthakriyākāritva* is treated by the Buddhist thinkers as the essence, or the characteristic, which is universally concomitant with all existence. Therefore, it is used in this sense in the course of this work.

2. Prabhācandra mentions four *doṣas*, viz., *asiddha, viruddha, anaikāntika* and *kālātyayāpadiṣṭa,* which are incidental to *kṣaṇikavāda* in its relation to *arthakriyākāritva*. See *NKC*, Vol. I, p. 379 ff.

called the *ekāntanityavāda* or *paryāyavāda*—although the Buddhist himself considers causal efficiency as the very essence of his doctrine. The Jaina endeavours to prove his contention by analysing the only possible two modes in which causal efficiency can function in a reality which consists of discrete and perishing moments (*pratikṣaṇavināśi-bhāva*) without any thread of inner necessity connecting them into some kind of unity. The two modes are succession or consecutiveness (*krama* or *paurvāparya*) and non-succession (*akrama*) or simultaneity.

The causal efficiency cannot, the Jaina maintains, function successively owing to the fact that the momentary existence (*kṣaṇas*) lack abiding nature and, therefore, can have neither spatial nor temporal extension. Succession—spatial or temporal—involves the notions of 'before' and 'after' which are absent from the moment. In confirmation of this contention both Hemacandra and Malliṣeṇa cite a stanza which may be rendered as follows : "Whatever is a a point of space is there alone and whatever is at an instant of time is also exclusively there. Thus in this (hypothesis, viz., the *paryāyaikāntavāda*) there is no spatial or temporal extension for the entities."[1]

If the Buddhist replies to this contention by stating that although the moments perish and have no extension in space or time they do form a continuous series (*santāna*), which

---

1. The stanza runs:

yo yatraiva sa tatraiva yo yadaiva tadaiva saḥ /
na deśakālayor vyāptir bhāvānām iha vidyate //

SM (text), p. 19.

does not perish and, therefore, enables the moments to be successive, then the Jaina propounds to his opponent an inescapable problem :

In the first place, *santāna* or the continuous series is an unreal fiction (*santānasyāvastutvāt*). Even the opponent has to admit this, since there is, according to him, nothing else than the self-sufficient moments.

Secondly, supposing the reality of *santāna* is conceded for the sake of the argument, even then the Buddhist position will be as illogical as before, for *santāna* also would then have to share, *ex hypothesi*, the momentary character of the units in it. This would be a needless duplication of momentariness in another medium (*santāna*) which is not merely imposed, falsely, on the momentary units, but also can never sustain any continuance in it.[1]

Lastly, if any continuance or non-momentariness is acquiesced in by the Buddhist, then the poignant sarcasm[2] (suggesting self-impeachment or self-conviction) of Jayanta and Hemacandra would be fully deserved by the Buddhist who thereby compromises his ardent passion for the notion

---

1. This Buddhistic notion of *santāna* like its analogous notion of "logical construction" or "symbolic fiction" as developed by Russell, has been criticised earlier. See pp. 44 (–50), f.n. 2.
2. Jayanta disarms his opponent by the following observation : *athāpi nityaṁ paramārthasantaṁ santānanāmānam upaiṣi bhāvam / uttiṣṭha bhikṣo phalitās tavāśāḥ so'yam samāptaḥ kṣaṇabhaṅgavādaḥ* // *NM*, p. 464 (quoted by Hemacandra also in *PMMS*, p. 27). Hemacandra also remarks in the same strain : *athākṣaṇikatvam; susthitaḥ paryāyaikāntavādaḥ*. *PMHS*, p. 26. See also *SM* (text), p. 19.

of exclusive momentariness (*bhedaikānta*) and admits what he has all along fought against.

The Buddhist fares no better in his plea for the other mode, viz., the simultaneous functioning of the causal efficiency which might be supposed to repose in the vanishing moments of his conception. This may be illustrated by means of the example of a fruit which simultaneously reveals diverse effects like colour, taste, etc. In this case a question which naturally arises is whether the 'colour-moment' (*rūpakṣaṇa*) and the 'taste-moment' (*rasakṣaṇa*) arise from an identical or single nature of the moment, or from different or many natures of it. If they were to arise from a single nature, then they would all be the same for the obvious reason that they arise from the self-same nature (*yadyekena svabhāvena janayet tadā teṣām*[1] *ekatvam syād ekasvabhāvajanyatvāt*[2]) and, therefore, would not admit of diversity. If they were to arise, on the contrary, from many natures—some effects like colour arising from a material cause (*upādānabhāvena*) and others like taste arising from co-operative auxiliary factors (*sahakāritvena*)—then the Jaina would ask whether the many natures are integral (*ātmabhūtāḥ*), or non-integral (*anātmabhūtāḥ*), to the causal moment. If they are non-integral—that is, if they do not belong—to the cause then evidently they cannot in any sense claim to constitute the intimate nature (*svabhāvatvahānih*) of the cause in question. If they are, on the contrary, integral to the nature of the cause, then either (a) they will lose their

1. That is, *rasādikṣaṇānām*.
2. *PMHS*, p. 27.

diversity or manyness, and become identically the same (*svabhāvānām vaikatvam prasajyeta*[1]) since they are said to proceed from a single cause, or, for that matter, become the cause itself, inasmuch as they are non-different from it (*tad avyatiriktatvāt teṣām tasya caikatvāt*)[2] or (b) the cause itself —which is admitted to be of a single or identical nature—will become diversified because of the fact that the plurality of natures and the variety of effects (*svabhāvabhedah kāryasāṅkaryañ ca*) will inevitably split its integrity. Arguing on the part of the Buddhist that this contingency of plurality of natures and diversity of effects would not arise in this case, owing to the fact that such plurality and diversity are due to the cause being *upādāna* (material) at one place (that is, with respect to *rūpa* or colour in the present example), and *sahakāri* (auxiliary) at another (that is, with respect to *rasa* or taste in the present example), would not be helpful to him.[3] For this plea will not, in the least, mitigate the tendency of the cause to diversity and plurality which are too obvious in the Buddhist arguments. Hence the argu-

---

1. *SM* (text), p. 19.
2. *Ibid.*
3. *SM* (text), p. 19. Moreover, if the Buddhist denies, as he does, interaction between the so-called *upādāna* and the *sahakāri* factors in a causal event he will fall into the error of treating a causal connection as a casual coincidence. For instance if the seed (*upādāna*) on the one hand and the co-operative (*sahakāri*) factors of soil water and light, etc., on the other are treated simply as several independent series of potencies extraneously conjointed to bring a sprout (the effect) into life, then how such erratically casual coincidences could form a nexus of uniformly recurrent cause-effect relation becomes hard to explain.

ment for the simultaneous functioning of the causal efficiency in a momentary real also becomes a nullity.[1]

Thus the above account indicates that neither in the *dravyaikāntavāda* nor in the *paryāyaikāntavāda* is there any logical warrant for the function of the principle of causal efficiency. That conjunction of these two hypotheses into a mechanical theory, called *ubhayavāda*, will also prove equally unsatisfactory in this regard will be shown in course of the treatment of the next question immediately following this.

The Jaina understands by *arthakriyāsāmarthya* a capacity for generating the practical consequences as indicated by Hemacandra in his *sūtra*: *arthakriyāsāmarthyāt.*[2] This meaning is the same as what the Buddhist means by causal efficiency. The Jaina maintains also that *arthakriyākāritva* constitutes a unique property (*asādhāraṇarūpa* or *lakṣana*) of a concrete real. This is laid down by Hemacandra in his *sūtra* on the subject: *tallakṣaṇatvādvastunaḥ.*[3] The concrete real, however, is an integral synthesis of continuity and transience or identity and difference. This is signified by his adherence to the *dravyaparyāyātmakatvavāda.*[4] Accordingly, the only kind of reality which offers an adequate field for the operative play of *arthakriyākāritva* is believed by the Jaina to be the one which is contemplated by his integral view.

---

1. *tasmātkṣaṇikasyāpi bhāvasyākrameṇārthakriyā durghaṭā* etc. *SM* (text), p. 20.
2. *Vide ibid., sūtra* 32 and the *vṛtti* thereon.
3. *Vide ibid., sūtra* 32 and the *vṛtti* thereon.
4. Cf. *dravyaparyāyātmakasyaiva vastuno'rthakriyāsamarthatvād ity arthaḥ. PMHS*, p. 25. Also cf. *kṣaṇo'pi na khalu so'sti yatra vastūtpādavyayadhrauvyātmakaṁ nāsti* (*SM*, text, p. 20).

It is noteworthy that, in this connection, Hemacandra observes that the urge for right knowledge springs from the need of practical consequences.[1] Here Hemacandra strikes an unmistakably pragmatic note. That action is the source as well as the test of knowledge is the fundamental principle of the many-sided developments of pragmatism in the West.

---

1. *arthakriyārthī hi sarvaḥ pramāṇam anveṣate.* Also see what follows.

CHAPTER VI

The Externalistic Doctrine of Identity-in-Difference (Ubhayavāda)

versus

The Doctrine of a Unique and Integral Synthesis of Identity-in-Difference (Jātyantaravāda)

CHAPTER VI

The Externalistic Doctrine of Identity-in-Difference (Ubhayavāda) versus The Doctrine of a Unique and Integral Synthesis of Identity-in-Difference (Jātyantaravāda)

Starting with a brief statement of the Jaina view of reality, as embodied in the basic formula of Umāsvāti, we have so far addressed ourselves to the task of seeking confirmation for that view from three great representative thinkers, and then of launching out on a dialectical examination of the implications of that view under a scheme of the statement and the refutation of four questions. Two of the four questions have been jointly stated and refuted. In the process of their examination the Jaina view has been found to be confronted with a series of objections, among which contradiction, confusion, infinite regress and a few others are notable ones. In order to clarify the Jaina stand against those objections, it has been found necessary to dilate upon, incidentally, the means by which being and non-being are synthesised in concrete reality, as well as upon the significance of negation as an element of reality. The treatment of the mode of synthesising being and non-being as well as of the significance of negation as a component element of reality is aimed at serving the dual purpose of having provided the necessary ontological background for the refutation of the various objections (contradiction being the most important one among them) referred to in the foregoing account, and of forming the basis of a discussion of the doctrines of *nayavāda* and the *syādvāda-saptabhaṅgī* which will be briefly presented in the sequel. Lastly, in the course of the Jaina answer to *bhedavāda* [the question (b)] we have tried to disprove the Buddhist contention that causal efficiency (*arthakriyākāritva*) can have an operative force only within the ontological scheme of *kṣaṇikavāda*, and to establish the validity of that principle within the exclusive sphere of a *dravya-paryāyātmaka* reality.

There still remain two more questions, viz., (c) and (d), which demand our attention before the treatment of the four-fold questionnaire is brought to a close. The question (c) concerns *ubhayavāda* or the theory of two-fold nature of reality, or of identity and difference, and the question (d) concerns *jātyantaravāda* or the theory of uniqueness—uniqueness obtaining in every manifestation of identity-in-difference constituting an object in reality—which aims at remedying the defects of *ubhayavāda*. We may begin with the first of these two questions.

Ubhayavāda

Ubhayavāda postulates that identity and difference are separate, or at any rate, separable, entities entering into the making of an object. It may be, therefore, described as a mechanical or a composite theory of reality in so far as it treats *dravya* and *paryāya* (*guṇa*) as external or independent[1] entities. This is why Guṇaratna describes this view as : *kāṇādayaugābhyupagata-parasparaviviktadravyaparyāyaikānte*, etc.[2], although it considers *dravya* as the substratum (*āśraya*) of the *guṇas*. The Vaiśeṣika[3] is the author of this view although it is falsely fathered upon the Jaina also by the Buddhist logicians, Arcaṭa and Durveka.[4] As a matter of fact, the Jaina thinkers[5] themselves, viz., Siddhasena, Abhayadeva,

---

1. Cf. : "Though thus dependent upon a *dravya*, they (*guṇas*) are conceived as altogether distinct from it, for they can by themselves be known and as such must, according to the doctrine (the Nyāya-Vaiśeṣika) be independent realities. They are what they are in complete independence of everything including the *dravyas* to which they belong ...." *OIP*, p. 232. See also *TS*, p. 82 (notes), where the *guṇas* are characterised as 'accidents' attaching to *substance*, the *Ens*.
2. *TRD*, p. 231. See also the following f.n.
3. In course of our treatment of *ubhayavāda* only the Vaiśeṣika (the *kāṇāda*) is referred to as the author of the theory, although the Naiyāyika (the *yauga*) also shares this view in important essentials.
4. Curiously enough Arcaṭa chooses the Jaina as the main target of his criticism against this *ubhayavāda* in his *Dravyaparyāyayor anekāntavāda-khaṇḍana*. *HBT*, pp. 104-107 (and the *Āloka* thereon), particularly the *kās*. 20, 25 and 24. The first two of these *kās*. have been quoted (*infra*) and the last one hints that the *dravyaparyāyavāda* would not be different from accepting a mixed view of *kūṭasthanityatā* in regard to *dravya* and *kṣaṇanāśita* in regard to *paryāya*, together. (As a matter of fact Ratnakīrti categorically affirms that there can be no third possibility beyond the alternatives of *kṣaṇikatva* and *akṣaṇikatva* in this regard : *kṣaṇikākṣaṇikaparihāreṇa rāśyantarābhāvāt*....p. 77, *SBNT*).

   The criticism of the Vaiśeṣika view, however, follows immediately the attack on the Jaina.
5. Siddhasena firmly repudiates the falsity (*micchāttam*) of the Vaiśeṣika position in *gā*. 49, *STP*, p. 656. Although the

Haribhadra, Hemacandra and Malliṣeṇa, have taken a strong line of criticism against this view of the Vaiśeṣika (*kaṇabhuṅmata*). A statement of the Vaiśeṣika school concerning the subordination of identity to difference has already been made earlier[1] by pointing out the predominant importance given to the concept of *viśeṣa* or particularity by the

Vaiśesika, like the Jaina, acknowledges the reality of both *dravya* and *paryāya* (*guṇa*), he treats each of them as being absolute and, therefore, as being mutually independent (*annonnaniravekkha*). He, therefore, resorts to *ubhayavāda* (*dohi vi naehi niam*). The two views, or *nayas*, which are mixed, or contained, in the *ubhayavāda* of the Vaiśeṣika, are the *dravyārthikanaya* (*davvātthiyanaya*) and *paryāyārthikanaya* (*pajjāvātthiyanaya*) each of which is severally illustrated by him in the following *gā.*, with reference to the Kāpila (the Sāṅkhya) *darśana* and the Śauddhodana (the Buddhist) *darśana* respectively:

jaṁ kāvilaṁ darisaṇam eyaṁ davvātthiyassa vattavvam /
suddhoana tanaassa u parisuddho pajjavaviappo // 48 //.

STP, p. 656.

Owing to their extreme (*suddha* or *pariśuddha*) or exclusive character the two *nayas* or doctrines, whether singly, as in the Kāpila *darśana* or Śauddhodana *darśana*, or jointly, as in the Vaiśeṣika *darśana*, are called the '*parasamayas*' or heresies. In his extensive com. on *gā.* 49, Abhayadeva expounds, and refutes, the most controversial problems of the Vaiśeṣika philosophy. The problem of *ubhayavāda* is, however, touched upon at the opening and the concluding parts of the com.

Hemacandra devotes to the Vaiśeṣika metaphysics as many as six *kās.* (4-9) in his *AVD* and a few brief but lucid passages specifically to *ubhayavāda* in his own com. on the *sūtras* 30-33 in his *Pramāṇamīmāṁsā* (pp. 25, 27 and 29, *PMHS*). Malliṣeṇa, in his elaborate com. on the six *kās.* of *AVD*, especially under the *kā.* 5, vividly brings out, in occasional polemical passages, the critical implications of this view (*SM*, pp. 10 ff. (text), especially pp. 13-20). Lastly, Haribhadra makes occasional critical observations on this question in his critique on the nature of reality in his *AJP*, Vol. I (particularly pp. 65-66 and 71-76).

1. See *supra*, pp. 107-112.

school. At present we are, therefore, concerned only with noticing how the mechanical hypothesis of *ubhayavāda* (which also applies to the Vaiśeṣika philosophy in so far as the predominant difference and the subordinate identity form a mechanical combination in the hypothesis) is unsatisfactory. This consideration will point to the necessity of treating *bheda* and *abheda* as two different aspects of an integral or vital synthesis instead of as two external entities conjoined in a composite object, which would evidently be two entities in one, although it (the composite object), is erroneously treated as one. It will also bring into the picture of reality the important trait of *jātyantaratā* by virtue of which each real would be cognised as something *sui generis.* The second factor, viz., *jātyantaratā*, will receive a greater stress in the next question, than the first one, because it has not figured so far in our inquiry into the nature of reality, except by a casual reference to its name on a few occasions.

To resume our consideration of the present question, the externalism between *dravya* and *paryāya* (*guṇa*) makes *ubhayavāda* not into one consistent theory which it is supposed to be, but into a conjunction[1], or mixture (*miśra* or *miśravāda*) of two independent, or even opposed[2] theories of *dravyavāda* and *paryāyavāda.* The reason for this is that *dravya* and *paryāya* are treated as numerically different entities, although they are supposed to exist as a single object. This is why Arcaṭa is right in urging against this theory that

1. Abhayadeva describes it as: *svaviṣayapradhānatāvyavasthitānyonyanirapekṣobhayanayāśritam / TBV*, p. 704.
2. Cf. *viruddhadharmayogena stambhakumbhādibhedavat / TSS, kā.* 561.

it lays itself open to the combined evils[1] of both Identity-view and Difference-view.

The initial error of *ubhayavāda* is, from the Jaina point of view, the acceptance of the idea that *dravya* and *guṇa* (*paryāya*) are 'completely independent'[2] despite the alleged 'dependence' of the latter (*guṇa*) on the former.

Besides robbing *dravya* and *paryāya* of their mutual dependence as complementary elements in an entity, this idea of absolute independence between *dravya* and *paryāya* leads the Vaiśeṣika to resort to a metaphysical tour de force, viz.,

---

1. Referring to the fictitiousness (*kalpanākṛta*) and falsity (*mṛṣārthatā*) of the Identity-view (*abhedavāda*) and Difference-view (*bhedavāda* or *paryāyavāda* or *dravyavāda*) individually Arcaṭa observes:

   abhedasyāparityāge bhedaḥ syāt kalpanākṛtaḥ /
   tasyāvitathabhāve vā syādabhede mṛṣārthatā //

   HBT, p. 106, *kā*. 20.

   Although the substance of this criticism against the two extreme views is the same as that of Siddhasena's criticism in his *gā*. 49 (*supra*, p. 187, f.n. 5), Arcaṭa treats the Jaina, as already noted, as the main target of this as well as of the following charge:

   bhedābhedoktadoṣāś ca tayor iṣṭāḥ katham na vā /
   pratyekam ye prasajyante dvayor bhāvāḥ katham na te //

   Ibid., *ka*. 25 (for a slight variation of the second line of this *ka*., as quoted by Hemacandra, see *PMHS*, p. 29, and p. 804, line 18).

   Both Hemacandra and Municandra agree with this criticism against *ubhayavāda*: *dravyaparyāyavādayoś ca yo doṣaḥ sa ubhayavāde'pi samānaḥ*. *PMHS*, p. 29. *idamuktam bhavati—kevalābhedapakṣe abhedapakṣe ca ye prāgeva nirūpitā doṣās ta ubhayapakṣābhyupagamam sutarām prāpnuvanti* / *AJPV* on Haribhadra's com. on *AJP*, Vol. I, p. 13.
2. *dravyaguṇayor asaṅkīrṇasvabhāvatvāt* / HBT, p. 107.
   dravyaguṇādibhyo vyāvṛttarūpāṇi / TBV, p. 656.
   Cf. also *supra*, p. 187, f n. 1.

the enunciation that a *dravya* can remain devoid[1] of a *guṇa* even though for an instant, after its birth, and that it can also outlast, by an instant, the destruction of the material cause from which it is produced.[2] Whatever the circumstances which might lead the Vaiśeṣika to perform this curious metaphysical feat, the acknowledgement of the separability between *dravya* and *guṇa* makes his position highly vulnerable[3] to the attack as to how the entities so external to each other get, when brought together, fused into such an intimate union as could be described as a single object.

---

1. Keśavamiśra observes: *dravyaṁ nirguṇam eva prathamam utpadyate.* Or again : *tasmāt prathame kṣaṇe nirguṇa eva ghaṭo guṇebhyaḥ purvabhāvīti...* *TB*, Pt. I, p. 8.

   "In consonance with the realistic and pluralistic spirit of the doctrine," a modern writer observes in this connection : "these qualities are all regarded as separately real or as having their own being, although they are never found by themselves. Theoretically a substance may, provided it is a product, exist without a quality for a little while." *EIP*, p. 93.
2. "....a jar for example is destroyed one instant after the destruction of the halves (*kapāla*) out of which it is made." The same writer further observes: "There is in this view the difficulty of satisfactorily explaining the continuance, for however short a period it may be, of the effect after its material cause is gone." *OIP*, p. 241.
3. There will arise several other objections also against the notion, viz., that *dravya* could be *nirguṇa* at the first moment: (1) How could a jar, for example, be perceived at the first moment while even the Vaiśeṣika accepts the rule that *guṇas* like colour and touch, are necessary for the perception of a *dravya*? (2) Would the jar be called a *dravya* at the moment when it is *nirguṇa* in the face of the definition, given by the Vaiśeṣika himself, that a *dravya* is a substratum of *guṇas* (*guṇāśraya*) (See *NKB*, p. 369)? Acceptance of imperceptibility as demanded by (1) and pleading, in answer to (2), that a '*dravya' may have capacity* for being a substratum of *guṇas* but may not be necessarily possessed of them always would be but evasive answers.

The tendency to externalise everything has also compelled the Vaiśeṣika to postulate a God (Īśvara or Maheśvara) for explaining the creation and destruction of the changing world. This *deus ex machina* amounts to a confession of failure in evolving an intrinsically self-sufficient notion of reality.

A further anomaly arising from the mechanistic conception of *ubhayavāda* in the Vaiśeṣika metaphysics is the division of *dravyas* into eternal (*nitya*) or permanent ones and non-eternal (*anitya*) or transient ones. The eternal ones are said to be primary or simple substances (*nityadravyaṁ tvasamavetam eva*[1]) and the non-eternal ones are said to be secondary or composite products derived from the simple ones (*anityadravyaṁ kāryarūpatvād avayavasamavetam*[2]). This assignment of eternality or permanence to one division and of transience or change[3] to another one results, at any rate according to the Jaina and the Buddhist critics, in a theory of two worlds in one of which, permanence enjoys an uninterrupted or lonely existence, and in the other there is the play of change in evidence initiated in a perpetually alternating cycle of creation and destruction by God or Maheśvara. From among the residents of the world a further order of substances is singled out. This order is said to consist of soul (*ātmā,* including *paramātmā* or God), space

---

1 & 2. See *NKB*, p. 370.

3. In keeping with the mechanistic temper of the system the Vaiśeṣika's idea of change does not signify any internal or dynamic transformation (*pariṇāma*) in a product but only its 'change of place' (*pariṣpanda*). Cf. *OPI*, p. 233.

(*dik*), *ākāśa*[1] and time (*kāla*). These substances are said to be so absolutely eternal that they do not give rise to the products (*dravyabhāvinaḥ*) of the transient realm.[2]

This bifurcation of the world into two or three independent orders of permanence and change, or identity and difference, does not commend itself to the Jaina.

Lastly, even *arthakriyākāritva* or causal efficiency cannot, according to the Jaina, come into play in such a world of being so sharply separated. How causal efficiency cannot operate in the static realm of a mere *dravya* has been already pointed out from the point of view of the Buddhist philosophy.[3] Hemacandra is in total agreement with the Buddhist in regard to the inapplicability of causal efficiency, either at the level of simultaneity or of succession, in a static *dravya*. He goes further in demonstrating how it cannot be operative even in a world of discreet momentariness which is the view of the Buddhist himself. This aspect of the problem also has been pointed out earlier.[4] The Vaiśeṣika's *ubhayavāda*,

1. *Dik* or space and *ākāśa* are different in the Vaiśeṣika system. *Ākāśa* is some 'ethereal substance' filling the space and having sound as its distinction.
2. Hemacandra describes the entire position as follows:
   kaṇādastu dravyaparyāyavubhāvapyupāgaman pṛthivyādīni guṇādyādhārarūpāṇi dravyāṇi, guṇādestvādheyatvāt paryāyaḥ/ te ca kecit kṣanikāḥ, kecit yāvaddravyabhāvinaḥ, kecin nityā iti kevalam itaretaravinirluṇṭhitadharmidharmābhyupagamāṁśasamīcīnavādinaḥ/
   He concludes the argument by stating :—
   ekāntabhinnānām kenacit kathañcit sambandhayogādityāhnikyapakṣe'pi viṣayavyavasthā / PMHS, p. 27.
3. See *supra*, pp. 52–56, and also the Sec. on *Arthakriyākāritvavāda* (p. 172 ff.).
4. See *supra*, p. 174 ff.

which is but a conjunction of *dravyavāda* and *kṣaṇikavāda* (*paryāyavāda*), is shown by Hemacandra and the other Jaina thinkers, to lend itself doubly[1] to the lack of any play of causal efficiency.

In view of the incongruities indicated in course of the present question the Jaina rejects *ubhayavāda* in favour of *jātyantaravāda* which is claimed to avoid the pitfalls met with in the present and the previous questions.

Jātyantaravāda

It has been discovered, in course of our attempt to answer the three questions (a), (b), and (c) concerning the nature of reality, that neither the pure identity-view (*dravyaikāntavāda*)[2], nor the pure difference-view (*paryāyaikāntavāda*), nor even the composite view of identity and difference (*ubhayavāda* or *parasparaviviktadravyaparyāyaikāntavāda*)[3] but only an integral view of

---

1. 'Doubly' because the Buddhist charges (with which the Jaina identifies himself subject to the two limitations indicated on p. 173, *supra*) made against the *paryāyaikāntavāda* (in the course of the previous question) of the Buddhist, will *together* hold against the mechanical theory of the Vaiśeṣika who conjoins the above two extreme theories into his *ubhayavāda*.
2. Although the Advaita view of reality is generally considered to be the *dravyaikāntavāda* (the identity-view) *par excellence*, the Sāṅkhya view is also considered by the Jaina writers to be a very good example of a *dravyaikāntavāda*. Therefore, the Jaina writers sometimes refer, in this connection, to both or to either (as Guṇaratna does in the phrase where reference to the *paryayaikānta* of the Buddhist also is made: *sāṅkhyasaugatābhimata-dravyaparyāyaikāntayoḥ* / *TRD*, p. 231) of the two.
3. See *supra*, p. 187 (f.), f.n. 5, etc.

identity-in-difference offers an adequate definition of reality.[1] The present question, the last in the series of four questions with which we started a critical exposition of the Jaina conception of reality, aims at dealing briefly with how and why the Jaina regards every real as not merely an indissoluble (*parasparānanuviddha*) union of identity-in-difference but also—this is the matter of immediate concern—as something *sui generis* (*jātyantara*)[2].

The Jaina ontologist maintains that a real is a synthesis of identity-in-difference and that each such synthesis is *jātyantara* or *sui generis*. That is, the combination of identity and difference in a real is not a numerical summation but a vital synthesis of the two elements. Each such synthesis is also said to be unique,[3] in the sense that when the real is analysed the two elements of identity and difference exhaust

---

1. *yata evotpādāditrayātmakaṁ paramārthasat* / *TRD*, p. 229
2. Cf. "A real is a unity and diversity in one, and the relation involved is neither one of absolute identity nor one of absolute otherness, but something different from both. It is *sui generis......*" *JPN*, p. 207.
3. Cf. *evaṁ hyubhayadoṣādidoṣā api na dūṣaṇam* /
   samyagjātyantaratvena bhedābhedaprasiddhitaḥ //
   AJP, Vol. I, p. 72.

   Akalaṅka also remarks : *ubhayadoṣa*(viz., *sadasadekāntapakṣa-doṣa*)*prasaṅga iti cet na jātyantaratvān narasiṁharūpavat* / *TRAG*, p. 225. Through expressing himself not merely against the view that a real is '*ubhayarūpa*' (composite) but also against the other two extreme dogmas, viz., that a real is merely '*dravyarūpa*' and that it (the real) is merely '*paryāyarūpa*', Hemacandra also asserts the manifold (*śabala*) and unique (*jātyantara*) character of the real as follows : *ayam arthaḥ—na dravyarūpaṁ na paryāyarūpaṁ nobhayarūpaṁ vastu, yena tattatpakṣabhāvī doṣaḥ syāt, kintu sthityutpādavyayātmakaṁ śabalaṁ jātyantarameva vastu* / *PMHS*, p. 29.

between themselves the entire content of the real, although they display a distinctive (*viśiṣṭa*) structural and functional individuality—not found in the individual constituent elements—in their combination. This is illustrated by the oft-quoted instance of Narasiṁha[1] (the Man-lion): As the name itself suggests, Narasiṁha is a combination of *nara* (man) and *siṁha* (lion). Nevertheless, it indicates a being which is somehow different[2], in its combination, from the parts severally entering into its making, although it is impossible to get such a being outside the parts in question.

Similarly jaggery (*guḍa*) and ginger (*nāgaram* or *suṇṭhi*) are said to cause phlegm (*kaphahetuḥ*) and bile (*pitta-*

---

1. Durveka explains this being as : *hiraṇyakaśipuvadhārthanirmita-narasiṁhātmakaḥ* / *HBTA*, p. 343.
2. Cf. *na naro nara eveti na siṁhaḥ siṁha eva vā* /
   śabdavijñānakāryāṇāṁ bhedājjātyantaraṁ hi tat //
   na naraḥ siṁharūpatvāt na siṁho nararūpataḥ /
   sāmānādhikaraṇyena narasiṁhaḥ prakīrtitaḥ //

   Quoted in *AJP*, Vol. I, p. 71, f.n. 1 and *NKC*, Vol. I, p. 369. The first verse is quoted also in Siddhasena Gaṇi's Com. on *Tattvārthādhigamasūtra*, Kapadia's edn., p. 377, as well as in *JTVS*, p. 11 (with slight variations in the last work). The verse following it in *JTVS* as well as in *TRD* and all the verses preceding it in *TRD* may also be seen.

   For a variant verse in which the same analogy is expressed, see *SM* (text), p. 20, and *TPSJ*, p. 79. Besides *TPSJ* see also *TSS*, *kās.* 325, 1733-1736 (together with *PK* on all these *kās.*), *HBT*, p. 104, and *HBTA*, p. 343 (in all of which reference is made to it either for a statement of, or a criticism against, the Jaina position). This analogy is cited in a few other non-Jaina works (e. g. *NVVS*, p. 261, the *tippaṇi* against p. 88, line 16), often in somewhat different contexts. See also *AGAV*, pp. 103 and 108, *TSV*, p. 435, *PKM*, p. 536, *TRD*, p. 245, *AJP*, Vol. I, pp. 65, 77 and 302, *SJPT*, pp. 214 and 215, *AVV*, p. 147, *NVVS*, pp. 87-88 and *SM* (text), p. 151.

kāraṇam) respectively but when compounded (*militayoḥ*), they lose their respective harmful effects (*doṣān*) and become something different[1] (*anyadeva, dravyāntaramidaṁ guḍa-nāgarākhyam* or *guḍanāgarabheṣajam*) despite the retention of the basic ingredients revealed in the analysis of the compound substance.

A more familiar example in this connection would be that of water and its constituent elements. When analysed, under electrolysis, water resolves itself into two molecules of hydrogen and one molecule of oxygen. That water is a distinctive or unique substance in comparison with its constituents is a scientific commonplace. These instances[2] indicate the lines on which the Jaina treats every entity as a unique phenomenon in relation to its constituent factors of identity and difference. This uniqueness is not a mere external[3] appendage but an inherent trait manifesting itself in the ceaseless vortex of causal interaction among the entities in the universe. In his Gifford Lectures Samuel Alexander makes a suggestive observation which brings out the spirit of the

---

1. Cf. *na cātra bhedābhedapakṣabhavī doṣo guḍanāgarasaṁjñita-vastvabhyupagamāt / taduktam—*

   gudaścet kaphahetuḥ syāt nāgaraṁ pittakāraṇaṁ /
   tannu amanyatevedaṁ guḍanāgarasaṁjñitam //

   NVVS, pp. 87-88 (with *tippaṇi* against p. 88, line 1, and p. 261), *HBT*, p. 106 (together with *HBTA*, p. 349).

2. Some of the other analogies given in illustration of the *jātyantara* character of a real are those of Umeśvara (*NKC*, Vol. I, p. 349), the multi-coloured (*citra* or *mecaka*) gem (*ibid.*) or *mayūrāṇḍa* (*TRD*, p. 244) etc.

3. That external factors like spatial and temporal considerations are not irrelevant is shown below (*supra*, p. 201 f.)

Jaina notion of *jātyantaratva* as an argument against a world of repetitive[1] cycle of entities and events : "Bare repetition it may be affirmed does not even exist. Manufactured articles are not identical though they may be identical within certain limits of precision. It is, however, true that the more closely instances reproduce each other the less useful they are for scientific discovery."[2]

Leibniz is more emphatically clear on this point. He states : "There is nothing in the universe which does not enjoy a certain singularity, which is to be found in no other thing."[3] He asserts, under the principle of the 'Identity of Indiscernibles'[4], that not even any two leaves of a tree or any two drops of water or of milk could be 'entirely alike' because of the fact that "The things are......distinguishable in themselves".[5]

The *jātyantara* trait of an entity is grounded in the fundamental manifoldness (*anekāntasvarūpatva*) which is believed by the Jaina to be at the heart of all reality. The

---

1. Repetitive in the sense of lack of individuality among entities.
2. *Space, Time and Deity*, S. Alexander (London, 1920), Vol. I, p. 231.
3. *Mon.*, p. 222, f.n. 15.
4. Explaining this principle of the 'Identity of Indiscernibles' with respect to a Monad, the Leibnizian conception of a real, Leibniz writes : "Indeed, each Monad must be different from every other. For in nature there are never two beings which are perfectly alike and in which it is not possible to find an internal difference or at least a difference founded upon an intrinsic quality". *Ibid.*, p. 222.
5. See *ibid.*, p. 37, f.n. 1 and *A Critical Exposition of the Philosophy of Leibniz*, B. Russell, (2nd Edition, 1949), pp. 55 ff. and 220.

existence of a simple real is thoroughly repugnant to the Jaina. Uniqueness or 'singularity' cannot, according to him, arise from such absolutely simple real whether the real be the Advaitic Brahman or the Buddhistic *kṣaṇikasantāna* (series of full stops as it were). For there is little room in such a real for anything else than its own bare subsistence (*sat*). Hence the truth underlying the Advaitic dictum: *naikasmin na sambhavāt*, or the Buddhistic dictum: *yo viruddhadharmavān nāsāvekaḥ*[1], betrays not the contradictoriness of the *anekānta* real but the logical consummation of the monolithic or simple form of reality. *Jātyantaratva* can, therefore, arise, it is believed, from the foundation of a manifold or variegated real which alone could afford the basis for the co-ordinate existence of diverse elements or components, as well as for their casual interplay, which in turn results in the emergence of a fully-fledged unique or singular entity. Therefore it is by no means an accident or a casual fancy that the Jaina conceives *anekāntasvarūpatva* as a synonym of *paramārthasat* (true reality) and conceives it as the pivot on which his entire philosophical—ontological and epistemological—developments turn. Thus *anekāntavāda*, with which alone the notion of *jātyantaratva* is affirmed to be concomitant, offers the most thoroughgoing ontological antithesis to the *ekānta* (extreme or monolithic) doctrine—single or composite—in Indian philosophy.[2]

---

1. See *infra*, p. 23-24 (and the footnotes).
2. For a reference to the synonymousness of *anekāntavāda* with *utpādavyayadhrauvyātmakavāda* and to its being the necessary basis for the notion of *jātyantaratva*, see *TRD*, pp. 229 f. and 244 ff.

There are two considerations—the one critical and the other constructive—which concurrently underlie the postulation of *jātyantaratva* as a trait in reality. Critically, the notion of *jātyantaratva* aims not merely at repudiating indirectly the *ekānta* doctrines just referred to of simple reals, but also at directly undermining the Vaiśeṣika's *ubhayavāda*, with which the *bhedābhedavāda* or the *anekāntavāda* (of which the *jātyantaravāda* is a corollary) is persistently confused by the Buddhistic thinkers. This is why Akalaṅka contrasts *jātyantaravāda* with the other theories by designating the former as a case of *pakṣāntara*[1] (a view which signifies the resultant real as a product distinct from—not merely as something interchangeable with—the constituent factors) and the latter as cases of *pakṣasaṅkara*[2] (a view which signifies the real as a confused complex).

---

1. Malliṣeṇa agrees with Akalaṅka in treating the Jaina as *pakṣāntara* : *nityānityapakṣavilakṣaṇasya pakṣāntarasyaṅgīkriyamāṇatvāt* / *SM* (text), p. 20.
2. Akalaṅka is inclined to use this epithet, viz., *pakṣasaṅkara*, for both the two *ekānta* doctrines of the identity-view (*sadvāda*) and the difference-view (*asadvāda*) as well as for the *ubhayavāda* (which is but a numerical summation of the two) although it is more appropriate in the latter (*ubhayavāda*) owing to the fact that, in the latter, there are two factors—identity and difference—which are mixed (*miśra*), *ex hypothesi*, in a mechanical togetherness. The only sense, however, in which the term would severally apply to the two *ekānta* doctrines also is when each of them is understood as mixing in a confused jumble : a real identity with an unreal difference (the *māyā* as superimposed on the *sat*) or a real difference with an unreal identity or continuity (the unreal *santāna* or continuity as superimposed on the discrete moments (*kṣaṇas*) the only reals recognised by *kṣaṇikavāda*). But this seems to be a rather far-fetched meaning; its indirect truthfulness is incontrovertible. It is, therefore, necessary to note that

The most serious objection associated with the confusion of the Jaina theory with that of the Vaiśeṣika—a critical reference has been already made to the other two *ekānta* theories at the beginning of the present question—is that the Jaina theory, like its erroneous counterpart, involves contradiction in the constitution of its real. The affirmation, on the part of the Jaina, of the mutual complimentariness or the integratedness of identity and difference in a real in contrast to the mere extraneous or composite togetherness of the two, as maintained by the *ubhayavādin*, has been observed under the treatment of *ubhayavāda*, to knock the bottom out of the charge of the contradiction. That is, the integrated or the indissoluble (*parasparānanuviddha*) structure of the real directly gives the lie to the opponents' charge of contradiction against the Jaina conception of a real. *Anekāntasvarūpatva*, the *raison d'être* of the integrated concreteness of a real, is hereby asserted to be the negation of contradictoriness, or the affirmation of complimentariness. The proof of contradiction would, therefore, mean the disproof of the *anekāntasvarūpatva* of all reality. But the possibility of such a proof is flatly denied by the Jaina on the strength of the warrant of experience, at perceptual and other levels, which is maintained to reveal the ultimacy of the *anekānta* truth in all reality.

Constructively, uniqueness or 'singularity' is a positive trait attending upon every phase of causal process which

---

the principle of *jātyantaravāda* or *pakṣāntaravāda* is proximately directed against *ubhayavāda* (which has the semblance of *jātyantaravāda*) although its indirect criticism against the other *ekānta* doctrines also is indubitably implicit.

marks a transition or evolution from an anterior manifold entity to a more inclusive or less inclusive posterior entity. It is conditioned by the determinate factors—external and internal within the fourfold range of the *dravya* (the material factor), the *kṣetra* (the spatial location), the *kāla* (the temporal reference) and the *bhāva* (the intrinsic nature), governing the context of the causal occurrence concerned. It is not traceable to any one of these factors singly but arises from the totality of all the factors prevailing in the causal setting from which a new entity emerges. Besides imprinting a certain distinctiveness or individuality upon the entities and events in the universe the presence of this factor, viz., *jātyantaratva*, saves the reality from becoming a universal mass of mere being or a conglomeration of incommunicable atomistic particulars, or a mere conjunction of such being and such particulars in a warring medium miscalled a real.

Briefly, the Jaina answer to the problem of the nature of reality—the problem which has been so far dealt with in course of the four questions—is that everything is a manifold entity, or an identity-in-differents, with an imprint of individuality in it, and that the world is a vast society of such entities which act and react upon one another in their ceaseless process of causal transformations.

CHAPTER VII

Is relation an Entity, or a Mental Construction, or a Structural Manifestation of Identity-in-Difference in Reality ?

CHAPTER VII

RELATION

Connectedness is an indubitable experience of reality. Whether it is (a) an independent entity alongside the various things of the Universe, or (b) a mental construction imposed on a disjoined heap of reality of the human mind, or (c) something which is objective, without being an entity, and an experience, which is not merely subjective—is a question which is supremely important in any inquiry into the nature of reality and knowledge. Hence a brief study of relation, with the necessary reference to its implications, for instance, whether it is external or internal and valid or invalid, may be attempted here. The entire discussion will, to anticipate the conclusion, reveal that relation is the structure of reality which is identity-in-difference.

A. Relation as an Objective Independent Entity:

The Naiyāyika[1], the extreme[2] realist, advances the theory

---

1. 'The Naiyāyika' and 'the Vaiśeṣika' are largely interchangeable in course of this discussion, except for an important difference of opinion between them, viz., that the former treats *samavāya* as perceptual, whereas the latter treats it as inferential. See *infra*, p. 212 (f.), f.n. 5.
2. The predominant note of this 'extreme' realism is the emphasis on the full knowableness and independence not merely

that relation is a real[1] (*vāstava*) entity intervening between two terms or the relata (*sambandhinau*) as a *tertium quid* (*padārthāntara*[2]) or a distinct 'link' connecting them into a relational unity.

---

of the world from the knowing mind, but also of each part from the others in the objective and pluralistic universe. This spirit is signified by the postulate that there can be no objectless knowledge (*na cāviṣaye kācid upalabdhiḥ*/ *NBV*, p. 220) as well as that what is 'cognitively distinguishable' is 'different' (*pratītibhedāt bhedo'sti* / *NM*, p. 312).

1. For the reality (*vastutva*) of relation, see *ILE*, 2, f.n. 2, p. 131.
2. Each of the two kinds of relation, viz., *saṁyoga* and *samavāya* (to be presently explained) is termed as '*padārtha*' or category. *Saṁyoga* (the conjunctive relation or conjunction), however, is said to a be quality and, therefore, *dependent upon*, though distinct from, a substance (*dravya*) which is the most important of the seven categories, whereas *samavāya* (the 'necessary relation') is treated as an independent category.

   While characterising *samavāya* as a '*padārtha*' a distinction is advanced by the Naiyāyika, viz., that *samavāya* is a 'subsistent' (*bhāva*), but not an 'existent' (*sattā*). (*BPV*, p. 30, *kā*. 13, and *SWK*, p. 107).

   Hiriyanna refers to this 'distinction between subsistence and existence' as 'quite fundamental to' as well as 'quite in accordance with' 'the basic principles' of Vaiśeṣika philosophy. (*IPC*, p. 162, and p. 163, f.n. 1).

   Cf. "Suppose, for instance," observes Russell, "that I am in my room. I exist, my room exists, but does 'in' exist? Yet obviously the word has a meaning; it denotes a relation which holds between me and my room. This relation is something, although we cannot say that it exists IN THE SAME SENSE in which I and my room exist". (*Problems*, p. 90). A little further he continues "....we shall say that they (universals in which relations are included, cf. *ibid*., p. 97) SUBSIST or HAVE BEING, where 'being' is opposed to 'existence' as timeless. The world of Universals, therefore, may also be described as the world of being". (*Ibid*., p. 100).

A relation[1] is 'conjunctive'[2] (*saṁyoga-saṁbandha*) when the relata are 'separable'[3] (*yutasiddha*), and 'necessary'[4] or 'intimate' (*samavāya-sambandha*) when they are 'inseparable' (*ayutasiddha*)[5].

The strict non-admission of any internality[6] between even the 'inseparable' relata under *samavāya* is a character-

---

1. *dvividhaḥ sambandhaḥ saṁyogaḥ samavāyaśceti* / *TB*, Pt. I, p. 5.
2. For conjunction as a 'transient' connection and its threefold distinction, see *Mis. Es.*, Vol. II, p. 302, and *BP* with *SMV*, *kās.* 114-116.
3. The relata are 'separable' (*yuta*) in the sense that they were separate before being conjoined, e.g., the hand and the book (*hasta-pustaka-saṁyoga*); *aprāptayos tu yā praptiḥ saiva saṁyoga īritaḥ* / *BP*, *kā.* 114, and they can be again separated at our will. Conjunction is, therefore, a purely adventitious or external relation.
4. 'Necessary' or 'intimate' relation seems to be a more satisfactory translation of *samavāya* than 'inherence', although the latter is more widely current, for 'inherence' is suggestive of an internal character, whereas *samavāya* is, as indicated in the next paragraph, an external, though inseparable (*apṛthak-siddha*) relation.
5. *tatrāyutasiddhayoḥ sambandhaḥ samavāyaḥ* / *TB*, Pt. I, p. 5. Also see *SDA*, p. 278, *kā.* 66, and *TRD* thereon.

   For the meanings of '*ayutasiddha*' and '*yutasiddha*' as well as for the gradual widening of the scope of the meaning of '*ayutasiddha*' from its original and narrow application to the relation of the container and the contained (*ādhārādheyabhāva*) to a five-fold one, see *PDS*, with *NK*, pp. 35-36.
6. Internality should mean, according to some critics, identity (*ātmarūpa*) of the relation with the relata. This would mean that the relation would be a constitutive or 'intrinsic' element in the being of the relata. (Cf. Bradley : "But every relation, as we have learnt, essentially penetrates into the being of its terms, and, in this sense, is intrinsical; in other words, every relation must be a relation of content." *AR*, p. 347. Also cf. "We should then have to ask if, in the end, every possible relation does not involve a something IN

istically significant feature about the Nyāya conception of relation. This is, of course, in consonance with the realistic and pluralistic ontology of this system. The relata in *samavāya* remain, therefore, mutually external,[1] although they are held together in an 'extrinsic' unity by *samavāya*. This externality is believed to guard *samavāya* against the

---

which it exists, as well as between which it exists, and it might be difficult to reconcile the claims of these prepositions." *PL*, Vol. I, p. 28. Elsewhere we come across the following remark: "A term in the end (we have seen) can stand in no relation into which it, itself, cannot enter". *CE*, Vol. II, p. 645). Acceptance of this position would eventually result in the total obliteration of relation as a distinctive entity owing to the fact that what constitutes the nature (*svabhāva*) of the relata cannot exist as an independent entity intervening between the relata which are alleged to be combined by the relation. Kumārila gives a brief but clear statement of this argument:

atha tasyātmarūpatvān nānyasambandhakalpanā /
abhedāt samavāyo'stu svarūpaṁ dharmadharmiṇoḥ //

MSV, p. 180, *kā*. 149 f., also see *NV* thereon.

1. The description of *samavāya*, by an eminent writer, as an "internal relation" does not, therefore, accord with the spirit of the Nyāya view of reality. Contrasting *saṁyoga* with *samavāya*, he observes, "*Saṁyoga* takes place between two things of the same nature which exist disconnectedly and are for a time brought into conjunction. It is external relation while *samavāya* is an internal relation". *IP*, Vol. II, p. 217. Hiriyanna, however, puts forth the correct view: "Even *samavāya*, it is necessary to add, has to be explained as an external relation, although it is usual to represent it as internal in modern works on the Nyāya-Vaiśeṣika." *OIP*, p. 230. Again, "...in all cases alike, *samavāya* leaves the terms it relates unaffected. (See f.n. under "unaffected" for reference to a Vaiśeṣika maxim and Muktāvali). In other words, it is an external relation like *saṁyoga*. The very fact that it is independent and relates ultimately simple factors shows that it cannot be an internal one". *IPC* (1927), p. 162.

danger of its becoming an identity and, thereby, playing the Naiyāyika into the hands of the Advaitin. For if the Naiyāyika were to accept even a partial interpenetration of the terms and their relation, there would be no stopping short, at any rate according to the Vedāntin, of being driven to a total merging of the two, rendering, thereby, the relation itself a superfluous entity. This would put him on the high-road to absolutism in which not merely the duality of the terms in a relation but also the entire scheme of reality will become a seamless[1] coat. Athalye is, therefore, perfectly right, from the Naiyāyika's point of view, when he observes that "....it is the theory (of *samavāya*) that makes them (the Naiyāyikas) so intensely realistic in marked opposition to idealistic schools like Vedānta".[2]

The other important characteristics[3] of *samavāya* are that it is eternal[4] (*nitya*), one[5] (*eka*) and all-pervasive[6] (*sarvavyāpaka* or *vyāpaka*).

Thus[7] according to the Nyāya ontology a relation—whether conjunctive or necessary—is an objectively real and

---

1. "Relations exist only in and through a whole which cannot in the end be resolved into relations and terms. 'And', 'together' and 'between' are all in the end senseless apart from such a whole." Additional Notes, *PL*, Vol. I, p. 112. Notes : 50.
2. *TS*, with *DNB*, Notes, p. 9, f. 8.
3. These involve one another.
4. What is meant by 'eternality' here is uncausedness (*akāraṇatva*) or improducibility and, therefore, indestructibility: *na hyasya kiñcit kāraṇam pramāṇata upalabhyate iti*. *PB*, p. 697. This is intended to be aimed at avoiding the fallacy of infinite regress (*anavasthā*) inasmuch as what is produced needs a productive agent and the pro-

ductive agent in turn, a further productive agent and so on. See *U* in *VD*, p. 350, where Śaṅkara Miśra repudiates the views that *samavāya* is other-caused or self-caused and affirms it is uncaused. See also *TS*, Notes, p. 97, *SP*, Notes, p. 6, and *RML*, pp. 148-149. The relata are, of course, said to be produced and destroyed while the relation (*samavāya*) is intact.

5. *samavāyas-tveka eva*, *TS*, p. 6, sec. 8 and *SP*, p. 5 (text), *kā*. 9; *sarvatraikaḥ samavāya iti gamyate*, *PB*, p. 697; *na ca saṁyogavan nānātvam*, *ibid.*, p. 696; *PBTS*, with *KR*, p. 172.

The absolute oneness or sameness of *samavāya* inevitably raises the question how it can avoid an 'intermixture of the categories' (*padārtha-saṅkara*) which would lead, for instance, cowhood to reside in men instead of in cows. To this the Vaiśeṣika replies that the distinctness of the categories is sustained by the difference of the substrata and their attributes (*ādhārādheya-niyamāt*); *nanu yady ekaḥ samavāyo dravyaguṇakarmaṇāṁ dravyatvaguṇatvakarmatvādiviśeṣaṇaiḥ saha sambandhaikatvāt padārthasaṅkara-prasaṅga iti, na ādhārādheyaniyamāt* (*PB*, p. 697; see also *U* on *VD*, VII. 2. 26, and cf. *SM*, p. 32 (text), line 29, as well as the note on p. 81 (notes), lines 29-30), where reference is made to different media or *avacchedakas* of *samavāya*.

The unique character of *samavāya*, corresponding to the substantiality (*dravyatva*) of substance (*dravya*) or to the attributeness (*guṇatva*) of attribute (*guṇa*), etc., is the cognitive pattern "this subsists in that" (*ihedaṁ-pratyaya-* or *iheti-pratyaya-darśana*). This pattern or mark is said to be the invariable feature of *samavāya* and, therefore, to denote the unity (oneness) or the sameness of *samavāya* in the diverse situations of its occurrence. See *PB*, p. 696.

The other important considerations adduced in support of the oneness of *samavāya* are 'economy (*lāghava*) and lack of evidence to the contrary: *yathā dravyaṁ sat guṇaḥ sat karma sadityekākārapratītiviṣayatvāt nānātvasādhakapramāṇābhāvāt lāghavāc ca sattā ekā, tathā ghaṭaḥ samavetaḥ paṭaḥ samaveta ityādy-anugatapratītiviṣayatvāt bhedakapramāṇābhāvāt-lāghavāc ca samavāyopyeka evetyarthaḥ / V on U, VD*, p. 35, see also *SPS*, with *M*, p. 18, *kā*. 8.

6. *samavāyasyaikatvān-nityatvād vyāpakatvāc ca / SM*, p. 41. Cf. also *ibid.*, intro. p. xcii.

7. The three characteristics, and their implications, just referred to, together with the others, in behalf of *samavāya*,

distinct entity co-existing with, and connecting, the relata in a relational situation.

An entirely opposite view to that of the Naiyāyika is held by the Buddhist[1] who maintains, with the

---

as well as of relations in general, will all come in, as will be seen in the sequel, for sharp criticisms at the hands of the Jaina and the non-Jaina thinkers. The Jaina does go some way with the Naiyāyika in so far as he (the Jaina) concedes relation as an objective fact, though not as an independent entity.

1. Dharmakīrti—with the exception of Śāntarakṣita and his lucid commentator, Kamalaśīla, who have addressed themselves to an acute criticism of a part of the problem, viz., *Samavāya* (*vide TSS*, *kās.* 823-866, and *PK.* thereon)—is the only Buddhist thinker who has developed a critique on the problem of relations in his works (e. g., *PVD* with *VM*, pp. 370-374) particularly in *Sambandhaparīkṣa* (see *HML*, p. 319) from which 22 *kārikās* have been preserved, in Sanskrit, by Prabhācandra in *PKM* (p. 504 ff.). While criticising Dharmakīrti, Prabhācandra adds, here and there, a few short explanatory comments. A few of these *kārikās* are found in the brief polemical accounts of Vidyānandin (*TSV*, pp. 148-149), Vādidevasūri (*SRK*, pp. 812 ff.) and of Prabhācandra himself in his other work (*NKC*, Vol. I, pp. 305-309).

An account of the twenty-four kinds of relations (*paccāyas*), as expounded in the seventh and the last work of the Buddhist Pāli canon, Abhidhamma Piṭaka, has been given, in Pāli, in *The Patthanuddesa Dipanī* (The Buddhist Philosophy of Relations), by Ledi Sayadaw, E. T., by S. V. Nyana, pub. by U. Ba Thah and Da Tin Tin, 1935, Rangoon. An earlier account by the same writer (spelt differently as Ledi Sadaw), given in course of three "letters", E. T. by S. L. Aung, is published under the title *On the Philosophy of Relations, JPTS*, 1915-1916, Ed. by Mrs. Rhys Davids, 1916, London. Two other accounts of the same topic are:—*The Compendium of Philosophy* (Abhidhammattha-saṅgaha), Pt. VIII, E. T. by S. L. Aung, Ed. by Mrs. Rhys Davids, *PTS*, 1910, London; and the article on "Relations" (Buddhist), by G. A. F. Rhys Davids, *ERE.* All these accounts deal with the subject of relations mainly from

Advaitin[1], a subjective view of relations. According to Dharmakīrti a relation, like a universal, is a conceptual fiction[2], fabricated by the mind, having no objective reality (*na vāstavah*), the only reals being the unrelated (*niranvaya* or unmixed or *amiśra*)[3] or simple moments enjoying, severally, an isolated or exclusive existence (*svātmanisthitāh; svayambhāvāh; vyāvṛttarūpāh*). Being neither perceptual nor inferable —perception and inference are the only two sources

---

the ethico-theological point of view of the early Pāli Buddhism, and do not, therefore, concern themselves with the philosophical development which the problem acquired at the hands of the dialectical masters like Diṅnāga and Dharmakīrti. Owing to the absence of any direct philosophical bearing on the treatment of the problem in this study no reference is made to these accounts.

1. See *infra*, p. 223 ff.
2. *sambandhaḥ kalpanākṛtaḥ, sambandhacintā, PVD,* III. 237; *vikalpite kalpanānirmite sambandhe...., MV,* p. 371; *na vastuvyatirekeṇa sambandho....kalpanāmātratvāt, TSV,* pp. 148-149. Cf. this position with Hume's notion "that all our distinct perceptions are distinct existences, and that the mind never perceives any real connection among distinct existences" (quoted) *JPPSM*, Vol. II, p. 33.
3. *tān (bhāvān) miśrayati kalpanā*, spd. *kā*. 5, and Prabhācandra's comments thereon, *PKM*, p. 506, and *NKC*, p. 306; see also *SRK*, pp. 813-814. On the basis of this conceptualist nature of relations the Buddhist denies any relation between a verb (*kriyā*) and its agent (*kāraka*) as, for instance, between 'drive away that white cow' and 'Devadatta' in the statement "Devadatta, drive away that white cow with your stick" (*devadatta, gām abhyāja śuklām daṇḍena*). *Vide* spd. *kā*. 6, and Prabhācandra's comment preceding it, *PKM*, p. 506.
4. For a critical exposition of this argument, as applied to the causal relation, from the Buddhist point of view, see *PKM*, p. 511 ff.

There is, it is necessary to note, a cardinal difference of opinion, between the Naiyāyika and the Vaiśeṣika concerning

of knowledge according to Buddhism—relation is unreal (*avastu*). Pursuing his demonstration of the unreality of relation Dharmakīrti makes a searching analysis into the possible kinds and the anatomy of a relational situation and endeavours to show that the Naiyāyika's defence of the reality of a relation is entirely baseless.[1]

Assuming the opponent's viewpoint, Dharmakīrti argues that the only two[2] possible ways of entertaining a relation in general, are by treating it as (a) *Dependence* (*pāratantrya*) or rather, interdependence, and (b) *Interpenetration* (*rūpaśleṣa*) or interfusion, of the relata entering into the relation in question. If we grant the first alternative, then the question arises whether the 'dependence' is between two full-fledged existents (*niṣpannayoḥ*) or between existents which have not yet emerged into full being (*aniṣpannayoḥ*). If it is, on the one hand, between two full-fledged existents, then the

---

the means of cognising *samavāya*; the former considers that *samavāya* is apprehended by perception and the latter by inference—*pratyakṣaḥ samavāya iti naiyāyikā āhuḥ* / *NKB*, p. 961; *samavāyo'tīndriyaḥ anumeya eva iti vaiśeṣikā āhuḥ* / *Ibid.*, p. 962; *pratyakṣaḥ samavāya iti naiyāyikās tadapy anupapannaṁ samavāyo'tīndriyaḥ...VD,* p. 353, and also *UV* thereon. *Saṁyoga* also is maintained, by the Naiyāyika, to be apprehended by perception but by two senses only. *Vide TS,* p. 87 (Notes).

1. See the last line of *kā*. 1, quoted *infra*, p. 214, f.n. 2.

2. *sambhandho'rthānāṁ pāratantryalakṣaṇo vā syād rūpaśleṣalakṣaṇo vā syāt? PKM*, p. 104. See also p. 214, f.n. 2. The context in which the problem is treated is the question of the relatedness among the atoms in a so-called concrete object. The Buddhist assumes an object to be an aggregation (*saṅghāta*) of unrelated (*asambaddha*) atoms.

Buddhist would argue, there is no need for a relation since such absolutely independent existents need no relating entity for the simple reason that they are, by hypothesis, severally self-sufficient entities and, therefore, admit of no dependence whatsoever (*pāratantryābhāvāt*)[1]. Such an imposition of dependence on two independent entities would, in Buddhist view, result in introducing contradiction in an otherwise relationless situation. If, on the other hand, the dependence is argued to be between two entities which are yet to come into being (*aniṣpannayoh*), then it would be absurd to talk about relating two entities which are yet to be.[2]

The second hypothesis of the interpenetration or interfusion of the relata fares, according to Dharmakīrti, no better, since here also, as in the other case, the argument is beset with a contradiction : the interfusing relata should, on this

---

1. *pāratantryavihīnatvāt siddhasyetyapare viduḥ* / *TSV*, p. 146, *kā*. 10. Vidyānanda uses '*siddha*' and '*asiddha*' also for '*niṣpanna*' and '*aniṣpanna*' respectively.

2. *prathamapakṣe kim asau niṣpannayoḥ sambandhinoḥ syād aniṣpannayor vā? na tāvad aniṣpannayoḥ, svarūpasyaivāsattvāt śaśāśvaviṣāṇavat niṣpannayoś ca pāratantryābhāvād asambandha eva* /

   Having thus stated the Buddhist argument Prabhācandra corroborates with the following *kā*. from Dharmakīrti :

   pāratantryaṁ hi sambandhaḥ siddhe kā paratantratā /
   tasmāt sarvasya bhāvasya sambandho nāsti tattvataḥ //

   PKM, spd., p. 504, *kā*. 1. Also see *SKR*, p. 812.

   Vidyānanda refers to another possible view which is not so much a third as the combined view of the two stated above. This combined view is also repudiated by the Buddhist as being liable to the defects of both the views together (*pakṣadvayabhāvidoṣānuṣaṅgāt*). *Vide PVD*, and *MV* thereon, III. 236, and TSV, p. 146.

hypothesis, remain *two*[1] in the resultant relational situation despite their mutual merging, inasmuch as a relation presupposes two disparate relational entities.[2] But, it is contended, how can the merging take place if the merging relata are not fused or transformed into one indistinguishable whole or identity in the process? In other words, the interfusing relata should satisfy the incompatible requirements of retaining their duality (*dviṣṭatva*) even in their resultant integration (*śleṣa*) into a relational whole,[3] and of becoming a perfectly related whole, in which case there results an identity (*aikya*)—identity, because the two become one—which goes against the fundamental pre-requisite of all relations that they should have two discreet entities.[4]

The moment the possibility of the two relata becoming a single relatum (identity) is accepted—this acceptance would be insisted upon by the Buddhist logician in conformity to the logical necessity of the argument: this is the reason why the Naiyāyika cautiously maintains the extrinsic[5] character of even *samavāya*—the duality of the relational structure will then disappear and along with it, the need for a relation also owing to the absurdity of attempting to relate a single entity.[6]

---

1. A *sambandha* always presupposes two things : *dviṣṭatvāt tasya (sambandhasya)*. *PKM*, p. 505.
2. *sambandhinor abhāve sambhandhāyogāt* / *Ibid.*, and *NKC*, p. 305.
3. Retaining duality would run counter to the integrating character of the *rūpaśleṣa* relation : *sambandhinor dvitve rūpaśleṣavirodhāt*. *PKM*, p. 505. *Vide* also *NKC* and *SRK*, p. 305 and p. 812 respectively.
4. See above f. n.
5. See *supra*, p. 207, and f.n. 6 thereon.
6. *tayor aikye vā sutarāṁ sambandho'bhāvaḥ* / *PKM*, p. 505. *tayor aikye'pi na sambandhaḥ sambandhinor abhāve tasyāghaṭanāt* / *TSV* p. 147. See also *SRK*, p. 812.

Another argument which is mentioned, in passing, as meeting with the Buddhist objection is tendency to treat the notion of 'continuousness'[1], or *nairantarya*—which means absence of any gap or interval (*antarabhāvarūpam*)[2] between the two terms—as constituting the *rūpaśleṣa* relation. This idea of continuousness is summarily rejected by the Buddhist as a negative (*atāttvika*[3] or *tāttvikatvāyoga*[4]) one (because the absence of something is passed for a positive entity which, in his opinion, militates against the opponents' (Naiyāyika's) acceptance of *sambandha* as a positive entity.

Stretching the argument further, the Buddhist questions why his opponent should not accept "the presence of a gap" (*sāntaratā*)[5] or the lack of continuousness, as the *rūpaśleṣa* relation. This implies that *nairantarya* is as arbitrary as

---

1. *nairantaryaṁ tayo rūpaśleṣaḥ; na / PKM*, p. 505. See also *TSV*, p. 147, and *SRK*, p. 812. Also the next f. n.
2. Vidyānanda vividly renders it as *chidramadhyaviraha*. *TSV*, p. 148. This notion of gaplessness attributed to the Naiyāyika, seems to be intended to defend his position against a split which cuts asunder a related whole into two independent, and therefore, unrelated entities. This is viewed, of course from the Buddhist angle. The Buddhist, however, contends, and rightly so, according to what *rūpaśleṣa* ought to be, that the acceptance of gaplessness does not, as stated at the end of the paragraph, save the Naiyāyika from playing into the hands of the Advaitin and accepting an unqualified identity.
3. The editor gives the equivalent of '*atāttvika*' as '*abhāva*' (*tucchabhāvarūpatvād abhāvasya*). *PKM*, p. 505, f.n. 3.
4. Both Vidyānanda and Vādidevasūri use this phrase. *TSV*, p. 147, and *SRK*, p. 812.
5. *nirantaratāyāś ca sambandharūpatve sāntaratā'pi kathaṁ sambandho na syāt ? PKM*, p. 505. *anyathā sāntaratvasya sambandhaprasaṅgatvāt / TSV*, p. 148, and *NKC*, Vol. I, p. 305.

sāntaratā and, therefore, that there is no logical bar against accepting the one or the other as the *rūpaśleṣa* relation, although both are equally absurd. The Naiyāyika, however, cannot concede *sāntaratā* between the relata since even the utmost closeness (*sāntaratā*) would not save him from the charge of the Buddhist who demands, under *rūpaśleṣa,* nothing short of a 'total merger' or fusion of the relata entering into the relation. Nor does such closeness banish duality or the separateness of the relata in the composite whole resulting from such admission. Acceding to a 'total merger' would inevitably land him in the forbidden region of identity, to the delight of the Advaitin.

A further dissection into the implications of the *rūpaśleṣa* relation is attributed to the Buddhist dialectitian: If the relata are interfused, is the fusion, he asks, total (*sarvātmanā*) or partial (*ekadeśena*)? If it is total, he answers, then the fusing relata become a single mass of identity. An aggregation, or a plurality, of atoms (*āṇūnāṁ piṇḍaḥ*) becomes on this hypothesis, indistinguishable from, or identical with, just a single atom (*aṇumātraḥ*) and then, on this score, the question of relation does not at all arise in the case of a single entity. If, on the other hand, the interfusion (*śleṣa*) is partial (*ekadeśena*)—that is, if a part of a relatum comes into contact with another part of the other relatum—then the problem arises whether each of the related parts is identical with (*ātmabhūtaḥ*) or different from (*parabhūtaḥ*) each of the corresponding unrelated parts in the relational whole. It cannot be said, he adds, that the related and the unrelated parts, within a relation, are identical. If it is so, a part of the relatum becomes identical with the whole of it and, in such circumstances, describing the relation as *partial* would become absurd. This also gives rise to the error of rejecting two entities, given by hypothesis, in favour of one entity which does not admit of any relation. In order to escape this dilemma, if the opponent (the Naiyāyika) accedes to the idea of a split, or distinction of parts, in the relatum—this would be inevitable if the present principle of relation is accepted—then arises the consequence of disintegrating a unitary relatum into two parts, one of which is in relation and the other out of the relation, which is an absurd proposition. For, once the compartmentalising a relatum into the related and the unrelated parts is acquiesced in, the Buddhist will naturally compel the opponent to accept the inevitable fallacy of an infinite regress. This is because division of a relatum gives rise to two parts—the one related and the other unrelated—and, again, division of the related part, leaving out the other one, gives rise to similar two parts, and then again, a further division into further two parts, and thus goes on a progression of successive and unending divisions.[1]

In the light of the above arguments Dharmakīrti concludes that there can be no *rūpaśleṣa sambandha* between two distinct entities, and that all entities are, therefore,

1. The elaboration of these implications is based on the following passage of Prabhācandra who puts the argument as follows: *kiñca asan rūpaśleṣaḥ sarvātmanā ekadeśena vā syāt ? sarvātmanā rupaśleṣe aṇūnāṁ piṇḍaḥ aṇumātraḥ syāt / ekadeśena tac-chleṣe kim ekadeśas tasyātmabhūtaḥ, parabhūtaḥ vā ? ātmabhutaś cet, na ekadeśena rūpaśleṣas tadabhāvāt / parabhūtaś cet; tair apy aṇūnāṁ sarvātmanaikadeśena rūpaśleṣe sa eva paryanuyogo'-navasthā ca syāt / PKM*, p. 505; also *NKC*, Vol. I, p. 350.

discreet by nature, and, as such, do not admit of any relation whatsoever.'

Then Dharmakīrti proceeds to unravel two more rifts in the conception of relation as a real entity combining two terms, or relational factors, involved in it.

It is impossible to conceive a relation without the relata it combines. It is, therefore, appropriate to consider relation, he pleads on behalf of his opponent, as involving, or forming the basis (*āśraya*) of, the duality (*dviṣṭatva*) of its terms. In other words relation cannot be conceived of as a distinct entity without its attribute (*dharma*) of the terms contained in it. When this is conceded Dharmakīrti probes into the implications of this view and tries to show an inconsistency. In view of the fact that relation is admitted as an objectively real and independent entity (*sat*) it ought to be, on the strength of this admission, a self-sufficient entity; that is to say, it should not have any lack[2] or 'expectancy' (*apekṣā*) for 'anything else' (*para*; the reason is described as *sarvanirāśaṁsatvāt*). If it shows any kind of 'lack' or 'expectancy', then it forfeits its claim for its very existence (*anyathā sattvavirodhāt*) owing to the fact that nothing can, according to the opponent, exist without the condition necessary for its existence—here the condition for its existence are its relata—being fulfilled. Therefore, if relation is to be considered an absolute entity it should not, the Buddhist

1. *rūpaśleṣo hi sambandho dvitve sa ca kathaṁ bhavet/
tasmāt prakṛtibhinnānāṁ sambandho nāsti tattvataḥ" //*
PKM, spd., p. 505, *kā*. 2.

2. The 'lack' here refers to the existence of relation being conditional upon the existence of the relata.

maintains, require the necessity of the relata in it and, consequently, should exist in its own right. An analysis of its requirements, however, exhibits the serious lack of dependence upon its relata for its existence. It cannot therefore exist, Dharmakīrti affirms, as a full-fledged and independent real (*tan na parāpekṣā nāma yadrūpaḥ sambandhah siddhyet*[1]).

When the truth of Dharmakīrti's contention in the above argument is recognised, the falsity of the converse of the argument could also be easily perceived : a non-existent relation cannot, as it has been just observed, exhibit any 'expectancy' for the necessity of the relata inasmuch as the relata will not, then, have any basis[2] for their subsistence (*apekṣādharmāśraya-virodhāt*[3]).

Lastly, Dharmakīrti scathingly brings out a major inconsistency which, from the Idealist point of view, is destructive of the opponent's strength in upholding the reality of relation. Relation is acknowledged, as it has been repeatedly pointed out, by the Naiyāyika to be a distinct entity besides the relata in a relational situation. This provokes the Buddhist dialectician to the presentation of a new dilemma inherent in the relationship between the consti-

---

1. *PKM*, p. 505.
2. *Ibid.*
3. The purport of this argument is contained in the following *kā.* of Dharmakīrti :—

   parāpekṣā hi sambandhaḥ so'san katham apekṣate/
   saṁs ca sarvanirāśaṁso bhāvaḥ katham apekṣate//

   PKM, spd., p. 505, *kā.* 3. See also *NKC*, Vol. I, p. 306, *SRK*, p. 813, and *TSV*, p. 148.

tuent elements of the situation, viz., the relation itself (*sambandha*) and its relata (*sambandhinau*). Is the relation, it is questioned, identical with (*abhinnah; anarthāntaram*) the relata, or different from (*bhinnaḥ; arthāntaram*) them ? If it is argued to be identical with them, then comes the Buddhist retort that there will either be the relata only (*sambandhināveva, na sambandhaḥ*[1]) or the relation only (*sa eva vā na tāviti*[2]), not the two together. If, on the contrary, the other position is advanced, viz., that the relation is different from the relata, then it would be asked, how could the relata which are absolutely (*kevalau*) independent of the relation be related by it at all ?[3] No two things, which lack some kind of mutual affinity can be related.

Further, granting the opponent's supposition that a relation is a distinctive entity alongside the relata (*sambandho'rthāntaram*) the Buddhist objects how the two relata could be related by one relation[4] at all ? Positing another relation in order to relate each relatum to the relation in question, would raise the difficulty of endlessly positing an increasing multiplicity of such relations landing the Naiyāyika in an in-

---

1. *PKM*, p. 505. Vidyānanda comments : ***Yady anarthāntaram tadā sambandhināveva prasajyete / tathā ca na sambandho nāma / TSV***, p. 148; also see *SRK*, p. 813.
2. *PKM*, p. 505.
3. ***sa (sambandhaḥ) tato'rthāntaraṁ cet sambandhinau kevalau kathaṁ sambaddhau syātām / TSV***, p. 148. See also *SRK*, p. 813. For a reference to Śaṅkara's view in this matter, ***vide*** p. 222, f.n. 1.
4. ***tenaikena sambandhena saha dvayoḥ sambandhinoḥ kaḥ sambandhaḥ ? PKM***, p. 505.

escapable *regressus ad infinitum* (*anavasthā*)[1]. In consequence of this 'absurd' (*atiprasaṅga*) hypothesis, and the other similar difficulties[2], the most important of which have been so far considered, Dharmakīrti finally, and categorically, rules out the notion of relation as an independent entity as a false one (*na vāstavī*)[3].

Śaṅkara and his follower[4] are at one with Dharmakīrti

---

1. *sambandāntarābhyupagame cānavasthā syāt tatrāpi sambandhāntarānuṣaṅgāt*/ *Ibid.*, p. 505-506; see also *SRK*, p. 813. *pareṇaikena sambandhād iti cet tenāpi na sambandhaḥ* / *TSV* p. 148.

   The consequence of *regressus ad infinitum*, as a result of recognizing two absolutely distinct relata, is clearly argued out by Śaṅkara. *Vide BBSB*, II. 2. 13. For the Jaina answer to this charge, see *infra*, p. 232 (ff.), f.n. 2.

2. Another criticism which Dharmakīrti brings in, is the stock Buddhist argument that a relation or the relata should, like everything real, satisfy the requirement of serviceability or usefulness (*arthakriyākāritva* or *upakāritva*). Referring to *samavāya*, in a similar context, he observes:

   nityasyānupakāritvād akurvāṇas ca nāṣrayaḥ /. *PVD*, III. 231 See also *PKM*., spd., p. 510, *kā*. 21.

   Prabhācandra meets this criticism, from the Jaina point of view, by carrying the fight into the enemy's camp. See *infra*, pp. 226-7.

3. *tan na sambandhinoḥ sambandhabuddhir vāstavī*..../ *PKM*, p. 506. Dharmakīrti expresses the purport of this argument in the following *kā*.:

   dvayor ekābhisambandhāt sambandho yadi tad dvayoḥ /
   kaḥ sambandho'navasthā ca na sambandhamatis tathā //
   PKM, spd., p. 506, *kā*. 4.

4. See, for instance, "The Refutation of Relation" (*sambandhakhaṇḍanam*) by Śrī Harṣa, *KKS*, pp. 1090-1099.

   Here, Śrī Harṣa's treatment of the problem is mainly concerned with the refutation of the relation of the 'container' (*ādhāra*) and the 'contained' as well as of *samavāya*, and does not make any significant novel contribution to the content of the subject.

in their denial of relation as an objective and independent entity intervening between the relational terms. It is needless to go into the elaborate subtleties—some of which have already been anticipated in substance, if not in letter, by Dharmakīrti—of the critique that both Śaṅkara, his commentators and others following him, have launched out on this subject. Just one or two[1] important features which indicate the Vedāntic attitude towards the problem may, however, be referred to here:

The Vedāntic view of reality is fundamentally based on the postulate that the effect is nothing other than 'a specific state-of-existence (*saṁsthānamātram*) of the cause itself'.[2] This doctrine has already been found to render the acceptance of any genuine or ultimate duality of any kind unreal and therefore illogical. But duality is, as has been frequently

---

1. For further criticisms see *BBSB* (text), II. 2. 3, *IP*, Vol. II, pp. 218-219.
2. *na hi kārya-kāraṇayor bheda āśritāśrayabhāvo vā vedāntavādibhir abhyupagamyate, kāraṇasya iva saṁsthānamātram kāryam ity abhyupagamāt* / *BBSB* (text), II. 2. 17, p. 62. See also *BBSB*, II. 1. 16, pp. 25-26 and *PHo* (E.T.); *upapattyanubhavābhyāṁ na kāryasya kāraṇād-anyatvam* / Bhāmati, *BSB*, p. 521.

   It is necessary to note, in this connection, that the Sāṅkhya also takes the same view of non-difference between the cause and the effect, or rather, that the effect already pre-exists in the cause. See *SKIS*, *kā*. 9. This evidently leads to the rejection of relation—particularly *samavāya*—in the Nyāya sense of the term, viz., that there should be two genuinely different entities for a relation (a third entity) to relate. Consequent upon the rejection of *samavāya* the Sāṅkhya comes somewhat nearer the Jaina on the particular point of viewing "the nature of object in question" as serving the purpose of the *samavāya* relation : "The category of inherence, *Samavāya*....is rejected in favour of the simpler view that what it means is really to be expressed by the nature of the object in question." *SSKH*, p. 105.

observed in course of this section, and, as confirmed by Śaṅkara[1] himself, the *sine qua non* of a relation. The incompatibility between the absolutistic or the monistic dogma and the dualistic requirement of relation leads the Vedāntin altogether to deny relation either of *saṁyoga* or of *samavāya*, and, to accept the principle that there can be nothing like a relation apart from the object supposed to be joined by it.[2]

In answer to the opponent's assertion that *saṁyoga* and *samavāya* are also 'subsistent' owing to the fact that we find, in experience, distinct designations or terms denoting their being (*śabdapratyayadarśanāt*),[3] Śaṅkara observes that even where there is only one object there may be many designations referring to it in accordance with its myriad 'intrinsic' (*svarūpa*) and 'extrinsic' (*bāhya*) predications. One and the same Devadatta, for instance, may be, Śaṅkara adds, the object of the epithets 'a man', 'a Brāhmaṇa', 'learned-in-Veda', 'affable', 'a boy', 'a youth', 'an old man', 'a father' and 'a son' etc.[4] Therefore the objects themselves (*sambandhināveva*) can be fittingly termed by the epithets '*saṁyoga*' and '*samavāya*' and, there need be no third entity

---

1. *dvayāyattatvāt sambandhasya* / *BBSB*(text), II. 2.19, p. 61.
2. *nāpi saṁyogasya samavāyasya vā sambandhasya sambandhivyatirekeṇāstitve kiñcit pramāṇam asti* / *Ibid.*
3. *Ibid.* See the next f.n. *infra*.
4. *sambandhiśabdapratyayavyatirekeṇa saṁyogasamavāyaśabdapratyayadarśanāt tayor astitvam iti cet* / *na* / *ekatve'pi svarūpabāhyarūpāpekṣayānekaśabdapratyayadarśanāt* / *yathaiko'pi san devadatto loke svarūpaṁ sambandhirūpam cāpekṣyānekaśabdapra.yayabhāg bhavati manuṣyo brahmaṇaḥ śrotriyo vadānyo bālo yuvā sthaviraḥ pitā putraḥ pautro bhrātā jāmāteti...* / *Ibid.*, p. 61f.

(*vyatiriktavastu*) existing apart from them (the objects).[1] In other words Śaṅkara's view of relation is that it has no existence apart from the objects which may be called the relata, by courtesy—and its use signifies neither a mechanical nor an inseparable connection among them but just a synonym for the objects themselves.

This negative attitude of Śaṅkara towards the problem of relation is essentially the same as that of Dharmakīrti except for the fact that the latter has brought a more acute and thorough dialectical analysis to bear upon the problem.

The Jaina View

In keeping with his reconciliatory metaphysical standpoint the Jaina offers a *via media* between the extreme externalism of the Naiyāyika and the equally extreme illusionism or idealism of the Buddhist and the Vedānta schools. An attempt is made here to state the Jaina view of relation, first, in relation to the Buddhistic and the Vedāntic approach, and then, to the Nyāya approach, to the problem.

The Jaina postulates the reality or the factuality of relation as a deliverance of the direct and objective experience. He, therefore, posits relation not merely as inferable[2], but

---

1. *tathā sambandhinor eva sambandhiśabdapratyayavyatirekeṇa saṁyoga-samavāyaśabdapratyayārhatvam, na vyatiriktavastvastitvena / Ibid.* p. 62.
2. *atas tad(sambandhaḥ)anyathānupapatteś cāsau siddhaḥ.* PKM p. 514.

also as an indubitably perceptual[1] fact. He does so in opposition to what he considers as the aprioristic dialectic of Buddhism, and by implication, of the Vedānta also, wherein the mind imposes its own forms upon, instead of obeying the dictates of the events of the objective realm. This is the spirit underlying Prabhācandra's contention that the Buddhist seriously errs, not merely by ignoring what is directly perceivable, viz., the relational element, but also in describing it as a conceptual fiction (*kalpanā*) which is anything but perceptible.[2] This does violence to a 'brute' fact of perceptual validity. If the Buddhist denial of the perceptual validity of relation is right, then, linen and its yarn, or the linen and its colour etc., ought to be seen as separate entities; but Prabhācandra rightly asserts that they are always perceived together. This constant togetherness is not conceived to be possible without the actual connecting factor of a relation.

One of the grounds on which the Buddhist bases the inadmissibility of relation is the lack of serviceability or practical utility[3] (*upakāritva, arthakriyākāritva*) attributed to relation. Prabhācandra effectively turns the table on the Buddhist by applying this test to the Buddhist conception of objects in general, and thereby shows how the relational element is a constituent factor in the make-up of the objects. If the atoms, for instance, are absolutely exclusive or discreet

---

1. *sambandhasyādhyakṣeṇaivārthānāṁ pratibhāsanāt/ Ibid.*
2. *kathaṁ ca sambandhe pratīyamāne pratīyamānaṣyāpyasambandhasya kalpanā pratītivirodhāt ? Ibid.*
3. See *supra*, p. 222, f.n. 2.

entities, as the Buddhist maintains, then Prabhācandra asks, atom A is unconnected with atom B, and atom B with atom C, and atom C in turn with atom D and so on in any concrete object, say, a pitcher. Being a conglomeration of such unconnected units or atoms, it ought not to be a 'pitcher' at all useful for fetching or holding water in. Similarly when a tender bamboo is pulled with a string tied to it, it ought not, on the Buddhist theory, to bend as it does. Such phenomena are inexplicable unless the atoms composing the objects are admitted to be cohesive, that is, capable of being connected or combined to become concrete and useful objects. The Buddhist cannot deny the occurrence of such phenomena and such undeniability amounts, according to the Jaina philosopher, to a covert admission of a relational factor in the texture of objective experience.

Alluding to Dharmakīrti's objection[1] to *pāratantrya-sambandha*, one of the only two possible kinds of relations conceded—conceded, of course, only for disproving, since no relation is accepted to be intrinsically valid—by the Buddhist logician, Prabhācandra remarks that far from being untrue it (*pāratantrya-sambandha*) is a matter of common knowledge (*pratītitaḥ suprasiddhatvāt*). However, Prabhācandra accepts its reality with the qualification that the essential nature of *pāratantrya* is unification of the relata (*ekatva-pariṇatilakṣaṇapāratantryasyārthānām*),[2] not mere 'dependence' as described by the Buddhist. In the eventual negation of the dependence-relation by the Buddhist, Prabhacāndra

---

1. See *supra*, pp. 213–214.
2. See *PKM*, p. 514.

sees the repetition of the error just referred to in the instances of the pitcher and the bamboo, viz., the impossibility of denying it without implying a tacit acceptance of its reality. Because the negation of pervasiveness with reference to the relata is itself an attempt to invest the relata with a relational trait. In other words, attributing a lack of dependence or pervasiveness to the relata amounts to positing a relation between the relata. No negation is, as a Western[1] idealist would say, absolute; it generally implies an affirmation of something. An attempt to deny the very thing which is, in some form (*kvacit*) accepted, is, according to Prabhācandra, a form of contradiction.

The consequence which is supposed, as already indicated, to result from accepting the *pāratantṛya-sambandha*, viz., the non-necessity for a relation between any two either 'full-fledged' or 'wholly finished' (*niṣpannayoḥ*) or 'not-yet-emerged' (*aniṣpannayoḥ*), entities is also resolved by Prabhācandra by his explanation that both alternatives are the two aspects of a single total situation which is identity of differents. A piece of linen, for instance, even prior to its coming into existence as a fabric, that is, when it is still *aniṣpanna*, exists (*paṭapariṇāmotpatteḥ prāg api sattvāt*) in the form of yarn which is already *niṣpanna* (*tantudravyatayā niṣpanna eva*). Or, conversely, the yarn as the material cause, or substance, is concurrently existent, as itself (*svarūpeṇa*), with the yarn as linen which is yet

1. "The bare form of negation is not adequate to fact; it contains mere emptiness or ignorance; we nowhere come upon a mere 'not-something'..every affirmative denies and every negative affirms." *EIB*, p. 134.

aniṣpanna, or non-existent, as its effect or modification.[1] In other words, the yarn, as the *dravya,* is the element of identity and the linen, as its *pariṇāma,* is the element of difference, both together constituting the relational situation. Here, as everywhere else, identity as the substantial element is the 'continuant' (or the continuing principle, *anvayī* or *dravya*) existing in the yarn as well as in the linen, but difference, as the modified form of the substance, is yet distinguishable—in the sense that linen is not quite the same as the yarn—from identity. Therefore, generically, the Jaina view of relation is that it is an identity of differents or different terms.

As regards Dharmakīrti's contention that the *rūpa-śleṣa-sambandha,* or the relation of interpenetration, the second possible relation, could have only two modes, viz., total (*sarvātmanā*) interfusion or partial (*ekadeśena*) interfusion, and that both are untenable for the reasons already adduced[2], Prabhācandra maintains that Dharmakīrti's analysis is both wrong and inexhaustive. It is wrong to say that we encounter any paradoxical[3] situation here, for relation could often be one of total merging, and at other times, of partial contact depending upon the nature of the relata involved. There is, for instance, a wholesale merging, or mutual permeation[4] between the

---

1. *tantudrayam api svarūpeṇa niṣpannaṁ paṭapariṇāmarūpatayā-niṣpannam* / *PKM,* p. 515.
2. See *infra,* p. 217 ff.
3. *Ibid.*
4. Prabhācandra describes this process as follows: *kvaccit tu nikhilapradeśānām anyonyapradeśānupraveśataḥ—yathā saktu-toyādīnām...PKM,* p. 515. It is, however, necessary to note here that in spite of such 'wholesale' permeation the relata retain their distinctness, and never become a single relatum. It is

meal[1] (*saktu*) and water (*toya*) blended with it, whereas there is only a partial contact[2] between the hand and the table when the palm of the hand comes into contact with the surface of

---

interesting to compare the Buddhist notion of 'merging' in which the relata are 'lost', and the Jaina notion in which the relata are 'distinct', with the distinctions made by Parker and William James: Parker distinguishes 'two types of unity'. "In one case", he observes, "the related elements interpenetrate and are lost; in another case, they remain distinct from one another" (*The Theory of Relations, SNdeW*, p. 272). Similarly, James also refers to a "partial conflux" or "a concatenated union" and contrasts it with a "total conflux" or a "through-and-through type of union". *The Thing and Its Relations, JPPSM*, Vol. II, p. 35.

1. The meal obtained from grinding fried corns.
2. In the case of a 'partial contact', that is, when the palm is in contact with the surface of the table, the Jaina does not posit that the contact is between the whole hand and the entire table. He admits that only a part of the hand is in contact with a part of the table. This admission of *parts* might immediately put the Buddhist on the offensive and provoke from him the retort how such admission of parts in or the divisibility of, the objects can accord with the Jaina notion of impartite, or indivisible, atoms. *nanv evam* (that is, *sāṁśatvavastuprakāreṇa*) *paramāṇūnām apy aṁśatvaprasaṅgaḥ syāt? PKM*, p. 515. The words in the round brackets are from the editor's note in f.n. 15, *ibid.* The whole passage, opening with this statement, is quoted later in this f.n. See next page.

   In this connection Prabhācandra offers a brief, suggestive and 'irrefragable' (*anuttaram*) answer on which McTaggart's remarks, also made in connection with relations, seem to make an unconscious *vārtika*. (The relevant remarks from both the authors are quoted, in appropriate places, in course of this note). Although his answer appears to be ingenious, it vividly brings out the spirit of manifoldness pervading the *Anekānta* philosophy : 'Parts' which mean divisions into which an atom is said to be divisible, do not, according to Prabhācandra, refer to the possibility of physically dividing an atom which is located in a particular spatial point, and, is really impartite, in the physical sense. They refer, it is suggested, to an infinite diversity, or to the fact of the infinitely manifold relatedness of an atom to the other atoms similarly located. The Jaina does not believe in the existence of absolutely simple entities. A real, say even an atom, is not a lonely being but a star in a constellation of similar entities, which assume, in their multitudinous groupings, various patterns and magnitudes which are determined by the laws of their internal compulsions and external pressure, and bear, accordingly, an infinity of relations, internal and external, total and partial, immediate and mediate, to the other phenomena in the universe. A real is, indeed, an independent existent but it is also a complex focus or network of relational forces. It is as it were a knot into which the strands of such forces are woven. The fact of the star or the knot being tethered to a point or a stretch of space, need not condemn it to a bare unrelated existence. The idea of the universe as a realm of interacting and interlocked elements of reality will be touched upon elsewhere (ch. IX.).

The aim of this note is somewhat to enlarge upon the implications of Prabhācandra's important distinction between the two meanings of "having parts" (*aṁśatva*) or divisibility, viz., (a) physical partition, and (b) infinite diversity or manifoldness of nature (*anantadharmātmakatva*) exhibiting a varied relational structure. He agrees with his Buddhist opponent on the impartiteness of the ultimate units or atoms of nature, but he also puts forward the other meaning which brings out the vital aspect of its manifold nature. As a matter of fact, he even suggests that such divisibility or manifoldness is possible because of the impartiteness of the units of nature. No fixed character can, after all, attach to a floating phantom or tyrannically isolated units of 'windowless monads'.

> *nanv evaṁ paramāṇūnām apy aṁśatvaprasaṅgaḥ syād ity apy anuttaram; yato'trāṁśa-śabdaḥ svabhāvārthaḥ, avayavārtho vā syāt? yadi svabhāvārthaḥ, na kaścid doṣas teṣāṁ vibhinnadigvibhāgavyavasthitānekāṇubhiḥ sambandhānyathānupapattyā tāvad vā svabhāvabhedopapatteḥ / avayavārthas tu tatrāsau nopapadyate/ teṣām abhedyatvenāvayavasambhavāt/ na caivaṁ teṣām avibhāgitvam virudhyate / yato'vibhāgitvaṁ bhedayitum aśakyatvam, na punar niḥsvābhavatvam /* (*PKM*, p. 515).

the table. In the infinitely variegated (*citra*) nature of things the one, or the other, or even both, might occur at a time and any kind of rigid legislation as to their occurrence could be motivated only by an artificial logic which does not take full cognizance of the plenitude and variety of the things in nature.

There are two very important considerations to be noticed in this connection. In the first place, however closely the

---

"We have come to the conclusion then, that no simple substance can exist, and that every substance that exists is divided into parts, which again have other parts, and so on, to infinity......If we are compelled to add to this, the further conclusion that no substance can, without contradiction, be divided into parts of parts to infinity, we could not escape from contradiction any way. If, on the other hand, we should find that infinite series of parts of parts would involve a contradiction unless the substances had a certain nature, we should be certain that all substances had that nature, since under no conditions could they have the infinite series of sets of parts which they do have. *NEMc*, Vol. I, p. 192.

Incidentally, the charge of *regressus ad infinitum* (*anavasthā*) directed by the Buddhist against the Realist (see *supra*, p. 222 and also f.n. 1 thereon) as resulting from an attempt to relate two 'absolutely distinct' entities, is suggestively answered by Prabhācandra, and his answer is borne out by McTaggart (*NEMc*, Vol. I, p. 142 ff.). The Buddhist would, indeed, be right if the relata are 'absolutely different' (*atyantabhede*) from each other. But, owing to the fact that they are, according to Prabhācandra, of the nature of identity and difference—which is entirely different from either view when each of them is taken singly and totally (*anekāntavastuno nātyantabhedābhedaṁ jātyantaratvāt / PKM*, p. 515)—the relation obtaining between is a unique synthesis partaking of both the elements which enter it. This consideration, combined with the fact that the relatedness of the relata is not something *ab extra* but is grounded in the very nature of the relata, sets at nought the accusation of the vicious infinite against the Jaina view. Cf. *PKM*, p. 515, and *NEMc*, Vol. I, ch. xxiii.

relata permeate each other, they do not lose their individuality. If they do, they cease to be as such. Here we see that the Jaina does accept a kind of internal relation but he does so in the same degree as he accepts internal change in the objects, and also consistently with the external changes happening to them. The change happening when a wooden stick is burnt to ashes is internal as compared with the conjunctional or external change occurring when a few such sticks are tied in a bundle. In adopting this attitude the Jaina avoids the two extremes of the Naiyāyika externalist with whom an effect makes a complete break with the cause (*ārambhavāda*), and, even *samavāya* is a mere external relation, and, of the Vedāntin with whom the cause alone is, and the effect is not, and, therefore, a relation, if any, can operate within the being of an identical entity.[1] That relation is an objective fact—not an objective entity—grounded in the relata themselves, and that it is internal or external in accordance with the relative proportions of the intimacy or distinctness of the relata concerned in a particular situation are the important consequences resulting from the attitude the Jaina has adopted toward the problem of relations.

The other consideration relates to the notion of 'uniqueness' (*jātyantararūpatva*) attaching to a relation : The Jaina looks upon the relation resulting from a combination of the relata in it as something unique (*jātyantara*), or *sui generis*, in comparison with the combining relata. That is, the resultant product emerging from the effectuation of the

1. As a matter of fact, a relation can never be substained on a strict absolute hypothesis.

relation is something novel and peculiar although it necessarily accommodates the respective natures of the combining relata. Necessity and novelty[1], to express the same in the idiom of western logic, are, therefore, the characteristics of the resultant relation. The uniqueness of relation is the element of novelty—not by any means a novel entity but a character or a trait—emerging from the relational transformation in which the natures of the relata are not totally annihilated but become overlaid with, as it were, a new informing trait. This idea is elucidated by the beautifully suggestive analogy of painting. A painted picture is indeed a product of a variety of paints and patterns, but yet it is not equivalent to a mechanical sum-

---

1. Necessity refers to the constituent factors, or the terms already existing, and novelty to the emergent feature attendant upon the fruition of a relation. The *satkāryavāda* of the Sāṅkhya system may, in spite of its evolutionary character, be said to exemplify the element of necessity inasmuch as the entire world-process derives, though gradually, from *prakṛti,* under the influence of *puruṣa.* Nothing new is created at any stage, since the history of the entire reality is an alternation of evolution and involution. The Nyāya-Vaiśeṣika seems, *prima facie,* to be what might be described as novelistic, in contrast to the necessitarian view of *satkāryavāda.* It is described as *ārambhavāda,* owing to the fact that the effect of a cause appears to be totally novel in comparison with its cause. But a closer examination shows that it is almost as necessitarian as the other; because it is more appropriate to describe the effect as merely different, not novel, from its cause. In the case of two different things, the question of novelty does not arise. Novelty is cognised to be so only against a background of necessity or permanence and when both form the ingredients of a single total situation. The notion of '*jātyantararūpatva*' seems to fit in appropriately only with the view of identity-in-difference.

mation of the paints and patterns. It is a unity and, at that, a novel unity, resulting from, and existing concurrently with, the paints and designs in a certain order. Similarly a relation is a unique combination of the constituent relata.

The Jaina is at one with the Nyāya-Vaiśeṣika in entertaining relation as a part of the real and objective world. There are, however, two points of significant difference which call for a brief reference although they have been anticipated at several places in course of this account. The first concerns the question of an independent existence of relation as a distinct entity, and, the second, of *samavāya-sambandha* (necessary relation).

The Jaina attitude to the first question is that relation is something which is integral to the terms but not something which is an absolutely independent entity. This does not at all mean that it is subjective or mental as the Buddhist means. It is indeed an objective fact serving as a link as it were between the terms of relation. The 'link' need not necessarily mean an independent existent. What is objective need not be an absolute or separate entity somehow penetrating into the being of the terms from without : A relation refers to the capacity of the terms for an 'intrinsic' or 'extrinsic' determination between themselves by virtue of the relational power seated in them. In spite of the diversities in the relatedness, between the terms, ranging from the most intimate or inseparable, to the most mechanical, or separable, kind, all relations are specific embodiments of identity-in-difference. This approach to relation as identity-in-difference containing, within itself, the power of bringing into connection the variegated contents of reality is sure to bring upon itself not merely the reproach of the idealists (the Buddhist and the Vedāntin whose views have already been examined) but also of the extreme realists, viz., the Naiyāyika to whom any reference to internality is disagreeable. The reproach from both sides would be that the Jaina holds a contradictory view owing to the incompatibility of identity and difference, or of internality and externality.

But once the manifold nature of things is granted, it is easy to understand that the Jaina position is inevitable. As Russell clearly points out a consistent monist finds relation needless for the obvious reason that there should be, for a relation, at least two entities which are irreducible to each other. But this is, *ex hypothesi*, impossible. Relationing is equally impossible with a consistent pluralist who subscribes to an unrelated series of momentary entities. Hence the Buddhist and the Vedāntin have repudiated, rightly from their respective points of view, relation as a part of reality. The Nyāya-Vaiśeṣika also admits relation as third entity but unless he accepts it as being, in some degree, grounded in the relata, it is impossible for him to avoid infinite regress. There cannot be a genuine relational 'transaction' between externally conjoined relata. Hence the theory of identity of differents seems to be the only possible hypothesis on which any genuine element of relation can work.

The most surprising fact about the development of the Nyāya philosophy is that it compromises, at the hands of the neo-Naiyāyikas, some of its fundamentals and arrives at a position which, if developed to its logical conclusion, will approach the Jaina viewpoint.[1] This fact becomes particularly evident in the case of *samāvaya* which, as will be presently seen, is given up all but in name.[2] The admission of *svabhāvasambandha*[3] or *svarūpasambandha*[4], the 'natural' or the 'simple' relation, offers the thin end of the wedge in dispensing with relation as a tertiary entity in a relational situation. This notion of *svarūpasambandha* connotes that the terms themselves contain, within their nature, the relational trait which is as objectively real[5] as

---

1. Cf. *JPN*, p. 232.
2. *saṁjñāmātreṇa, na vastutathābhāvaḥ* / *STP*, p. 704.
3. Cf. Śrī Harṣa's observation that the Naiyāyika regards the 'nature' of things also as their 'determinant' : *svabhāvasyāpi bhavatā niyamakatvāṅgīkārāt* / *KKS*, p. 1091. Chatterjee writes: "Unlike the relations of conjunction and inherence *Svarūpasambandha* is not distinct from the terms related by it. Rather, the relation is itself constituted by one of the relata....the relation is constituted by the object, or is due to the nature of the object." *NTN*, p. 188.

   The distinction, in the Nyāya philosophy, between relation as a 'third unity' (an independent entity) and relation 'without a third relating unity' as Stcherbatsky renders it expresses the difference between 'separable conjunction' (*saṁyoga*) and 'inseparable conjunction' (*samavāya*) on the one hand, and 'the simple relation' (*svabhāvasambandha*) on the other. The former is found with the reality of the 'link' (*anubhūyamāna sambandha*, or *vigrahavān sambandha*) and the latter 'without the reality of the link' but yet objective. Cf. *Log.*, Vol. II, f.n. 3, p. 287.
4. Cf. *JPN*, p. 232, and *RML*, pp. 153–154. Regarding the directness of the temporal and spatial relation, Ingalls writes : "Everything resides directly in time by a temporal relation. Time thus acts like space (*dik*) in that it is a substratum, for all entities." *NNLI*, p. 78.
5. Just because relatedness is 'resident' in the relata, the ideal-

the terms themselves. Its application is unfortunately restricted to the cases of *viṣayaviṣayībhāva* (the subject-object relation) and *viśeṣaṇaviśeṣyabhāva* (the substance-attribute relation, such as (a) the absent jar and 'the empty space' (*bhāvābhāvayoḥ*) and (b) (i) the spatial relations

---

ist objection that relatedness disappears, or becomes, under the circumstances, merely a 'way of looking at things' (conceptualistic), is not endorsed by the Naiyāyika (in this respect the Jaina is with the Naiyāyika). The Naiyāyika never accepts the position of non-relatedness of even the 'natural property' (*svabhāvadharma*) of things : cf. "We have to accept it (*svarūpa*) as a relation because without some relation we cannot explain our sense of one thing being resident in another." *RML*, p. 153.

It is a significant fact that *svarūpasambandha* is attributed, by the Naiyāyika, even to *samavāya*, although it is normally distinguished from the latter, and definitely from *saṁyoga*, as 'a third relation' (see *NTN*, p. 188) and is said to 'explain' such cases as do not come under either *samāvaya* or *saṁyoga*. Cf. *IPC*, 1927, p. 165, where Hiriyanna, while discussing the nature of *samavāya*, remarks that "it (*samavāya*) is directly connected with the relata", and then, adds, in a f.n., "This is technically described as *svarūpasambandha*, i. e., it is self-related not unrelated". Its self-relatedness is said to be due to the fact that it cannot, being an independent category (*padārtha*), abide in a *dravya* or a cause. The important fact to be noted, in this connection, is that eventually, even the Naiyāyika has to admit the 'nature' of things as the determining factor of at least one kind of relation. A wider scope of its applicability is not resorted to by him owing to his commitment to a radical pluralism. As for the Jaina, anything which does not have its own nature, which is the source of all relations, is to be described with Malliṣeṇa, as '*nissvabhāva*' '*avastu*', *śaśaviṣāṇa*, or nothing (*SM* (text), p. 33). The compelling truth of 'nature' as the determining factor is somewhat indicated by the Naiyāyika's limited acceptance of *svabhāvasambandha*. Treating all relata as 'naturally' related will save the Naiyāyika from an unduly formal and hyper-realistic procedure.

(*daiśikaviśeṣaṇatā*) and (ii) the temporal relations (*kālikaviśeṣaṇatā*).[1]

Nevertheless its extension to cover the entire range of the relational nature of things is but the logical culmination of such a limited acceptance. Moreover, the consideration of the economy of thought (*lāghava*) and the faithfulness to experience demands such extension.

Kumārila[2] also supports this thesis and admits that there is nothing like a separate relational link which is an independent intermediary between the relata and that the terms contain within themselves the relational trait which brings about the contact between things. The acceptance of this fact, viz., that relation is an objective factor residing in the relata themselves, and is, therefore, their (*svabhāva* or *svarūpa*) leads him to the conclusion that relation is nothing else than identity-in-difference which constitutes the nature of things. The Jaina concurs fully with this view and believes that objects have a natural disposition (*yogyatā*) for mutual contact at all levels and this disposition, described as relation, forms an integral aspect of the nature of things as identity-in-difference.

The untenability of the Nyāya position is particularly evidenced[3] in its surrendering, at the hands of the

---

1. See *Bud. Log.*, Vol. II, f.n. 3, p. 287, and f.n. 8, p. 290. Also, *RML* pp. 153-154.
2. He characterises *samavāya* as *svarūpaṁ dharmadharmiṇoḥ*; see *supra*, p. 222, f.n. 2.
3. *Vide* Intro, *SN*, p. xcii, *JPN*, pp. 232–233.
   "There is *samavāya* of smell in earth and not in water; so the *samavāya* is many, say moderns". Dinakarī, quoted in *MML*, f.n. 1. (The statement runs as: *pṛthivyāṁ gandhasya*

later[1] Naiyāyikas, the oneness (*ekatva*), and the eternality (*nityatva*) of *samavāya*, for manyness (*anekatva*) and transcience (*anityatva*). Consequently, with the admission of manyness what was conceived as all-pervasive (*vyāpaka*) became something which is restricted to individual objects.

This triple change in the conception of *samavāya* has been actuated by the compelling force of the opponent schools like the Buddhists, the Vedāntins, the Mīmāṁsakas and the Jainas. The Jaina does not concede[2] the occurrence of the '*ihapratyaya*' or *ihabuddhi* ('in-ness')—e.g., the linen is in the yarns (*iha tantuṣu paṭah*)—which is held by the

---

samavāyaḥ, na jale ityādi pratīteḥ samavāyasya nānātvam iti navyāḥ / *BPVK*, p. 113.) Also see *NNLI*, f.n. 162, p. 75, and f.n. 165, p. 76. "The later Naiyāyikas and the Mīmāṁsakas following Prabhākara refuse to view *samavāya* either as eternal or one." *IPC*, 1927, p. 162, f.n. 3. (The references indicate the Prabhākara view of *samavāya* : *samavāyo nānā nityaś ceti Prabhākaraḥ*, *U* on *VD*, p. 353, also see *V* thereon.) "*Samavāya*, Inherence, cannot be regarded as everlasting, because it is actually found to be ephemeral; for instance, the Inherence between the Community and the Individual comes into existence when the Individual is produced, and perishes as soon as that Individual perishes." *PMS*, p. 63. See also, *ibid.*, p. 93, where "Eternal contact" is regarded as a contradiction in terms. Dhruva maintains that the "earlier logicians" could not accept a plurality of *samavāyas* since they feared that the quality of *number* would be associated with it. See Notes, *SM*, p. 81. But it is difficult to see how they could avoid accepting even "*one*" as a number.

1. For the statement of the early Naiyāyikas on the oneness, the eternality and all-pervasiveness of *samavāya*, see *supra*, p. 209 and the footnotes thereon.
2. Abhayadeva describes this as a fancy induced by the bias towards one's own system : *svasamayahitavāsanāprakalpita iva*. *TBV*, p. 700 ff. Cf. *tadeha ihavijñānaṁ pareṣām eva vartate, svasiddhāntānurāgeṇa nādartuṁ laukikaṁ tu tat* / *TSS*, *kā*. 827.

Vaiśeṣika to be the *sine qua non* of *samavāya*. According to him, no such 'in-ness' intervenes between the terms. Nor does he admit the relation of *samavāya* as something which conditions the terms.[1] He postulates spontaneity (*svabhāva*) of relatedness which is immediate or direct (*svataeva*) between the terms[2] themselves. This applies not merely to *samavāya* but to the whole range of relatedness in propositions which embody, within the being of their terms, the objective content which is identity-in-difference. In the instance[3] of the yarn and the linen 'yarn' is the identical or 'continuant', and 'linen' the changing (modificational) or 'occurrent', element. The 'continuant' (*dravya*) and the 'occurrent' are no doubt interrelated and this interrelatedness is as objective[4] a feature as the relata themselves. It is in the very nature (*svabhāva*) of the relata to be mutually and appositely or appropriately—this latter feature is implied by the term '*yogyatā*' and is intended as an answer to the objection of 'intermixture' (*saṅkara*) of the relata—related. Śaṅkara[5] and his followers also are inclined to treat

---

1. *na ca vṛkṣe śākhā ityādikāpi matiḥ samavāyanibandhanā* / *TBV*, p. 701.
2. *padārthā api svata eva parasparam abhisambaddhā bhavanti* / *SRK*, p. 790. The next fn. gives the instance.
3. Or better still in the example of *ātman* and *jñāna* (knowledge).
4. Cf. The following observation of William James: ".... the relations that connect experience must themselves be experienced relations, and any kind of relation experienced must be accounted as 'real' as anything else in the system". *JPPSM*, Vol. I, p. 534 (James has put these words entirely in italics).
5. *nāpi saṁyogasya samavāyasya vā sambandhasya sambandhivyatirekeṇāstitve kiñcit pramāṇam asti* / *BSB*, II. 17, p. 521 f.

"It is absolutely necessary for you (the Naiyāyika) to regard the nature of all things as determinants (as it is only

16

'naturalness' (*svabhāvatā*) of relation—or relation as a part (*atmabhūta*) of the terms themselves—as a less unsatisfactory hypothesis for the Naiyāyika. The difference, however, between Jainism and Vedāntism (and for that matter, also Buddhism, which takes relation as merely conceptualistic) is that the former takes relation as a real and objective trait whereas the latter as unreal and a subjective fancy.

The Naiyāyika's fallacy, according to the Jaina view, is that relation is treated as an independent entity. The indefensibility of the Nyāya position is pointed out to be inherent in the view held by the Nyāya pluralist: He rigidly clings to the argument that not merely the relata are absolutely different (*atīva bheda*) from each other but also that even the relation combining them is totally different from either of the relata.[1]

---

by means of its nature that anything can ever be determined"; *IT*, Vol. V, p. 273 (ET. *Khaṇḍana-khaṇḍa-khādya*, II. 85).

tādātmyapratīteś ca dravyaguṇādīnāṁ samavāyakalpanānarthakyam / *BSB*, II. 1. 18, p. 486. *tasmāt kāraṇasyātmabhūtā śaktiḥ śakteś cātmabhūtaṁ kāryam* / *Ibid.*

Vācaspati Miśra also observes : *sattvaṁ tu svabhāvata eva sad iti na sattvāntarayogam apekṣate, tathā sāmavāyaḥ samavāyibhyāṁ sambaddhuṁ na saṁbandhāntarayogam apekṣate svayaṁ sambandharūpatvād iti* / Bhāmati on II.1.18, *ibid.*, p. 468.

All that we cognise are the two relata, one of which is the *dharmi* (substratum : *dharmāṇāmaśrayabhūto dharmī*) and the other, *dharma* (attribute), and no third independent entity —corresponding to 'lac' (rāla) rivetting two separate stones (*śilāśakalayugala*)—is, according to Hemacandra, cognised besides these two, either by perception or by inference : *ayaṁ dharmī ime cāsya dharmā ayaṁ caitatsambandhanibandhanasamavāya ityetat tritayaṁ vastutrayaṁ na cakāsti jñānaviṣayatayā na pratibhāsate yathā kila śilāśakalayugalasya mitho-'nusandhāyakaṁ rālādidravyaṁ tasmāt pṛthak tṛtīyatayā pratibhāsate..... / SM* (text) p. 32.

1. As a matter of fact, between any two totally different entities the very distinction that the one is *dharmi*, and the

This naturally raised the legitimate objection that the two absolutely different relata cannot be related by a relation—whether it be *saṁyoga* or *samavāya*—without a further relation relating the relata to the initial relation. The second relation, again, necessitates a third, and the third, in turn, a fourth, and so on, interminably, landing the Naiyāyika in the muddle of an infinite regress.[1]

By extending the notion of *svarūpasambandha*, which has already been accepted in some form, within a limited sphere of experience, over the entire range of experienced reality and, thereby, conceiving the relational element to be embedded in the terms themselves, the Naiyāyika can avoid the above difficulties. This would tone down his close adherence to difference and bring him nearer to the

---

other *dharma*, cannot arise; much less does, therefore, the question of relating them arise if only for the reason that no such tertiary entity is vouchsafed to us in our experience; *na dharmadharmitvam atīvabhede vṛttyāsti cen na tritayaṁ cakāsti* / *AVD*, p. 31, *kā*. 7. *SM* (text); see also *SM* on the *kā*.

The acceptance of such an absolute distinction leads the Naiyāyika to the curious position of holding *caitanya* or *jñāna* (*caitanyaṁ jñānam*, p. 38, *SM*) to be absolutely separate from *ātman* connected with it (*ātman*) by *samavāyasambandha*. This *samavāyasambandha* is supposed to avoid the contingency of why the *jñāna* of Caitra should not belong to Maitra since *jñāna* is adventitious to both persons alike. But this *sambandha* does not seem to help the Naiyāyika—*samavāya* being one, eternal and all-pervasive, and therefore identically the same (*sarvatra vṛtter aviśeṣāt*) in both persons. *Vide SM*, p. 41.

The Jaina also accepts difference between the *dharmi* and the *dharma* (cf. *prativastusvabhāvabhedād iti* / *SM* (text), p. 32) but not in the absolute sense. See Note 8, p. 80 (Notes), *SM*.

1. *samavāyasya samavāyāntareṇa vṛttyabhyupagame tu, tatrāpyaparasamavāyakalpane'navasthā nātidustarā* / *SDS*, p. 252 f., *TRD*.

acceptance of the view that relation is of the nature of identity-and-difference to which the Jaina subscribes. The Śāṅkara and the Saugata view, which treats relation to be mind-created, contradictory and even illusory, shows scant regard to the intrinsic objectivity of the relational element in the make-up of things.

These considerations leave the Jaina view of relation as identity-of-differents[1] unaffected. It strikes a golden mean between regarding relation as a solid and independent entity and a fanciful myth in the subjective realm.

---

1. It is interesting to note that in recent contemporary Western philosophy also a similar development of thought, concerning the problem of relations, has taken place. F. H. Bradley's view approximates to that of the idealist Śaṅkara and Dharmakīrti. Russell opposes Bradley and takes the line of the Naiyāyikas. Several writers like Parker, William James and McTaggart have views which come between the two extremes of Bradley and Russell. There are, of course, fundamental differences in their metaphysical postulates, not merely among these western thinkers themselves but also between them and the Indian philosophers. There is, however, an unmistakable correspondence, in the three major trends of relational thinking between the western thinkers and their Indian counterparts. The following few statements and references from some of the western writers will indicate their respective alignments :

   Bradley : "Relational experience must hence in its very essence be called self-contradictory....it can claim no title higher in the end than that of a necessary makeshift." *CE*, Vol. II, p. 635. A little further he writes that accepting "relational truth as final" leaves us "hopelessly in a blind maze of unending regress" *ibid.*, p. 641, and the chap. on Relations, p. 62, f.n. 1. See also p. 207, f.n. 6, in this work.

   Russell : "Hence we admit that the relation, like the term it relates, is not dependent upon thought, but belongs to the independent world which thought apprehends but does not create." *Problems*, p. 98. "When it ('a fact') consists of a relation between two things, it has three constituents, the things and the relation. When it consists of a relation between three things, it has four constituents, and so on." *OKEW*, p. 61.

Between these two extremes we have the others whose views correspond, at least in some essentials, to the Jaina viewpoint :

De Witt Parker : "They (relations) are neither divided up among the terms, as Leibnitz thought, nor suspended between them, as Russell would have us believe, but character of the terms when united. We should not think of the unity which relation involves as a link or a tie or as glue, as a thing which externally affixes itself to elements and thus unites them. We should think of relations as rather running through terms, as embedded in them....; or if we cannot help thinking of them as bonds, we should picture them as so tight that they cut into the flesh and leave no space between." *The Theory of Relations*, *SNDeW*, pp. 250–251. See also *ibid.*, p. 260. "Since everything exists both on account of itself and of other things, there would be a part of the thing which would remain the same before the entrance into the new relationship and another part which would be different." (p. 261). See also p. 241 (the last paragraph wherein he suggests a compromise between 'different theories'), pp. 258-260 (where he replies to an 'objection'), and *ibid.*, pp. 271-272, para. Nos. 1, 7 and 8.

William James characterises the relational experience as a "primordial and empirically incorrigible" and "intelligible factor" of reality. "Continuities and discontinuities" (which may be taken to be equivalent to the factors of identity and difference which, according to the Jaina, together form the nature of things) are said to be factors which "compenetrate harmoniously" and are said to be "co-ordinate". *JPPSM*, Vol. II, p. 30 and p. 35. *The Thing and its Relations, CPP*, pp. 29-41.

Striking a note of finality on the nature or "constitution" of things as the basis of the co-ordinate elements of "continuities" and "discontinuities" James writes : "Somewhere we must leave off with a *constitution* behind which there is nothing". *Ibid.*, p. 39, f.n. 14. See also "A Treatment of Relations", "A World of Pure Experience", 2 articles: 1. pp. 533-543 and 2. pp. 561–570, *JPPSM*, Vol. I. For reference to some important points of resemblance between McTaggart's and the Jaina theory of relations, see *supra*, pp. 230, f.n. 2.

CHAPTER VIII

A Consideration of Two Controversies Concerning Dravya and Guṇa (and/or Paryāya) with a view to Clarifying the Nature of Both :

(1) How far could a Dravya be treated as A Concrete Universal ?

(2) Are Guṇas the Same as, or Different from, Paryāyas ?

CHAPTER VIII

A Consideration of Two Controversies Concerning Dravya (Substance) and Guna (and/or Paryāya) with a View to Clarifying the Nature of Both

Our investigation so far has led us to the conclusion that reality is a co-ordinate synthesis of identity-in-difference and that every real accordingly is a unique embodiment of identity-in-differents. There are, however, two controversies which further elucidate the nature of *dravya* and of *paryāyas in the anekānta* ontology. One of them owes its genesis to an impact of recent Western philosophy (Hegelianism and neo-Hegelianism) on Indian thought and is, therefore, modern, and the other is a natural development arising from an impulse to obviate an inherent inconsistency and dates back, at any rate in its more conscious form, to the times of Siddhasena Divākara. These controversial problems are : A. whether a *dravya* could be described as a concrete universal, and B. whether the *paryāyas* are the same as, or different from, the *guṇas*, in a *dravya*. They deserve at least a brief notice and, therefore, an attempt may be made to consider their salient features.

A. How far could a Dravya be treated as a Concrete Universal?

In a fit of Hegelian enthusiasm, two critics, Nahar and Ghosh, have attempted to find in the Jaina notion of *dravya* an echo of the Hegelian and the neo-Hegelian idea of the concrete universal.[1] For Hegel, as for Bradley and Bosanquet,

---

1. Describing a real in Jainism as 'The Absolute' the two critics proceed: "The Absolute is the Universal. This Universal is not the abstract Universal of the formal logic but the concrete Universal. The absolute expresses itself in A ...... A is the particularisation of the Universal......The Universal comes out of Itself and particularises Itself in the particular objects......" etc. *EJNG*, p. 166. A passage like this could be taken, almost at random, from any page in Hegel, Bradley, or Bosanquet. The last sentence, in particular, looks like a faithful parody on the well-known Hegelian dictum: that the Absolute goes out of itself, returns to itself to be itself.

   The tendency to compromise the co-ordinate status of difference in a manifold real as a result of this bold Hegelianisation of Jainism is too obvious. This is corroborated, on the side of Western philosophy, by Bosanquet who, in course of his treatment of the 'concrete universal', observes: "The universal is just that character of experience *which overcomes the 'is not' by reducing it to an element harmonious with and corroborative of the 'is'*. It is 'the self in the other'." *The Principle of Individuality and Value* (1912), p. 46.

   The concepts of the 'is' and the 'is not' have been noted already to signify identity and difference respectively. 'Reducing' the 'is not' to a foil which sets off the glory of the 'is' is a familiar idealistic rigmarole.

   Expounding Hegel's view, Stace observes that "*the universal is the absolute and ultimate being which is the foundation of all things, which produces the world out of itself*". (Italics in the text). *The Philosophy of Hegel* (Macmillan and Co., Ltd., London, 1924), p. 14.

   The neo-Hegelian Bradley writes: "But in the concrete universal, which has guided our steps, and which has appeared as the identity of analysis and synthesis, we have turned to truth and made our peace with reality." *PL*, Vol. II, p. 487, (22nd edn., 1940).

   While controverting the view of Bosanquet, the other great neo-Hegelian, N. K. Smith, points out that the doctrine of the concrete universal is "Hegelian in origin" (*Mind*, 1927, p. 156) and S. Alexander adds that this doctrine is "nowhere

the two great modern heirs of Hegelian absolutism, the Absolute, which is identity par excellence, is the supreme consummation, and the sole presupposition, of our entire philosophical quest. Furthermore, it (the Absolute) is also said to be the perfect concrete universal.[1] Being 'completely identical with itself'[2] this 'being' of the concrete universal does not admit

---

expounded with more effect and enthusiasm than by Mr. Bosanquet". *Space, Time and Deity,* Vol. I, p. 233, S. Alexander, (The Humanities Press, New York, 1950). We notice this 'enthusiasm' in Bosanquet's own words: "The recognition of this logical form (the concrete universal) as the true type of universality is the key to all sound philosophy." *The Principle of Individuality and Value.*

It may be doubted, for a moment, that the words "logical form", in the above statement of Bosanquet, do not bring out the ontological significance of the concrete universal. But that they do so will be realised when it is remembered that 'the identity of knowing and being' (and therefore of the 'thought' and the 'thing'), as will be pointed out later in course of this topic (*infra,* p. 255) forms "the basic principle of all idealism".

This truth of the ontological significance of the concrete universal is further demonstrated by the self-contradictory idealistic argument that the true (the concrete) universal is the perfect 'Individual' and that the only such perfect 'Individual' is of course the supremely 'Real' (the ontological principle), or the Absolute. Cf. "We say then with Bradley, following, of course, Plato and Hegel, that the Individual which, as we have seen, is the only true form of the universal, is the Real." Bosanquet, *op. cit.*, p. 68, f.n. 3. (See also *PL,* Vol. II, p. 487).

1. "......the Absolute is the concrete universal". P. T. Raju's *Thought and Reality* (George Allen and Unwin, Ltd., London, 1937), p. 174.
2. Hegel no doubt speaks, as already observed (*supra,* p. 98, f.n. 2) of mere identity as 'pure light' and of mere difference as 'pure night', and of both as 'two voids'. This seems to be opposed to such a description of the Absolute, which is the

of difference (of which change, plurality, etc. are but variant forms) or otherness or, as it is otherwise called, 'the opposite', being lastingly and coordinately rooted in reality. At best it allows difference, in its course of 'self-dispersion', as a 'transitional' phenomenon which appears for a moment only to dissolve itself into the matrix of identity—identity which, in the course of its development, culminates in the supreme state of the Absolute. In brief, this entire development is one of the Absolute going out of itself and finally returning unto itself.[1] This fact that Absolute Idealism celebrates, under

---

concrete universal, as being 'completely identical with itself'. From the Hegelian point of view, however, difference figures as a transitional, and even necessary, element, but it does so only during the relatively imperfect stages of the development of reality towards the ultimate stage of the absolute. But when the development reaches its consummation in the Absolute, the Absolute, conducting itself as an all-enveloping identity in which difference, *if it exists at all*, would be hushed into a a silent or theoretic existent and would, therefore, be functionally effete. Hence the description of the Absolute as being "completely identical with itself" would be, it will be explained, perfectly right.

To the Jaina at any rate, this treatment of difference, viz., recognising its necessity at the so-called transitional stages of development and trifling with it eventually (by assigning to it a theoretically subordinate status which logically amounts almost to an actual cancellation or annulment) at the supreme level of the Absolute, will appear as hunting with the hound and running with the hare.

1. Cf. "Hence we have now reached the idea of *a being which in passing outwards into its opposite passes only* into itself, and this opposite does not become anything different, *but remains even in the opposition, completely identical with itself*." Stace, *op. cit.* p. 222. (Italics in the text.)

A little further on Stace adds: "Hence in determining B (the opposite) A determines itself."

the notion of the concrete universal, the triumph of identity, ignoring the primal importance due to difference, is too obvious to need any further treatment at length. Identifying the Jaina concept of a *dravya*, which accords to difference an equally primordial status to that of identity, with the Hegelian concrete universal, therefore, does violence to an important point of principle.

Besides the non-recognition of difference also as a co-ordinating primal element of reality, the Absolute Idealism, with its adherence to the doctrine of the concrete universal, treats all reality as ultimately 'spiritual' [1] or 'mental' [2]. This 'panlogism' or mentalism leads the idealist to

---

1. Concluding his great work, Bradley observes: "We may fairly close this work then by insisting that Reality is spiritual. There is a great saying of Hegel's, a saying too well known, and one which without some explanation I should not like to endorse. But I will end with something not very different, something perhaps more certainly the message of Hegel. Outside of spirit there is not, and there cannot be, any reality, and the more anything is spiritual, so much the more is it veritably real." *AR* (9–10th imp., 1930), p. 489. Hegel himself observes: "The aim of knowledge is to divest the objective world that stands opposed to us of its strangeness, and, as the phrase is, to find ourselves at home in it: which means no more than to trace the objective world back to the notion,—to our inmost self." *The Logic of Hegel* (Trd. by W. Wallace, 1892, Oxford), p. 335.
2. Cf. "The universe is nothing but the content of consciousness." Stace, *op. cit.*, p. 73. "The absolutely concrete is the mind." *The Logic of Hegel*, p. 295. "The Notion of the Absolute fully realised, in and for itself, is thus 'Mind'...." *ERE*, Vol. VI, p. 574.

   Not satisfied with reducing 'the objects' to 'minds' the Absolute Mentalist proceeds to reducing them to one 'mind'. Cf. Alexander's remark while criticising Bosanquet's view:

uphold the identity[1] of 'the real' and 'the rational', 'the thing' and 'the thought', 'the experienced' and 'the experience'. "The real is the rational" and "the rational is the real" is a Hegelian commonplace signifying the interchangeability or the eventual identity of reality and rationality. The Jaina, who, as a realist, firmly believes in an ultimately or irreducibly dualistic reality of souls and the material world, does not, therefore, subscribe to this idealistic spiritualisation of the world. This second radical difference, in the approach to reality, between the Jaina on the one hand and Hegel and the neo-Hegelians on the other, prevents a facile identification of the Jaina conception of reality—whether this reality be the macrocosmic dualistic universe of spirits and the physical world, or the microcosmic real of *dravya* and *paryāya*—with the mentalistic concrete universal into which the principle of difference (macrocosmically the physical

---

"The very objects of the mind themselves, it is urged, are, not indeed minds, but mind...." *The Basis of Realism* (The Annual Philosophical Address to the British Academy, 1914), p. 28. Contrasting his own position with that of the Absolute, Alexander adds: "....the realist does not commit the mistake of declaring, therefore, that things are, in their real and deep seated nature, mind." *Ibid.*, p. 29.

1. "The identity of knowing and being is, in fact, the basic principle of all idealism." Stace, *op. cit.*, p. 73.

"That the *thing* is identical with the *thought*—this means that there is no absolute separation between subject and object, for the object is *within* the subject." *Ibid.* (Italics in the book.) This is why the absolutist asserts that, finally, there is only—and that would be only one—experience: cf. "And there is no distinction here between the experience and what is experienced." Bradley's *Essays on Truth and Reality* (1914, Oxford), p. 196. Further, Bradley adds elsewhere : "And Reality is one experience self-pervading..etc." *AR* (9th imp., 1930), p. 489.

universe and microscosmically, the *paryāyas*) or 'the Other' would be untraceably 'absorbed'.[2]

These two major divergences—not to speak of the other cognate ones concerning, for instance, unity and plurality, or the non-occurrence or the otherwise of the 'compresence' of the universal and particular in a real—militate against a wholesale comparison being made—except with reference to the earlier phase of Hegelianism, and, within the limits to which a reference has been made earlier—between the absolutistic idea of the concrete universal and the Jaina notion of a real. But the authors of *An Epitome of Jainism* seem to ignore these divergences, and, to reduce Jainism to an imperfect copy of the Hegelianism in respect of the problem in question. In their attempt at comparison of the two schools they write, for instance, that "everything which is real is rational", and add, as if by way of elucidating this truth: "The thinker and the object thought of are nothing apart from each other. They are twain and yet

---

1. "The Other, which it asserts, is found on enquiry, to be really no Other....And the form of otherness or of opposition again has no sense, save as an internal aspect of that which it endeavours to oppose." *AR* (9th imp., 1930), p. 463.
2. "....Mind on its part is not merely a world beyond Nature and nothing more : it is really, and with full proof, seen to be mind, only when it involves Nature as *absorbed* in itself." *The Logic of Hegel*, p. 180. (Italics mine.) Bradley confirms this truth: "Nature is an abstraction from experience, and in experience it is not co-ordinate with spirit or mind. For mind, we have seen, has a reality higher than Nature, and the essence of the physical world already implies that in which it is absorbed and transcended. Nature by itself is but an indefensible division in the whole experience." *AR* (9th imp., 1930), p. 470.

one....They have no meaning or existence taken individually and in their union they are not two separate things stuck together but two that have lost or dissolved their duality in a higher unity."[1] This passage, like the other several passages in the book which are suffused with a "blind adoration to the German Idealism", as Chakravarti describes,[2]

---

1. *EJNG*, p. 109 and p. 114.
2. By a curious irony this critic also becomes, eventually, a victim to the Hegelian hypnosis of which he is initially critical in the authors of the *Epitome* and goes to the extent of even declaring firmly that "The Jaina metaphysics does not contemplate the Hegelian absolute." (*PSKC*, Intro., p. li). Referring to the Jaina conception of *dravya* as an 'organic unity' of 'permanency in change' he writes, in a later passage: "Hegel is responsible for introducing such a conception of reality in modern thought. Jainas in their conception of Dravya have anticipated such a modern idea, several centuries in advance. Of course the concept was not fully worked out because of other limitations peculiar to their age." *Op. cit.*, p. 5.

   One might concede that there is, as it has been already pointed out earlier (*supra*, pp. 98-101), a certain similarity between the Jaina view of reality and that of Hegelianism with respect to the latter's 'relative' or 'transitional' phases. But it cannot be conceded that the Jaina view, when 'fully worked out' would, unless there was a radical departure from its fundamental ontological presupposion (viz., the *bhedābheda* nature of reality), ever take the Hegelian view in its (the latter's) final form of absolutism (*abhedavāda* or the identity view) by which Hegel firmly swears. But Chakravarti seems to regret that the Jaina view did not take the final form of Hegelianism "because of other limitations peculiar to their (the Jainas') age." While admitting that the Jaina metaphysics has, in general, remained comparatively stagnant in its growth, it would be wrong to think, on this specific issue, that it would be more logical if it had gone the way of Hegel in search of an Absolute. If it did so it would fall into the very pitfall which it has been doing its best to avoid throughout its polemical history.

exhibits a complete lack of the awareness of the divergences just referred to. The mentalizing tendency of a real is indicated in the dictum, repeated almost verbatim from Hegel, that 'everything which is real is rational' as well as in what follows, and the primacy attached to identity over difference is indicated in the reference, at the end of the passage, to the loss and the dissolution of 'their duality in a higher unity'.

These two important considerations do not, therefore support the close comparison which Nahar and Ghosh have made between the Jaina notion of reality and that of the absolutistic concrete universal, although there are some comparable traits between the former school and the pre-absolutistic, or 'the relative' phases of Hegelianism to which a reference has been already made at some length.[1]

B. Are Guṇas the same as, or different from, Paryāyas ?

Having briefly occupied ourselves with the controversy, given rise to by some modern Hegelian enthusiasts, whether a *dravya* could be treated as a case of a concrete universal, and found that it cannot be, we may now proceed to a study of a considerably earlier controversy concerning the relation between a *paryāya* (modification or mode) and a *guṇa* (quality or property) in a *dravya*. There are three views[2]

---

1. See *supra*, p. 98 ff.
2. The third 'view' is, as will be indicated later (*infra*, p. 265), more a tendency than a well-defined doctrine.

involved in this controversy which aim at the determination of the principle of change or difference which is constituted by these elements of *paryāya* and *guṇa*: First, that the two, viz., *paryāya* and *guṇa*, refer to the same unitary principle of change under two different names; secondly, that the two are two distinctive elements or aspects, the one, viz., the *paryāya*, being an external mode and the other, *viz.*, the *guṇa*, being an internal attribute, the two together constituting the principle of change; and, thirdly, that the two are mutually identical as well as different. The three views are described as the Abhedavāda, the Bhedavāda and the Bhedābhedavāda respectively, and the authors of each view will be referred to in the appropriate places.

1. Abhedavāda

Siddhasena Divākara is the champion of this view that *paryāya* and *guṇa* are synonyms[1] (*tullatthā* or *tulyārthau*) signifying the principle of change. This change consists in the external and the internal transformations of all entities consistently, of course, with the continuance of the entities. In proving the identity of *paryāya* and *guṇa*, Divākara, bold as he is in often departing from tradition, appeals to revelation[2] (*desaṇā*) as almost the sole argument on his

---

1. This topic has been discussed in *STP*, ch. III, *gās*. 9-14. Prefacing the *gā*. 12 the Commentator, Abhayadeva, remarks: *atha tatra guṇa eva paryāyaśabdenoktaḥ tulyārthavat* / *TBV*, p. 635.
2. Continuing the line (after *tulyārthatvāt*), cited in the above f.n., Abhayadeva adds "*āgamāśca*", and quotes the following statement from the *āgama*: *ya eva paryāyaḥ sa eva guṇaḥ* / *Ibid.*

side : "Lord Mahāvira has," he observes, "once and for all, acknowledged only two points of view namely *Dravyāstika* and *Paryāyāstika*; now if the idea of *Guṇa* would have been altogether different from the *Paryāya*, he would have certainly admitted a third viewpoint, namely that of *Guṇāstika*."[1] This appeal to tradition has a special force in view of the fact that the theory of *abhedavāda*, propounded by Divākara, is not widely held and is strongly opposed by even Kundakunda, Umāsvāti and others. Divākara is, however, supported in his view by Siddhasena Gaṇi[2], Haribhadra[3], Hemacandra[4], Yaśovijaya and, among modern critics, by Hermann Jacobi[5].

---

1. *STP*, *gā.* 10. Tr. Athavale and Gopani (*ST*, ch. III, p. 120). The *gāthā* runs as follows :
   do una nayā bhagavayā davvātthiya-pajjavātthiyā niyaya /
   etto ya guṇavisese guṇātthiyanao vi jujjanto //
   See also Abhayadeva's introductory statement to this *gā.*)
2. *vastutaḥ paryāyaḥ guṇa ityaikāntikam /* Siddhasena Gaṇi's *Tattvārthaṭīkā*, Pt. I, (ed. H. R. Kapadia, Bombay, 1926), p. 428.
3. Cf. The lengthy passage, in *STP*, p. 633 (f. n.) from *Śāstravārtāsamuccaya*, wherein Haribhadra offers, in substance, the same arguments as Siddhasena Divākara.
4. Hemacandra's attitude to the problem is indicated by the total absence of any reference to the concept of *guṇa* in his treatment of the real (*vastu*) in either the relevant *sūtra* (viz. *pramāṇasya viṣayo dravyaparyāyātmakaṁ vastu*) or his own com. thereon, in his work *Pramāṇamīmāṁsā*. *Vide PMHS*, pp. 24-25.
5. Jacobi's view is that there was "no room for an independent category 'quality' at the early epoch in the development of metaphysics" and that *paryāya* included the qualities. To quote his own words, "....the ancient Jaina texts usually speak only of substances, *dravyas*, and their development or modifications, *paryāyas*, and when they mention *guṇas*, qualities, besides, which however is done but rarely in the *Sūtras* and regularly in comparatively modern books only, this seems to be a later innovation due to the influence which the

Yaśovijaya distinguishes between the '*sahabhāvi*', the simultaneous or the intrinsic aspect, and '*kramabhāvi*', the successive or the extrinsic aspect, of *paryāya*, and identifies *guṇa* with the former. He observes that each of the two names is a specific sign (*viśeṣasaṁjñā*) for its corresponding aspect and brings the two signs together under the generic sign (*sāmānyasaṁjña*) of *paryāya*. By thus treating *guṇa* as a kind of *paryāya* he is able to assert, with Divākara, that the twofold[1] framework of *dravyāstika* and *paryāyāstika* is adequate to comprise the full content of reality.

---

philosophy and terminology of Nyāya-Vaiśeṣika gradually gained over the scientific thoughts of the Hindus. For on the side of *paryāya*, of development or modification, there seems to be no room for an independent category 'quality' since *paryāya* is a state in which a thing, *dravya*, is at any moment of its existence, and this must, therefore, include qualities, as seems to be actually the view embodied in the oldest text." *JSJ*, Pt. II, p. xxxiv. He also refers to this view of *paryāya* as a "mark of antiquity" of Jainism.

Whatever might be the date of the "ancient Jaina texts" or "*Sūtras*" in which the problem of *paryāya* has been treated, it is hard to think of Kundakunda's *Pravacanasāda* or Umāsvāti's *Tattvārthādhigamasūtra*, works which 'mention regularly' the distinct category of *guṇa*, as 'comparatively modern books only'. It would, perhaps, be better to recognise that postulating the distinct category of *guṇa* must have been done at a considerably early period, may be in the early centuries of the Christian era, posterior, of course, to the period when *paryāya* alone was accepted as the more inclusive category. This must have come about from the spontaneous perception of an obvious gap in the ontological picture of a *dravya* as well as from the "influence" of the Nyāya-Vaiśeṣika philosophy as suggested by Jacobi and Upadhaye (see *PrSKU*, Intro., p. lxvii f.).

1. *iti dravyaparyāyārthikabhedāddvaividhyameva* / Vivṛti on Yaśovijaya's *Nyāyālokaḥ* (The Śrī Jaina Grantha Prakāśaka Sabha, Ahmedabad, *vik. sam.* 1974), p. 203. See also the early part

2. Bhedavāda

Bhedavāda, the opposite of the view held by Siddhasena Divākara and some others, is championed by Kundakunda, Umāsvāti, Pūjyapāda and Vidyānanda. This upholds the distinction of *paryāya* and *guṇa*.

Kundakunda describes the protagonists of the *Abhedavāda*, or the *Paryāyavāda* as it is otherwise called owing to its belief in the oneness (*aikantikam*) of *paryāya* and *guṇa*, as 'false believers (*parasamayā*) who are deluded by modifications (*pajjayamūḍhā*)'[1]. As against their view he expresses his own dualism of *guṇa* and *paryāya* which, in combination with the *dhrauvya* (or *dravya*) element, give rise to the triune conception of a real (*attho*) which reveals itself as of "*dravyaguṇaparyāyasvabhāva*". This triune conception is described by Amṛtacandra as the true (*parameśvarī*) one.[2] In the words of Kundakunda himself : "The object of knowledge

---

of the passage. In this connection the following line is quoted : *davvātthiyo ya pajjavanayo ya sesā vigappā siṁ*/

1. See *PrSKU*, ch. II. *gā*. 1. Commenting on "*pajjayamūḍhā hi parasamayā*" in the *gā*. Jayasena observes : *yasmāditthambhūtadravyaguṇaparyāyaparijñanamūḍhā .... bhedavijñānamūḍhāś ca parasamayā mithyādṛṣṭayo bhavantīti* / In the same connection Amṛtacandra writes: *hato hi bahavo'pi paryāyamātramevāvalambya tattvapratipattilakṣaṇaṁ mohamupagacchantaḥ parasamayā bhavanti* / *Ibid.*, pp. 121-122.

2. *iyaṁ hi sarvapadārthānāṁ dravyaguṇaparyāyasvabhāvaprakāśikā parameśvarī vyavasthā sadhīyasī, na punaritarā*/ *Ibid.*, p. 121. Although *guṇa* and *paryāya* may be collectively designated as attributes, *guṇa* is generally rendered as equality and *paryāya* as modification or mode.

is made up of substances, which are said to be characterised by qualities, and with which, moreover, are (associated) the modifications."[1] A substance is, therefore, that which is endowed with qualities and accompanied by modifications.[2]

Despite their common abode, there is, between *guṇa* and *paryāya*, a considerable difference : a *guṇa* is, according to Kundakunda, a trait which is deeply embedded in the being of a *dravya* and is therefore called '*sahabhāvi*', simultaneous or intrinsic. A *paryāya*, on the contrary, is a relatively extrinsic feature appearing in a *dravya* for a time and disappearing later giving place to another *paryāya*. It is, therefore, called '*kramabhāvi*'[3]—successive or extrinsic.

It is, however, necessary, to remember that a *dravya* is invariably accompanied not merely by the ever-inseparable

---

1. *attho khalu davvamao davvāṇi guṇappagāni bhaṇidāni /*
tehiṁ puno pajjaya......
PrSKU, ch. II. See also the comms. on this *gā*. In his comm. Amṛtacandra refers to '*vistāra*' and '*āyata*' as synonyms of *guṇa* and *paryāya* respectively and also distinguishes two kinds of *paryāya*, the '*svabhāva*' and the '*vibhāva*'. *Ibid*. p. 119.
2. *guṇavaṁ ca sapajjāyaṁ jaṁ taṁ davvaṁ hi vucchanti // Ibid*., ch. II, *gā*. 3. See also, *gās*. 4 & 15, *ibid*., and 10, 13 in *PSKC*.
3. *Guṇa* and *paryāya* are also called *anvayi*, or inclusive, and *vyatireki*, or exclusive, respectively. Evidenty, the inclusiveness refers to the inwardness of *guṇa* in *dravya* and the exclusiveness refers to the separation of one *paryāya* from another in the succession of *paryāyas* happening in a *dravya*. *Vide PrSKU*, p. 121, Jayasena's Com.

It is necessary to note here the difference between Kundakunda's and Yaśovijaya's use of the terms '*sahabhāvi*' and '*kramabhāvi*'. Kundakunda treats the term as referring to two distinct existents (*bhāvāntarau*) while Yaśovijaya does so as referring to two aspects of the single principle, viz., *paryāya* (*vide supra*, p. 260).

guṇa[1] which is either generic (*sāmānya*) or specific (*viśeṣa*)[2] but also by some *paryāya* or the other. That is, a *dravy* may be, at a particular moment, without this or that *paryāya* but it can never be without some *paryāya* going with it.[3] In this sense *paryāya* is as essential[4] an attribute in a *dravya* as a *guṇa,* although the former is internal and the latter external. In modern parlance, *guṇa* and *paryāya* together constitute the 'what' whereas *dhrauvya* constitutes the 'that' of a *vastu.*

---

1. This prefix 'ever', though apparently superfluous, has been advisedly used here in order to distinguish the Jaina idea of inseparableness of *dravya* and *guṇa* from that of the Nyāya-Vaiśeṣika. According to the Nyāya-Vaiśeṣika a *guṇa*, though intimately or 'inseparably' related (*samaveta*) to *dravya,* is said to enter into the *dravya* a moment after the latter's birth, and to cease to be a moment after the latter's cessation. The Jaina, on the contrary, does not entertain such a paradoxical situation. He believes in the unconditional inseparability of *dravya* and *guṇa* without prejudice, of course, to their distinctions.
2. *svakīyaviśeṣasāmānyaguṇebhyaḥ....sarvadravyāṇi guṇātmakāni bhavanti*/ *PrSKU*, p. 121. The distinction between a *sāmānyaguṇa* and a *viśeṣaguṇa* may be illustrated by a simple instance: *amūrtatva* or formlessness is a generic or common quality (*sāmānyaguṇa*) between space (*ākāśa*) and a pure soul. Being a receptacle for (*avakāśasthānayogyatvam*) objects is the specific quality (*viśeṣaguṇa*) of space and consciousness (*cetanā*) of a soul.
3. Cf. *PrSKU*, ch. I, *gā.* 10, the Comms. thereon and Intro., p. lxviii.
4. While comparing *guṇa* and *paryāya* A. N. Upadhye refers to them as "inseparable and separable accidents" respectively (*PrSKU*, Intro., p. lxvi). This does not seem to be happy even as a 'rough' comparison, for *paryāya*, like *guṇa*, is, despite its extrinsic character, almost as 'inseparable' from *dravya* as a *guṇa* in as much as no *dravya*, in the Jaina view, could be ever found without some *paryāya*. Upadhye himself is not unaware of this fact of inseparableness of *paryāya* and

Another difference which is said to be observed between *guṇa* and *paryāya* is that when the one remains the same the other may vary. The qualities of gold, for instance, will remain the same when it is transformed into the various modifications like a ring, a bangle or a chain. Conversely, the modification of jarness will remain the same among several jars made from different substances like gold, silver or clay which vary in qualities from one another. Thus *guṇa* and *paryāya* are two distinct elements constituting, in their togetherness, the nature of a *dravya* in the Jaina ontology as expounded by Kundakunda and his commentators.

It is needless to give individual statements of the views held, among others, by Umāsvāti, Pūjyapāda and Vidyānanda, since all these writers substantially concur with Kundakunda in maintaining the distinction between *guṇa* and *paryāya*.

Umāsvāti's view may, however, be briefly mentioned. He enunciates his *bhedavāda* in the *sūtra* : Substance is possessed of qualities and modifications (*guṇaparyāyavad dravyam*).[1] In contrast with Siddhasena's view that *paryāya* comprehends, and is another symbol (*saṁjñāntaram*) for, *guṇa*, he categorically declares that *paryāya* is not merely a

---

dravya (*vide*, *ibid*., p. lxv), although he chooses a comparison which understates the case. Moreover, the epithet 'accident' as applied, in particular, to *guṇa*, is, despite the adjective 'inseparable', inappropriate in view of the fact that no 'accident', however 'inseparable' it is from a *dravya*, can adequately represent the depth of the intimateness commanded by a *guṇa* in its *dravya*.

1. *STSU*, V, *Sū*. 37.

different symbol but also a distinct subsistent (*bhāvāntaram*)[1] existing, along with *guṇa*, in the substance.

3. Bhedābhedavāda

The third 'view', viz., *bhedābhedavāda*, could be described more as a tendency than as a well-developed attitude. It suggests a coalescence of mutual identity and difference between *guṇa* and *paryāya* in a substance. Akalaṅka an Vādideva seem to hold this view. Akalaṅka, for instance, holds at once that *guṇas* themselves are, or are identical with, *paryāyas* (*tato guṇa eva paryāyaḥ*)[2], and that they (*guṇas*) are also a distinct category from *paryāyas*, a fact which is sanctioned, according to Akalaṅka, by scriptural authority (*guṇābhāvādayuktiriti cennārhatpravacanahṛdayādiṣu guṇopadeśāt*). It is interesting to observe that both Akalaṅka and Siddhasena derive sanction of the same divine authority for their contrary views on the present question.

---

1. *bhāvāntaraṁ saṁjñāntaraṁ ca paryāyaḥ. Ibid.* The Com. on *Sū.* 37. For definitions of *guṇa* and *paryāya* (or *pariṇāma*) see *ibid.*, V, *Sūtras* 40-44 and the Com. thereon.

2. Concerning the *abheda* side of the problem, Akalaṅka remarks : *guṇa eva paryāya iti vā nirdeṣaḥ/ athavā utpādavyayadhrauvyāṇi na paryāyaḥ/ na tebhyo'nye guṇāḥ santi tato guṇa eva paryāyaḥ iti.../* Supplementing this, and as if in answer to Siddhasena's repudiation of the independent status of the category of *guṇa* on the basis of the scriptural authority (*infra*, p. 258) Akalaṅka refers to the *bheda* view of the matter as follows : *guṇābhāvādayuktiriti cennārhatpravacanahṛdayādiṣu guṇopadeśāt/ uktaṁ hi arhatpravacane "dravyaśrayā nirguṇā guṇā" iti/* etc... *TRAG*, p. 243. These statements concerning both the views, occur in course of the com. on the *sūtra* of Umāsvāti already referred to on p. 170. The manner in which Akalaṅka has

Vādideva approaches the problem under consideration on the same lines as, but more consistently than, Akalaṅka: "The question may be asked," he observes, "'Why are *guṇas* and *paryāyas*, which are presumably the same, differentiated?' The answer would be that while *guṇas* always (*kālābhedāpekṣayā*) inhere in an entity, *paryāyas* come one after another (*kālavibhedāpekṣayā*). (Hence the two, viz., *guṇa* and *paryāya*, are different). It may, however, be observed that the difference between the two is not absolute (*sarvathā*) because of the fact that they are partly identical, which is not at all an incompatible circumstance[1] (with their difference). Surely the difference between the two is not (as great) as it is between a pillar and a jar; nor is the identity (*abheda*) between them (as indissolubly intimate) as it is between a thing and its nature (*svarūpavat*). The difference consists in the peculiar nature (*svarūpāpekṣayā*) of each and the identity in their (common) abode (*dharmyapeksayā*)".[2]

---

merely juxtaposed the two views does not seem to be very convincing; it even tends to leave the impression that the two views are somewhat paradoxical and that they are not properly synthesised into the form of a *bhedābhedavāda*. Vādideva puts the matter in a more consistent form. Reference to Vādideva's view will presently follow.

1. *kathañcidabhedasyāpyavirodhāt* / See the following f. n.
2. *nanvevaṁ ta eva gunasthā eva ca paryāyā iti kathaṁ teṣāṁ bheda iti cet / maivam / kālabhedavibhedāpekṣayā tadbhedasyānubhūyamānatvāt/....na caivameṣāṁ sarvathā bheda ityapi mantavyam / kathañcidabhedasyāpyavirodhatvāt / na khalveṣāṁ stambhakumbhavadbhedo—nāpi svarūpavadabhedaḥ / kintu dharmyapekṣayābhedaḥ / svarūpāpekṣayā bheda iti / SRK*, p. 736.

The English rendering is mine and is free, including the transposition of the last two sentences as well as the simple and obvious correction of "*kālabheda....*" into "*kālābheda*" of the Sanskrit original.

Thus we see a divergence of opinion among the three views so far outlined, regarding the relation between *guṇa* and *paryāya*. But it does not materially affect the fundamental conception of a real which is the foundation of the Jaina metaphysics: A real has been observed in Jaina ontology to be an enfoldment of the permanent and the changing elements within its being. Whether the changing element is a comprehensive and unitary (*abheda*) concept, designated by Divākara as *Paryāya*, or a dual (*bheda*) concept consisting of two distinct elements known as *guṇa* and *pāryāya*, it does not impair the basic structure of the real in so far as it (the changing element) remains an inseparable complement of permanence. This approach has been envisaged by Vādideva who endeavours to combine the two elements in his *bhedābhedavāda*[1] in which *bheda* is represented severally by the 'peculiar nature' (*svarūpāpekṣayā*) of *guṇa* and of *paryāya* and *abheda* by the common residence (*dharmyapekṣayā*) of *guṇa* and *paryāya*, in their inseparable togetherness in the *dharmi*.

On a critical analysis of this situation we find that the spirit of Vādideva's argument is largely agreed to by the two so-called extreme theorists also, viz., the *abhedavādin* and the *bhedavādin*. For, all the three schools now under consideration agree on the following three factors as being indispensable for anything to be a real: 1. Continuance (*dhrauvya*); 2. Quality which is internal to (*sahabhāvi*) the real; and 3 transformation (*pariṇāma*) which consists in the process of

---

[1] See *supra*, pp. 265-6.

successive (*kramabhāvi*), more or less extraneous events happening in the real. The main difficulty which has led to the disagreement on the relation between *guṇa* and *paryāya* is that *abhedavādin* considers himself a nominalist (hence the belief that the difference between *guṇa* and *paryāya* is one of name only) and *bhedavādin* a realist (hence the assertion that *guṇa* and *paryāya* are not merely two different names but also that they signify two distinct existents corresponding to the names). But the *abhedavādin* is not quite right in thinking that he is a nominalist owing to the fact that he does recognise the existence of *guṇa* also, even though in an indirect form, viz., as something which is incorporated in *paryāya*. As a matter of fact Yaśovijaya even goes to the extent of singling out *sahabhāviparyāya* and naming it specially as *guṇa*.[1]

Hence the rift between the *abhedavādin* and the *bhedavādin* is not so great as to disrupt the uniform agreement between them on the basic structure of a real which is the foundation of the Jaina ontology. Vādideva's statement of the case, in the form of his *bhedābhedavāda*, not merely embodies a compromise between the other two rather extreme viewpoints but also suggests the right solution which is in consonance with the basic ontological presupposition of the Jaina philosophy.

---

1. See *supra*, p. 260.

PART II

ETISTEMOLOGY

A. ANEKĀNTAVĀDA, the Theory of Manifoldness, the Most Consistent Form of Realism;

B. NAYAVĀDA, the Theory of Standpoints;

C. SYĀDVĀDA, or Saptabhaṅgī, the Dialectic or Conditional or Sevenfold Predication.

CHAPTER IX

Anekāntavāda or The Theory of Manifoldness

CHAPTER IX

Anekāntavāda or the Theory of Manifoldness
The Most Consistent Form of Realism

Anekāntavāda is the heart of Jaina metaphysics and *Nayavāda* and *Syādvāda* (or *Saptabhaṅgī*) are its main arteries. Or, to use a happier metaphor, the bird of *anekāntavāda* flies on its two wings of *nayavāda* and *syādvāda*. It is beyond the scope of the present work to give a full exposition, not to mention an ample critical assessment, of even some of the most essential aspects of these three topics. The traditional viewpoints are, of course, presented in the old Prākṛt and Sanskrit works. But no sizeable literature, which is commensurate with the magnitude and importance of these problems, and which represents any significant effort for achieving a reorientation of these problems to the trends of modern thought, has yet come into existence although the need of such effort cannot be exaggerated. However, consistently with the aim of the present study that it should confine itself to certain important problems which have received inadequate or little attention, we may discuss, in the present chapter, how *anekāntavāda*—the theory of manifoldness or indetermination—manifests itself as the most consistent form of realism in Indian philosophy. A glimpse into some significant implications of *nayavāda* and *syādvāda* will also follow the inquiry into *anekāntavāda*.

As already shown, while repudiating the idealistic notion of the concrete universal, the theory of identity-in-difference, the metaphysical presupposition of *anekāntavāda*, animating all the spheres of Jaina philosophical thinking, recognises the objectivity of the material universe. The objectivity of the universe signifies the fact that the universe is independent of the mind or consciousness. This independence, or the duality of consciousness and the material universe, necessarily presupposes the principle of distinction, which exerts a compulsive force until the logical goal of this principle is reached in the form of the development of the Jaina concepts of reality and knowledge into the comprehensive scheme of *anekānta* realism. In other words, once the initial step is taken, namely the recognition of the principle of distinction as being at the root of the duality of the mind and the world, there is no stopping short of working out, to their logical conclusion, the consequences of the operation of the principle of distinction. The claim that *anekāntavāda* is the most consistent form of realism lies in the fact that Jainism has allowed the principle of distinction to run its full course until it reaches its logical terminus, the theory of manifoldness of reality and knowledge.

The first significant step to be taken, once the operative principle of distinction is accepted, is the postulation of a multiplicity of ultimate reals constituting the cosmos. The material or the objective world is constituted, according to Jaina ontology, by five ultimate reals : viz., matter (*pudgala*) space (*ākāśa*), time (*kāla*), the medium of motion (*dharma*) and the medium of rest (*adharma*); and the mental or the subjective world consists of an infinity of independent minds, or spirits, in their conditioned or free existence. An analysis, on the physical as well as on the mental side, reveals, therefore, a multiple or pluralistic universe.

The other step, which, along with the corollary to be referred to a little later in this chapter, fulfils the purpose of the ubiquitously operative principle of distinction, and which imparts the name of '*anekāntavāda*', after which the entire Jaina metaphysics is often known, is the postulation of manifoldness, or inherent complexity, within each of the reals in the universe. In other words, reality, according to Jainism, is not merely multiple but each real, in its turn, is manifold or complex to its core. Reality is thus a complex web of manyness (*aneka*) and manifoldness (*anekānta*). The central thesis of the Jaina is, according to a modern critic, "that there is not only diversity but each real is equally diversified".[1]

The 'diversification' or manifoldness—also described as indeterminateness' or 'indefiniteness'—may be illustrated by the two instances of matter and space in the physical universe. Dealing with the atomic theory of matter and space in Jainism Hiriyanna observes: "The atoms, according to it (Jainism) are all of the same kind, but they can yet give rise to the infinite variety of things so that matter as considered here is of quite an indefinite nature. *Pudgala* has, as we know, certain inalienable features, but within the limits imposed by them it can become anything through qualitative

1. *JPNM*, p. 70.

differentiations. The transmutation of elements is quite possible in this view and is not a mere dream of the alchemist."[1] The material world evolves from the diversification of these homogeneous atoms into aggregates of earth, water, fire and air. It is pointed out that "Jainism also, like Upaniṣads, does not stop in the analysis of the physical universe at the elements of *pṛthvī*, etc. It pushes it farther back where qualitative differentiation has not yet taken place. But while in the latter the ultimate stage is represented by the monistic principle of Brahman, here it is taken by an infinity of atoms."[2] Indicating that the character of indefiniteness or indeterminateness is extended to the sphere of quality also the same writer further observes: "It is not qualitatively only that matter is indefinite. Quantitatively also it is regarded as undetermined. It may increase or decrease in volume without addition or loss."[3] A further treatment of the notion of manifoldness of matter has been offered in the chapter on Relations, in connection with the problem whether an atom has, and if so in what sense it has, an infinite part (*aṁśa*), despite the fact it is impartite (*niravayava*) in its nature. In the course of the treatment of the problem we have met with an occasion to discuss the light which is shed on it by three thinkers, viz., Prabhācandra and McTaggart on the one hand and Abhayadeva

---

1. *OIP*, p. 212 f.
2. *Ibid.* The phrase 'an infinity of atoms' may be substituted, without being incorrect, 'an infinity of diversified atoms'.
3. *Ibid.* Cf. the following fragment of Empedocles in Greek philosophy: "Earth increases its own mass and Air swells the bulk of Air." Burnet's *Early Greek Philosophy*, the edn. Adam & Charles Black, London, 1952, p. 212.

on the other. Again, in the present instance of matter[1], the brief hints hitherto given of the Jaina atomic theory sufficiently indicate the nature of indeterminateness or manifoldness in reality.

Space or *ākāśa* is another example of a manifold real.[2] Its manifoldness is connoted, as in the case of matter, by its possession of parts.[3] According to Abhayadeva as well as Prabhācandra even an incorporeal or formless real may contain parts or divisions, as evidenced by the obvious instance of *ātman*[4], which contains cognitive and other powers. Abhayadeva points out further that to be divisible does not necessarily mean that the parts[5] should be put together at some point of time prior to division. In other words the divisibility of space is a spontaneous feature.

The entire argument on the manifoldness of space, as well as of other reals, is developed by Abhayadeva in his polemic against the Naiyāyika view of *ākāśa*. According to

---

1. For a somewhat clearer view of the problem, this account of the indeterminateness of matter may be read in conjunction with the controversy regarding the *sāvayavatva* or otherwise of an atom in an earlier chapter (ch. VII).
2. Cf. *nanvanārabdhamūrtimaddravyāvayavatve gaganādīnāṁ niravayavatvaprasakter anekāntatva ekatvavyāghātaḥ, na...TBV*, p. 641, For an explanation of the term *anārabdha*, occurring in this quotation, see *infra*, f. n. 5.
3. *ākāśasya...sāvayavatvaṁ ghaṭāder ivopapannaṁ sāvayavamākāśaṁ himavat—vindhyāvaruddhavibhinnadeśatvāt / Ibid.*
4. *Ibid.*, p. 642, lines 9-11; cp. *amūrtasyāpyātmano jñānādyadhikaraṇatvapratīteḥ / PKM*, p. 563.
5. The term for the state in which the parts need not be put together prior to division is *anārabdha*.

the Naiyāyika *ākāśa* or 'ether'[1] is one (*eka*)[2] or partless (*na nānā or niravayavi*) and, consequently, it is all-pervading (*vibhu*)[3] and eternal (*nitya*)[4]—the distinctions, therefore, like *ghaṭākāśa* and *maṭhākāśa* are, like the concepts 'here' and 'there', a superimposition (*upādhi*)[5] upon that eternally unchanging medium.

But the Jaina believes in the genuine divisions of infinite *pradeśas* which are as much objectively existent as the medium of which they are divisions. Were it not so, the two towns, say, Paṭaliputra and Mathurā which, like the two mountains, the Himavat and the Vindhya,[6] occupy different locations of space (*nānākāśapradesāḥ*), would, he affirms,

---

1. Besides *ākāśa* or 'ether' the Naiyāyika recognises another entity, viz., *dik*, which is translated as 'space'. But in actual fact it is *ākāśa*, not *dik*, which corresponds to the Jaina conception of 'space'.
2. *nanvākāśamapi kiṁ pṛthivyādivan nānā/netyāha—taccaikamiti / bhede pramāṇābhāvādityarthaḥ/ Tarkadīpikā* on the *sū*. 14 of *TS* (text, p. 11) which runs as : *śabdaguṇamākāśaṁ/ taccaikaṁ vibhu nityaṁ ca //*
3. *ekatvādeva sarvatropalabdher vibhutvamaṅgīkartavyamityāha—vibhviti / Ibid.*
4. *vibhutvādevātmavan nityamityāha—nityaṁ ceti / Ibid.*
5. Cf. "The epithet one implies that the mention of numerous *ākāśas* such as *ghaṭākāśa* and *maṭhākāśa* in common parlance is due to *upādhi* and cannot be real". *Ibid.*, Notes, pp. 127-128. Akalaṅka's term for '*upādhi*' is '*aupacārikī*' or '*adhyāropa*'. Calling the person 'Māṇavaka' a 'lion' because of the former's fierceness (*kraurya*) and bravery (*śaurya*) etc., is cited as an example of *upacāra*. Similarly, the attribution of *pradeśas* or parts to the partless medium of *ākāśa* is from the point of view of the Naiyāyika, a case of *upādhi*, or *upacāra*: *pradeśa-kalpanā niravayavatvādaupacārikī siṁhavat // TRAG*, p. 202, *kā*. 9.
6. *Vide TBV*, p. 642.

tend to be at one location (*taddeśabhāvinyeva*) which is an absurd proposition.[1]

But the Naiyāyika may advance a more ingenious argument[2] by stating that the *sāvayavatva* of *ākāśa* is like a monkey in relation to a tree (*kapivṛkṣasaṁyogavat*). That is, the statement that 'the monkey is sitting on the tree' denotes that the monkey in question is sitting on the branch of the tree (*śākhāvacchedena*) but not on the tree itself, or rather on the root of the tree (*mūlāvacchedena*). This analogical argument indicates the truth that just as the idea of the tree in its relation to the idea of the monkey does not pervade the latter fully (*vyāpyavṛttitvam* or *sāmastyavṛttitvam*)[3] but does so, if at all, only partially, so also does *ākāśa* pervade its so-called *avayavas* at best only partially. This partial pervasion of the tree in the monkey, or of the *akaśa* in the parts, is described as *avyāpyavṛttitvam* or *avyāpyavṛtti*. This relation of *avyāpyavṛtti* aims at suggesting that, eventually, *ākāśa* does not directly possess the *avayavas*, or if it does possess any at all, it does so only in a remote and superficial way so that it would not be far wrong to say that the parts are almost unreal. The Jaina would, of course, turn the tables on the Naiyāyika by

1. Commenting on his own *kā*. (16), viz., *dravyāṇāṁ pratiniyatapradeśāvasthānāt*, Akalaṅka observes : *Ihānyeṣu ākāśapradeśeṣu pāṭaliputraṁ sthitam anyeṣu ca mathurā ato nānākāśapradeśāḥ / yasyaikāntenāpradeśam ākāśaṁ tasya yaddeśe pāṭaliputraṁ taddeśabhāvinyeva mathurāpi syāt / Ibid.*, p. 203.
2. This argument and the supplementary argument on *saṁyoga* as described in the following paragraph are elaborated on the basis of suggestive hints thrown in by Abhayadeva in the course of his commentary. See *TBV*, p. 602.
3. *vyāpyavṛttitvaṁ tu sāmastyavṛttitvam / Ibid.*

rejoining that all the latter's verbal subtleties have not succeeded in ruling out a reference in the latter's argument—however indirectly it might be—to the *avayavas* with regard to *ākāśa.* It is, as a matter of fact, quite obvious that the Naiyāyika's analogy of the tree and the monkey would fall to the ground if the essential element of the branch of the tree is removed from it.

Another important consideration which undermines the Naiyāyika's thesis of indivisibility (*niravayavatva*) of *ākāśa* in the above argument of *kapivṛkṣasaṁyoga* hinges on the relation of *saṁyoga* figuring in it. The sitting monkey is conjoined to the branch of the trees by way of *saṁyoga* or external relation. *Saṁyoga* is admitted by the Naiyāyika himself as a *guṇa*, and a *guṇa* in turn is admitted to need a *dravya* for its *āsraya*[1], or support. The support in the analogy under consideration is the tree and, correspondingly, the support for the *avayavas* of *ākāśa*, is evidently *ākāśa* itself. This means that the *avayavas* of *ākāśa* are not a case of either *upādhi* or *avyāpyavṛtti* as is evidenced by the grounds admitted by the Naiyāyika himself. Thus this as well as the previous argument as advanced by the Nyāya school presupposes, at any rate indirectly, the Jaina thesis of the *sāvayavatva* of *ākāśa.*

Akalaṅka also does not see eye to eye with the Naiyāyika on the question of impartite *ākāśa.* He is inclined to feel that the divisibility of *ākāśa* would be incompatible with the divisibility of a material object. In other words, the

---

1. *saṁyogasya gunatvena dravyāśritatvāt tadabhāve ca tadabhāvāt* / *Ibid.* See also *TS*, *sū*. 4.

indivisible *ākāśa* is not a favourable receptacle for the divisibility of an object like a jar[1] (*dravyavibhāgābhāvāt*).

The last significant argument which is brought by Abhayadeva to bear upon the present issue concerns the Nyāya view of sound (*śabda*) as the special quality (*viśeṣaguṇa*) of *ākāśa*. It is a commonplace universal experience that a particular sound prevails (*vartate*) only at a particular place (*ekadeśe eva*) but not everywhere (*na sarvatra*) and that the sound subsequently fades away (*vinaśyati*) from where it is heard. If the Nyāya thesis of the partless—or unitary and, consequently, of the eternal—*ākāśa* were right, then every sound, for that matter even the distant word uttered by the divine Brahman (*brahmabhāṣitam*) would be straightaway heard by us[2] everywhere (*sarvagatatvaṁ syāt*), and would remain everlasting (*nityam*)[3]. In point of fact even the usage (*vyapadeśa*) that "a particular sound prevails only at a particular place but not everywhere" would be evidently impossible under the conception of a partless *ākāśa*.[4] Besides even the established fact of the transitoriness of *śabda* would militate against the Nyāya conception of an all-pervasive

---

1. Commenting on his own *kā*. (5), *niravayavatvānupapattiriti cen na dravyavibhāgābhāvāt* /, Akalaṅka observes: *yathā ghaṭo dravyato vibhāgavān sāvayavaḥ na ca tathaiṣāṁ dravyavibhāgostīti niravayatvaṁ prayujyate* // *TRAG*, p. 202.
2. Cf. *yadi ca sāvayavaṁ nabho na bhavet tadā śrotrākāśasamavetasya śabdasya brahmabhāṣitasyāpyupālambho'smadāder bhavet niravayavaikākāśaśrotrasamavetatvāt*/ *TBV*, p. 641.
3. *yadi ca sāvayavam ākāśaṁ na bhavet, śabdasya nityatvaṁ sarvāyatatvaṁ ca syāt* / *Ibid*.
4. *na hi niravayavatve 'tasyaikadeśe eva śabdo vartate na sarvatra' iti vyapadeśaḥ sangacchate*/ *Ibid*.

(*vibhu*) *ākāśa*. Nor does the Nyāya belief in what might be described as the wave theory of sound[1]—that is, the theory according to which sound is transmitted by waves—work without presupposing a divisible *ākāśa*. Hence the Nyāya view of *ākāśa*[2] points, according to Abhayadeva, to the Jaina thesis of the *sāvayava* nature of *ākāśa*.

Thus the Jaina view of *ākāśa* is that it is an objective real having infinite parts[3] or *pradeśas*[4] ('space-points') which signify its *anekānta* nature (*nānātvam ityanekāntaḥ*[5]).

---

1. Cf. *na ca niravayavatve ākāśasya santānavṛttyā āgatasya śabdasya śrotreṇāpyupalabdhiḥ sambhavati anyānyākāśadeśotpattidvāreṇa tasya śrotrasamavetasyānupapatteḥ jalataraṅganyāyenāparāparākāśadeśādāvaparāparaśabdotpattiprakalpanāyāṁ kathaṁ nākāśasya sāvayavatvam* / *TBV*, p. 642.
2. For a further reference to a few other consequences resulting from the Nyāya view of *ākāśa*, see *ibid.*, pp. 641-642.
3. *anantabhāgapramitam ākāśadravyam* / Brahmadeva's *Dravyasaṅgrahavṛtti* (*Davva-saṁgaha* by Nemicandra S. Chakravarti, ed. S. C. Ghosal, Arrah, 1917), p. 24.
4. A *pradeśa* or 'space-point' is 'the space occupied by an atom'. *PrSKU*, p. 17 (E. Tr.), f. n. 4. The *pradeśas* are, however, limited to 'physical space' (*lokākāśa*) only, the other part of *ākāśa* being a 'non-physical space' (*alokākāśa*). *Ibid.*
5. *Vide TRAG*, p. 203, *gā*. 19 and the com. thereon.

   The manifoldness of time is indicated not merely by an infinity of intrinsically real (*pāramārthika*) units called *kālāṇus* or 'time-atoms' which form the basis of the conventionally temporal (*vyāvahārika*) distinctions like the minute, the hour, the day, the year and so on, but also by the diverse effects which are brought about by the instrumentality of the *kālāṇus* which permeate the events in the universe. Cf. *so'nantasamayaḥ*/ *TSVJ*, V. 40, "The Jaina Theory of Time", Y. G. Padmarajiah (a paper read in the Indian Philosophical Congress Trivandrum, 1947) and *TRAG*, V. *sū*. 22, especially the *kā*. 14, and the comm. on both. For further light on the manifoldness in various senses, of *ākāśa* as well as on *dharma* and *adharma*,

Lastly the soul or *ātman*, an individual centre of experience among an infinity of similar centres in the realm of consciousness, is the subjectivistic instance of manifoldness in Jainism. It is needless to enlarge upon the manifold nature of an *ātman* since it is evident in every one of the infinite states (*anantabhāvas* or *pariṇāmas*) as well as in the multiple powers which are attributed to *ātman*.[1] There are at least two considerations which indicate the manifoldness of *ātman*: First, an *ātman*, like the Liebnizian entelechy, mirrors the the entire universe within itself as a unique centre of experience. The universe it mirrors, or comprehends, is an infinitely complex one. Hence its experiential powers must be manifold, or commensurate with the complexity of the experienced universe. This is an implication of Vādideva's idea that difference in the cognised (*viṣaya*) signifies a (corresponding) difference in the cognition (*vikalpa*) concerned[2] as well as of the characteristically Jaina idea of relativity of knowledge, which signifies that "the full knowledge of everything is inextricably bound up with the full knowledge of everything and (*vice versa*)".

---

the medium of motion and that of rest respectively, see *TRAG*, p. 210 ff., *sū*. 12, *kā*. 27 and its comm. It is, however, necessary to observe that the nature of manifoldness in the case of *dharma* and *adharma* has not been very clearly developed, although their conformity to the supreme law of the entire reality as expressed in the celebrated formula of Umāsvāti, viz., *utpādavyayadhrauvyayuktaṁ sat*, has been clearly stressed. *Vide TB* on *ST*, p. 641 f., *gā*. 33.

1. Cf. the *Vivṛti* and Prabhācandra's comm. thereon—*NKC*, Vol. II, p. 686 and p. 689 respectively.

2. *viṣayabhede hi siddhe vikalpabhedaḥ sidhyati* / *SRK*, p. 755.

Secondly, *ātman,* as conceived by the Jaina thinkers, is the exact antithesis of the Advaitic Brahman. The Advaitic Brahman, as pointed out on several occasions in the course of this work, is a monolithic conception, or an unredeemed identity. Being antithetical to this extreme Advaitic conception the Jaina notion of *ātman* is that of an infinitely diversified centre of experience.

The significance of manifoldness characterising the consciousness in the latter's function of apprehending the many-faceted universe has crystallized itself into the twofold dialectic of the *nayavāda* and the *syādvāda* to which reference will be made in the course of this section.

In our endeavour to trace the logical steps which have led the Jaina conception of reality to the most consistent form of realism in Indian philosophy, we have been able to observe that in consequence of recognising the force of the principle of distinction inherent in all realistic procedure, the Jaina has postulated an independent objective world as against the world of consciousness, and has proceeded to posit manyness in reality and manifoldness in each real. The progress from multiplicity of reals to manifoldness of each such real consists chiefly in advancing from the number to the nature of the reals. The last step, which completes the logical picture of this realistic procedure, is an implicit recognition of what may be called, after Kant, the Principle of 'Reciprocity', or of 'Interaction', or of 'Community', among the reals in the universe.

Except for an occasional hint here and there the principle of Reciprocity or Interaction is more implied than expressly stated or developed in Jainism. Nevertheless its necessity and importance are undoubtedly clear. It would not, therefore, be inappropriate if we approach Kant for an explicit formulation of this idea which is germane to the fundamental notion of *Anekānta* in Jainism.

It has been observed earlier that the *Anekāntavādin* postulates the interrelatedness of all reals in the universe, and, therefore, that one who has a total cognisance of one thing would have a total cognisance of everything and *vice versa.* This interrelatedness or relativity of nature evidently involves, at any rate in its narrow sense, the permeation of the relational factor in reality, but does not explicitly specify the dynamical element of interaction among the reals. It is this dynamical or active element which is provided for by the principle of 'reciprocity' or 'interaction', or 'community'[1] (*commercium*)[2].

Without 'the reciprocity of the manifold' the inter-relatedness, therefore, becomes 'merely an ideal relation', whereas with it the inter-relatedness becomes a 'real one'. This is the significance of the description of reciprocity as "the action and reaction of quite different substances, of which each determines the other's state..". Prichard's instance of

1. Kant formulates this principle under his 'Third Analogy', as: "All substances, so far as they coexist, stand in thorough-going community, that is, in mutual interaction". In his earlier formulation (first edition) Kant uses 'reciprocity' in place of 'community'. *KCPR*, p. 233.

2. This is one of the two Latin meanings of the original German 'Gemeinschaft'. See *KCPR* (1923), p. 381, f.n. 5.

the 'reciprocal influence'[1] between 'a lump of ice' and 'fire' clearly illustrates this idea of interaction.[2] Describing reciprocity as a 'double refraction....of objects upon each other', Caird refers to it, in Kant's own words, as "the condition of the possibility of the things themselves as objects of experience"[3].

In Kantianism, as in Jainism, the principle of reciprocity goes beyond the 'co-existence' or the interrelatedness of the substances, and explains the 'dynamical community' among them. This is in sharp contrast with the 'isolation of the individual substances' as found in the individualism of Leibniz or the momentariness of Hume and Buddhism.

The terms like *anyonyātmakatva*[4] (mutuality) or *anyonya-vyāptibhāva*[5] (mutual pervasiveness), used by Abhayadeva and Haribhadra in the somewhat limited context of a concrete real, correspond, at least in a limited degree, to the Kantian idea of 'reciprocity' or 'dynamical community' among the reals in Jainism. When we consider, however, the Jaina view of the universe as a fully interrelated or relativistic[6] (*sāpekṣa*) system of reals, which in turn are causally efficient[7] (*artha-kriyākāri*) it is not difficult to see that the feature of Kantian

---

1. For the slight difference in the meaning between 'influence' and 'community or reciprocity', see *KCPR*, p. 234.
2. *KJKP*, p. 303 f. The last sentence, in the description of the illustration (p. 304) refers to "the determination of the *unobserved states* coexists with the observed states".
3. *CPKE* (Vol. I), p. 535.
4. *TBV*, p. 645.
5. *AJP*, Vol. I, p. 132.
6. *Vide infra*, p. 157 ff. (together with the footnotes).
7. *Vide infra*, the section on *Arthakriyākāritvavāda*, especially the last page.

'reciprocity' is implicitly contained in the structure of reality as envisaged by Jainism.[1]

In course of this brief enquiry into, and the illustration of, the steps in the development of the spirit of distinction involved in the theory of the *Anekānta* (the manifold or indeterminate) nature of reality we have observed that the notion of manifoldness not merely presupposes the notion of manyness or pluralism, but also contains the activistic implication of reciprocity or interaction among the reals in the universe. Although manifoldness is the most significant step in the dialectical analysis of the Jaina conception of reality, it comprehends and presupposes the other steps within its scope as a logical necessity. That is, independence (of consciousness and the world), pluralism, interrelatedness and reciprocity or dynamism are component factors in the amplitude of the ontological as well as the epistemological significance of the relativistic notion of manifoldness or indetermination with which the entire reality is, according to Jainism, stamped (*syādvādamudrāṅkitam*).

Before proceeding, finally, to consider the theories of standpoints (*nayavāda*) and of the Conditional Predication (*syādvāda*) or the Sevenfold Dialectic (*saptabhaṅgīvāda*, as *syādvāda* is otherwise called), it is necessary to point out that the whole above account of the nature of *anekāntavāda*,

---

1. The notion of a mere interrelated universe has an idealistic flavour. The Jaina is a thoroughgoing realist. This realistic spirit cannot, therefore, remain satisfied with a mere interrelatedness, but demands an impact or 'a double refraction', among the dynamic reals which influence or impinge upon one another proximately or remotely.

has aimed at progressively demonstrating the fact that *anekāntavāda* is the most consistent form of realism in Indian philosophy.

The claim that *Anekāntavāda* is the most consistent form of realism in Indian philosophy hinges mainly on the fact that it has allowed the maximum scope for distinction to play its role. It will take us far afield if we go closely into the problem of elucidating how the analytical function of distinction is inherent in any realistic procedure. This problem deserves to be specifically brought within the focus of the discussion of comparative Indian philosophical thought although some broader questions—like how the notion of *anekānta* is found, in some measure and form, even in some non-*anekanta*[1] schools of philosophy, a conscious,

---

1. The reconciliatory spirit (*samanvayadṛṣṭi*) which consists in an endeavour to harmonise, by various methods, different or apparently conflicting views in a new synthesis, is found, in however imperfect a manner it may be from the Jaina point of view, among the several non-Jaina schools of philosophy. Some of the notable instances are: (a) the *Ajñānavāda* (agnosticism) of Sañjaya (*vide* B. M. Barua's A *History of Pre-Buddhistic Indian Philosophy*, Calcutta Univ., 1925), pp. 328-330; and *JSJ*, Pt. II, Intro. p. XXVIII-IX, (b) the *Vibhajyavāda* ('the Critical Method of Investigation' as contrasted with what the Buddha himself describes as the *Ekāntavāda*, or the one-sided method, in *Majjhima-nikāya, Sutta* 99, *vide NVVS*, Prastāvanā, p. 11) or the *Madhyamapratipada* (*samyutta, vide PMHS*, Bhāṣāṭippaṇāni, p. 62) of the Buddha which induced him 'to treat prevalent opinions with all due consideration' (*JSJ*, Pt. II, Intro., p. XXIX); (c) the celebrated four-fold (*catuṣkoṭi*) antinomial method of the Mādhyamika founder, Nāgārjuna (cf. *atastattvaṁ sadasadubhayānubhātmakacatuṣkoṭivinirmuktaṁ śūnyameva / Sarva-darśana-saṅgraha*, Ed. V. S. Abhyankar, Govt. Oriental (Hindu) Series, Poona, 1924; see also pp. 572-3 in

balanced and systematic treatment of it being a special feature of Jainism—have been noticed with some degree

---

Nāgārjuna's *Mūlamādhyamikakārikā*, Ed. la Vallee Poussin, Bib. Bud., St. Petersbourg, 1913); and (d) the critique, on the eight doctrines, of Gautama (vide ch. IV, *Āhnika, sūtras* 14-43 in Gautama's *Nyāyasūtras*, E. T. Ganganatha Jha, Poona Oriental Series, Poona, 1939). Despite the fact that these methods are treated in the respective systems with which they are severally associated, in the spirit and form resembling the *Anekāntavāda*, they have not been considered to be so fundamental and pervasive (*vyāpaka*) as they have been in Jainism. It is, therefore, no surprise that the early critics of *Anekāntavāda* like Dharmakīrti (see *PVD*, ch. III, *kās.* 180-1 and *MV* thereon, and f.n. 3), and Śaṅkara, the earliest commentator on the *Brahmasūtras* of Bādarāyaṇa, make Jainism the target of their polemic against *Anekāntavāda*. This is done on an even more elaborate scale by Arcaṭa also (*HBT*, pp. 104-107).

Furthermore, some schools like the *Bhedābhedavāda*, especially of Bhartṛprapañca whose system is even referred to as '*anekānta*' (*vide PMHS*, *Bhāṣāṭippaṇāni*, p. 62, f.n. 3); the *Bhaṭṭa-Mīmāṁsā* and the Sāṁkhya have an *anekānta* bias with respect to some of their methods and ideas. While criticising the concept of '*vaicitrya*' which is so vital to *Anekāntavāda*, Śāntarakṣita significantly attributes it to the Mīmāṁsā (*Vipra*) as well as the Sāṁkhya (*Kāpila*) systems also (*kalpanāracitasyaiva vaicitryasyopavarṇane / ko nāmātiśayaḥ prokto vipranirgranthakāpilā// TSS*, *kā*. 1776). Arcaṭa, who also chiefly attributes it to Jainism and criticises, describes it as '*vaicitryam*' or '*vicitram*' as: *vicitraṁ hi rūpaṁ śabalamucyate*; or, *vicitratā ca nānāsvabhāvatā* (*HBT*, p.104). These considerations indicate the influence which the notion of *anekānta* has, unwittingly or otherwise, in various forms and degrees, on the systems other than Jainism in Indian philosophy. For two further references bearing on this thesis see the next two footnotes. For a brief treatment (with occasional references to, and quotations from the texts) of this topic with regard to the non-Jaina systems see *PMHS*, *Bhāṣāṭippaṇāni*, pp. 61-63, *NVVS*, *Prastāvanā*, p. 11 ff.; and *ST*, Intro. 150-2.

of attention by a few old writers[1] and contemporary critics.[2] A brief attempt has, however, been made in the immediately preceding pages to show how the impelling logic of distinction, inherent in all realistic metaphysics, has led to the evolution of the Jaina conception of reality from the simple notion of dualism to the complex one of manifoldness or indetermination. All that is necessary for our purpose now is to indicate how this notion of manifoldness or indetermination is the most consistent and inevitable manifestation of the realistic spirit in Indian philosophy.

This fact, that the theory of manifold or indeterminate reality is the most significant form of realism in Indian philosophy, could be adduced from the following two considerations : First, that the Jaina conception of reality admits of the principle of distinction which is the universal and basic axiom of all realistic metaphysics. Having admitted it the Jaina view allows this principle to exercise its full logical function so that every detail of the universe, physical and mental, becomes an infinitely diversified fact of nature. Secondly, the Advaita absolute, which is the exact logical antithesis to the Jaina conception of the diversified real, does

---

1. For instance, by Siddhasena Divākara, at several places in his *STP*, Ch. III; by Malliṣeṇa in his *SM*, pp.16-17 (the systems referred to are those of the Svāyambhuvas and the Prakrāntavādins, or the Vaiśeṣikas. See the Editor's explanations of these terms in his Notes, pp. 45-58); and, by Guṇaratna in his *TRD*, pp. 237-244 (the systems referred to are those of Buddhism in general, as well as the Vaiśeṣikas and the Sauntrāntikas in particular, the Naiyāyikas, the Vaiśeṣikas, the Sāṁkhyas and the Mīmāṁsakas).

2. See the end of f.n. 1, and *AGAM*, *Prastāvanā*, p. 90.

not admit of distinction in any form in its ultimate nature of pure being (*sat*), and, therefore, develops itself, inevitably, into a spiritualistic *ekāntavāda* par excellence. This fact proves, indirectly, that once the initial assumption of distinction is allowed to operate—as it should be, since distinction is an irrefutable fact of reality—it leads to the Jaina view, as a logical necessity, of an indeterminate reality. In other words, the developments of the two contrasting conceptions of reality, the Jaina and the Advaita, reveal the truth that if we follow a strictly monistic hypothesis of Advaitism we must inevitably accept some kind of mentalism or spiritualism which asserts the identity of the knower and the known, or rather the reality of the knower and the falsity of the known which, consequently, is treated as a projection of the knower. It is, therefore, not a surprise that Advaitism in India, like its Hegelian counterpart in the West, received the characteristically subjectivistic interpretation of the *dṛṣṭisṛṣṭivāda* of Prakāśānanda, which has its counterpart in the Berkeleyan theory of *esse est percipi.* Alternatively, in order to avoid a mentalistic or subjectivistic orientation in our approach to reality, if distinction or objectivity is admitted to be real, *anekāntavāda* represents the most logical form which such a realistic procedure can take. Owing to the decisive significance of this issue the two considerations just outlined deserve a some-what closer notice here. We may start with the second one first :

I. The Advaitic absolute is what may be described as a monolithic conception. It is also driven home to us, repeatedly, that its nature, like that of the Hegelian absolute, is mentalistic or epistemic (*prātītikasattvam*).[1] Nothing else than it is real.[2] This pan-psychic reality cannot, in the nature of the case, admit of objectivity or an independent non-mental principle. Hence the question of distinction cannot arise in it. If it does, we have to find something which is to be distinguished from the absolute. There is nothing answering such a description. It is not possible to speak of a distinction in a real where there is no possibility of an actual separableness in some genuine sense. This is the story of all idealism, viz., that the real therein stages its duel with itself, or, at best, its shadow; it enacts a play in which the *dramatis personae* consist of one character only; or it constitutes a musical scale which consists of one note only—namely, itself. Not merely this, it is also the duel as well as the participant in it; the play as well as the player; and the music as well as the musician. Hegel at least tries to integrate difference in the ascending order of his triadic dialectic but, eventually, with the same result as his Indian counterpart.

It may, however, be argued that Śaṅkara does recognise

---

1. *Prātītikasattvaṁ sarvasyeti siddham/* p. 537, *Advaitasiddhi* of Madhusūdanasarasvatī (with three commentaries, ed. N. S. Ananta Krishna Sastri, Bombay, 1917). *avidyāyonayo bhāvāḥ sarve'mī budbudā iva / kṣaṇamudbhūya gacchanti jñānaikajaladhau layam // Ibid.* (quoted by the author from *Śruti*). *etat sarvaṁ mana eva /* (quoted in *Gauḍabrahmānandī*, a com. on the above work *Ibid.*, p. 537). *jagato manaḥpariṇāmatvamuktam / Ibid.* Lastly, *asmādātmanaḥ sarve prāṇāḥ sarve lokāḥ sarve vedāḥ sarvāṇi bhūtani /* (quoted by Nyāyāmṛtakāra) *Ibid.*, p. 538.

2. See the above f.n., particularly the second quotation.

some kind of objectivity at the so-called empirical level of existence (*vyāvahārikasattā*). But he does so only as a mere 'epistemic' phenomenon which is not of the substance of the real in a straightforward way. His grand *tour de force* only proves the obstinacy of objectivity, which cannot be explained away even by his logical genius. Hence the term 'objective' in the so-called Objective Idealism is a misnomer. It attributes 'objectivism' to a philosophy of objectless reality.

Further, the mental realm, the realm of souls which are the centres of experience, should and does command its legitimate place and importance in any reasonable scheme of reality, but the total mentalization of the objective world by the schools of idealism imports into their scheme a kind of anthropomorphism. Had it not been for this Alexander would not have proclaimed his mission to "de-anthropomorphise" philosophy. Despite its length his statement on this question bears reproducing here. Writing under "The Spirit of Realism" he observes: "The temper of realism is to *de-anthropomorphise*: to order man and mind to their proper place among the world of finite things; on the one hand to divest physical things of the colouring which they have received from the vanity or arrogance of mind, and on the other to assign them along with minds their due measure of self-existence. But so deeply is the self-flattering habit of supposing that mind, in its distinctive character of mind, is in special sense the superior of physical things, so that in the absence of mind there would be no physical existence at all, that Realism in questioning its prerogative appears to some to degrade mind and rob it of its richness and value."[1]

The mere magnification of the mental principle into a cosmic one and the description of its function as an act of objectivisation does not make the real either any the less mental or the more objective. The ghost of objectivity or independence cannot be laid by the magic of verbal trickery. It comes back in some kind of awkward form as an 'empirical' or 'epistemic' phenomenon or an 'antithesis'.

There is, therefore, nothing strange in the fact that the mind-ridden Absolute Idealism gave rise to the curious doctrine of *Dṛṣṭisṛṣṭivāda* or *Jñātasattāvāda* of Prakāśānanda and others, which affirms that a thing exists only when it is perceived. In this view the "blue", for instance, "and its awareness are one, and there is no external object apart from its cognition."[2] Alluding to this view an Indian critic observes: "The whole world is thus only a psychic modification and has no reality outside the mind."[3] Prakāśānanda himself observes: "The wise maintain the psychological ideality of the world, the ignorant its objective reality."[4]

---

1. "The Basis of Realism" (p. 1), an Address by S. Alexander to the British Academy in 1914.
2. P. N. Srinivasachari's *Aspects of Advaita* (Sri Krishna Library series, Madras, 1949), p. 16.
3. *Ibid.* See also pp. 97-98.
4. *Jñānasvarūpamevāhur jagadetadvicakṣaṇāḥ / arthasvarūpaṁ bhrāmyantaḥ paśyanteti kudṛṣṭayaḥ //* The following line also expresses the same idea more pithily: *dṛṣṭireva bhavet sṛṣṭirdṛṣṭisṛṣṭimate../*

   These lines have been quoted in M. N. Sircar's *The System of Vedāntic Thought and Culture* (published by University of

This view, in which 'spirit greets the spirit', or *dṛṣṭi* is *sṛṣṭi*, has its close parallel in the well-known Berkeleyan view *esse* is *percipi*. Referring to the relation of the 'unthinking things' of the objective world to this 'intuitive or self-evident' principle Berkeley observes: "Their *esse* is *percipi*; nor is it possible they should have any existence out of the minds or thinking things which perceive them." [1]

Dṛṣṭisṛṣṭivāda and its close Western parallel have been mentioned here, not merely because they are a particular school of idealism but because they represent the tendency of all idealism towards subjectivism.[2] As a critic observes:

Calcutta, 1925), p. 126, footnotes 1 and 2. See also pp. 125-26 (the text).

Madhusūdana also observes: *imameva ca dṛṣṭisṛṣṭivādamācakṣate asmiṁś ca pakṣe jīva eva svajñānavaśājjagadupādānanimittaṁ ca / dravyaṁ ca sarvaṁ prātītikam / Siddhāntabindu* (of Madhusūdana with a Com. by Puruśottama, ed. P. E. Divan, *GOS*, Baroda, 1933), p. 29. See also *Advaitasiddhi* and Prakāśānanda's *Siddhāntamuktāvali* (E. T. by Arthur Venis, Reprint from the Pandit, Benares, 1890), p. 25 ff. (text).

Even the so-called 'opposite view' to this (*dṛṣṭisṛṣṭivāda*) viz., *sṛṣṭidṛṣṭivāda*, also retains the character of mentalism in so far as it maintains that the world is a "creation or emanation" from Brahman (see *Siddhāntamuktāvali*, Pref. p. II, f. n. 1). The difference, if there is any at all, is that in *sṛṣṭidṛṣṭivāda* the world is supposed to 'precede' our knowledge of it, while in *dṛṣṭisṛṣṭivāda* it is said to be concurrent with (because it is also the creation of) our knowledge. The difference, however, is not material owing to the fact that Brahman is only an extension of the individual psychic principle.

1. *Of the Principles of Human Knowledge* (Vol. I of *The Works of George Berkeley*, in 4 Vols., ed. A.C. Fraser, Oxford, 1901), p. 259.
2. Cf. Russell's observation that "...very many philosophers, perhaps a majority, have held that there is nothing except minds and their ideas. Such philosophers are called 'ideal ists" etc. *Problems*, p. 14; see also p. 37.

"The forms of idealism like objective idealism and absolute idealism are only *attenuated forms* of subjective idealism and the true subject transcends the subject-object relation."[1] In his celebrated essay "The Reputation of Idealism", G. E. Moore also is in full accord with this criticism. He characterises the notion of *esse* is *percipi*—conceding generously to the idealist that *percipi* need not mean 'sensation' only but 'thought' also, both of course being 'forms' of consciousness —as the 'ultimate premise of Idealism' in general.[2] Confirming his attitude to the same notion, he further observes: "I believe that Idealists all hold this important falsehood."[3] His choice of this notion as the most vulnerable point for attack in idealism has considerably strengthened the realistic stand for objectivity or independence in the analysis of the nature of reality.[4]

---

1. Srinivasachari in *Aspects of Advaita*, pp. 14-15 (the italics are mine). L. T. Hobhouse demonstrates this truth in a lucid and critical note wherein he analyses the positions of T. H. Green and B. Bosanquet. See his *The Theory of Knowledge* (third ed. London, 1921), p. 537 f., f. n. 2.
2. *Philosophical Studies* (The International Library of Psychology, Philosophy, and Scientific Method, 1951 (reprinted), London), pp. 7-8.
3. *Ibid.*, p. 12.
4. The following witticisms make an interesting reading: It would be more appropriate, in this context, to substitute 'percept' wherever the term 'idea' occurs. So Beattie told Hume that the idea (or image) of a roaring lion is not a roaring idea, and that the image of an ass is not a long-eared sluggish idea; and he put some 'clownish questions' to Berkeley in the same spirit. "Where," he asked, "is the harm of my believing that if I were to fall down yonder precipice and break my neck, I should be no more a man of this world? My neck, Sir, may be an idea to you, but to me it is a reality and

an important one too. Where is the harm of my believing that if, in this severe weather, I were to neglect to throw (what you call) the idea of a coat over the ideas of my shoulders, the idea of cold would produce the idea of such pain and disorder that might possibly terminate in my real death?" *A Study in Realism* (John Laird, C. U. P., 1920, Cambridge), p. 63.

Repudiating the claim that the Modern Einsteinian Theory of Relativity supports idealism, Russell writes under the heading 'Realism in Relativity'; "It is a mistake to suppose that relativity adopts an idealistic picture of the world—using 'idealism' in the technical sense, in which it implies that there can be nothing which is not experience. The observer who is often mentioned in expositions of relativity need not be a mind, but may be a photographic plate or any kind of recording instrument. The fundamental assumption of relativity is realistic, namely, that these respects in which all observers agree when they record a given phenomenon may be regarded as objective, and not as contributed by the observers." Bertrand Russell on 'Relativity', *Encyclopaedia Britannica Inc.*, The Univ. of Chicago, 1950. See also his *The A. B. C. of Relativity* (London, 1925), pp. 219-20.

Max Born, the great theoretical physicist, also offers a similar vindication of the 'reality' of the pre-existing external material world. This is done in answer to Herbert Dingle's thesis. Dingle puts to himself the fundamental question, viz. "What exactly is it that physicists are doing?" The answer: "That can be answered satisfactorily only in terms of experience, not of the external world." In his reply to Dingle, Max Born describes the former's viewpoint as "a standpoint of extreme subjectivism" or "physical solipsism" and endeavours to restore, by means of several technical and lay arguments, common sense to the relativistic, quantum, (for an unequivocal support of Max Plank to an external world "which is 'independent of ourselves', something absolute that we are facing..." see *Albert Einstein: Philosopher-scientist,* 2nd ed., ed. P. A. Schilpp, New York, 1951, p. 136 f.) and other theories of science and, thereby, to philosophy. (Vide H. Dingle's lecture to the British Association, 1951, on "Philosophy and Physics", 1850-1950, in *Nature* (London), Vol. 168, pp. 630-36, especially p. 634, para 2, and Max Born's article on "Physical Reality" in the *Philosophical Quarterly* (ed. T. M. Knox), Vol. III No. 11 for April 1953, pp. 139-149.) A. P. Ushenko is

II. Thus the Advaitic attempt at building up a structure of reality from which the independence of the objective world is explained away has been revealed, in our analysis so far, to tend towards some form of mentalism. Even if any other school of idealism attempts to bring anything in *ab extra* into the being of its ultimate realm the attempt would be foredoomed to failure in the same measure as its denial of self-existence to the objective universe. Nothing short of a forthright recognition of the independent and intrinsic nature of reality will ever succeed in avoiding the mentalization or spiritualization of the non-spiritual realm of reality.

Once the claim of independence as an integral part of reality is initially conceded, then, it becomes the thin edge of the wedge; that is, the operative force of the principle of distinction thus introduced in the real will work itself out, through various stages of increasing approximation like duality, plurality and reciprocity towards the *anekānta* view of reality. The dialectical evolution of these approximations

---

another fierce critic who joins issue with Dingle: "If I am asked to mention," he observed, "some particular metaphysics which clearly does not fit in with the theory of relativity, I should name solipsism." *Albert Einstein*, p. 613.

Yet another writer of today to whose views on the present problem Einstein himself has paid a serious attention is Henry Margenau. Margenau's argument for the reality or objectivity of the universe, under Einstein's theory, cannot be cited here, but merits our attention. Vide his article on "Einstein's Conception of Relativity" in *Albert Einstein* (see 4, pp. 252-57), and his recent work, *The Nature of Physical Reality*, The Graw-Hill Book Co. Inc., New York, the sections on The Reality of Data, Other Selves, pp. 297-9, and the Real World, pp. 299-305; and the entire chap. (21) on The Contours of Reality, pp. 448-67.

or stages has been already traced out earlier in course of this section. According to the Jaina dialecticians the several schools which do recognise the independent objectivity of the world have inevitably, though often unwittingly, been confronted with the necessity of acknowledging the *anekānta* view, at least in some aspects of their conception of reality as well as of knowledge. The instances, which, among others include the Mīmāṁsā, the Sāṅkhya, and the Vaiśeṣika schools, have already been mentioned elsewhere. He feels that they all have stopped short of consciously allowing the principle of distinction to reach its logical conclusion in an indeterminate approach to the problem. If the compulsive force of the spirit of *anekānta* is allowed to have its sway, then, according to him, reality would be infinitely diversified.[1] The optimum point of the restless force of distinction is represented in the inexhaustible diversification of every detail in the physical and the mental universe consistently, of course, with the equally enduring identities in nature. The theory of manifoldness is therefore the story of the gradual unfoldment of the implications of distinction which is at the heart of everything. If this cardinal truth is disproved, then the entire structure of the *anekānta* philosophy will collapse like a house of cards.

To summarise the entire argument: The essence of realism is the principle objectivity, independence, or dis-

---

1. The Vaiśeṣika comes nearest, particularly with respect to his atomism, to *anekavāda*, but he stops at the level of what may be described as mechanical pluralism, rather than in determinate relativism of the Jainas. Cf. *supra*, ch. on *Arthakriyākāritvam* and the Vaiśeṣika's *Ubhayavāda*.

tinction. The alternative to the non-acceptance of this principle in reality is some form of idealism which is generically inadequate and has a tendency towards subjectivism. Acceptance of the intrinsic objectivity of the world marks the starting point of the functioning of distinction which progressively develops until the point of culmination is reached in the fact of the indeterminate and manifold nature of reality. It is in the logical necessity of the development from the initial simple state of distinction to that of infinite diversification of everything real, physical or mental, that the justification of the claim of *Anekāntavāda* as the most consistent form of realism lies.

CHAPTER X

Nayavāda
or
The Theory of Standpoints

CHAPTER X

NAYAVĀDA
(The Theory of Standpoints)

Anekāntavāda as a theory of reality, according to which reality is infinitely manifold, or relativistic in its determinations, has been observed to be inherent in the co-ordinate conception of identity-in-difference. It has also been pointed out, at the beginning of our treatment of *anekāntavāda* that the *nayavāda*, or the method of standpoints, and *syādvāda*, or the method of dialectical predications, are the two main wings of *anekāntavāda*. A brief attempt may be made, in this part, to bring out how the two theories, viz., *nayavāda* and *syādvāda*, bring out and sustain the relativistic character of reality.

Logically, *nayavāda* and *syādvāda* are two complementary processes forming a natural and inevitable development of the relativistic presupposition of the Jaina metaphysics. They form a scheme which is pre-eminently one of correlative methods[1] rather than of theories of reality although they both presuppose and explain the primordial notion that all reality is relativistic. *Nayavāda* is principally an analytical

---

1. While dealing, principally, with *nayavāda* Rao characterises 'Jainism' as follows : "It is essentially a method and an attitude." *The Half-Yearly Journal of the Mysore University*, New Series, Section A—Art, March 1942, p. 79.

method investigating a particular standpoint of a factual situation according to the purpose and the level of equipment of the experient (*jñātṛ*). The particular standpoint thus investigated is one among a multitude of different viewpoints which, in their totality, reflect the full nature of the situation. *Syādvāda*, or *Saptabhaṅgī*, is, essentially, a synthetical method designed to harmonise the different viewpoints arrived at by *nayavada*.[1]

Making a further distinction between *nayavāda* and *syādvāda* Upadhye[2] maintains that the former is "primarily conceptual" and the latter "mainly verbal". Although not quite incorrect, this distinction is apt to be somewhat mis-

---

1. Cf. "...each of the *nayas* comprehends things from only one particular standpoint, knowledge derived from a *naya* therefore is partial and incomplete. To comprehend things in all their aspects, therefore, a special mode or form must be found. This, according to the Jains, is their *Syādvāda* or the doctrine of many possibilities." *The Nyāyāvatāra* (Ed. by P. L. Vaidya, Bombay, 1928), Intro. p. XL. 1.

   "The *nayas* refer to the parts of the thing, whereas the *saptabhaṅgī* refers to the things as a whole; *nayas* have relation to analysis, whereas *saptabhaṅgī* relates to synthesis; *nayavāda* is the analytical method of knowledge, whereas *saptabhaṅgī* is the synthetical method of knowing a thing." H. L. Jhaveri's *The First Principles of the Jaina Philosophy*, London, 1910, p. 42. See also *NKV*, Intro. pp. 21-22. Also,

   nayānāmekaniṣṭhānāṁ pravṛtteḥ sṛtavartmani /
   sampūrṅārthaviniścāyī syādvādaśrutamucyate //

   The Nyāyāvatāra, kā. 30. See also Siddharṣi's Comm. thereon.

2. He observes: "*Syādvāda* is a corollary of *Nayavāda*: the latter is analytical and primarily conceptual and the former is synthetical and mainy verbal". *PrSKU*, Intro. p. LXXXV. Incidentally (see *SJJ*, p. 17 and p. 52), it would be more correct to say, with Jacobi, that *syādvāda* is a 'logical complement' than a 'corollary' of *nayavāda*.

understood if we are not aware of the background against which it is made. This is because the so-called 'primarily conceptual' method is also verbal, inasmuch as it not merely requires the aid of words for the expression of its various standpoints but also has as many as three, among its seven, standpoints which are exclusively concerned with the verbal problems, and are therefore designated as *śabdanayas*. Similarly, in contradistinction to the verbal elements of the 'conceptual' *nayavāda*, the 'mainly verbal' method of *syādvāda* is so much charged with the epistemological character that we might say that its verbal side is more instrumental than intrinsic in value. The term 'conceptual' may, however, be applied to the four *dravyanayas*, under *nayavāda*, with relatively greater propriety. But under *syādvāda* no distinctions, such as the verbal modes of *syādvāda* and the non-verbal or the epistemological modes of *syādvāda*, can be made since all modes are both verbal and epistemological. This is so in spite of the fact that much care and exactitude are needed in the verbal formulation and manipulation of the modal judgments.

Leaving aside the epistemological content of the modal judgments for the moment, the description of all the modes of *syādvāda* as verbal also may give rise to a possible objection that such a description should not be applied to the mode which contains the 'inexpressible' (*avaktavya*) as its predicate. For the 'inexpressible' is, *ex hypothesi*, a verbal failure insofar as it is incapable of a 'co-presentation' or a simultaneous expression of the positive and the negative traits of a real in a single attempt. Describing a mode as verbal when a signal verbal failure is inscribed on it would, therefore, be, according to the possible objector, paradoxically objectionable. Deferring a fuller discussion of the modal predicate, the 'inexpressible', to the next chapter, we may briefly indicate here the line of argument the Jaina would take in answering the present objection. The Jaina answer to this objection, it may be noted, necessarily entails a reference to the third mode of *syādvāda* also :

The predicate 'the inexpressible' does indeed record a signal verbal failure in expressing, at once, the great amplitude of the variegated reality as embodied in every factual event. But this failure is not due to the inherent unknowability, and, consequently, of the inexpressibility of reality, as in the case of the theories underlying the formulae like "*sa eṣa neti neti*" or "*catuṣkoṭivinirmuktatvam*" or "*anirvacanīyatā*". It is, on the contrary, due to the bewildering wealth of impressions directly pouring into the human mind whose limitations of powers are such that it cannot at once grapple with all the impressions by way of all-comprehending attention and precise expression. Hence the postulation of the predicate in question. The only verbal feature of the predicate is the symbol (*saṁjñā*) '*avaktavya*' employed in designating the predicate. This symbol declares the inadequacy of the verbal machinery when confronted with such cognitive situations. But this does not mean that *avaktavya* is the last word in our cognitive venture and, consequently, that we are inescapably condemned to be cognitively overwhelmed and verbally dumb. What is not simultaneously expressible can be expressed by a gradual process in the order of the attention severally paid to the manifold features in the situation concerned. This fact introduces a sequential outlet (*kramārpaṇa*) for what would otherwise remain a 'paradoxically objectionable' position. In other words, if the mode of *avaktavya* were an absolute position (*sarvathaikāntadṛṣṭi*) it would certainly be 'a paradoxically objectionable' position, but since the mode represents a relative position (*kathañcidekāntadṛṣṭi*) it leaves room for a sequential alternative which guarantees a gradual unfoldment of the entire complex structure of the factual situation in hand.

Words have a vital role to play in the process of the unfoldment of the complex or the simple meanings of reality in spite of their limitations as noticed under the 'inexpressible' (*avaktavya*) mode. Communication of the meanings of reality either to us (*svārthaḥ*) or from us to others (*parārthaḥ*) is said to be an inherent power (*svābhāvikī śaktiḥ*)[1] in words. Devabhadra, for instance, observes that every specific meaning is resident in a particular

---

1. Referring to this *śaktiḥ* or *yogyatā* Prabhācandra observes: *yogyatā hi śabdārthayoḥ pratipādyapratipādakaśaktiḥ, jñānajñeyayor jñāpyajnāpakaśaktivat*/ *NKC*, Vol. II, p. 538. See also *PKM*, p. 428, where also he writes to the same effect when commenting on the following *Parīkṣāmukha sūtra* : *sahajayogyatāsaṅketavaśāddhi śabdādayaḥ vastupratipattihetavaḥ*/ *Ibid.*, p. 427. (Here '*śabdādayaḥ*', or words etc., means words, gestures made by fingers, etc. (*aṅgulyādivākya*) and any similar signs.) In *NKC*, Vol. II, p. 541, the same writer again observes : *śaktis tu svābhāvikī yathā rūpaprakāśane cakṣurādeḥ tathā arthaprakāśane śabdasyāpi* / Vādideva also makes similar observations on this question. See *SRK*, pp. 702-3. A brief comment of Kumārila also is of interest in this connection : *sarvo hi śabdo'rthapratyayanārthaṁ prayujyate* (*Tantravārtika*, I. 3. 8).

word.[1] Siddharṣi supports this idea from another angle by remarking that there are no objects (*artha*) without names.[2] Maladhāri Hemacandra believes that everything cognisable is also expressible in some way.[3]

The Jaina is, however, cautious in not stretching this belief in the natural power of words to the extent of advocating the identity (*tādātmya*) of essence between the word and its meaning. Had it not been so he would find himself an ally of Bhartṛhari and the other grammarian philosophers who maintain the doctrine of *śabdādvaitavāda*. According to the Jaina words are only expressive (*vācaka*) or, as Yaśovijaya puts it, suggestive (*jnāpaka*) symbols rather than productive (*kāraka*[4]) entities of meanings. In other words, what is meant by the remark that a meaning resides in a word is nothing more than forcefully stating that the word has the natural power of expressing the meaning which is not produced by, or derived from, it. The meaning is eventually rooted in the nature of things in reality, but is conveyed to us through the natural expressive capacity of words.

The main purpose of introducing here the above brief discussion on the linguistic aspect of *syādvāda* has been to show how far *syādvāda* can be described as 'mainly verbal', or, for that matter, a 'verbal' method at all. The discussion

---

1. *pratyarthaṁ śabdanivāsād iti*/ *Nyāyāvatāra* (of Siddhasena Divākara, with Siddharṣi's *Vivṛti* and Devabhadra's *Tippaṇa*, ed. P. L. Vaidya, 1928, Bombay), p. 81.
2. *nirabhidhānārthābhāvāt* / *Ibid*., p. 80.
3. *kaścit tu gamyatayā sarvo'bhilapyaḥ..*/ *SHM*, on *gā*. 143, *VBJ*.
4. *sabdānāṁ ca arthajñāpakatvam na tu kārakatvam* / *SKL*, p. 250.

indicates the undoubted necessity for a precise scheme of linguistic symbols (*vacanavinyāsa*). But the scheme of linguistic symbols is only the garb of the modal judgments which represent a system of alternative and exhaustive aspects of truth of a particular factual situation investigated by *syādvāda*. The content being such judgments *syādvāda* is essentially an epistemological method. This pre-eminently epistemological character of it becomes more evident when we remember that the knowledge obtained by its use is conceived to be the human analogue of the perfect knowledge (*kevalajnāna*) attained by the perfect souls (*kevalins*), the difference between the two being that the one is mediate (*asākṣāt*) and the other immediate (*sāksāt*[1]).

The purport of the entire argument is that the distinction between 'conceptual' and 'verbal' is a relative one, and therefore that when it is associated with the two methods under consideration, it should be done subject to the consideration outlined in course of the argument.

The logical justification for the formulation of these two methods of *nayavāda* and *syādvāda* consists in the fact that the immense complexity of the relativistic universe is too baffling for the human mind, with its limited range of perceptual and other capacities, to penetrate at once, into its full secrets. In the process of grasping the bewildering universe analysis, or *nayavāda*, naturally precedes synthesis, or *syādvāda*, and the two methods together offer an articulated knowledge of the universe. After this comparative estimate

---

1. Cf. *syādvādakevalajñāne sarvatattvaprakāśane / bhedaḥ sākṣādasākṣāc ca..... // AMS, kā.* 105.

of the two methods we may now proceed to consider them in their natural order.

The Definition of Nayavāda

A *naya* is defined[1] as a particular opinion or (*abhiprāya* or *abhimata*) or a viewpoint (*apekṣā*)—a viewpoint which does not rule out other different viewpoints and is, thereby, expressive of a partial truth (*vastvaṁśagrāhī*) about an object (*vastu*)—as entertained by a knowing agent (*jñātṛ*[2]). A *naya* is a particular viewpoint about an object or an event, there being many other viewpoints which do not enter into, or interfere

---

1. This is the general definition (*sāmānya lakṣaṇa*) of a *naya*. The specific feature (*viśeṣa lakṣaṇa*) of each particular *naya* will be noticed later on.

2. To express the nature of a *naya*, in the words of Prabhāchandra: *anirākṛtapratipakṣo vastvaṁśagrāhī jñāturabhiprāyo nayaḥ / PKM*, p. 676. There are numerous variant forms of the definition of a *naya*. But they all express substantially, but often more elaborately, the whole, or a part, of the connotation so briefly indicated by Prabhāchandra's definition. See, for instance, *NKC*, Vol. II, p. 606 f., f.n. 1, in which the editor has enumerated about as many as thirty such variant forms. In *AGAM*, pp. 142-3 (*tippaṇāni*), under '*naya*' the same editor has made a few editions to the forms. The following, not necessarily found in the above-mentioned two places, may, however, be cited here:

   arthasyānekarūpasya dhīḥ pramāṇaṁ tadaṁśadhīḥ /
   nayo dharmāntarāpekṣī durnayas tannirākṛtiḥ //
   AŚA on *AMS*, 1.47.

   pramāṇaparicchinnasya anantadharmātmakasya vastuna ekadeśagrāhiṇaḥ taditarāṁśapratikṣepiṇo adhyavasāyavid eṣa nayaḥ/. *JTBY*, p. 21 (cf. *PNTA*, VII. 1, and *SRK* thereon, in *SRK*, p. 1044). *nayantīti nayāḥ anekadharmātmakaṁ vastu ekadharmeṇa nityamevedam anityameveti vā nirūpayanti/*" See *NKC*, Vol. II, p. 606 f., f.n. 1.

with, the particular viewpoint under discussion. Although the other viewpoints do not enter into the perspective[1] of the particular viewpoints under discussion they constantly, as it were, attack its frontiers, and await its reconciliation with them in the sphere of a fuller and more[2] valid knowledge which is the sphere of *pramāṇa*.

---

1 Cf. *audāsīnyaparāyaṇās tadapare cāṁśe bhaveyur nayāḥ*/ *ABHI*, p. 1853.

2. This phrase "more valid" is advisedly used here. This becomes clear when we notice the controversy, met with in Jaina works, as to whether the partial truth conveyed by a *naya* is as valid as the full truth conveyed by *pramāṇa*. Vidyānanda attempts an answer to this by employing an analogical argument, often repeated by writers since, in which he compares *naya* to a part of a sea which is *pramāṇa* (*TSU*, p. 118, *kā*. 5 and the *ṭīkā* thereon). See also *SRK*, pp. 1044-7. Insofar as the part is identical with the whole—*it is identical* since it is a legitimate part of the whole—a *naya* shares the validity, at any rate in some measure, of *pramāṇa*. But, insofar as it is different from the whole—*it is different* from the whole, in some sense, otherwise the part and the whole become indistinguishable—a *naya* is invalid. The conclusion implied is a simple one, viz., that a part(*naya*) is not eschewed by the whole (*pramāṇa*); that the whole itself would not be but for the combination of such parts; that the part is valid (*mānātmako nayaḥ*; *nāpyasatyo nayaḥ*) so far as it goes, and that it becomes invalid when its partial truth is taken to be the whole truth when it is called a *nayābhāsa*, or *kunaya*, or *durnaya*.

The above conclusion is generally agreed to in spirit if not in letter also, but most writers including Vidyānanda, Jinabhadra and his commentator Maladhāri Hemacandra, however, do not seem to accede to this conclusion whole-heartedly, although they do not eventually disagree with it (see *VBJ*, *gā*. 2277 and *SHM* thereon). For some of the expressions with which they describe the nature of *nayas* are more appropriate to the description of the nature of *nayābhāsas* or *durnayas*. For instance, *nayas* are said to be incapable of being *vastuno gamakāḥ* (*pratyekāvasthāyāṁ tadagamakatvāt*). Further, they

Theoretically the viewpoints from which an object or an event could be perceived are not merely numerous[1] (*aneka-vikalpa*) but infinite[2] in number (*anantaprakāram*) because even the humblest fact of existence is infinitely manifold and therefore can be an object of various modes of analysis. But this way of looking at the subject is too broad (*vyāsa* or *vistāra*[3]) or gross (*sthūla*) and, therefore, does not vouchsafe to us a compact view of reality on the basis of which we can develop a practicable analytical method by means of which we may tackle reality piecemeal and obtain partial glimpses of its truth. The view of reality, conceived under the great division consisting of two inclusive categories, viz., *dravyārthikanaya* or the substantive view, and *paryāyārthikanaya* or the modal (or the modificational) view, is, however, considered to be an answer to the demand.[4] The categories are

---

are said to be heretical (*mithyātmadṛṣṭitvāt*), contradictory (*virodhato*, or *virodhitvāt*), inimical (*vairivat*) in their character.

Another factor which seems to confirm the attitude of Jinabhadra, more especially of his great commentator, is the quotation, by the latter, of a devotional verse, the second line of which is in tune with the view suggested by the two writers:

udadhāviva sarvasindhavaḥ samudīrṇāstvayi nātha dṛṣṭayaḥ /
na ca tāsu bhavān pradṛśyate pravibhaktāsu saritsvivodadhiḥ//

See *VBJ*, *gā.* 2266 and *SHM*, on 2265-6.

1. *jāvaiyā vayanavahā tāvaiyā honti nayavāyā / STP*, III. 47. *jāvanto vayanapahā tāvanto vā nayāvi sāhāvo / VBJ*, *gā.* 2265. *vyāsato'nekavikalpā iti / PNTA*, VII. 4 and the *SRK* thereon in *SRK*, p. 1047.

2. *nayāś cānantāḥ / SM* (text), p. 161.

3. See *PNTA*, VII. 4 and the *SRK* thereon.

4. Cf. *dravyaparyāyarūpasya sakalasyāpi vastunaḥ/ nayāvaṁśena netārau sakalasyāpi vastunaḥ // Tattvārthasāra*, *kā.* 38. Vādideva brings out very clearly and elaborately, the

also called, briefly, as *dravyanaya* and *paryāyanaya* respectively. The view of reality conceived under the division is described as the concise (*sankṣepa* or *samāsa*[1]) one in contrast to the other (the broad) one.

By a process of further analysis the Jaina thinkers have been led to the formulation of the methodological scheme consisting of seven ways of looking at reality. They are enumerated in the following order of decreasing denotation[2]: *naigama, saṅgraha, vyavahāra, ṛjusūtra, śabda, samabhirūḍha,* and *evambhūta*[3]. Generally among these the first three are considered to be *dravyanayas* or substantive standpoints and the other four *paryāyanayas* or modal standpoints[4]. Reserving to a later stage[5] the consideration of the question whether the number of these seven ways of viewpoints can be reduced to six, or five, or even less, either by elimination of any of them, or by subsumption of some of them under the one or the other of the seven viewpoints, we may now proceed to point out, with illustrations, the nature and function of these seven viewpoints.

---

progressive decrease in denotation, from every preceding *naya* to its succeeding one, in the course of as many as seven *sūtras* and his own comm. thereon. See *ONTA,* VII. 46-52 and the *SRK* thereon.

1. See *PNTA,* VII. 5 and the *SRK* thereon.
2. Cf. *pūrvaḥ pūrvanayo bhūmaviṣayaḥ kāraṇātmakaḥ / paraḥ paraḥ punaḥ sūkṣmagocaro hetumāniha// Nayavivaraṇa, kā.* 98.
3. See *TSUJ,* I. 33.
4. *dravyārtho vyavahārāntaḥ paryāyārthas tatoparaḥ / TSV,* p. 268.
5. See *infra.*

Naigamanaya (*the teleological or the universal-particular standpoint*)

Naigamanaya relates to the purpose (*saṅkalpa*)[1] or the end of a certain continuous series of actions which are represented by one or a few of their number. For instance, a person carrying fuel, water, and rice, when asked "What are you doing?" says "I am cooking" instead of saying "I am carrying fuel" and so forth.[2] This means that the general purpose of cooking controls the entire series of actions which are represented by one or more of them such as carrying the materials or drawing water enabling us thereby to grasp the purpose which governs the individual factors relating to it. This is the aim or function of the *naigama* standpoint.

According to another interpretation *naigamanaya* is described as the standpoint of the 'non-distinguished'[3]. By the 'non-distinguished' is meant the absence of distinction or discrimination between the universal or the generic and the particular or the specific elements of the object under review. Accordingly, the meaning of the term *naigama* is analysed as 'not' (*na*) 'one' (*eko*) 'understanding' (*gamaḥ*), that is, not understanding or distinguishing either the generic element alone, or the specific element alone, but taking the object in in its concrete unity.[4] One of the instances given in illustration of this non-distinction is that of the term 'bamboo'. When we use this term in a statement such as "Bamboo

---

1. *arthasaṅkalpamātragrāhī naigamaḥ* / *TRAG*, p. 65, *kā*. 2. *aniṣpannārthasaṅkalpamātragrāhī naigama iti nigamo hi saṅkalpaḥ tatrabhavaḥ tatprayojano vā naigamaḥ* / *SRK*, p. 1052.
2. Cf. *SRK*, p. 1052 f. See also *Tattvārthasāraḥ*, *kā*. 44.
3. *yadvā naikaṁ gamo yo'tra sa satāṁ naigamo mataḥ*/ *TSV*, p. 269.
4. *NKC*, *kā*. 5.

grows here in plenty", from the 'non-distinguished' point of view, the distinction between the generic and the specific features of the bamboo is not within the focus of our attention, although it is undoubtedly at the back of our minds. This truth, namely, that when some aspect of concrete situation in reality is in the foreground of our attention the other aspects recede into the background, is one of the cardinal principles of the modern Gestalt, or Configurationist, school of psychology. Also, it holds good of not merely the 'non-distinguished' standpoint, but also of all the others under the present method.

Although the two interpretations of *naigamanaya*, the one emphasising its teleological character and the other its 'non-distinguished' character, are mentioned to be different, the difference between them does not seem to be always sharp and material. This is evident when we notice that the principle of non-distinction between the universal and the particular is inherent in, or, at any rate, is not repugnant to, the purpose governing the actions in the relevant context such as the above-mentioned instance of cooking. It must, however, be admitted that when a 'non-distinguished' instance like "the bamboo grows here in plenty" is viewed from the angle of the first interpretation the teleological element is not so evident, although it would not be an impossible idea to think of some instances wherein the two elements could go together. Taking both sides of the argument into consideration we may safely conclude that at least in a considerable number of instances, the difference between the elements of teleology and non-distinction is a matter of difference in emphasis. This view does not, however, bar the possibility of even a radical difference between the two interpretations in a certain number of situations considered under the present standpoint.

The non-distinction of the *naigama* standpoint is not, as just indicated, absolute. It does imply distinction but in a relative sense only. If the distinction is asserted absolutely, then arises the fallacy called *naigamābhāsa*, of which the Nyāya-Vaiśeṣika[1] system, which maintains an absolute distinction (*atyantabhinnatva*) between its categories, is an illustration.

Saṅgrahanaya (*the class view*)

This standpoint concerns itself with the general[2] or the class character of a factual situation, unlike the *naigama* standpoint which includes the specific character as well. Just as *naigamanaya* is not hostile to the intermingled character of concrete existence, so also *saṅgrahanaya* is not repugnant[3] to the complementary feature of *viśeṣa* which is not included in it. *Saṅgrahanaya* marks a step further from *naigamanaya* in that it differentiates, in its analytical process, the common character from the universal-cum-particular complex which every real is. For instance, when, pointing to a solitary tree at some distance from you, you observe to a stranger asking for direction, "turn left near the tree there", it is not relevant to

---

1. See *PNTA*, VII. 12 and the *SRK* thereon. See also *Nayapradīpa*, p. 101, and *Nyāyāvatāra* (P. L. Vaidya's edn.), p. 82.
2. *sāmānyamātragrāhī parāmarśaḥ saṅgraha iti*/ *PNTA*, VII. 13. See also the *SRK* thereon, as well as *TSV*, p. 270, *kā*. 51.
3. See *NKV*, *kā*. 6.

the occasion to mention whether "the tree there" is mango, banyan, or any other, although "the tree" must be one of these. For there can be no universal without a particular[1], or a genus without species, although in a particular context the mention of the former will serve the purpose in hand. Similarly, when we state that everything is *sat*[2] (being) it makes a perfectly understandable proposition, although it provisionally shuts out its necessary complement of *asat* (non-being).

Laying such an exaggerated emphasis[3] on the universal as to leave no room at all for the particular leads to *saṅgrahābhāsa*, a fallacy of which the Sāṅkhya and the Advaita schools of philosophy are notable instances.[4]

Vyavahāranaya[5] *(the standpoint of the particular)*

In contrast with the *saṅgraha* standpoint the *vyavahāra* standpoint specialises itself in being concerned with the speci-

---

1. *Ibid.*
2. *viśvamekaṁ sadaviśeṣāditi*/ *PNTA*, VII. 16.
3. *saṅgraho'pyaśeṣaviśeṣāviśeṣapratikṣepamukhena sāmānyamekaṁ samarthayamāno durnayaḥ....* / *Nyāyāvatāra* (P. L. Vaidya's edn.), p. 85.
4. *saṅgrahābhiprāyapravṛttāḥ sarve'pyadvaitavādāḥ sāṅkhyadarśanaṁ ca.* / See also *PNTA*, VII. 17 and 18 and the *SRK* thereon. The reason why the Sāṅkhya system is instanced here is stated by Prabhācandra: *vikāravikāriṇoḥ sāṅkhyaistādātmyābhyupagamāt*/ *NKL*, Vol. II, p. 629.
5. This *vyavahāranaya* should be distinguished from another *naya*, bearing the same name and occurring in a different classification of *nayas* into *niścayanaya* (the true viewpoint) and *vyavahāranaya* (the conventional or empirical viewpoint). There is nothing common between the two except the name.

fic features[1] of the object concerned, without, of course, losing sight of the fact that they cannot stand by themselves without the support of the generic properties in the larger setting of concrete reality. For example, when a person is asked to bring a mango fruit he attempts to bring mango, but not any other fruit, although he is aware of the fact that mango is only a species in the genus of fruit.[2]

When the generic correlative of a specific feature is entirely ignored the resultant fallacy comes to have only the semblance of the *vyavahāra* standpoint (*vyavahāranayābhāsa*) of which there can be no better example than the materialism of Cārvāka[3] in Indian philosophy.

The above three standpoints, viz., *naigama*, *saṅgraha* and *vyavahāra*, come under the first comprehensive category, viz., *dravyārthikanaya.* This is so because these standpoints concern themselves with the durable side (*dravyasaṁsparśī*) of concrete reality. The remaining four standpoints, viz., *ṛjusūtra, śabda, samabhirūḍha* and *evambhūta*, engage themselves in the analysis of the fleeting side (*paryāyasaṁsparśī*) of concrete reality. Hence their collective designation (*paryāyārthikanaya*), the second of the two comprehensive categories.

Among the four *paryāyanayas* only the first one, viz., *ṛjusūtranaya*, which will presently be dealt with, makes a direct ontological reference to an aspect of reality, viz., the

---

1. *viśeṣātmakamevārthaṁ vyavahāraś ca manyate/ viśeṣabhinnaṁ sāmānyam asatkharaviṣāṇavat//* NKV, *kā.* 8.
2. *Ibid., kārikās* 9 and 10.
3. *PNTA*, VII. 26. For two other instances see *LTB, V, kā.* 42 and the *NKC* thereon in *NKC,* Vol. II, pp. 631-5.

aspect of flux (*paryāya*). The other three are concerned with the verbal questions of the meanings of the modal side of reality. On the basis of this distinction, viz., the aspect involving an ontological reference and the aspects involving verbal references, the standpoints are also classified as *arthanayas* (or *arthatantra*), and *śabdanayas* (or *śabdatantra*), the former class including within itself the first four, and the latter class, the last three.[1]

Jinabhadra, however, chooses to treat *ṛjusūtranaya* as one of the *dravyanayas* on the ostensible ground that it has a direct ontological reference like the other *dravyanayas*.[2] But this is not widely accepted. Now the treatment of the four *paryāyanayas* or the modal standpoints may be resumed.

Ṛjusūtra (*the standpoint of momentariness*)

The *ṛjusūtra* standpoint relates to the momentary nature of a thing.[3] It is narrower than the *vyavahāra* standpoint in that it looks at a particular thing as the thing appears at a particular moment.[4] This standpoint is in operation

1. *tatrarjusūtraparyantāḥ catvāro'rthanayā matāḥ/ trayaḥ śabdanayāḥ śeṣāḥ śabdavācyārthagocarāḥ// Nayavivaraṇam* (by an unknown author, ed. Pannalal Caudhuri, Digambara Jaina Grantha Bhāṇḍāra, Kāśī, Vīra Saṁvat 2451), *kā*. 97. See also *Tattvārthāsava*, *kā*. 43.
2. *VBJ*, p. 2262, *kā*. 77.
3. Cf. *ṛjusūtraḥ sa vijñeyo yena paryāyamātrakam/ vartamānaikasamayaviṣayaṁ parigṛhyate// Tattvārthasāraḥ* (by Amṛtacandrasūri, printed in the *Prathamagucchaka*, Śrī Digambara Grantha Bhāṇḍāra, Kāśī, Vīra Saṁ. 2451), *kā*. 47. See also *JTBY*, p. 22.
4. Siddharṣi explains *ṛjusūtranaya* as follows : *tatrarjupraguṇamakuṭilam atītānāgatavakraparityāgāt vartamānakṣanavivarti vastuno rūpaṁ sūtrayati niṣṭaṅkitaṁ darśayatīti ṛjusūtraḥ/ Nyāyāvatāra* (P. L. Vaidya's edn.), p. 77. See also *NKV*, *kārikās* 11 and 12.

when, for instance, we treat an actor, who is enacting the role of a king on the stage, as the king for the moment.

While recognising the importance and the relative validity of this 'occurrent' aspect in the life of reality we are not expected to lose sight of the 'continuant' character of reality.

An over-emphasis[1] on the fleeting aspect of concrete reality has, according to *nayavādin,* led the Buddhist to treat this partial truth as the sole foundation of his conception of reality.

Śabdanaya (*the standpoint of synonyms*)

Among the remaining three *paryāyanayas* or the modal standpoints *śabdanaya* is the first verbal viewpoint. Besides referring to this specific viewpoint the term '*śabdanaya*'[2] is also employed as a collective designation for all the three viewpoints, including the present one, because of the fact that all the three are mainly concerned with verbal problems. In order to distinguish the present verbal standpoint from the other two similar viewpoints we may specifically designate the present one as the viewpoint of synonyms since it is largely concerned with synonymous words[3].

The present standpoint of synonyms refers to the function of synonymous words which, despite their differences in

---

1. For an elaborate criticism of the various schools of Buddhism, as illustrating this *nayābhāsa,* see *TBV,* (on *STP,* I, *gā.* 5), p.317 ff.
2. *śabdaḥ samabhirūḍhaivambhūtau te śabdabhedagāḥ / Tattvārthasāra, kā.* 42.
3. *tasmādeka eva paryāyaśabdānāmartha iti śabdaḥ / Nyāyāvatāra* (P. L. Vaidya's edn.), p. 80. See also *NKV, kā.* 14, *TSV,* p. 274, *kā.* 87 and *Nayavivaraṇa, kārikās* 90-91.

tense, case-endings, gender, number and so forth, convey the same meanings.[1] For instance, the words *kumbha, kalaśa* and *ghaṭa* denote the same object (*ekārthavācakāḥ*), viz., a jar which is one of the forms taken by clay. Similarly the words Indra, Śakra and Purandara denote one and the same individual in the same manner as the words globe, orb and sphere denote, despite their several differences, the same circular entity.

A misapplication of this standpoint by treating, for instance, two synonymous words as being utterly identical in their meanings is said to lead to the fallacy called *śabdanayābhāsa*. The *śabdādvaitavādins* and a few other schools in Indian philosophy are said to have committed[2] this fallacy.

Samabhirūḍhanaya (*the etymological standpoint*)

The etymological standpoint represents an advance upon the standpoint of synonyms although it is narrower in its scope than the latter. Its advance consists in the fact that it distinguishes the meanings of synonymous words purely on their etymological grounds.[3] The synonyms Indra, Śakra and

---

1. *yo vartanaṁ ca manyate ekārthe bhinnaliṅgādīnāṁ/ sa śabdanayo bhaṇitaḥ..// Laghunayacakram, kā.* 40. Also : *śabdapṛṣṭhato'rthagrahaṇapravaṇaḥ śabdanayaḥ liṅgasaṅkhyākālakārakapuruṣopagrahavyabhicāranivṛttiparatvāt/ Dhavalaṭīkā* (quoted in *GAM, tippaṇāni*, p. 147).
2. See *Nyāyāvatāra* (P. L. Vaidya's edn.), pp. 82 and 90; and *NVUS, tippaṇāni*, p. 277.
3. *paryāyaśabdabhedena bhinnārthasyādhirohaṇāt/ nayaḥ samabhirūḍhaḥ syāt....// TSV*, p. 273, *kā.* 76. *paryāyaśabdeṣu niruktibhedena bhinnamarthaṁ samabhirohan samabhirūḍha iti/ PNTA*, VII. 36, and *NKC*, Vol. II, p. 638, f.n. 1, the extracts from *Dhavalaṭīkā* and *Jayadhavalā*.

Purandara denote, according to the conventional approach (*ruḍhiḥ, upacāraḥ*) of *śabdanaya,* the same individual whereas they do not do so if their difference in their etymological derivation is taken into consideration.[1] Indra, for instance, signifies one who is 'all prosperous' and the other two names signify one who is 'the all powerful' and the destroyer of the enemies'[2] respectively.

"Hence the difference in the roots" as a critic remarks in this connection "must mean a corresponding difference in the terms and therefore in their meanings." Had it not been for this standpoint a jar (*ghaṭa*), in the opinion of an old writer, would become indistinguishable from linen (*paṭa*).

The truth of this viewpoint is based on the following two principles in the Jaina philosophy of language : The first principle is that whatever is knowable is also expressible. That is, knowledge, or the meaning of anything in reality, is not possible except through the means of words.[3] The second

---

1. *śabdanayo hi paryāyabhede'pi arthabhedamabhipraiti, samabhirūḍhastu paryāyabhede bhinnānarthānabhimanyate*/ *JTBY,* p. 22. Devasūri also confirms this: *tannaikārthavācino dhvanayaḥ santi, ruḍhiḥ punaravicāritatadarthanamiti samabhirūdhaḥ*/ *Nyāyāvatāra* (P. L. Vaidya's edn.) This writer contrasts *ruḍhita-śabdas* (conventional words) from *vyutpatti-śabdas* (words based on their etymological derivations). See *ibid.*, p. 74.

2. *śacīpatireko'pyartha indanaśakanapuradāraṇabhedāt bhidyate / indatītīndraḥ/ śaknotīti śakraḥ/ puraṁ dārayatīti purandara iti/ Tattvārthasūtra* (with Bhāskaranandi's *Sukhabodha,* ed. by A. Shantiraja Sastry, Mysore, 1944), p. 25.

3. Cf. *ye nirabhidhānā vartante arthāḥ teṣāṁ śabdāt pārthakyena vastutvasiddhiriti cet na, nirabhidhānārthābhāvāt.../ tataś ca sarve'rthā vidyamānasvavācakāḥ, arthatvāt, ghaṭārthavaditi pramāṇāt../*

principle is that, strictly speaking, there can be only one word for one meaning and *vice versa*.[1] Accordingly, several words which are conventionally supposed to convey one and the same meaning, have in actual fact as many meanings as the number of words found there.[2] That is, this priniciple does not recognise any synonymous terms but maintains a determinate relation between a meaning and its word (*vācya-vācakaniyama*). It may be contended that the non-recognition of synonymous terms under *samabhirūḍhanaya* contradicts the recognition of such terms under *śabdanaya*. The *nayavādin* does not see any contradiction between the two viewpoints. This is so because, according to him, *samabhirūdhanaya* applies stricter canons of etymological derivation and grammatical propriety than is done by *śabdanaya* which treats words in a rough and ready manner at the level of uncritically accepted conventions or usage. Since the two principles, just referred to, are going to be dealt with at some length in the process of

---

Nyāyāvatāra (P. L. Vaidya's edn.), p. 80. Devabhadra also observes: *pratyartham śabdanivāsāditi/ Ibid.*, p. 81. Referring to the interdependence (*anyonyāpekṣā*) of word and meaning Siddhasena Gaṇi adds: *yadi yathā vyañjanam tathārtho yathā cārthaḥ tathā vyañjanam, evam hi sati vācyavācakasambandho ghaṭate anyathā na../ Tattvārthādhigamasūtram* (Kapadia's edn.), Vol. I, p. 24. On '*vyañjanam*' and '*arthaḥ*' he remarks: *vyañjanam vācakaḥ śabdaḥ, artho'bhidheyo vācyaḥ/ Ibid.* See also *SHM* on *gā*. 143, *VBJ*, p. 90.

1. *śabdārūḍho'rtho'rthārūḍhaḥ tathaiva punaḥ śabdaḥ/ Nayācāra* (*kā*. 42).
2. *tato yāvanto'rthasya svābhidhāyakā dhvanayaḥ tāvanto'rthabhedāḥ/* Devabhadra on *Nyāyāvatāra* (P. L. Vaidya's edn.), p. 81. See also the passages dealing with the principle of *avaktavya* under *syādvāda*.

their application to some important problems in *syādvāda*, it is unnecessary to enlarge upon their further implications here.

Evambhūtanaya (*the 'such-like' standpoint*)

Evambhūtanaya, or the 'such-like' standpoint, is a further specialised form of the application of the verbal method. It calls for a different designation for each of the different attitudes which the same object assumes under different conditions. It is even more rigorous than the etymological viewpoint in that it treats the different attitudes of the object denoted by different designations as numerically different entities.[1] Purandara, for instance, should be, according to this *naya*, designated as such only when he is actually engaged in the act of destroying his enemies. Similarly the designation Śakra is appropriate only when he is actually manifesting his prowess. A cow ceases to be a cow when she is not in actual motion; and the onomatopoeic designation of a *ghaṭa* would no more denote the *ghaṭa* when the *ghaṭa* is not producing the peculiar sound 'ghaṭ, ghaṭ'. Consequently, because of this insistence that designations should be derived from the different functional states of what is ordinarily known as the same object, Purandara becomes as different from Śakra as a cow is different from a jar.

Before concluding this chapter we may briefly notice the difference of opinions among the writers on *nayavāda* on the question whether the number of *nayas*, viz., seven, can be

---

1. See *PNTA*, VII. 40, and *NKV*, *kārikās* 17-18.

reduced. There are mainly three traditions (*paramparās*) which are based on the number of *nayas* occurring in the classification adopted by each of them within the framework of reality which is conceived to be fundamentally *dravyaparyāyātmaka* (identity-in-difference) or *sāmānyaviśeṣātmaka* (universal-cum-particular). The first one adopts a classification of seven *nayas*. Our treatment of the subject has been based on this classification. The order in which the seven *nayas* have been treated in our account, viz., *naigama, saṅgraha, vyavahāra ṛjusūtra, śabda, samabhirūḍha,* and *evambhūta*, has also been recognised by this tradition. The second tradition adopts a classification of six *nayas* eliminating, from its classification, *naigamanaya* which is the first among the seven *nayas* recognised by the first tradition. The third tradition reduces the number from seven to five[1] by subsuming *samabhirūḍhanaya* and *evambhūtanaya*, the last two standpoints within the first classification, under *śabdanaya*, and thus treating them as two subdivisions of the latter.

Umāsvāti himself is largely responsible for the first[2] and the third traditions. For the concerned *sūtra* of his great work, *Tattvārthādhigamasūtra,* gives, in its Digambara version, the enunciation of the seven *nayas*[3], in their natural order, whereas the same *sūtra* gives, in the Śvetāmbara

---

1. *naigamasaṅgrahavyavahārarjusūtraśabdā nayāḥ / Sabhāṣyatattvādhigamasūtrāṇi* (ed. by Motital Laghaji, Poona, Vīra Saṁ. 2453), I. 34.
2. *naigamasaṅgrahavyavahārarjusūtraśabdasamabhirūḍhaivambhūtā nayāḥ/ TSUJ*, I. 33.
3. See the above f. n.

version of his work, the enunciation of only five *nayas*, treating the last two *nayas* as subdivisions of *śabdanaya*. All the Digambara writers and most of the Śvetāmbara writers also adhere to the former tradition[1]. The latter tradition is confined to the relevant *sūtra* by Umāsvāti in the Śvetāmbara version of his work, as well as to the Bhāṣya which is ascribed to Umāsvāti himself by the Śvetāmbara writers. The second tradition, the tradition of the six *nayas*, is maintained by Siddhasena Divākara[2] with his characteristic vigour and independent judgment.

Besides these three traditions there are four more views according to which the number of *nayas* is severally one, two, three or four. A passing mention may be made of these views :

When our attention is focussed on the aspect of the generic universal (*mahāsāmānya*), viz., being (*sattā*), the entire gamut of reality, which, on a fuller analysis, is universal-cum-particular, appears as one[3] pure and uniform existence. This abstract way of looking at reality is described as the pure and the absolute viewpoint (*śuddhaniścayanaya*[4]).

---

1. See, for instance, *TSV*, I. 33, *TRAG*, I. 33, etc. The notable instances among the works of the Śvetambara writers, are *PNJA*, Ch. VII, *SRK* thereon, and *SM* (text), p. 161.
2. Cf. *ST*, Intro. pp. 141-2. Jinabhadra Gaṇi also follows Siddhasena Divākara on this point. *Ibid.*
3. Cf. *sāmānyādeśatastāvadeka eva nayaḥ sthitaḥ*/ *TSV*, I. 33, *kā*. 2. This line is found in *Nayavivaraṇa* also : see *kā*. 18.
4. No material difference seems to exist between this viewpoint and one of the subdivisions of *saṅgrahanaya*, viz., *parasaṅgrahanaya*. Cf. *parasaṅgrahastāvat sarvaṁ saditi saṅgṛhṇāti*/ *TSV*, p. 271. Cf. also *PNTA*, VII. 15.

The *nayavādins* consider this standpoint as a class by itself. This is the first of the four views just referred to.

Reality may often be viewed either from the generic or the specific angle of vision. When it is the former we are said to be governed by the generic viewpoint or *sāmānya-naya,* and when it is the latter we are said to be governed by the specific viewpoint or *viśeṣanaya.* This classification[1] is the same as the substantive (*dravyārthika*) and the modal (*paryāyārthika*) viewpoints. This classification, which consists of two members, is the second of the four views.

Siddhasena Divākara suggests a classification of three standpoints although he generally accepts a classification of six standpoints. He does so by subsuming *śabda, samabhiruḍha* and *evambhuta nayas* under *ṛjusūtranaya.* This is because he considers *ṛjusūtranaya* as the foundation of the entire modal (*paryāyāstika*) approach to reality and, therefore, the other three as its sub-divisions (*suhumabheya*)[2]. This reduction of four *nayas* to one, viz., *ṛjusūtranaya,* coupled with the further elimination of *naigamanaya,* leaves only three *nayas,* viz., *saṅgraha, vyavahāra,* and *ṛjusūtra.*

Lastly, *Samavāyāṅgaṭīkā* formulates a method by which we obtain a classification of four *nayas.* It divides *naigama-naya* into two subdivisions, viz., *sāmānyanaigama* (that which comprehends the universal aspect in reality) and *viśeṣa-naigama* (that which comprehends the particular aspect in reality), and subsumes them under *saṅgrahanaya* and *vyava-*

---

1. Cf. *Syādvādamañjarī* (J. C. Jain's edn.), p. 323 f.
2. See *STP, gā.* 5 and the extensive comm. (*TBV*) thereon.

hāranaya, respectively. Further, it brings *samabhiruḍhanaya* and *evambhūtanaya* under *śabdanaya* so that the resultant classification we obtain under this scheme consists of *saṅgraha, vyavahāra, ṛjusūtra* and *śabda nayas*.[1]

Thus we find that we can obtain many classifications, based on different methods, even within the framework of the substantive and modal categories and of the seven standpoints based on these categories. There are many minor classifications outside the scheme of the standpoints treated in this chapter. As a matter of fact there are several subdivisions under each of the standpoints dealt with here. Any attempt at cataloguing the numerous classifications and enumerating the more numerous subdivisions will be needlessly cumbrous.[2] For such an attempt, even if feasible,

---

1. *naigamanayo dvividhaḥ sāmānyagrāhī viśeṣagrāhī ca / tatra yaḥ sāmānyagrāhī sa saṅgrahe'ntarbhūtaḥ, viśeṣagrāhī tu vyavahāre / tadevaṁ saṅgrahavyavahārarjusūtraśabdāditrayaṁ caika iti catvāro nayāḥ/ Samavāyāṅgaṭīkā* (quoted in J. C. Jain's edn. of *Syādvādamañjarī*, p. 324, f. n. 2). See also the following observation by Maladhāri Hemacandra: *saṅgrahavyavahārarjusūtralakṣaṇāh trayo'tra nayāḥ vivakṣyante/ ekastu śabdanayaḥ paryāyāstikaḥ tadā catvāro mūlanayā bhavanti/* Comm. on *VBJ*, *gā*. 2264.

2. For an account of such classifications and subdivisions (*upanayas*) of the various *nayas* see Devasena's *Laghunayacakram* and *Nayādhikaraṇa* (both printed in *Nayacakrādisaṅgrahaḥ*, ed. by Vaṁśīdhara, Bombay, 1920): Amṛtacandra's *Tattvārthasāra*, Devasena's *Ālāpapaddhati*, and *Nayavivaraṇa* by an unknown author (all these three works published in the *Prathamagucchaka*, Digambara Grantha Bhāṇḍara, Kaśī, ed. by Pannalal Chaudhari, Vikram Saṁ. 1982); Yaśovijaya's *Nayarahasya* and *Nayapradīpa* (included in a collection of works: *Adhyātmasāra*, etc., Nyāyācārya-Yaśovijayajīkṛta Granthamālā, Bhavanagar, 1909); and the portions dealing with *nayavāda* in the

is not likely to give considerably more light on the nature, the significance and the function of the analytical method of *nayavāda* than can be done by a consideration of the most fundamental division of categories (viz. *dravyārthikanaya* and *paryāyārthikanaya*) and of the seven viewpoints based thereon. Hence the present chapter has confined itself to the treatment of only the essential aspects of the subject.

The various standpoints outlined in course of this chapter offer an analysis of the manifold reality from their respective angles of vision. Such an analysis results in a wealth of partial truths which will be harmonised into a coherent scheme of knowledge by the employment of the synthetical method of *syādvāda*[1] which will be dealt with in the next chapter. The complementary functions of the two methods, viz., *nayavāda* and *syādvāda,* remind us of the oft-quoted parable of the elephant and the blind men. To express the same truth after Siddhasena Divākara's analogy *nayas* offer the discrete (*visañjutta*) or individual jewels (*maṇi*) which are strung together, by means of *syādvāda,* into a necklace (*rayaṇāvali*).[2]

---

standard works like *UBJ* and its comm., *SRK, TSV, STP* and its comm., and *NKC*.

1. The mutual necessity, or the complementary character of the two methods, viz., *nayavāda* and *syādvāda*, as well as the corrective character of *nayavāda*, in relation to the dogmatic (*ekānta*) character of the 'closed' systems of philosophy (this aspect of the problem will be presently touched upon in the next paragraph) is suggestively expressed by Devasena as follows: *yasmānnayena vinā bhavati narasya syādvādapratipattiḥ// tamāt sa boddhavya ekāntaṁ hantukāmena// Laghunayacakram, kā*. 3.
2. See *STP*, I, *gāthas* 22-25.

Further, the philosophy of standpoints is also a warning against, as well as a corrective to, the 'closed' or the 'architectonic' systems. Describing *nayavāda* as a 'philosophy of standpoints' a critic observes: "It is a revolt against the tendency in philosophers to build closed systems of philosophy. According to Jainism, the universe in which we live is an active universe, plastic and full of possibilities and no particular current of thought can fully comprehend it. In order to do justice to the complexity and variety of such a universe, thought must not be hurried to any easy terminus but must be allowed to follow its course freely and meander through the whole field of experience, crossing and recrossing it, so as to create a great confluence of standpoints rather than a closed system. The tendency ingrained in the philosophers to build architectonic systems is inimical to the adventure of thought......Each philosopher approaching reality from a particular and a partial standpoint, looks upon the one he adopts as the only true standpoint. Jainism rejects the idea of the absolute which is playing havoc in the field of philosophy by creating absolute monisms, absolute pluralisms, and absolute nihilisms. By thus rejecting the absolute and the one-sided, it claims to save philosophy from the chaos of conflicting opinions. Without partiality to any one it promises to give us a theory of relativity which harmonises all standpoints."[1]

---

1. G. H. Rao : *The Half-Yearly Journal of the Mysore University*, March, 1942, pp. 79-80.

CHAPTER XI

Syādvāda

or

The Dialectic of Conditional Predication

CHAPTER XI

SYĀDVĀDA (The Conditional Dialectic)
or
SAPTABHAṄGĪ (The Theory of Sevenfold Predication)

In the course of our treatment of *nayavāda* or the theory of standpoints, it has already been observed that *syādvāda* is a method which is complementary to that of *nayavāda*, and that while *nayavāda* is analytical in character, *syādvāda* functions as a synthetical method.[1] That is, *nayavāda* analyses one of the standpoints under the aspect of identity (*dravyārthikanaya*) or of difference (*paryāyārthikanaya*); and *syādvāda* further investigates the various strands of the truth delivered by a *naya*, and integrates them into a consistent and comprehensive synthesis. Each such strand is called a *bhaṅga* which is referred to, variously, as a mode, or a predication or an alternative or a possible truth. Describing the relation between the two methods Dasgupta observes: "There is no universal or absolute position or negation, and all judgments are valid only conditionally. The relation of the *naya* doctrine with the *syādvāda* doctrine is therefore this, that for any judgment according to any and every *naya* there are as many alternatives as are indicated by *Syādvāda*."[2] The indeterminate or *anekānta* reality is

1. *Supra*, p. 303 ff.
2. *HIP*, Vol. I, p. 181.

thus analysed into various standpoints and each standpoint in turn is examined with respect to its various strands of truth and, finally, all the strands are woven together into the synthesis of the conditional dialectic. Owing to their function of analysis and synthesis the methods of *nayavāda* and *syādvāda* may also be described as the disjunctive dialectic and the conjunctive dialectic, respectively.

Further, *saptabhaṅgī*, or the theory of sevenfold predication, is treated as synonymous with *syādvāda* owing to the fact that the number of possible or alternative truths under the conditional method of *syādvāda* are, as will be noticed hereafter, seven only.

The fact that the term '*syādvāda*' is often treated as standing for the entire Jaina philosophy is due to the great importance attached to the method of the conditional dialectic with which it (the term) is most intimately connected.[1] The controversy as to whether '*syādvāda*' is a synonym of '*saptabhaṅgī*' or of the entire Jaina philosophy is, therefore, a needlessly scholastic one[2], at any rate from the philosophical standpoint.

---

1. Cf. "The doctrine of the Indefiniteness of Being is upheld by a very strange dialectical method called *Syādvāda,* to which the Jains attach so much importance that this name frequently is used as a synonym for the Jaina system itself." *Studies in Jm.,* p. 16.

2. In his introduction to *AJP*, Vol. I, p. X, Kapadia states that the term *syādvāda* is synonymous with the term *anekāntavāda*, and, therefore, is wider in its scope than the term *saptabhaṅgī* which is only a part of it. He is, however, not sure of his position although he had adduced a few authorities in his support. But as Jacobi suggests, as seen in the above f.n., *syādvāda* could

Before we set forth the modes of *syādvāda* and their principal features, and, at the end, a few relevant criticisms against the method as a whole, it would be helpful to remember here what has already been stated[1] with regard to the two groups of factors which, together, determine the nature of a real. The first group of such factors is the positive one referring to the material (*dravya*) of the make, the spatio-temporal setting (*kṣetra* and *kāla*) and the state (*bhāva*), like black or red, or big or small and so forth, of a jar (*ghaṭa*) which may be cited here as an example. The second group of factors is a negative one referring to the material, and so on, of things like linen (*paṭa*) which form the negative counterpart (*niṣedha-pratiyogi*) of the jarness (*ghaṭatva*) of the jar. The negative counterpart (*paṭatva*, etc.) is, as has already been noticed, as much constitutive of the full-fledged nature of the jar as the positive one. These groups of factors are briefly described in Sanskrit as *svadravyādicatuṣṭaya* and

---

be used in an inclusive sense of *anekāntavāda* owing to the paramount importance attached to *saptabhaṅgī* with which it (*syādvāda*) is primarily synonymous. Moreover, none of the authorities adduced by Kapadia decisively supports his thesis. There is at least one great and old authoritative writer, viz., Prabhācandra, who contradicts Kapadia's thesis. (Interpreting Akalaṅka's phrase '*syādvādekṣaṇasaptakam*', Prabhācandra writes: *syādastītyādi saptabhaṅgamayo vādaḥ*/ See the Comm. on *LTP*, *kā*. 51, in *NKC*, Vol. II, p. 655). But over and above all these considerations the reason why *syādvāda* is generally and rightly treated as synonymous with *saptabhaṅgī* is that the particle *syāt* invariably accompanies every *bhaṅga* (or mode) in *saptabhaṅgī*. It would, therefore, be perfectly natural to describe *saptabhaṅgī* alternatively as *syādvāda* or the doctrine of *syāt*. It is rather strange that this obvious reason has not even suggested itself to Kapadia.

1. *Supra*, pp. 154-155 etc.

paradravyādicatuṣṭaya, respectively. They may be referred to, briefly, in English, as self-quaternary and other-quaternary. After these few preliminary observations we may now proceed to elucidate the nature and the modes of the method of the sevenfold predication.

Syādvāda[1] (The Conditional Dialectic) or Saptabhaṅgī (The Theory of Sevenfold Predication)

Syādvāda or *Saptabhaṅgī* is that conditional method in in which the modes, or predications (*bhaṅgāḥ*) affirm (*vidhi*), negate (*niṣedha*) or both affirm and negate, severally (*pṛthagbhūta*) or jointly (*samudita*), in seven different ways, a certain attribute (*dharma*) of a thing (*vastu*) without incompatibility[2] (*avirodhena*) in a certain context (*praśnavaśāt*).[3]

---

1. Although '*syādvāda*' is the most popular name it has various synonyms like *saṁhāravāda, sarvavastuśabalavāda, ākulavāda saṅkīrṇavāda, tadatattvavāda,* and *vibhajyavāda*. See *AJP*, Vol. I, Intro. p. IX and f. n. 5 thereon.
2. Incompatibility includes not merely consistency with the other modes, in the method, but also with the valid knowledge, perceptual (*pratyakṣa*) or otherwise (*parokṣa*).
3. Cf. Malliṣeṇa's definition : *ekatra jīvādau vastuni ekaikasattvādidharmaviṣayapraśnavaśāt avirodhena pratyakṣādibādhāparihāreṇa pṛthagbhutayoḥ samuditayoś ca vidhiniṣedhayoḥ paryālocanayā kṛtvā syācchabdalāñchito vakṣyamāṇaḥ saptabhiḥ prakāraiḥ vacanavinyāsaḥ saptabhaṅgīti gīyate*/ *SM*, pp. 142-3. Akalaṅka puts the same, cryptically, as follows: *praśnavaśāt ekatra vastuni avirodhena vidhipratiṣedhakalpanā saptabhaṅgī*/ *TRAG*, p. 24.

The following two definitions are by Vādideva and Vimaladāsa, respectively : *Ekatra vastuni ekaikadharmaparyanuyogavaśāt avirodhena vyastayoḥ samastayoś ca vidhiniṣedhayoḥ kalpanayā syātkārāṅkitaḥ saptadhā vākyaprayogaḥ saptabhaṅgī*/ *PNTA, EV* 14 in *SRK*, p. 716. *tallakṣaṇaṁ tu prāśnikapraśnajñāna-prayojyatve sati ekavastuviśeṣyaka-aviruddhavidhipratiṣedhātmaka-dharmaprakāraka-bodhajanaka-saptavākyaparyāpta-samudāyatvam*/ *SBT*, p. 3.

That is, no modal assertion, or proposition,—simple or complex; affirmative, negative or both,—can, at once, express anything other than an aspect (*prakāra*) of the truth of a thing. The full truth, or rather the synthesis of truths, can result only from a well-ordered scheme of propositions (*vacanavinyāsa*). Each proposition is, therefore, relative to, or alternative with, the other propositions which, in their totality, present the full of the thing with respect to the particular attribute predicated of it. The Jaina maintains that *saptabhaṅgī* offers such a well-ordered scheme in which the modes (*bhaṅgas*) are exclusive of one another, but are at the same time, in their totality, exhaustive of the many-sided truth of the indeterminate real under discussion.

It has just been noted that the term '*syādvāda*' means conditional or relativistic dialectic and is synonymous with '*saptabhaṅgī*'. We may examine, somewhat more closely, the meaning of this term owing to its well-merited importance in the system: The name '*syādvāda*' is due to the prefix '*syāt*' which is an invariable accompaniment of every predication. This particle '*syāt*' which is treated by most of the Jaina writers as an indeclinable[1] (*avyaya*) although, generally, modern writers—some of them perhaps unknowingly—consider it in its obvious sense of being a form derived from the Sanskrit root '*as*' (to be) in the potential mood, third form, singular.[2] Another term equi-

1. See *infra*, p. 338, f.n. 3. See also *Nyāyakusumāñjali* by Muni Nyāyavijaya, ed. H. R. Kapadia, Bombay, 1922, p. 177. For the 'other several meanings' of '*syāt*' as an indeclinable, see *AJP*, Vol. II, Intro. p. CXV, f.n. 2.
2. *OIP*, p. 163.

valent to '*syāt*' is '*kathañcit*'[1] and no word or phrase in English is adequate to bring out precisely the significance of either word. Some of the suggested English equivalents like 'probably', 'may be', 'perhaps', 'indefinitely' and so forth are inadequate, if not somewhat misleading. Its main significance lies in its emphasis on the indeterminate or manifold nature of the real which—like all other reals—comes within its purview. Indeterminateness or manifoldness means that the "reals cannot be determined as possessing only such and such attributes and not the rest". Discussing the spirit of *syādvāda* a modern critic observes : "It signifies that the universe can be looked at from many points of view, and that each viewpoint yields a different conclusion (*anekānta*). The nature of reality is expressed completely by none of them for in its concrete richness it admits all predicates. Every proposition is therefore in strictness only conditional. Absolute affirmation and absolute negation are both erroneous".[2] It is this conception of reality 'as extremely indeterminate in nature' that is suggested or 'illumined' by the term '*syāt*'.[3] A phrase which will approximately bring out this indeterministic significance of '*syāt*' would be 'from a certain point of view', or 'in a certain sense', or some other equivalent form.

Another Sanskrit word which is used to suggest that each of the conclusions signified by the seven modes is exclusive —that is, does not encroach upon the province of the conclu-

---

1. *SM*, p. 151 (text).
2. *OIP*, p. 163.
3. *Syādityavyayamanekāntadyotakam* / *SM*, p. 151 (text).

sions pointed out by the other modes—is '*eva*' which may be translated as 'only' or 'certainly' (or in some equivalent form such as 'there is no doubt', or 'without doubt'). For instance, the first mode, *syādastyeva ghaṭaḥ*, means: "In a certain sense, the jar exists without doubt." This sense of exclusion[1] (*vyāvṛtyartham*) seems to be more prominent than that of 'definiteness' (*avadhāraṇārtham*) although the one implies the other and both the functions[2]—which may also be described as restrictive force and the definitive (or deterministic) force, respectively—are inherent in the word.

The *syādvādins* warn us against allowing '*eva*' to proceed beyond its prescribed limits of exercising the restrictive and deterministically articulating influence on the mode within which it functions. That is, its force (*sāmarthya*) is confined to the avoidance of intrusions from the other modes and to the bringing of a definitive articulation into the mode with which it is connected. If, on the contrary, it leads to the extreme position of setting up the particular mode or aspect, with which it is connected, as the sole manifestation of the truth of the object concerned, then it

1. In the words of Vidyānanda '*eva*' is '*vyavacchedaprayojanaḥ*' *TSV*, p. 137. Contrast the difference in the emphasis of the two functions of the word in *JPN*, p. 147, and *Nyāyakusumāñjali*, p. 178.
2. Cf. *avadhāraṇaṁ ca atra bhaṅgenābhimatārthavyāvṛtyartham upāttam / itarathā anabhihitatulyataivāsya vākyasya prasajyeta, pratiniyatasvārthānabhidhānāt/ taduktaṁ vākye'vadhāraṇaṁ tāvad aniṣṭārthanivṛttaye/ kartavyo'yam anyathānuktasamatvāt tasya kutracit //* *SRK*, p. 717. For further elucidation of the idea contained in this passage as well as for the three distinctions of '*evakāra*' *viz.*, *ayogabodhakatva, anyayogabodhakatva,* and *atyantāyogabodhakatva*, see *SBT*, pp. 21-29.

gives rise to an absolutism which does not recognise the fact that there are other aspects (*apekṣāḥ*) of truth, in the object, than the one reflected by it.

Schools which build up their systems on the foundation of some single concept or the other, which represents only one facet of the many-sided truth in reality, illustrate this narrow and dogmatic approach.[1] They are called *nirapekṣavādas* in contrast to *sāpekṣavada* which is another name for *syādvāda*.

Thus whatever the aspect represented by a mode, under the conditional method of sevenfold predication the term '*syāt*' is an invariable accompaniment[2] of the mode for the very reason that it suggests that the determinate context of the mode is carved out as it were from the indeterminate richness of reality, and the term '*eva*' holds forth the determinate context in its clear outline.[3] But it is necessary to note here that the two terms '*syāt*' and '*eva*' need not necessarily be stated explicitly in a modal proposition. They are always logically inherent in the nature of a modal judgment whether or not they are verbally specified.[4]

---

1. Cf. *kārtsnyaikadeśena ca tattvārthādhigamānupapatteḥ*/*TSV*, p. 142.
2. *sarvatra syātkāro'bhyupagantavyaḥ*/ *NKC*, Vol. II, p. 692.
3. Cf. *syācchabdaprayoge sarvathaikāntavyavacchedena anekāntapratipatterasambhavāt, evakāravacane vivakṣitārthapratipattivat* / *SBT*, p. 30. Cf. also the following *kā.* by Vidyānanda: *syācchabdādapyanekāntasāmānyasyāvabodhane / śabdāntaraprayogo'tra viśeṣapratipattaye*// *TSV*, p. 136, *kā.* 55.
4. *sāmarthyāc ca aprayoge'rtho gamyaḥ syādevakārayoḥ* / Quoted from *Siddhiviniścaya Ṭīkā* in *NKC*, Vol. II, p. 961, f.n. 6. *nanvaprayukto'pi syācchabdo vastuno'nekāntasvarūpatvasāmarthyāt pratīyate, sarvatraivakāravat, iti cet satyam* / *SBT*, p. 31. Also: *aprayukto'pi sarvatra syātkaro'rthāt pratīyate*/ *vidhau nīṣedhe'pyanyatra kuśalaś cet prayojakaḥ* // *LTB* and *NKC* thereon, in *NKC*, Vol. II, p. 692. See also *SM* (text) p. 143 f. and *TSV*, p. 137, *kā.* 56 and the comm. thereon.

Now the seven modes, or predications, and their characteristics may be treated with reference to the stock example of a jar (*ghaṭa*) and its negative counterpart (*niṣedha-pratiyogi*) linen (*paṭa*). In doing so we may first enumerate the seven modes, then explain the three primary concepts, viz., the being (*astitva*), non-being (*nāstitva*) and the inexpressible (*avaktavyatva*), together with the elementary or simple propositions given rise to by them; and, lastly, point out the remaining complex[1] propositions which result from combining two or more simple ones.

The seven modes are :—

(1) In a certain sense, the jar is (*syādasti*[2] *ghaṭaḥ*).

(2) In a certain sense, the jar is not (*syānnasti ghaṭaḥ*).

(3) In a certain sense, the jar is and is not (*syādasti nāsti ca ghaṭaḥ*[3]).

---

1. A slight departure from the procedure laid down here will be made in the case of the third mode (*syādastināsti*) which, complex proposition, will be treated jointly with the fourth simple proposition (*syādavaktavya*). This will be done in order to bring out the important difference between the concepts of 'consecutive presentation' (*kramārpaṇa*) and co-presentation (*sahārpaṇa*) involved in the two modes, respectively.
2. For brevity the adverb '*eva*' is dropped in all the modal statements here, but the indeclinable '*syāt*' is retained.
3. Some writers interchange the sequence between the third and the fourth modes, but this does not make any material difference. While dealing with the fourth mode, Vādideva observes, in this connection :—*ayaṁ ca bhaṅgaḥ kaiścit tṛtīyabhaṅgasthāne paṭhyate, tṛtīyaścaitasya sthāne/ na caivamapi kaściddoṣaḥ, arthaviśeṣasyābhāvāt/ SRK*, p. 719.

   As a matter of fact the same ancient author, Kundakunda, states these two modes in a different order in his two works. Cf. *PrSKU*, II. 23, and *PSKC*, *gā*. 14.

(4) In a certain sense, the jar is inexpressible (*syādavaktavyo ghaṭaḥ*).

(5) In a certain sense, the jar is and is inexpressible (*syādastyavaktavyaśca ghaṭaḥ*).

(6) In a certain sense, the jar is not and is inexpressible (*syānnāstyavaktavyaśca ghaṭaḥ*).

(7) In a certain sense, the jar is, is not and is inexpressible (*syādastināsti cāvaktavyaśca ghaṭaḥ*).

The three fundamental concepts making up the seven predicates, in the seven modes, singly, in twos, or all together, are 'is' (*asti*), 'is not' (*nāsti*) and 'inexpressible' (*avaktavya*). A predicate containing any one of them involves a simple judgment, and a predicate containing any two or all the three of them involves a complex judgment. Consequently, the first two modes, and the fourth mode, are assertions of simple judgments and the remaining four of complex judgments. These judgments, whether simple or complex, are always made against the background of the indeterminate reality which is suggested by the qualifying term '*syāt*'.

Not being absolute or independent the concepts of the 'being' (*astitva*) and the 'not-being' (*nāstitva*) cannot be fully explained except in their mutual relation. Mere 'being' is fictitious without the co-ordinate element of 'non-being' and *vice versa*.[1] Each can, however, be described as an isolated aspect of, or abstraction from, a concrete real.

---

1. *vastuno'stitvaṁ nāstitvenāvinābhūtaṁ nāstītvaṁ ca teneti*/ *SM*, p. 144 (text). This idea that a real is a positive-negative complex is expressed by Candraprabhasūri as follows: *svaparātmanopādānāpohanavyavasthāpanādyaṁ hi vastutvam* / Candraprabhasūri's *Prameya-Ratna-Kośa*, ed. L. Suali, Bhavanagar, 1912.

The first mode, represented by the proposition, "In a certain sense the jar is", asserts the existent or positive aspect of the jar. By virtue of the fact that the existence of the jar is inseparably bound up with the non-existence of linen (*paṭa*) etc. in it, what the proposition signifies is that for some reason at the moment of our making the assertion, our attention is being focussed primarily[1] (*pradhānatayā*) on the existent aspect of the jar. As already explained earlier[2], the existent aspect of the jar is to be understood in terms of its self-quaternary, and the non-existent aspect, in terms of the other-quaternary. If, on the contrary, the jar is understood to be capable of being the linen as well (*itararūpāpattyāpi*), then it will surely lose its very nature (*svarūpahāniprasaṅgaḥ*) as a distinctive existent[3], *viz.*, a jar. This claim for a distinctive existence is guaranteed by the implicitly understood term '*eva*' in the proposition.[4]

---

1. *vivakṣāvasāc cānayoḥ pradhānopasarjanabhāvaḥ/ SM*, p. 144 (text). *prathame bhaṅge sattvasya pradhānabhāvena pratītiḥ, etc. SBT*, p. 9. This idea is beautifully expressed by Amṛtacandra in the following stanza: *ekenākarṣantī*.........

2. See *supra*, pp. 335-336; see also pp. 154-155.

3. *syātkathañcit svadravyakṣetrakālabhāvarūpeṇa astyeva sarvaṁ kumbhādi, na punaḥ paradravyakṣetrakālabhāvarūpeṇa/ tathā hi kumbho dravyataḥ pārthivattvenāsti, na jalādirūpatvena, kṣetrataḥ pāṭaliputrakatvena, na kānyakubjāditvena, kālataḥ śaiśiratvena, na vasantāditvena, bhāvataḥ śyāmatvena, na raktatvādinā/ anyathā itararūpāpattyā svarūpahāniprasaṅga iti / SRK*, p. 717. For a discussion on *svadravyādicatuṣṭaya* and its negative counterpart see *supra*.

4. *tatra svarūpādibhiḥ astitvamiva nāstitvamapi syādityaniṣṭārthasya nivṛttaye syādastyevetyevakāraḥ/ tena ca svarūpādibhirastitvameva na nāstitvamityavadhāryate/ SBT*, p. 21.

The second fundamental concept is 'non-being' (*asat*). It is embodied in the second predication, *viz.*, 'the jar is not'. This concept is easier to understand after recognising the nature and function of its positive counterpart (*vidhi-pratigogi*), viz., 'being' (*sat*). It is the negative (*niṣedha*) element in the determinate context of the concrete nature of the jar in the example. That is, despite its name 'negative element' this concept is a co-ordinate and constituent element in the full make-up of the jar. The fact that negation constitutes a necessary element in reality has already been dealt with, at some length, in an earlier chapter[1] and, therefore, nothing more than the mere mention of it is called for here. This important fact warrants the formulation of a distinctive conditional predication which is provided for in the second mode. The main significance of the second mode lies not in the false statement that the jar does not exist as the jar but in the irrefutable statement that the jar does not exist as linen or anything else. When we focus our attention exclusively (*pradhānatayā*) on this negative aspect of the jar, as we do under certain conditions, we are said to be viewing the jar in the perspective of the second mode. Non-existence in the second predication is not, therefore, a vacuous predicate but is the obverse of the existent side of the object. In other words, non-existence or 'non-being' is a determinate fact with a content and not a void. This is so because under the category of the 'non-being' all that should not figure within the 'being' of the jar is sought to be ruled out.

---

1. For a discussion on negation see *supra*, pp. 153 ff.

An objection to treating the present mode as a logical complement to the previous mode is that the two modes being mutually opposed, are self-contradictory. A refutation of this objection forms the subject of a specific account in an earlier chapter[1] and, indeed, runs as an undercurrent throughout the body of this work. It is, therefore, sufficient to remember here that the two elements, constituting the two modes, are not merely non-contradictory—because, if they were, the qualification 'without incompatibility'[2] (*avirodhena*) in the definition of *syādvāda*, would be meaningless—but are mutually necessary complements in the real. Contradiction would arise if the opposition were between the two absolute assertions "the jar exists" and "the jar does not exist". The source of such a fault lies in the objector's mistake in construing the latter assertion, *viz.*, "the jar does not exist", as being equivalent to "the jar does not exist as a jar". The true interpretation of it should be that "the jar does not exist as linen, or water etc." There is surely no contradiction in the latter interpretation because of the fact that it is based on the assumption that the assertion is a relative (*kathañcit*) and determinate (*niyata*) abstraction from a complex and concrete real.[3]

The third and the fourth modes may be treated jointly

---

1. See *supra*, pp. 142-144 and pp. 163-169 (with f. notes).
2. See *supra*, p. 336.
3. For a refutation of a further charge that *syādvāda* brings about a situation of doubt (*saṁśayaviṣayatvasambhava*) owing to the co-existence of the relative concept of the non-existence (*kathañcidasattvam*) with that of the existence (*kathañcitsattvam*), see *SBT*, pp. 6-7 and *TRAG*, p. 26.

in order to bring out their difference more clearly. They are enunciated as : "In a certain sense the jar is and is not", and "In a certain sense, the jar is inexpressible", respectively. These two modes present the 'being' (*astitva*) and the 'non-being' (*nāstitva*) together. But there is a great difference in the presentation (*arpaṇabheda*) they make of the togetherness of the two modes. The third mode offers successive presentation (*kramārpaṇa*) and the fourth one offers a simultaneous presentation (*sahārpaṇa*) of the two concepts. These two kinds of presentation are also translated as "consecutive presentation" or "differenced togetherness", and "co-presentation" or "undifferenced togetherness".[1] Although the third mode appears to be one proposition, it entails, in actual fact, two propositions which are expressed as one owing to a certain verbal facility. But the verbal togetherness does not signify a logical compresence of the propositions, or the concepts they embody.

The fourth mode introduces the third primary concept, viz., the inexpressible[2] (*avaktavya*) in its predicate. Before dealing with the Jaina conception of the inexpressible and its difference from the consecutive predicate, in the third mode, it would be of some interest to trace the dialectical stages

---

1. See *JTA*, pp. 45 and 47.
2. *avaktavya* is often translated as "the unspeakable" or "the undescribable". Commenting on the eminent suitability of this term '*avaktavya*', in an attempt to express the two primary aspects of a real (*ghaṭa*) Akalaṅka remarks : *na cānyaḥ śabdaḥ tadubhayātmāvasthātattvābhidhāyī vidyate/ ato'sau ghaṭaḥ vacanagocarātītatvāt syādavaktavya ityucyate/ TRAG*, p. 25. The nature and the importance of this concept, viz., *avaktavya*, will be hereafter clarified.

through which the concept of the inexpressible has evolved in Indian philosophy. An account of the evolution will not merely give us an estimate of the general significance of the concept, but also will indicate the relation in which the concept stands to similar concepts in other Indian schools. A brief account of it may, therefore, be attempted here.

We may distinguish four stages through which the concept of the inexpressible has passed in its evolutionary process. These stages, it should be noted, at the outset, do not necessarily represent a chronological order of development but a logical one.

In the first place, we meet with a tendency in the *Ṛgveda* which is suggestive of a negative attitude to the problem. The seer, confronted with the mystery of the universe which reveals both *sat* (being) and *asat* (non-being), tends to feel that the universe is neither being nor non-being (cf. the primal state of reality, he says. "Then was not non-existent nor existent...." *Ṛgveda*, the "Song of Creation", Bk. X, Hymn 129, E. T. by R. T. H. Griffith). This somewhat naïve and negative attitude that the real is neither being nor non-being may be described as one of *anubhaya*.

The next tendency is a positive one, and is represented by certain Upaniṣadic utterances like : "*sadasadvareṇyam*" ('The great Being' as 'being and not being', *Muṇḍakopaniṣad*, II. 2. 1; *tathākṣāt dvividhāḥ somya bhāvāḥ prajāyante....* *Ibid.*, II. 1. 1) and "*saṁyuktametat kṣaramakṣaraṁ ca vyaktāvyaktaṁ bharate viśvamīśaḥ*" (That which is joined together as perishable and imperishable, as manifest and unmanifest—the Lord ... supports it all. *Śvetāśvataro-*

paniṣad, I. 8). It conceives both being and non-being as inherent in reality. Owing to the positive character this tendency may be described as the *ubhaya* phase (in which *both* are real) of the concept.

Before touching upon the third phase in the evolution of the concept it is necessary to note two significant features in the above two tendencies. First, although both attitudes refer to the elements of being and non-being they suggest the two elements as being merely together. As yet there does not seem to be any attempt to weld the elements into a single complex mode. Nor has any definite awareness of the impossibility of expressing the two elements, simultaneously, in a single concept dawned upon these poet-philosophers. Secondly, the two elements are conceived to be mutually opposed rather than complementary.

The third phase is met with, again, in certain other Upaniṣadic utterances like "*sa eṣa neti neti*" (*Bṛhadāraṇyakopaniṣad*, IV. 5. 15); "*yato vāco nivartante aprāpya manasā saha*" (*Taittirīyopaniṣad*, II. 4); or "*naiva vācā na manasa prāptuṁ śakyaḥ*" (*Kaṭhopaniṣad*, II. 6. 12). In this phase there is a clear awareness of the unutterableness of the ultimate owing to the fact that an attempt at utterance is beset with contradictoriness. Hence, although this phase is also negative[1] like that of the *Rgveda* it marks an

---

1. Cf. "This world, O Kaccana,....generally proceeds on a duality, on the 'it is' and the 'it is not'. But O Kaccana, whoever perceives in truth and wisdom how things originate in the world, in his eyes there is no 'it is not' in this world. Whoever, Kaccana, perceives in truth and wisdom how things pass away in this world, in his eyes there is no 'it is' in this world...." Quoted in H. Oldenberg's *Buddha*, (E. T. by W. Koey, 1882, London), p. 249.

advance upon the naïvete of the latter in so far as it is distinctly aware of the inexpressibility of the ultimate. In order to distinguish this logically sophisticated phase from the simple negative tendency of the *Ṛgveda* we may call this the stage of *avaktavya*, or *anirvacanīyatā*, after the Vedāntic usage. Not merely the modes (*koṭis*) of *sat* and *asat* but also the mode of *sadasat* are associated with *anirvacanīyatā*. Although *anirvacanīyatā* signifies unutterableness like the Jaina notion of *avaktavyatva* it differs from the latter by insisting upon absolute (*sarvathā*) unutterableness. The specific term by which the Jaina refers to this *absolute* type of *avaktavyatva* is *avyapadeśya* which is in contrast with his own relativistic notion according to which *sat* and *asat* are jointly or consecutively (*kramārpaṇayā*) expressible (*kathañcidvyapadeśya*). Incidentally, one is reminded, here, of the fact that the Buddha's '*avyākṛtas*' and Nāgārjuna's conception of the ultimate as being '*catuṣkoṭivinirmukta*'[1] are, after making allowance for the respective differences in the metaphysical tenets and, consequently, in the modes

1. The paradoxical situation involved in the absolute unutterableness (*anabhilapyatva*) of the position of *catuṣkoṭivinirmuktatvam* comes in for a sharp polemic by Sāmantabhadra and his two commentators, Vasunandi and Akalaṅka. Sāmantabhadra contends that a strict insistence on the principle of '*anabhilapyatvam*' should prevent its advocates from indulging in the description of what cannot, *ex hypothesi*, be described (*avaktavyacatuṣkoṭivikalpopi na kathyatām*/ *AMS*, *kā*. 46). Consequently, referring to the distinctions (*koṭis*) like *sat*, *asat*, etc. in relation to 'the indescribable' (or possibly the Void or *Śūnya*) is like introducing an adjective or a qualification where there is no substantive or the qualified (*asarvāntamavastu syāt aviśeṣyaviśeṣaṇam*/ *Ibid*). For the entire argument, see *ibid.*, *kārikās* 45-50 and the comms. *VVas* and *ASA* thereon.

of expressing the concept of the inexpressible, cognate with the concept of *anirvacanīyatā*, or *avyapadeśya*, as the Jaina would call them.

Another important difference of this *anirvacanīya* view from that of the relativistic inexpressible of the Jaina, is that the former assumes *sat* and *asat*, singly or jointly, to be absolutely independent and contradictory while the latter assumes them to be relative and complementary. On the basis of this difference the former view is designated as *nirapekṣavāda* and the latter *sāpekṣavāda.* The attribution of absolute independence to *sat* and *asat* in their combination as *sadasat* paves the way for the development of the conception of the ultimate absolute (*brahman*) which utterly transcends words and eventually constitutes itself into the transcendental realm of truth (*parasatya* or *paramārthasat*). In other words, the verbal and logical transcendentalism becomes the metaphysical transcendentalism which relegates the antinomies of *sat, asat* and *sadasat* to the intrinsically unreal empirical realm.

The last phase in the dialectical evolution of the idea of the inexpressible is represented by the relativistic (*sāpekṣa*) view of *syādvādin.* The distinctive features of relativism and complementariness in the Jaina view of the inexpressible have already been brought out while contrasting them with the absolutistic view of the *anirvacanīyavādin.* Instead of fighting shy of their supposed contradictoriness and other difficulties the Jania treats the two elements of *sat* and *asat,* in their combination, as a necessary, inevitable and distinctive feature of our objective experience and, consequently, tries to assign them a place in the framework of his dialectical scheme of modal propositions.

In the above account of the four stages in the evolution of the notion of the inexpressible, in Indian philosophy, an attempt has been made to show the relation in which the Jaina notion of the inexpressible stands to the views of certain other schools about the same notion. Incidentally, certain general features like the relativism (*sāpekṣatva*) and the complementariness of the combining concepts of being and non-being, in the same predication, have also been brought out in the account. Now, the status and the significance of this notion, in the scheme of the conditional dialectic (*syādvāda*), as well as the manner in which this notion is to be differentiated from the consecutive concept involved in the third predication of the dialectic, are yet to be further elucidated. But such an elucidatory attempt presupposes a knowledge of the Jaina view of the relation between a word and its meaning, since the development of the concept of the inexpressible is directly based on that view. Hence a brief reference may be made to show how the Jaina treats language as a medium of the meaning of reality.

It is a well-known fact, in Indian philosophy, that Bhartṛhari, the author of the great classic on the philosophy of grammar, the *Vākyapadīya*, puts forth a well-finished, elaborate, and powerful thesis that "the whole order of reality, subjective and objective, is but the manifestation of word".[1]

---

1. *JPN*, p. 111; also cf. *Vākyapadīya*, with Puṇyarāja's Comm. (Ed. by Gangadhara Sastri Manavalli, Benares, 1887), I.119. The relevant *kā.* in *Vākyapadīya* is prefaced by Puṇyarāja as follows: *idānīm śabdasyaiva jaganmūlatvaṁ prapañcayati.* Then

Expression, according to him, is "the very essence of consciousness and, hence, all that exists. Therefore, whatever exists and whatever is thought of, is *completely expressible.*"[2] This thesis represents an extreme viewpoint.

An antithesis to Bhartṛhari's viewpoint is presented by certain utterances of the Upaniṣads which, as noticed during the treatment of the third phase in the development of the indefinable,[3] were, later on, developed into the well-articulated theories of *anirvacanīyatā* in Advaitism, and similar ideas in certain trends of Buddhism. This antithetical view maintains that the ultimate is absolutely beyond the reach of words, and, when any attempt is made to 'reach' the ultimate through words they are found utterly to conceal, nay, even distort it.

---

follows the *kā.* beginning with: *śabdeṣvevāśritā śaktirviśvasyāsya nibandhanī/* Commenting on this Puṇyarāja further observes: *sarvā apyarthajātayaḥ sūkṣmarūpeṇa śabdādhiṣṭhānāḥ /*

2. According to Bhartṛhari "There is no cognition which is not interpenetrated with word. Thought is impossible without verbal expression. It is language that makes cognition illuminative of its objects." This item is beautifully expressed by the following celebrated *kā.* of Bhartṛhari: *na so'sti pratyayo loke yaḥ śabdānugamādṛte/ anuviddhamiva jñānaṁ sarvaṁ śabdena bhāṣate// Vākyapadīya,* I. 124, and for its E. T. see *JPN*, p. 111. For a similar importance attached to *Śabda* by the author of *Kāvyādarśa* see *The Philosophy of Sanskrit Grammar* (P. C. Chakravarti, Calcutta University, 1936), p. 39, especially n. 2 thereon. This *Philosophy of Grammar* as well as his "Linguistic Speculations of the Hindus" in the *Journal of the Department of Letters,* Vol. XII, University of Calcutta, 1925, give an exposition of Bhartṛhari's general position in relation to the Mīmāṁsakas, the Naiyāyikas and others.

3. See *supra*, pp. 348-350.

Here again the Jaina strikes the balance between the two extremes and maintains that reality is both[1] expressible and inexpressible, and, that there is no contradiction in holding this position since reality is so from different points of view.[2] It is in defence of this position that the Jaina view of the relation between a word and its meaning comes into the picture.

According to *syādvādin* one word expresses one meaning only. The relationship between a word and its meaning is designated by the Jaina as *vācyavācakaniyama* or *ekārthatva-niyama*[3], and, by some non-Jaina writers, on the subject, as *nānāśabdavāda*[4]. Both these designations affirm their common essential conviction that a word, which appears to convey more meanings than one, is to be treated, not as one word, but as as many words as the number of meanings it appears

---

1. Expressibility is a consecutive possibility and inexpressibility is an attempt at a co-presentation and, therefore, is a verbal impossibility.

2. Commenting on his own *kā.*, viz., *arpaṇabhedādavirodhaḥ pitṛ-putrādisambandhavat*, Akalaṅka writes : *tadyathā ekasya deva-dattasya jātikularūpasaṁjñāvyapadeśaviśiṣṭasya pitā putro bhrātā bhāgineya ityevamprakārāḥ sambandhā janyajanakatvādiśaktyar-paṇabhedāt na virudhyante/ na hyekāpekṣayā piteti śeṣāpekṣayāpi pitā bhavati/ śeṣāpekṣayā tu putrādivyapadeśabhāk/ na ca pitā-putrādikṛtaṁ sambandhabahutvaṁ devadattaikasya na/ virudhyate-tadvad astitvādayo na yānti virodham ekatra/ TRAG*, p. 26.

3. See *SBT*, p. 61.

4. Although their actual designation is not used Vidyānanda ex-presses its meaning in the following statement : *śabdasya ca prativiṣayaṁ mānatvāt sarvaguṇānām ekaśabdavācyatāyāṁ sarvār-thānām ekaśabdavācyatāpatteḥ śabdāntaravaiphalyāt/ TSV*, p. 136.

to convey.[1] We have already met with an expression of this attitude towards the present question under the etymological standpoint (*samabhirūḍhanaya*[2]) in the chapter on Nayavāda. For instance, the word '*gauḥ*'—we say the 'word' in the singular in conformity to popular usage, we should say, in strictness, a multitude of words—is said to convey a cow (*paśu*), a *vāhika*, earth (*pṛthivī*), heaven (*svarga*), a point of compass, a word (*pada*), and 'a ray of light' (*kiraṇa*).[3] Similarly the English words like play, pound, file, etc. stand for more than one meaning. But the Jaina does not agree with the popular view that the very same word, among such words, can convey all the meanings associated with it by commonsense and listed against it by lexicographers. He believes[4],

---

1. Besides indicating this idea Vimaladāsa also points out the consequences of its violation : *nanu sarveṣāṁ padānām ekārthaniyame nānārthapadocchedāpattiriti cenna, gavādipadasyāpi svargādyanekārthaviṣayatayā prasiddhasya tattvato'nekatvāt, sādṛśyopacārādeva tasyaikatvena vyavaharaṇāt/anyathā sakalārthasyāpi ekaśabdavācyatvāpatteḥ arthabhedena anekaśabdaprayogavaiphalyāt/ SBT*, p. 61.
2. See *supra*, pp. 321-324, and *SBT*, p. 61, where the author writes : *yathaiva hi samabhirūḍhanayāpekṣayā śabdabhedād dhruvo'rthabhedaḥ tathā arthabhedādapi śabdabhedaḥ siddha eva/ anyathā vācyavācakaniyamavyavahāravilopāt/*
3. Four of these meanings are given in the Hindi comm. on *SBT*, p. 61, and five of them (with the addition of the meaning, a 'word') are given in *JPN*, p. 117. *Vāhika*, though not given in either work, is widely referred to in *Vākyapadīya* and other works.
4. Prabhācandra puts forth this idea of one word for one meaning in a somewhat different form (substituting that simultaneous inexpressibility of the positive and the negative meaning of a word for a similar inexpressibility of more than one meaning of a so-called synonymous word) in a polemic against a particular theory of the import of words (*apohavāda*). Although the theory controverted is not specifically mentioned

with Bhāmaha[1], that in spite of the common structural and phonetic pattern the word '*gauḥ*', when uttered or written against any one of the several meanings, is a specific symbol different from what appears to be—and structurally and phonologically is—the same symbol against another meaning connected with it. In other words, the word '*gauḥ*' as meaning 'a cow' is different from the word '*gauḥ*' as meaning a '*vāhika*'. The fact that two or more

---

by him it is evidently the theory, sponsored by Ratnākaraśānti, which propounds "that a word denotes something positive, and at the same time differentiates it from all others. The two acts, one positive and the other negative, are", according to this theory, "simultaneous. It is not a positive action followed by negation nor is it a negative act followed by assertion.' (*SBNT*, preface, p. 1). To quote the words of Ratnākaraśānti himself: *nāsmābhirapohaśabdena vidhireva kevalo'bhipretaḥ/ nāpyanyavyāvṛttimātram, kintvanyāpohaviśiṣṭo vidhiḥ śabdānāmarthaḥ/ Ibid.*, p. 3. This view is opposed to the widely accepted view of *apoha* which consists in 'mutual negation' (*parasparaparihāra* or *anyavyāvṛtti*, as referred to by Ratnākaraśānti in the above quotation) between point-instants (see Stcherbatsky's *The Conception of Buddhist Nirvāṇa*, p. 157, f. n. 3). Criticising the above view, of Ratnākaraśānti, that one word (*dhvani*) may generate in us two cognitions (*vijñānadvaya*), one positive and the other negative, at once, Prabhācandra writes: *athaikenaiva gośabdena buddhidvayasya utpādāt na paro dhvanir mṛgyaḥ ; na ekasya vidhikāriṇo niṣedhakāriṇo vā dhvaner yugapat vijñānadvayalakṣaṇaphalānupalambhāt/ vidhiniṣedhajñānayoś ca anyonyaṁ virodhāt katham ekasmāt sambhavaḥ/ PKM*, pp. 431-2. Bhāmaha is at one with Prabhācandra on this question. See the following f. n.

1. Bhāmaha, like *syādvādin*, holds that "no single word can have two fruits" or meanings, as is evidenced by the following *kā.* quoted with approval by Prabhācandra: *nanu jñānaphalāḥ śabdā na caikasya phaladvayam/ apavādavidhijñānaṁ phalamekasya vaḥ katham // Ibid.*, p. 432. Commenting on this *kā.*, quoted also by Śāntarakṣita, Kamalaśīla observes: *na hyekasya vidhikāriṇaḥ niṣedhakāriṇo vā śabdasya yugapadvijñā nadvayalakṣaṇaṁ phalam/ TSS.*, *kā.* 913, and the P. thereon.

meanings have the same linguistic symbol (*saṁjñā*) is, according to the Jaina, simply a matter of linguistic coincidence just as in the case of two persons, who are entirely different from each other in many respects, having the same name, say Devadatta. The farthest that the Jaina could go concerning the question of the occurrence of the same symbol against several meanings is that he can conceive every instance of its occurrence as being only *similar* (*sādṛśyopacārādeva*)[1], linguistically, to the other instances.

In the general position[2] taken up by the Jaina on the problems of the philosophy of language our concern here is with the specific problem[3] of the relation between word and

---

1. See *supra*, p. 354, f. n. 1.
2. The following works deserve attention for their treatment of the problems concerning the philosophy of language from the Jaina point of view : *PKM*, ch. III, pp. 391-465; *NKC*, Vol. II, ch. IV, pp. 530-604, ch. V, pp. 636-54, ch. VI, pp. 690-766.
3. Closely allied to this problem of word-meaning relation is the question whether the meaning of a word resides in the word as a natural power (*svabhāva*) or is associated with it as a mere convention. In the debate on this question the Mīmāṁsaka takes the former view and the Naiyāyika takes the latter view. In conformity with his reconciliatory attitude the Jaina takes the middle position between these two extremes. Accordingly, he believes that although meaning is natural potency of a word it needs the aid of convention for its discovery as well as its expressive use. "The power," it is said, "is natural, but is made effective only by convention. We have to learn the relation of words to facts and this shows that knowledge of convention is necessary for understanding the meanings of words. But the knowledge of convention is only a means to the discovery of the power of the word and does not make the postulation of power unnecessary or redundant." (*JPN*, p. 119). But whatever the relative proportions of the role played by power and convention, the stand taken by the Jaina with regard to the problem of word-meaning relation is consistently maintained (cf. *ekapa-*

meaning (*saṁjñāsaṁjñi-sambandha*). Having noticed that he favours the view that every distinctive meaning needs a distinctive word (*pratiniyatavācyavācakabhāva*) for its medium, we may now resume our treatment of the co-presentative predicate of the inexpressible (*avaktavya*) and of its differentiation from the consecutive-presentative, in their respective modes, under the method of seven-fold predication.

If the above principle of one word for one meaning is granted, then the concept of the inexpressible in *syādvāda* lends itself to an easy grasp. The fourth mode, viz., "The jar is inexpressible", is an attempt to present the aspects of 'being' and 'non-being' in the jar, *at once* (*yugapat*), and, as *primary meanings.*

Although both these aspects are the inalienable features of the jar a simultaneous attention to both aspects is a psychological and logical impossibility. Moreover 'being' conveys the meaning of one aspect and 'non-being' of the other. A conveyance of both meanings at once is incompatible with the established rule, viz., *vācyavācaka-niyama*. To say that one word, like *avaktavya* in the present

---

dasya pradhānatayā anekadharmavacchinnabodhakatvaṁ nāstīti niyamasyoktatvāt / *SBT*, p. 66. See also *supra*, pp. 42, 354 (f. ns. 1, 2 and 4) and 374 (f. n. 1), as well as pp. 42, 43 (f. n. 3), 44 (f. n. 1). For a further discussion on how collective terms like army (*senā*), forest (*vana*) etc., and how terms expressing plural number, like trees (*vṛkṣāḥ*) etc., can be explained in terms of the Jaina conception of word-meaning relation, see *SBT*, pp. 63-67. The relevant grammatical points, bearing on the explanation of these terms, especially the terms involving the plural number, are also mentioned by the way, often in opposition to Paṇini's view on the matter (*ibid.*).

context, can convey both the meanings at once would not be correct, according to the Jaina, because of two reasons: first that no word can convey more than one meaning at a time, and secondly, even if it can, our mind can attend to them only in a successive order. A further mention of these difficulties incident to the concept will presently be made.

No such difficulties arise in the case of the third predication which is concerned with presenting, consecutively (*kramārpaṇayā*), the two aspects of 'being' and 'non-being', although it is expressed in the shortened form of a single proposition. It is because of this consecutive element that this mode is aptly called 'differenced togetherness' (or distinguishable togetherness) in contrast to the phrase 'undifferenced togetherness' (or undistinguishable togetherness) which signifies *avaktavya*. Both aspects are 'primitive', co-ordinate and mutually irreducible. Our mental (perceptual and other) as well as expressive (*bodhanasāmarthyam* and *vacanasāmarthyam*) faculties being ill-adapted for comprehending and asserting both of them at once in their primary togetherness (*ubhayaprādhānyam*) we can grasp and assert them either successively or confess to our inability to do if asked to do it at a single stroke.[1] This is precisely what is done under the third and the fourth modes, respectively.[2]

It is contended that the third mode is redundant, or

---

1. *iti sakalavācakarahitatvādavaktavyaṁ vastu yugapatsattvāsattvābhyām pradhānabhāvārpitābhyām ākrāntaṁ vyavatiṣṭhate*/ *SM*, p. 145.
2. See *SBT*, p. 62, *PNTA,* IV. 15, and *SRK* thereon in *SRK*, pp. 718-719.

superfluous, and, therefore, is unjustifiable[1] as a distinctive alternative in the dialectical scheme of conditional predications. The reason pleaded for this contention is that it does not exhibit any unique or novel feature of objective reality, being almost a mechanical conjunction of the two simple predicates contained, severally, in the first and second modes. While not denying the fact that it is a conjunctive predication, the Jaina does not agree with the contention that it is redundant. A conjunctive proposition embodies a judgment of consecutive togetherness which is no less a unique or distinctive moment of factual significance than any other, and, cannot, therefore, be expunged from a methodological scheme which pretends to synthesise, exhaustively, all possible moments, or alternatives, within its fold.

A similar consideration applies to the concept of the inexpressible. This concept confronts us with a logical, psychological, and verbal failure to embody, within any one symbol (*saṅketa*), the two fundamental aspects of reality, with equal prominence. This is indeed an inconvenient predicament inevitable in any effort to take in, in one sweep, the whole range of truth. But the inconvenient or the impossible is not necessarily illogical or untrue. Limitations in the range of human powers of thinking and expression entail such a failure. But even this failure is a necessary step to be reckoned with in the dialectical method of *syādvāda*. Being at once an inescapable and unique fact in our grappling with reality it cannot but be provided for as a dialectically

---

1. See *SBT*, p. 69 f.

possible or alternative position. K. C. Bhattacharya clearly expresses this position in the following words: "It (the inexpressible) is objective as given: it cannot be said to be not a particular position nor to be non-existent. At the same time it is not the definite distinction of position and existence: it represents a category by itself. The common-sense principle implied in its recognition is that what is given cannot be rejected simply because it is not expressible by a single positive concept. A truth has to be admitted if it cannot be got rid of even if it is not understood."[1]

The remaining three[2] modes are derived from combining the three primary concepts in such a way that these three, combined with the four modes hitherto expounded, exhaust all the possible or alternative aspects of truth concerning the object in question (the jar in the present instance).

The fifth mode, viz., "In a certain sense, the jar is, and is inexpressible", asserts the truth of the 'being' of the jar conjointly with the inexpressible truth of the compresence (or co-presentation) of the being and the non-being of the same object.[3] This is a combined mode derived from

---

1. *JTA*, p. 48.
2. After mentioning the four 'ways' or 'steps' of the 'formula' (*syādvāda*) Hiriyanna observes: "It may seem that the formula might stop here. But there are still other ways in which the alternatives can be combined. To avoid the impression that those predicates are excluded, three more steps are added. The resulting description becomes exhaustive, leaving no room for the charge of dogma in any form." *OIP*, p. 165.
3. Cf. *yugapad asāṅketikenaikenaiva śabdena vaktuṁ vivakṣitaḥ kumbhaḥ saṁś ca vaktavyaś ca bhavati, ghaṭo'vaktavyaś ca bhavatītyarthaḥ deśe tasya ghaṭatvāt, deśe cāvaktavyatvād iti/ SHM* in *VBJ*, *gā*. 2232.

bringing together the first and the fourth predicates in a complex expressed judgment.

The sixth mode, viz., "In a certain sense, the jar is not, and is inexpressible", asserts the truth of non-being of the jar conjointly with the inexpressible truth of the compresence of the 'being' and the 'non-being' of the same object.[1] This, again, is a combined mode resulting from bringing together the second and the fourth predicates in a complex expressed judgment.

The seventh and last mode, viz., "In a certain sense, the jar is, is not, and is inexpressible", combines the consecutive presentation of the 'being' and the 'non-being', conjointly with the co-presentation or compresence, of the 'being' and the 'non-being' of the jar.[2] This mode is evidently a resultant of bringing together, within its fold, the third and the fourth predicates of the conditional dialectic.

Unlike the first two and the fourth predications, each of which contains a simple predicate involving one of the three primary concepts, the fifth, the sixth and the seventh predications are, severally, complex in structure, the last one being the most complex among them. This is so because they are assertions of complex judgments.

These are the seven modes each of which contains one

---

1. Cf. *tathā, ekadeśe paraparyāyaiḥ asadbhāvenārpito viśeṣito'nyasmins tu deśe svaparaparyāyaiḥ śadbhāvāsadbhāvābhyāṁ sattvāsattvābhyām yugapad asāṅketikenaikena śabdena vaktuṁ vivakṣitaḥ kumbho'sannavaktavyaś ca bhavati / Ibid.*
2. *Ibid.*

alternative truth while all together contain the total truth[1] of a situation in which any feature predicated of a real is investigated. The reason why the number of modes is neither more nor less than seven is because, it is believed, any complex situation is amenable to treatment by this seven-fold technique if one is an adept in using it. It means every conceivable problem[2] regarding a factual situation can be reduced to the terms of these seven angles from which it can be viewed. Any attempt to add or subtract a mode will be found to be impossible since addition finds the mode already there, among one of the existing seven modes, and subtraction will mutilate an essential limb from the scheme.[3] In the event of a fresh situation arising with regard

---

1. Jinabhadragaṇi sums up the complex position of *Syādvāda* in the following *gāthā*: *sabbhāvāsabbhāvobhayappio saparapajjaobhayao/ kumbhākumbhāvattavvobhayarūvāibheo so// VBJ., gā.* 2232. Explaining this *gā.* Maladhāri observes:.. *tathā hi—svaparyāyaiḥ, paraparyāyaiḥ, ubhayaparyāyaiś ca sadbhāvena, asadbhāvena, ubhayena, cārpito viśeṣitaḥ kumbhaḥ kumbhākumbhāvaktavyobhayarūpādibhedo bhavati—saptabhaṅgī pratipadyata ityarthaḥ / SHM* in *VBJ*, p. 910. In a similar manner Vidyānanda and Sāmantabhadra sum up the entire position in two and four *kārikās*, respectively. See *AMS*, 14 and 16; and *TSV*, p. 128, 49-52.
2. For instance, applying *syādvāda* to the postulation that reality is one we get the following conclusions: the reality is one (*syādekaḥ*); the reality is non-one or many (*syādanekaḥ*); the reality is both one and many (*syādekaścānekaśca*); the reality is inexpressible (*syādavaktavyaḥ*); the reality is one and also inexpressible (*syādekaścāvaktavyaḥ*); the reality is many and also inexpressible (*syādanekaścāvaktavyaḥ*); and, the reality is one, many and also inexpressible (*syādekaścānekaścāvaktavyaśca*).
3. Cf. *bhaṅgāssattvādayassapta saṁśayāssapta tadgatāḥ/ jijñāsāssapta sapta syuḥ praśnāssaptottarāṇi ca//* quoted in *SBT*, p.8. This refutes objections such as the one by Kumārila who feels that "When

to the same problem under a different setting it can again be dealt with by the application of this method. All the conclusions accumulating from the varied application of this method will, eventually, give us a conspectus of the complex truth with regard to a problem. The whole method, therefore, may be said to be one which helps a patient inquiring mind in its adventure of mapping out the winding paths running into the faintly known or unknown regions of reality and bringing them within the bounds of human knowledge.

Now we may consider some important criticisms directed against *syādvāda.*

A few criticisms, considered by the critics directing them to be fatal to *syādvāda,* come from the *vedāntic* quarters, especially *advaitic* absolutism. This is inevitable since *advaitic* absolutism and *syādvādic* relativism are diametrically opposed to each other in their fundamental presuppositions. Although these criticisms originated with the founders of the *vedāntic* schools it would be better to see them (the criticisms) through the eyes of the modern exponents of *vedānta.* An elaborate refutation of them lies outside the limits of this work. A few remarks may, however, be made in answer to them inserting, here and there, some observations of the critics themselves who, to some extent, answer, perhaps somewhat unwittingly, their fellow-critics.

---

seven principles are admitted then there may also be a hundred" (*saptabhaṅgī prasādena śatabhaṅgyapi jāyate*) *PSKC*, p. 14. Chakravarti observes in this connection: "The complex nature of a real object or *dravya* is amenable to description by the above seven and only seven propositions." *Ibid.*, p. 12.

Hiriyanna, by no means an unsympathetic exponent even of Jainism, observes : "The half-hearted character of the Jaina enquiry is reflected in the seven-fold mode of predication (*sapta-bhaṅgī*), which stops at giving us the several partial views together, without attempting to overcome the opposition in them by a proper synthesis. It is all right so far as it cautions us against one-sided conclusions but it leaves us in the end....with little more than one-sided solutions. The reason for it, if it is not prejudice against absolutism, is the desire to keep close to common beliefs."[1] In another work of his also the same criticism is made with some more incisive touches on one or two points. One additional point mentioned there, on the authority of Bādarayaṇa, Śaṅkara, and other absolutists, is that "If all our knowledge concerning reality is relative, they say (the old Indian critics like Śaṅkara, Rāmānuja etc.), the Jaina view must also be relative. To deny this conclusion would be to admit, at least, one absolute truth; and to admit it would leave the doctrine with no settled view of reality, and thus turn it into a variety of scepticism."[2]

From these observations we may elicit two points of criticism : The first one is that *syādvāda* is a form of "electicism" because it is "a mere putting together of the several partial truths"[3] without "a proper synthesis". This is expressed even more trenchantly by a follower of Hiriyanna who, after characterising "The Jaina Philosophy of Relativity" as

1. *OIP*, p. 172 f.
2. *EIP*, p. 69.
3. *Ibid.*, p. 68.

"refreshingly modern"[1] and as "a happy blend of naturalistic and spiritualistic, realistic and idealistic tendencies", observes: "'Just the philosophy' is perhaps what many contemporary philosophers would say. But on close scrutiny, it fails to satisfy some of the deepest metaphysical and religious aspirations of mankind. Its fascination is the fascination of an *eclecticism*—a philosophy of compromise."[2] This is said to be "the central defect" arising from the relativism of *syādvāda.*

The second criticism of *syādvāda*, made by Hiriyanna, is that it (*syādvāda*) is "variety of scepticism". "Prejudice against absolutism", the reason imputed by Hiriyanna for such "scepticism", is even more conclusively advanced by Radhakrishnan, who, after mentioning "the strong points of the theory of knowledge of the Jainas and defending it against the attacks of the Vedantins" remarks : "Yet in our opinion the Jaina logic leads to a monistic idealism (by which he means 'the hypothesis of the absolute') and so far as the Jainas shrink from it they are untrue to their own logic."[3]

After casually complementing *syādvāda* as the "most searching dialectic"[4] Belvalkar gives such a twist to his statement of *syādvāda* that it is made to sound like scepticism,

---

1. "Anekāntavāda or The Jaina Philosophy of Relativity", G. Hanumantha Rao, *The Half-yearly Journal of the Mysore University*, March, 1942, p. 79.
2. *Ibid.*, p. 87 f.
3. *IP*, Vol. I, p. 305.
4. "The Undercurrents of Jainism" (an article in the *Indian Philosophical Review*, Vol. I, No. 1, 1917, edited by A. C. Widgery and R. D. Ranade, Bombay), p. 33.

or rather, the even more non-committal attitude of "agnosticism". He writes : "As is well-known, this theory denies the possibility of any predication : S may be, or may not be, or may both be and not be, P. With such a purely negative or agnostic attitude one cannot have any dogma; and Śankarācārya lays his finger accurately on the weakest point in the system when he says—'As thus the means of knowledge, the knowing subject, and the act of knowledge, are all alike, indefinite, how can the Tīrthaṅkara (Jaina) teach with any claim to authority, and how can his followers act on a doctrine the matter of which is altogether indeterminate?' "[1]

Besides this charge of agnosticism Belvalkar manages to raise a fresh issue which, however, he links up with agnosticism. He remarks that "the dialectic (of *syādvāda*) could not have sprung up from the same teacher or one and the same philosophical background".[2] This means that, according to him, *syādvāda* is incompatible with, or at any rate, does not naturally emerge from, the Jaina philosophy of identity-in-difference. Connecting this issue with his favourite charge of agnosticism he writes in his notes on *Brahmasūtrabhāṣya*, "Śaṅkarācārya, no less than the Sūtrakara,.... succeeds in proving that, as a mere '*anaikāntika*' (*sic*) theory of predication, the Syādvāda must return upon itself and end in doubting the doubter himself".[3] Rao strengthens him by placing in his hands a further weapon in the form of charging *syādvāda* with "self-contradiction". To quote Rao's own

1. *Ibid.*, p. 32.
2. *Ibid.*
3. *BBSB*, p. 181 (Notes).

words: "We see the tendency to please everybody and to compromise and in trying to compromise it involves itself in self-contradiction; the saviour of all systems is committing suicide".[1] From this joint attack of Belvalkar and Rao emerges the third charge that *syādvāda* is contradictory to the Jaina philosophical position in general as well as that it is self-contradictory.

A systematically elaborate answer to each of these three charges, viz., eclecticism, agnosticism and contradiction including self-contradiction, lies, as already mentioned, outside the scope of this work. Moreover, if a glance is cast over the various chapters of this work, especially these last three parts, it will be seen that these criticisms have been met in spirit, if not in letter, according to the lights vouchsafed to the Jaina thinkers. We may, therefore, confine ourselves to a few remarks against each charge drawing upon, wherever possible, the remarks by the critics themselves who, on certain points, answer one another.

We may begin with the first criticism: Is *syādvāda* an eclecticism? Eclecticism is a "term applied to a system of philosophy or theology that strives to incorporate the truth of all systems, or the method by which it is made". "Since an eclectic system is a loose piece of mosaic work, rather than an organised body of original thought", it is said, "the term in philosophy has come to be one of reproach".[2]

---

1. "The Jaina Instrumental Theory of Knowledge" (*Proceedings of the First Indian Philosophical Congress*, 1925, Calcutta University, Calcutta, 1927), p. 135.
2. *The New Schaff-Herzog Encyclopaedia of Religious Knowledge*, ed. by S. M. Jackson, New York and London, 1909, Vol. IV, p. 71.

We may examine *syādvāda* in the light of the definition of eclecticism as given here. So far as the first statement in the definition of eclecticism is concerned, there is nothing objectionable to *syādvāda*. For *syādvāda* is a "system of philosophy" which, "strives to incorporate the truth of all systems"[1] as well as a "method by which it (that is, 'incorporating the truth of all systems') is made." The critics also do not grudge this claim on the part of Jainism but they are doubtful whether Jainism can provide an adequate answer to the charge that it is "a loose piece of mosaic work rather than an organised body of original thought". Further, even as regards this charge they are keen not so much on the point of *syādvāda* being a product of "an original thought" as on that of its being "a loose piece" in which the parts do not hang together in an organised or systematic closeness. This emphasis on the question of closeness should be the leading factor in our refutation of the present charge.

That the seven modes of *syādvāda* express "partial truths" which do not firmly hang together, as a logical necessity, is only the *prima facie* view of *syādvāda*. That

1. The types of the absolute (*nirapekṣa*) doctrines repudiated by each of the seven modes may be gathered from the following passage: *sāṁkhyena yat sattvaikāntyam upāgataṁ tannivṛttaya ādyo bhaṅgaḥ/ śūnyatvavādyupāgata-asattvaikāntyanivṛttaye dvitīyo bhaṅgaḥ/ kālābhedena sattvāsattve tārkikopāgate tadanaikāntyāya tṛtiyo bhaṅgaḥ/ vedāntinā anirvacanīyatvam upāgamyate tadanaikāntyāya caturtho bhaṅgaḥ/ sattvavādinaṁ prati sattvenānirvacanīyatvaṁ pūrvapakṣiṇodbhāvitam, asattvavādinaṁ prati asattvenānirvacanīyatvaṁ pūrvapakṣiṇodbhāvitam, sadasattvavādinaṁ prati tābhyāmanirvacanīyatvaṁ pūrvapakṣavādinodbhāvitam, tadanaikāntyadyotanāya avaśiṣṭāstrayo bhaṅgāḥ/* Quoted in *BBSB* (Notes), p. 183.

their truths are severally partial is true. But from this it does not necessarily follow that they are an odd collection of arbitrary 'half truths' lacking in proper synthesis, or system. The fact that the truths presented by them are alternative truths which individually touch every aspect, and, together, all the aspects, of a situation in a systematic way has been borne in upon us, in some measure, in the course of the present chapter. A certain actuality, like the jar, an example with which the modes have been illustrated, is looked at from the possible seven angles and the deliverance of these modal judgments does represent a synthesis which is neither 'loose' nor unsystematic. Unfortunately no non-absolutistic system can provide the sort of idealistic 'synthesis' which "can satisfy the deepest metaphysical and religious aspirations of mankind". Under the absolutistic prescription a 'proper synthesis' can proceed from the sole real, viz., the absolute. But one fails to understand where the need for a 'synthesis' arises in the case of a secondless absolute. A 'synthesis' of any description is possible when there are more alternatives, loose or firm, than one. If it is so, it is impossible to understand the protests of the absolutists against any lack of synthesis when no synthesis at all is possible with a unitary absolute. By 'synthesis', therefore, the absolutist critics mean an obliteration of alternative truths in favour of the one asserted by the fourth mode in *syādvāda*. It is not a mere 'prejudice against absolutism'[1]

1. Ascribing this 'prejudice' to the *syādvādin* has elicited a counter-charge of a 'speculative bias' from a critic in rather strong terms : "...And it would be the height of sacrilege to the system of Jaina speculation to attempt an unnecessary twisting

but a deep difference in the approach of philosophical analysis that prevents *syādvādin* from throwing in his lot with a despotic absolute which brooks no rivalry from coexistent truths and, therefore, should raise no issue of synthesis. It is the love of a superficial reconciliation that lies at the back of the claim that *syādvāda* is a "halfway house to absolutism". Thus the synthesis achieved by *syādvāda* is one of discriminative unity rather than of a secondless unit which cannot be approached either by synthesis or by analysis. The conception of a unitary absolute has been, no doubt, a constant lure for mysticism and poetry. But the sphere of reality is often less lofty and very much less ethereal. Absolutism escapes from the harrowing problems of existence under the master excuse of the absolute. But it is through a tortuous process of analysis and synthesis that the secrets of elusive reality grudgingly yield themselves. This is provided for by *nayavāda* and *syādvāda* respectively.

If by lack of 'proper synthesis' *syādvādin* does not instal an absolute at the centre as well as on the periphery of his philosophy and logic *syādvāda* pleads guilty to the charge and will be satisfied to remain an unrepentent sinner. The threat of its modes not hanging together does not baffle him since he is not unwilling to retain to some extent distinctive-

---

of facts, to impose an absolutist or monist interpretation on their conception of truth and reality, as has been done in some quarters, on the plea of pseudo-simplicity, or perhaps owing to speculative bias". Narimohana Bhattacharya's paper on "The Jaina Conception of Truth and Reality" (*Proceedings of the First Indian Philosophical Congress*, 1925, Calcutta University, Calcutta, 1927), p. 165.

ness or even exclusiveness in the modal conclusions. He feels perhaps that the distinctions of the modal truths look to an absolutist eye grossly exaggerated. But they are bound together also by the unity of the dialectical principle under which the aspects of a factual situation are investigated and synthesised. *Syādvāda* may be an eclectic synthesis from the point of view of absolutism which demands a 'block' universe or a 'seamless coat' but is not unfaithful to the genius of its own philosophical position which demands a discriminative synthesis which it undoubtedly is. The next charge against *syādvāda*, viz., that it is "a variety of scepticism" or "agnosticism", may now be examined. A sceptical or agnostic philosophy or method is based on "the opinion that real knowledge of any kind is unattainable".[1] More particularly agnosticism is an attitude of "know-nothingness". Therefore a sceptic is defined as "One who, like Pyrrho and his followers in Greek antiquity, doubts the possibility of knowledge of any kind, who holds that there are no adequate grounds for certainty as to the truth of any proposition whatever".[2]

It is not possible to see how *syādvāda* could be called sceptical or agnostic while it firmly repudiates any such association and has its genesis, at least partially, in an attempt to fight, as will be presently shown, the agnosticism (*ajñānavāda*) of Sañjaya. According to *syādvāda* each modal truth is valid so far as it goes, and, instead of being annulled, it is supplemented and transfigured, by the other six

1. *O. E. D.* under "scepticism".
2. *Ibid.* under "sceptic".

modal truths, all the seven truths together giving us a full range of the complex truth concerning a particular problem of a fact in reality. Each truth is as it were a single note in the full scale of seven notes which are severally distinctive, in respect of place and function, and, in their totality, interdependent and exhaustive. The aim of *syādvāda* being to achieve such a comprehensive synthesis which includes the specific cognitive manifestations it is not correct to describe the doctrine—either as a theory or as a method—as sceptical or agnostic. Often it is true that a doctrine leads to results contrary to those it intends to achieve. But *syādvāda* seems to be such a one to a superficial observer. Speaking of *anekāntavāda* in general, a writer makes the following statement which is fully applicable to *syādvāda* which is an essential method of *anekāntavāda*. "Unfortunately", he observes, "it has been a neglected branch of study; it is often misunderstood or half-understood; that is why it is often adversely criticised".[1] It is of paramount importance that a philosophical theory or method must be first understood in terms of its own canons or motives before it is subjected to any critical examination by alien criteria. From the exposition of *syādvāda* in the present chapter, as well as from the few remarks specifically made here, in answer to the present charge, one will find, at least in some measure, that the charge of scepticism is not well-founded. Because nowhere do we come across, in the accounts of *syādvāda*, the expression of the attitude of "know-nothingness" or of

1. "References to *Syādvāda* in the Ardhamāgadhi Canon", *Proceedings and Transactions of the Ninth All India Oriental Conference, Trivandrum, Dec. 1937*, Trivandrum 1940, p. 668.

"the opinion that real knowledge of any kind is unattainable".

In the light of these few observations on the non-sceptical attitude of *syādvāda* we find that Belvalkar gives a rather misleading twist to the nature of the method as a whole by stating the doctrine in such form as he has done.[1] As has already been remarked, even historically *syādvāda* arose in an appreciable degree, 'as a happy way leading out of the maze of the *ajñānavāda*' (agnosticism). This is expressed by Jacobi in the following passage: "Would any philosopher have enunciated such truisms, unless they served to silence

---

1. An attempt to assess the historical claims of the different opinions on the development of *syādvāda* and its modes will take us far afield. However, for some information on these opinions, see *SM*, Intro. pp. LXXIV-LXXVIII; *Syādvādamañjarī* (by Mallişeṇa, Ed. with Hindi Tr. by Jagadīśacandra, Bombay, 1935) 26-29; *NVVS*, Prastāvanā, pp. 35-50; *AJP*, Vol. II, Intro. pp. CX-CXII; *PrSKU*, pp. LXXXVI-LXXXVIII: A. N. Upadhye's paper on "References to *Syādvāda* in the Ardhamāgadhī Canon", *Proceedings and Transactions of the Ninth All India Oriental Conference, Trivandrum, Dec. 1937*, Trivandrum, 1940 pp. 669-672, and *The Canonical Literature of the Jainas* (H. R. Kapadia, 1941, Bombay), pp. 218-220.

   Whatever might be the value of the opinions as to the nature, the extent and the sources of influence on the development of *syādvāda* and its modes, we may safely assert that, philosophically speaking, *syādvāda* was an inherent necessity in the system of *anekāntavāda*. This fact of its having been an inherent philosophical necessity need not invalidate the equally important fact that *syādvāda* enlarged its range in answer to a varied external demand. No doctrine or method, particularly the latter, can, after all, arise from an atmosphere of a philosophical vacuum. The great critical philosophy and the critical method, of Kant, if it could possibly arise at all, would be little more than an idle speculation were it not for the rationalistic dogmatism of Descartes, Spinoza, and Leibniz as well as for the empiristic scepticism of Locke, Berkeley, and Hume. Any genuine growth in philosophical thinking is thus a story of action and reaction between vital ideas.

some dangerous opponents? The subtle discussion of the agnostics had probably bewildered and misled many of their contemporaries. Consequently the *syādvāda* must have appeared to them as a happy way leading out of the maze of the *ajñānavāda*. It was the weapon with which the agnostics assailed the enemy, turned against themselves. Who knows how many of their followers went over to Mahāvīra's creed convinced by the truth of *saptabhaṅgīnaya* ?"[1]

As regards the third charge, directed by Belvalkar, that *syādvāda* cannot spring from "one and the same philosophical background", and the supplementary charge, directed by Rao, that *syādvāda* itself suffers from "self-contradiction", we may allow the charges to be answered by three of their fellow critics themselves. Answering Rao and Belvalkar in order, of course unwittingly, Radhakrishnan observes: "Śaṅkara and Rāmānuja criticise the *Saptabhaṅgī* view on the ground of the impossibility of contradictory attributes co-existing in the same thing". After quoting the relevant passage from Rāmānuja he proceeds to say: "The Jains admit that a thing cannot have self-contradictory attributes at the same time and in the same sense. All that they say is that everything is of a complex nature, and identity in difference. The real comprehends and reconciles differences in itself. Attributes which are contradictory in the abstract co-exist in life and experience. The tree is moving in that its branches are moving and it is not moving since it is fixed to its place in the ground".[2] Then incidentally dis-

1. *JSJ*, Pt. II, Intro. p. XXVIII.
2. *IP*, Vol. I, p. 304.

missing another point of criticism that "the *Saptabhaṅgī* doctrine is of no practical utility" or "an expression of personal opinion over which we need not linger", the same critic proceeds to answer the specific charge by Belvalkar: "Nor can it be contended" he observes, "that the *Saptabhaṅgī* doctrine is inconsistent with the other views of the Jaina philosophy. It is a logical corollary of the *anekāntavāda*, the doctrine of the manyness of reality. Since reality is 'multiform' and ever changing, nothing can be considered to be existing everywhere and at all times and in all ways and places, and it is impossible to pledge ourselves to an inflexible creed".[1] Confirming Radhakrishnan on the second point of criticism, which is the main charge of Belvalkar, Hiriyanna briefly observes: "The thought underlying it (*saptabhaṅgī*) is inherent in the doctrine, although its clear enunciation seems to belong to the present period." The same opinion is suggestively expressed by R. G. Bhandarkar also.

Incidentally Belvalkar's misleading interpretation of '*anekāntavāda*' as an 'indefinite' doctrine—which in turn means a shifting or evasive doctrine—is corrected by Hiriyanna's correct description of it: Interpreting '*anekānta*' as meaning 'indeterminate in nature' Hiriyanna remarks: "This does not, however, mean that it is altogether indefinite but only that it cannot be defined absolutely. It is this idea that is conveyed by the sevenfold statement as a whole and it expresses the nature of reality in several steps, because no single mode of doing so is adequate to it."

---

1. *Ibid., EIP*, p. 67.

We gather from a consideration of the present charge, as well as of the other two charges, that the critics advance contrary criticisms even on the same point, as well as from the same viewpoint, viz., monistic absolutism. The irony of the situation is particularly evident in the fact that contradictory arguments are presented on the very issue of alleged contradiction and self-contradiction in *syādvāda*. Among others there seem to be two important reasons underlying the misconceived criticisms of the critics on *syādvāda* : The first is that they do not note an explicit reference in the very definition of *syādvāda* to the important condition that the modal judgments should not be 'incompatible' (*avirodha*) not merely with the other modal judgments within the sphere of *syādvāda*, but also with 'valid knowledge, perceptual, or otherwise', in the entire sphere of experience. Had this been fully recognised Rao's criticism on 'self-contradiction' would perhaps be not as strong as it is now. Then, 'the Saviour of all systems' would be found not 'committing suicide' but performing its benevolent mission of saving the absolutisms from their excessive dogmatism.

The second reason is their failure to realize the true significance, place and function of negation in Jaina philosophy, in general, and in *syādvāda* in particular. Since this subject has been dealt with, at several places, it is needless to enlarge upon it any further.

In concluding this chapter it would not be out of place to quote a passage by R. B. Perry which bears a striking resemblance to *syādvāda* in suggesting a procedure which, as in *syādvāda*, is at once a critique on 'vicious intellectualism' (which brings in its train errors like 'exclusive particularity') and a positive programme of dealing with reality. Perry observes ".... 'vicious intellectualism'[1] proceeds as though a conceptual truth about a thing were the exclusive truth about the thing; whereas it is true only *so far as it goes.* Thus the world may be truly conceived as permanent and unified, since it is such *in a certain respect.* But this should not lead us, as it has led certain intellectualists, to suppose that the world is therefore not changing and plural. We must not identify our world with one conception of it. In its concrete richness it lends itself to many conceptions. And the same is true of the least thing in the world. It has many aspects, none of which is exhaustive of it. It may be taken in many relations or orders, and be given different names accordingly. As it is immediately presented it contains all these aspects as potentialities for the discriminating and abstracting operations of thought. 'Vicious intellectualism' thus rests on the errors that I have already referred to as 'exclusive particularity' and 'definition by initial predication': the false supposition that because a thing has one definable character, it cannot also have others and that because it has been named first for one of its aspects, the others must be reduced to it or deduced from it."

Continuing further, he writes: "Now the fault of 'vicious intellectualism' evidently lies in the misuse of concepts, and not in the nature of the concepts themselves. There is nothing to prevent our supposing that the abstractness of

---

1. 'Vicious intellectualism' is explained as follows: "To conceive a thing as *a*, and then assume that it is *only a*, is to be 'viciously' intellectual." (p. 234).

single concepts can be compensated for by the addition of further concepts, or by some conceptual system in which the presence and interrelation of many concepts is specially provided for. In this case the remedy for the shortcomings of concepts would be more concepts. . . . ."

Syādvāda gives, in its own way, such a "conceptual system in which the presence and interrelation of many concepts is specially provided for". Or, rather, the "concepts", or to put the matter in terms of *syādvāda*, "the modes of truth" are "not merely *many* truths, but alternative truths" under the "conceptual system" of *syādvāda*.

CONCLUSION

This study commenced with a search for a balanced view of reality in which the elements of identity and difference would find their due place. The search led us to the formulation of a scheme involving five possible approaches to the problem. The first four approaches were examined and found wanting. Mere identity was recognised to be as inadequate as mere difference as an explanation of the total experience of reality. Nor did the other two possibilities, viz., identity-in-difference in which identity subordinates difference and identity-in-difference in which difference subordinates identity, prove to be any more satisfactory. Only a co-ordinate view of identity-in-difference, it was discovered, could serve as a satisfactory basis for the totality of our ontological experience. Confirmation for this view was sought from the schools of Kumārila, Kant and Whitehead.

Next, certain flaws or fallacies (*doṣas*) alleged to vitiate the Jaina view—the most important being that of contradiction—was examined and refuted from the Jaina viewpoint. The analysis revealed that some critics who claimed to discern these fallacies were labouring under a misapprehension as to the nature and importance of the idea of significant or determinate negation which forms the pivot of the Jaina viewpoint. Others, it was pointed out, confused the externalistic view of identity and difference (designated as *ubhayavāda* or *miśravāda*) with the integral view of identity-in-difference which is the Jaina view of reality. It was found that in order to expose this confusion the Jaina thinkers had to emphasise the necessity of treating everything real as not merely a co-ordinate and integral synthesis, but also as a unique (*jātyantara*) one.

A further pursuit of our inquiry into some aspects of reality brought out the truth that only the principle of a co-ordinate synthesis could form an adequate basis for their existence and function. It was noticed, for example, that outside the framework of identity-in-difference the solution to the problem of relation (*sambandha*) would have to take the form either of crude realism or of subjectivism. Similarly, it was found that the principle of causal efficiency (*artha-kriyākāritvam*) could not function in a reality which was not a co-ordinate synthesis of identity-in-difference.

After discussing two controversies which shed some light on the notions of substance (*dravya*) and attribute (*paryāya* as well as *guṇa*) the ontological part of the present study was concluded.

The second part of the work concerned itself with some problems of epistemology with particular emphasis on *anekāntavāda*, *nayavāda* and *syādvāda*. It was not possible to treat other questions of epistemology, e. g., the ways of knowing and the nature of validity.

Anekāntavāda—the doctrine of manifoldness (or 'indeterminateness')—was shown to be not so much a method as the source or presupposition of the other two methods. When viewed in the light of this doctrine reality was seen to reveal itself not merely as many (*anantātmakam*) but also as infinitely manifold (*anantadharmātmakam*) or indeterminate in every detail. The principle of distinction, the motive force of realism in any form, was observed to have reached its logical terminus in this doctrine. Hence the claim that *anekānta-vāda* is the most consistent form of realism in Indian philosophy. In the process of substantiating this claim the several logical phases in the evolution of *anekāntavāda* (from a simple state of distinction to that of infinite diversification, encompassing the physical and the mental realms) were traced and illustrated.

It was next pointed out that *Nayavāda*, the doctrine of standpoints (the analytical method or methods), and *Syādvāda*, the dialectic of conditional predication, or simply the conditional dialectic (the synthetical method), stemmed from *Anekāntavāda*. The first was observed to be a scheme of analytical methods and the second a synthetical method involving seven progressive steps. Together the two methods were looked upon as forming a comprehensive scheme of correlative instruments designed to aid an apprehension of the complex structure of reality. Each method, or each step involved in it, was individually treated and its significance and implications were duly noted.

The work has aimed throughout at a comparative treatment of the problems under discussion. It was endeavoured to avoid strained and far-fetched comparisons or contrasts. Further, the treatment in this study of criticisms and controversies has been undertaken not from the citadel of sectarian dogmas but from the standpoint of a certain system of logic, a system deserving of better attention than it has hitherto received.

BIBLIOGRAPHY

Abbreviations, in alphabetical order, of the works consulted or quoted

ABHI	*Abhidhānarājendra* (a lexicon of Jaina Prakrit, explained in Sanskrit) by Vijayarājendra, 7 vols., etd. by Dīpavijaya and others, Ratlam, 1910-1925.
AGAM with *AGAV*	*Akalaṅka-Granthatrayam* by Akalaṅka, with his own Comm. *Vivṛti* (*AGAV*), etd. by Mahendra Kumar Sastri, Singhi Jaina Granthamala, Ahmedabad-Calcutta, 1939.
AGAV	See *AGAM* with *AGAV*.
AJP with *AJPV*	*Anekāntajayapatākā* by Haribhadra, 2 vols., with Haribhadra's own Comm., and with *Vivaraṇa* (*AJPV*)- Supercomm. by Municandra, etd. by H. R. Kapadia, Baroda, 1940 (vol. I) and 1947 (vol. II).
AMS with *VVas* and *ASA*	*Apta-Mīmāṁsā* by Sāmantabhadra, with Vṛitti (*VVas*) by Vasunandi and *Aṣṭaśatī* (*ASA*) by Akalaṅka, etd. by Gajadharalal Jain, Sanatana Jaina Granthamala, Kāśī, 1914.
AR	*Appearance and Reality*, by F. H. Bradley, Oxford, 1940, (10th impression).
ASA	See *AMS*.
AVD with *SM*	*Anyayogavyavacchedadvātriṁśikā* by Hemacandra, with Malliṣeṇa's Comm. *Syādvādamañjarī*, etd. by A. B. Dhruva, Bom. Sans. and Prak. Ser., Bombay 1933.
AVV	*Aṣṭasahasrī* by Vidyānanda, etd. by Vaṁśīdhara, Nirnayasagar Press, Bombay, 1915.
BBSB	*The Brahmasūtra of Bādarayana with Śaṅkara's Bhāṣya*, 2nd edn., etd. by S. K. Belvalkar with E.T. and Notes, Poona, 1931.
Bib. Ind.	*Bibliotheca Indica.*

Bom. Sans. and Prak. Ser.	*Bombay Sanskrit and Prakrit Series.*
BP with *SMV*	*Bhāṣāpariccheda* with *Siddhānta-Muktāvali* of Viśvanātha Pañcānana, etd. by E. Roer, Bib. Ind., Calcutta, 1850.
BPV	*Bhāṣapariccheda* by Viśvanātha, etd. with E. T. by J. R. Ballantyne, Calcutta, 1851.
BPVK	*Bhāṣāpariccheda* (or *Kārikāvali*) by Viśvanātha Pañcānana, with Comms. *Muktāvali, Dinakarīya* and *Rāmarudrīya,* etd. by Laksmana Sastry, Kāśī Sans. Ser., Benares, Saṁvat 1890.
BSB	*The Brahmasūtra Śāṅkara Bhāṣya*, with Comms. *Bhāmatī, Kalpataru* and *Parimala*, etd. by Anantakrisna Sastry, Nirnayasagar Press, Bombay 1938.
Bud. Log.	*Buddhist Logic* by Th. Stcherbatsky, 2 vols., Leningrad, 1930 (vol. II) and 1932 (vol. I).
CCBS	*The Central Conception of Buddhism*, by Th. Stcherbatsky, Price Publication Fund, London, 1923.
CE	*Collected Essays*, by F. H. Bradley, 2 vols., Oxford, 1935.
Chow. Sans. Ser.	*Chowkhamba Sanskrit Series.*
CKCPR	*A Commentary to Kant's Critique of Pure Reason* by Norman Kemp Smith, Macmillan & Co., London, 1930.
CP	*Compendium of Philosophy* (*Abhidhammāttha-saṅgaha*), PTS edn., London, 1910. This work contains "A Compendium of Relations" in Pt. VIII.
CPKE	*The Critical Philosophy of Kant*, 2nd. edn., by Edward Caird, 2 vols., James Madehose & Sons, Glasgow, 1909.
CPRM	*Critique of Pure Reason* by Kant, E. T. by J. M. D. Meiklejohn, George Bell & Sons, London, 1887.

CPRMax *Immanuel Kant's Critique of Pure Reason*, E. T. by F. Max Muller, Macmillan & Co., London, 1881.

EIP *The Essentials of Indian Philosophy*, by M. Hiriyanna, George Allen and Unwin, London, 1949.

EJNG *An Epitome of Jainism*, by P. C. Nahar and K. C. Ghosh, Calcutta, 1917.

ELB *The Essentials of Logic*, by Bernard Bosanquet, London, 1903.

ERE *Encyclopaedia of Religion and Ethics*, etd. by James Hastings, Edinburgh, 1918.

GOS *Gaekwad's Oriental Series.*

HBT with *HBTA* *Hetubinduṭīkā of Arcaṭa*, with *Āloka* by Durveka, etd. by Sukhlalji Sanghavi and Muni Shree Jinavijayaji, GOS, Baroda, 1949.

HBTA See *HBT*.

HIP *A History of Indian Philosophy*, by S. N. Dasgupta, 4 vols., Cambridge, 1922, 1932, 1940, and 1949.

ILE *Indian Logic in Early Schools*, by H. N. Randle, London, 1930.

IP *Indian Philosophy*, by S. Radhakrishnan, 2nd edn., 2 vols., George Allen & Unwin Ltd., London, 1931.

IPC *Proceedings of the Indian Philosophical Congress*, 1927, Calcutta Univ., 1929, pp. 159–166 ("What is Samavāya", by M. Hiriyanna).

IT *Indian Thought*, a Quarterly Journal devoted to Sanskrit Literature, etd. by G. Thibaut and Ganganatha Jha, Allahabad (not continuing now).

JAOS *Journal of the American Oriental Society.*

JPN *The Jaina Philosophy of Non-Absolutism*, by Satkari Mookerjee, Bharati Mahavidyalaya Publications, Jaina Series, No. 2, Calcutta, 1944.

JPPSM *The Journal of Philosophy, Psychology and Scientific Methods*, etd. by Frederick J. D. Woodbridge, 2 vols.

Vol. I, Jan.-Dec., 1904. (This contains two articles by William James on "A World of Pure Experience" : (i) pp. 533-543 and (ii) pp. 561-570.)

Vol. II, Jan.-Dec., 1905. (This contains an article by William James entitled "The Thing and Its Relations", pp. 29–41. This article and the two articles in Vol. I deal with the problem of relations.)

JPTS — *Journal of the Pāli Text Society.*

JSJ — *Jaina Sūtras*, Pt. I and Pt. II, E. T. by H. Jacobi, Oxford, 1895. (*The Sacred Books of the East*, Vols. XXII and XLV respectively.)

JTA — *The Jaina Theory of Anekāntavāda,* by K. C. Bhattacharya. An article in the Philosophical Quarterly, the Indian Institute of Philosophy, Amalner, April, 1925.

JTBY — *Jaina Tarkabhāṣā* by Yaśovijaya, etd. by Sukhalalji Sanghavi, Ahmedabad–Calcutta, 1938.

JTVS — *Jainatarkavārtikam* with the Vṛtti by Śantyācārya, etd. by Vitthal Shastri, Benares, 1917.

Ka. — *Kārikā.*

KCPR — *Immanuel Kant's Critique of Pure Reason*, by Norman Kemp Smith, Macmillan & Co., London. 1950.

KKS — *Khaṇḍanakhaṇḍakhādya* by Śrī Harṣa (with extracts from the Comms. of Ānandapūrṇa, Citsukha, Śaṅkaramiśra and Raghunātha), etd. by Lakshmana Sastri Dravida, Chow. Sans. Ser., Benares, 1914.

KMEP — *Kant's Metaphysic of Experience*, by H. J. Paton, 2 vols., George Allen & Unwin Ltd., London, 1936.

KR — See *PBTS*.

KTKP — *Kant's Theory of Knowledge*, by H. A. Prichard, Oxford, 1909.

M — See *SPS*.

Mis. Es. — *H. T. Colebrooke's Miscellaneous Essays*, etd. by T. E. Colebrooke, 2 vols., London, 1873.

Mon.	*The Monadology and the other Philosophical Writings* by Leibniz, E. T. by Robert Latta, O. U. P., London, 1951.
MSV with *NR*	*Mīmāṁsa-śloka-vārtika* of Kumārila with *Nyāyaratnākara* of Parthasārathi Miśra, etd. by Rama Sastry Tailanga, Chow. Sans. Ser., Kāśī, 1898.
MV	See *PVD*.
NB	See *TS* with *TD* and *NB*.
NBD	See *NBTD*.
NBTD with *NBD*	*The Nyāyabindu-ṭīkā* with the *Nyāyabindu*, both by Dharmottara, etd. by P. Peterson, Bib. Ind., Calcutta, 1929.
NBV	See *ND*.
ND with *NBV*	*The Nyāya-Darśana with the Nyāya-Bhāṣya of Vātsāyana*, Bib. Ind., Calcutta, 1865.
NEMc	*The Nature of Existence*, by J. M. E. McTaggart, 2 vols., Cambridge University Press, Cambridge, 1921.
NK	See *PDS*.
NKB	*Nyāyakośa*, by Bhimacarya Jhalakikar, 3rd edn., Bom. Sans. and Prak. Ser., Poona, 1928.
NKC Comm. on *LTB*	*Nyāya-kumuda-candra*, by Prabhācandra, a Comm. on *Laghīyastraya* of Bhaṭṭākalaṅka, etd. by Mahendra Kumar Shastri, Manik Chandra Digambar Jain Series, Bombay, 1938.
NKV	*The Naya-Karṇikā* by Vinaya Vijaya, etd. with E. T. by M. D. Desai, The Library of Jaina Literature, Vol. III, Arrah, 1915.
NM	*Nyāyamañjarī* by Jayanta Bhaṭṭa, etd. by G. Sastri Tailanga, Viz. Sans. Ser., Benares, 1895.
NNLI	*Materials for the Study of Navya-Nyāya Logic*, by D. H. Ingalls, Harvard Oriental Series, Cambridge (Mass.), 1951.
NR	See *MSV*.
NTN	*The Nyāya Theory of Knowledge*, by S. C. Chatterjee, Calcutta University, 1939.

NVTT — *Nyāyavārtikatātparyaṭīkā* by Vācaspati Miśra, etd. by Rajeshwara Sastri Dravid, Kāśī Sans. Ser., Benares, 1925.

NVVS — *Nyāyāvatāravārtika-vṛtti* by Śānti Sūri, etd. by Dalsukh Malvania, Singhi Jain Series, Bombay, 1949.

OIP — *Outlines of Indian Philosophy*, by M. Hiriyanna, George Allen & Unwin Ltd., London, 1931.

OKEW — *Our Knowledge of the External World*, by Bertrand Russell, reprinted, George Allen & Unwin Ltd., London, 1949.

PB — *Praśastapādabhāṣyam*, with *Sūkti*, *Setu* and *Vyomavatī*, etd. by Gopinath Kaviraj and Dhundiraj Sastri, Chow. Sans. Ser., Benares, 1924.

PBTS with *KR* — *Praśastapādabhāṣyaṭīkāsaṅgraha*, with *Kāṇādarahasya*, by Śaṅkara Miśra, etd. by Vindhyesvari Prasada Dvivedin, Chow. Sans. Ser., Benares, 1917.

PC — See *SP*.

PDS with *NK* — *The Padārthadharmasaṅgraha* of Praśastapāda, with the *Nyāyakandalī* of Śrīdhara, E. T. by G. Jha, reprint from the Pandit, Benares, 1916.

PKEW — *The Philosophy of Kant Explained*, by John Watson, James Madehose & Sons, Glasgow, 1908.

PK — See *TSS* with *PK*.

PKJha — See *TSS* with *PKJha*.

PKM — *Prameya-Kamala-Mārtaṇḍa* by Prabhācandra, 2nd edn., a Comm. on *Parīkṣāmukha-Sūtra* of Māṇikyanandi, etd. by Mahendra Kumar Shastri, Bombay, 1941.

PL — *Principles of Logic* by F. H. Bradley, 2nd edn., 2 vols., Oxford, 1940.

PMHS — *Pramāṇa-Mīmāṁsā* by Hemacandra, etd. with *Bhāṣā-ṭippaṇa*, by Pt. Sukhlalji Sanghavi, Singhi Jaina Granthamala, Ahmedabad–Calcutta, 1939.

PMS — *Pūrva-Mīmāṁsā in its Sources* by Ganganatha Jha, etd. with a Critical Bibliography, by Umesha Mishra, Benares Hindu University, Benares, 1942.

Problems — *The Problems of Philosophy* by Bertrand Russell, Reprinted, Home University Library, London, 1951.

PrSKU — *Pravacanasāra* by Kundakundācārya, with the Sk. Comms. of Amṛtacandra and Jayasena and the Hindi Comm. of Pande Hemaraja, etd. with Eng. Intro. and E. T. by A. N. Upadhye, Bombay, 1935.

PSKC — *Pañcāstikāyasāra* by Kundakunda, etd. with Eng. Intro. and E. T. by A. Chakravarti, The Sacred Books of the Jaina Series, Arrah, 1920.

PVD with *MV* — *Pramāṇavārtika* by Dharmakīrti, with a Vṛtti by Manorathanandin, etd. by Rahula Sankrityayana, published as Appendixes to BORSJ, Vols. XXIV XXXI, 1938-40.

RML — *Relations in Modern Logic*, by Rasvihari Das, in Calcutta Review, Nov.-Dec. 1932.

RRS — *Reign of Realism in Indian Philosophy*, by R. Naga Raja Sarma, Madras, 1937.

SBE — *Sacred Books of the East.*

SBNT — *Six Buddhist Nyāya Tracts*, etd. by Haraprasad Shastri, Bib. Ind., Calcutta, 1910.

SBT — *Saptabhaṅgītaraṅgiṇī* by Vimaladāsa, Rayacandra Granthamala, Nirnayasagar Press, Bombay, Vīra Saṁvat 2431.

SCKCE — *A Short Commentary on Kant's Critique of Pure Reason*, by A. C. Ewing, Methuen & Co. Ltd., London, 1938.

SDS with *TRD* — *Saḍdarśana-samuccaya*, by Haribhadra, with *Tarkarahasyadīpikā* by Guṇaratna, etd. by L. Suali, Calcutta, 1905.

SDSC — *The Sarva-darśana-saṁgraha* by Mādhava Acārya, E. T. by E. B. Cowell and A. G. Gough, Kegan Paul, Trench, Trubner & Co., Ltd., London, 1914.

SHM — See *VBJ* with *SHM*.

SJJ — *Studies in Jainism*, containing three articles by H. Jacobi, Jaina Sahitya Samsodhaka Studies, No. 1, etd. by Jina Vijaya Muni, Ahmedabad, 1946.

SJPT — *Studies in Jaina Philosophy*, by Nathmal Tatia, pubd. by the Jaina Cultural Research Society, Benares, 1951.

SKIS — *The Sāṅkhyakārikā of Īśvarakṛṣṇa*, etd. with E. T. by S. S. Suryanarayana Sastri, Univ. of Madras, 1948.

SKL — See *SVS*.

SM — See *AVD* with *SM*.

SMV — See *BP*.

SNDeW — *The Self and Nature* (containing "The Theory of Relations", ch. IX, pp. 212-273), by DeWitt H. Parker, Harvard Univ. Press, Cambridge, 1917.

SP with *PC* — *Saptapadārthī* by Śivāditya, with *Padārtha-candrikā* by Śeṣānanta, etd. by V. S. Ghate, 2nd edn., Bombay, 1919.

SPD — *Saṁbandha-parīkṣā* by Dharmakīrti. Kārikās from this work have been quoted in *PKM*, p. 504 ff.

SPS with *M* — *Saptapadārthī* by Śivāditya, with *Mitabhāṣiṇī* by Mādhava, and two other Comms., etd. by Amarendra Mohan and Narendra Chandra, Calcutta Sans. Ser., Calcutta, 1934.

SRK Comm. on *PTNA* — *Syādvāda-ratnākara*, 5 parts, by Vādidevasūri, a Comm. on *Pramāṇanayatattvālokālaṅkāra* by the same author, Ārhata-mata-prabhākara Ser., etd. by Motilal Laghaji, Poona, Vīra Saṁ. 2452-2457.

SSKH — *The Sāṅkhya System*, by A. B. Keith, 2nd edn., The Heritage of India, Calcutta, 1924.

ST — *Sanmati-Tarka* by Siddhasena Divākara, etd. by Sukhalal Sanghavi and Bechardas Doshi, E. T. from Gujarati, Dalsukh Malvania, Bombay, 1939.

STBS — *The Soul Theory of the Buddhists* (The Appendix to the Abhidharmakośa of Vasubandu), E. T. with Intro. and Notes by Stcherbatsky, Petrograd, 1920.

STP — *Sanmati-tarka-prakaraṇa*, 5 pts., by Siddhasena Divākara, with the Comm. *Tattvabodha-vidhāyinī* (also known as *Vāda-mahārṇava*) by Abhayadeva Sūri, etd. by Sukhlal Sanghavi and Bechardas Doshi, Gujarat Puratattva Mandira Granthavali, Ahmedabad, Saṁ. 1980.

SVJha — *Ślokavārtika*, E. T. by Ganganatha Jha, Bib. Ind., Calcutta, 1901.

SVS with *SKL* — *Śāstra-vārtā-samuccaya* of Haribhadra, with the ṭīkā *Syadvādakalpalatā* by Yaśovijaya, etd. by Pt. Hargovinddas Trikamchand Shaw, Sethi Devchand Lalbhai Jain Pustakoddhar Series, No. 16, Bombay, 1914.

SVTJ — *Ślokavārtikaṭīkā* (*Śārkarikā*) by Bhaṭṭiputrajayamiśra, etd. by C. Kunhan Raja, University of Madras, Madras Univ. Sans. Ser., Madras, 1946.

SWK — *Six Ways of Knowing,* by D. M. Datta, George Allen and Unwin Ltd., London, 1932.

TB — *Tarkabhāṣā of Keśavamiśra*, Pts. I and II, etd. by A. B. Gajendragadkar and R. D. Karmarkar, Poona, 1934.

TD — See *TS* with *TD* and *ND*.

TPSJ — *Tattvopaplavasiṁha* by Jayarāśi Bhaṭṭa, etd. by Sukhlalji Sanghavi and R. C. Parikh, GOS, Baroda, 1940.

TRAG — *Tattvārtharājavārtika*, a Comm. on Umāsvāti's *Tattvārthādhigamasūtra* by Akalaṅka, etd. by Gajadharalal Jain, Sanatana Jaina Granthamala, Kāśī, 1915.

TRD — See *SDS*.

TS with *TD* and *NB* — *Tarka-Saṅgraha* and *Dīpikā*, by Annaṁbhaṭṭa, with *Nyāya-bodhinī* by Govardhana, etd. by Y. V. Athalye and M. R. Bodas, 2nd edn., reimpression, Bombay Sans. and Prak. Ser., Bombay, 1930.

TSS with *PK* — *Tattvasaṅgraha* by Śāntarakṣita, with *Pañcikā* by Kamalaśīla, 2 vols., etd. by Embar Krishnamacharya, GOS, Baroda, 1929.

TSS with *PKJha* — *TSS* with *PK*, E. T. by Ganganatha Jha, 2 vols., GOS, Baroda, 1937 and 1939.

TSUJ — *Tattvārthādhigamasūtra* by Umāsvāti, etd. with E. T. by J. L. Jaini, Sacred Books of the Jainas, Arrah, 1920.

TSV (Comm. on *TSU*) — *Tattvārtha-śloka-vārtika* by Vidyānanda, a Comm. on *Tattvārthādhigamasūtra* by Umāsvāti, etd. by Manoharlal Sastry, Nirnayasagar Press, Bombay, Vīra Saṁ. 2444.

UV — See *VD* with *UV*.

VBJ with *SHM* — *The Viśeṣāvaśyaka Bhāṣya* by Jinabhadra Gaṇi Kṣamāśramaṇa, with the Vivṛti *Śiṣyahitā* by Maladhāri Hemacandra, etd. by Haragovinda, Benares, Vīra Saṁ. 2437.

VD with *UV* — *The Vaiśeṣika Darśana* of Kaṇāda with the Comm. *Upaskāra* by Śaṅkara Miśra, etd. with his own Vivṛti by J. Tarka Panchanana, Bib. Ind., Calcutta, 1891.

Viz. Sans. Ser. — *Vizianagaram Sanskrit Series.*

VND — *Vādanyāya* by Dharmakīrti, with Śantarakṣita's Comm. *Vipañcitārtha*, etd. by Rahula Sankrityayana, Appendix to JBORS, Vol. XXI, Pt. IV, Patna, 1935.

VPSN — *Vedānta-Pārijāta-Saurabha* of Nimbārka and *Vedānta-Kaustubha* of Śrīnivāsa (Comms. on the *Brahmasūtras*), 3 Pts., E. T. by Roma Bose, Calcutta, 1940, 1941, and 1943.

VVas — See *AMS*.

Some works, which have not been widely used, have been referred to, with full particulars in the course of the text itself.

INDEXES

I (A). INDEX TO WORKS MENTIONED IN THE BIBLIOGRAPHY (in abbreviated form)

I (B). INDEX TO OTHER WORKS

II. INDEX TO NAMES OF AUTHORS, ETC.

[N=footnotes. References that follow N are to the footnotes.]

III. INDEX TO THE PHILOSOPHICAL SECTS AND TENETS &C.

[N=footnotes. References that follow N are to the footnotes.]

V. INDEX TO SANSKRIT AND PRAKRIT WORDS

[N=footnotes. References that follow N are to the footnotes.]